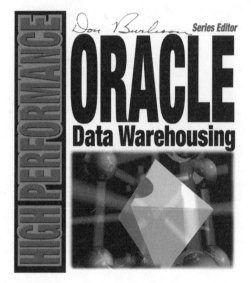

HIGH PERFORMANCE

Don Burleson Series Editor

ORACLE
Data Warehousing

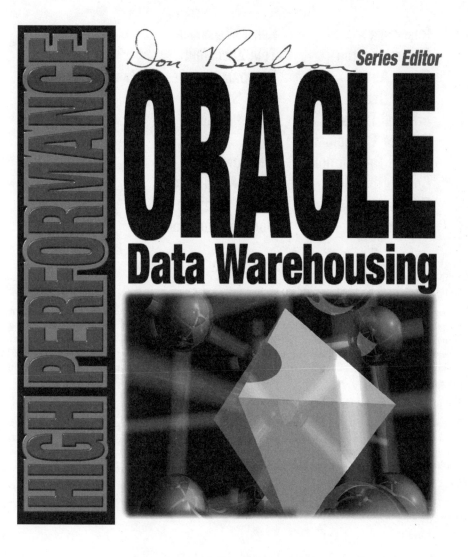

HIGH PERFORMANCE

Don Burleson **Series Editor**

ORACLE
Data Warehousing

Donald Burleson

 **CORIOLIS GROUP BOOKS**

an International Thomson Publishing company I(T)P®

Albany, NY • Belmont, CA • Bonn • Boston • Cincinnati • Detroit • Johannesburg • London
Madrid • Melbourne • Mexico City • New York • Paris • Singapore • Tokyo • Toronto • Washington

PUBLISHER	KEITH WEISKAMP
PROJECT EDITOR	TONI ZUCCARINI
COVER ARTIST	PERFORMANCE DESIGN/GARY SMITH
COVER DESIGN	TONY STOCK
INTERIOR DESIGN	NICOLE COLÓN
PROJECT COORDINATOR/	
LAYOUT PRODUCTION	KIM EOFF
COPYEDITOR	MARY MILLHOLLON
PROOFREADER	SHELLY CROSSEN
INDEXER	DONALD BURLESON

High Performance Oracle Data Warehousing
ISBN: 1-57610-154-1
Copyright © 1997 by The Coriolis Group, Inc.

Limits of Liability and Disclaimer of Warranty

The author and publisher of this book have used their best efforts in preparing the book and the programs contained in it. These efforts include the development, research, and testing of the theories and programs to determine their effectiveness. The author and publisher make no warranty of any kind, expressed or implied, with regard to these programs or the documentation contained in this book.

The author and publisher shall not be liable in the event of incidental or consequential damages in connection with, or arising out of, the furnishing, performance, or use of the programs, associated instructions, and/or claims of productivity gains.

Trademarks

Trademarked names appear throughout this book. Rather than list the names and entities that own the trademarks or insert a trademark symbol with each mention of the trademarked name, the publisher states that it is using the names for editorial purposes only and to the benefit of the trademark owner, with no intention of infringing upon that trademark.

The Coriolis Group, Inc.
An International Thomson Publishing Company
14455 N. Hayden Road, Suite 220
Scottsdale, Arizona 85260

602/483-0192
FAX 602/483-0193
http://www.coriolis.com

Printed in the United States of America
10 9 8 7 6 5 4 3 2 1

To Andy, whose enthusiasm and energy were instrumental to my motivation.

To Jenny, whose unconditional love inspired me.

And special thanks to Toni Zuccarini, whose talents were instrumental in making this book a success.

The woods are cool, the forest deep,

But I have promises to keep,

And miles to go before I sleep,

And miles to go before I sleep.

Stopping by Woods on a Snowy Evening
–Robert Frost

A Note From Donald Burleson

Today's Oracle professionals are standing at the turning point. As Oracle technology moves into the twenty-first century we are seeing the complexity of database systems becoming almost unfathomable. Today's Oracle professional must be an expert in database performance and tuning, database administration, data warehousing, using Oracle with the Web, using OLAP and spatial data, and many other areas. These robust new features of Oracle present unique challenges to anyone who must use Oracle technology to deliver solutions to complex data-oriented challenges.

Oracle, the world's leading database management system, provides a mind-boggling wealth of features and options—far more than one Oracle professional can easily digest. The Oracle market is filled with new possibilities as Oracle introduces the management of objects, data warehouses, and Web-enabled applications; Oracle professionals everywhere are struggling to understand how to exploit these new features.

It is no longer acceptable for Oracle professionals to be generalists—they must become intimately familiar with all facets of Oracle technology and understand how these technologies interoperate. Rather than simply breadth of knowledge, the Oracle professional must have enough depth to effectively apply the technology. To get this knowledge we must rely on experts to guide us through the labyrinth of complicated tools and techniques, and we do not have the luxury of wading through mundane technical manuals.

What we need is clear, concise advice from seasoned Oracle professionals. That is the purpose of The Coriolis Group's High Performance Oracle series. As you are challenged to keep pace with this exciting new technology, we are challenged to provide on-point books to help guide you through the myriad of Oracle features and ensure your success.

Don Burleson
Rochester, New York

Contents

Introduction

While the concepts of data warehousing and decision support have been around for decades, the availability of cheap disk storage is making large-scale data warehousing a reality for major corporations. Unfortunately, the techniques for developing, populating, and using data warehouses are both nascent and confusing. Data warehouse developers are faced with a huge choice of tools, techniques, and approaches, and it is not always evident which choice is the best for any particular type of data warehouse. Providing expert guidance on using these features is the primary purpose of this book.

The advent of Oracle database software has changed the face of data warehousing. Because of its huge installed base, Oracle is dominating the market, and data warehouse developers are now creating warehouses that conform to the Oracle architecture. Oracle Corporation has also made a commitment to support data warehouse applications, as evidenced by the numerous tools and features (including Oracle Express, formerly the IRI Express multidimensional database) designed especially to support very large data repositories. But having the tools is only a part of the solution—we must understand how to effectively apply these tools to real-world systems.

Unfortunately, until now there have been no books on the market that explain how to use Oracle to create effective data warehouses. The existing books are terse and difficult to understand, and fail to provide insight into the "tricks" that an experienced Oracle DBA would use to create a successful data warehouse.

The basic tenet of this book is one simple principle: The use of computers to solve abstract business problems is not new. What is new is the availability of a large, robust online data repository to speed up the decision process. This book focuses on the use of the Oracle database engine as the vehicle for planning and implementing a data repository that will allow all types of decision support.

What makes *High Performance Oracle Data Warehousing* unique is the fact that it applies the timeworn principles of decision support systems to the Oracle database architecture. It is only by associating the principles of decision support with Oracle that a full understanding of the power of the Oracle engine can be gained.

This book is structured to provide the maximum amount of value to the Oracle professional who must design and implement a data warehouse—only those features that directly apply to data warehousing are discussed. Plus, the material in this book is drawn from my years of experience designing and implementing some of the world's largest Oracle data warehouses.

Unlike other books on data warehousing, this book describes invaluable tools and techniques that can be found in no other document. While there may be no substitute for experience, this book provides pragmatic, real-world tips on effectively exploiting the Oracle architecture. The code snippets provided on the CD-ROM, alone, will pay for the cost of this book during their first use.

High Performance Oracle Data Warehousing is structured to take the reader step-by-step through all of the information needed to create and implement first-rate Oracle data warehouses. But unlike other data warehouse books that feel compelled to discuss every feature of Oracle, this book only addresses the Oracle features that directly relate to Oracle data warehousing.

And we cannot get this information from the Oracle documentation. While the Oracle documentation describes the features of Oracle, it does not tell the reader how to apply the features effectively, especially when dealing with very large and complex systems. This book provides insights that cannot be found in any manual.

Best of all, this book warns the reader about all of the potential pitfalls that can cripple a data warehouse development effort. It provides a simple, easy-to-understand approach to the development of Oracle data warehouses. By following the advice in this book, you can ensure your success and gain confidence that your new data warehouse is running at its maximum potential.

Today, Oracle shows no signs of relinquishing its hold on the data warehousing market. This commitment is sure to manifest itself in even more exciting data warehousing features. It is my hope that you will be able to apply my tips and techniques efficiently and use my insights to create robust and powerful Oracle data warehouses.

The Evolution Of The Data Warehouse

CHAPTER

1

HIGH PERFORMANCE

The Evolution Of The Data Warehouse

While the use of databases as a vehicle for complex data analysis is new, the need to perform complex data analysis has been with us for centuries. Answering "what-if" questions, simulating the introduction of a new product, or determining the most profitable products are all legitimate business needs, and the advent of the data warehouse did not herald the first time that computers had been used to solve these types of tasks.

In fact, computers have been used to solve complex types of data analysis problems since their earliest commercial inception in the 1950s. Essentially, the nature of the questions that data warehouses solve has not changed in four decades. The summarization of numbers, the aggregation of associated data, and data variance analysis is nothing new.

The Evolution Of Data Management Platforms

Regardless of the sophistication of a database manager, it remains true that all databases are constructed from simple data structures such as linked lists, B-trees, and hashed files. In reviewing the building blocks of database systems, it is possible to gain a historical perspective on the evolution of databases, and to remember the past, so that we are not condemned to repeat it.

The following pages are a historical review of database evolution, showing each of the enhancements that were introduced with each new architecture. It is also important to review the problems inherent to each database architecture. As you will see, there are striking similarities between object-oriented databases and earlier database architectures. By understanding the historical reason that object-oriented databases have evolved into their present form, we can gain insight into the future trend and directions of databases.

Pre-Disk Data Storage

On the earliest commercial computers, drum storage was far too expensive to hold large volumes of transaction data. Consequently, transactions were keyed onto punched cards, and these cards were sorted and copied to a daily transaction tape. This daily transaction tape was then processed against the previous day's sorted master tape (see Figure 1.1).

In this fashion, the data processing site collected a historical archive of each day's transactions. These daily transaction tapes were used as the input to statistical programs that

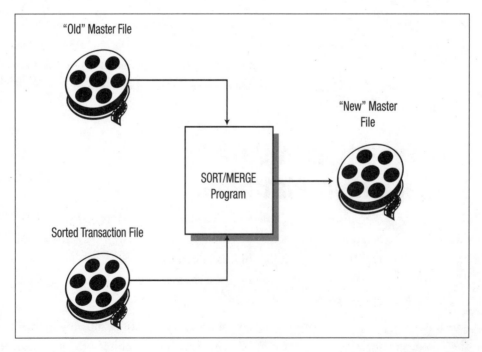

Figure 1.1

Transaction processing with magnetic tapes.

read and aggregated the transactions according to predefined rules, writing the aggregate summaries onto another tape (see Figure 1.2). These tapes, in turn, were used by managers to answer decision support queries similar to the queries serviced by today's data warehouses.

Early Disk-Based Data Storage

Prior to the development of early commercial databases such as IMS, many "database" systems were nothing more than a loose conglomeration of flat-file storage methods on magnetic disks and drums. The term *flat file* includes physical-sequential storage as well as the indexed sequential access method (ISAM) and virtual sequential access method (VSAM). Early flat-file systems such as ISAM and VSAM were actually little more than physical-sequential files with indexes stored on disks or drums.

The data access methods used by these early disk systems were very primitive when compared to today's commercial databases. One of the most common disk access methods was commonly known as *BDAM* (Basic Direct Access Method). BDAM was used for data records that required fast access and retrieval of information. BDAM uses a *hashing algorithm*, which takes a symbolic key and converts it into a location address on a disk (a disk address). Unfortunately, the range of addresses generated by hashing

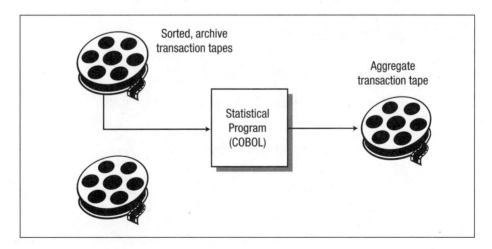

Figure 1.2
Data aggregation on magnetic tapes.

algorithms requires careful management. Because a hashing algorithm always produces the same key each time it reads an input value, duplicate keys have to be avoided. BDAM file structures also consume large amounts of disk storage. Because records are randomly distributed across the disk device, it is common to see hashed files with more unused spaces than occupied spaces. In most cases, a BDAM file is considered "logically" full if more than 70 percent of the space contains data records.

Despite these problems, hashing is still used within commercial data warehouses, and it remains one of the fastest ways to store and retrieve disk information. Most Unix systems can take a symbolic key and convert it into a disk address in as little as 50 milliseconds. While hashing is a very old technique, it is still a very powerful method. Many C++ programmers use hashing to store and retrieve records within their object-oriented applications.

While the hashing technique is still very popular for fast storage and retrieval of individual records, it is not suitable for the type of full scans that we see in a data warehouse. As we would expect from a random key generator, records are not stored contiguously on a disk. Rather, they are randomly distributed across the disk device. While an index can help speed retrieval of hashed records, we still do not see the high I/O throughput that we see when records are stored contiguously on data blocks (see Figure 1.3). With contiguous record storage (such as a relational database), we see

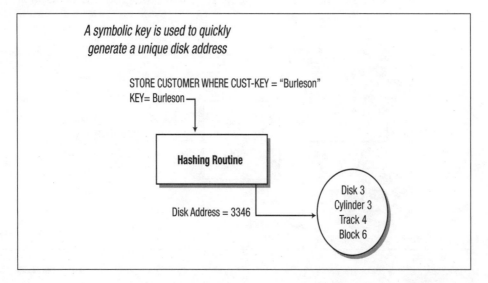

Figure 1.3
Hashing for disk data storage.

that an 8 K file I/O will read hundreds of records into an out buffer with one I/O. We do not get this luxury with hashed file storage techniques.

It is interesting that in the early 1990s, more data was stored on magnetic tapes than in all of the other file formats combined. In fact, even now, companies with terabytes of data warehouses continue to use magnetic tapes for systems that contain large amounts of unchanging, infrequently used data. Magnetic tapes, which remain more than 10,000 times cheaper than disk storage, are still the most economical way to store large volumes of data.

Overall, data warehouse applications that access data stored in ISAM and VSAM data structures remain popular. Commercial engines such as the Informix-SE database are basically ISAM files that are accessed by the data warehouse.

However, the lack of robust commercial databases made sophisticated data analysis very cumbersome. The problems inherent in early disk-based systems were very serious, and an effort was undertaken to rethink the entire concept of data storage. These problems included the following issues:

- *Data relationships could not be maintained.* Early flat-file systems could not easily recognize and manage the natural relationships between data items. One-to-many and many-to-many data relationships were often ignored, and widespread denormalization of the data occurred.

- *"Islands of information" developed within organizations,* as different departments developed independent flat-file systems. These departmental "islands" were often written in different programming languages, with different file structures, and it was very difficult for a department to share information with other departments. (See Figure 1.4.)

- *Widespread data redundancy developed.* Each department within the corporate database often duplicated information, leading to the increased costs of data storage, and the possibility of update anomalies when an item was changed within one department but not another.

- *Maintenance nightmares ensued.* Because these systems had no repository of *metadata*, program changes became very cumbersome. Whenever a file changed in structure, the programs that referred to the file could not readily be identified, and every program that referenced that file had to be modified and recompiled.

Accounting—COBOL with Flat files

Finance—Fortran with VSAM

Marketing—PL/1 with BDAM files

Figure 1.4
Islands of information.

- *Tightly-coupled data and programs led to maintenance problems.* Because many application programs defined and maintained their own data structures, there was a problem as all new programs were forced to adhere to the calling procedures of the existing programs. The same communications problems exist within object-oriented systems. The Common Object Request Broker (CORBA) standard for object-oriented systems was designed to ensure that this problem will not resurface in the future.

- *No concurrency control or recovery mechanisms.* Systems had no method for simultaneously updating information and no way to roll-forward information in case of disk failure.

- *No method for establishing relationships between data items.* The relationships between data items are generally lost or introduced with cumbersome data structures, such as repeating fields within records.

Early Commercial Databases

The problems associated with flat-file systems led to the development of the first commercial database—IMS (Information Management System), from IBM. IMS is considered a *hierarchical database*, meaning that pointers are used to establish the data relationships. IMS remains very popular today, and it is well-suited for modeling systems in which the entities are naturally hierarchical in nature. The data relationships are established with *child* and *twin* pointers, and these pointers are embedded into the prefix of every record in the database (see Figure 1.5).

Many data warehouses are populated from data extracted from IMS databases, so a discussion of the internals of IMS will help the warehouse administrator develop a plan for extraction from IMS.

While IMS is very good at modeling naturally hierarchical data relationships, complex data relationships, such as many-to-many and bill-of-materials relationships, have to be implemented in a very clumsy fashion, with the use of *phantom* records. The IMS database also suffers from its own complexity. Learning to program and administer an IMS database requires many months of training, and, consequently, IMS development remains very slow and cumbersome.

It is interesting to note that while IMS is considered a dinosaur by today's computer standards, IBM continues to sell new copies of IMS, and IMS is still used

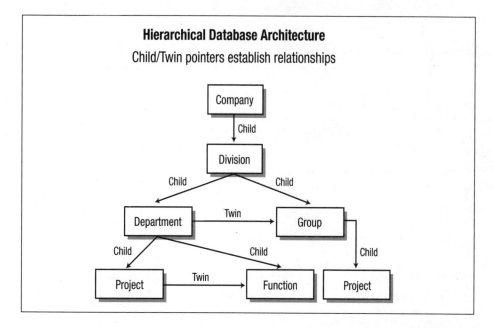

Figure 1.5
Hierarchical databases.

by hundreds of corporations that require high-speed Online Teleprocessing (OLTP) applications. While some of these systems are *legacy systems*, which are not easily converted to modern technology, many corporations continue to use IMS because of its high speed. A hybrid of IMS, called *IMS/FASTPATH*, is one of the fastest commercial databases available, even by today's standards. IMS/FASTPATH is used at companies that may have hundreds, or even thousands, of concurrent transactions, and some IMS configurations have surpassed the 1,000 transactions per second barrier.

As fast as IMS is for highly normalized OLTP systems, the denormalized nature of data warehousing makes much of the fast access of IMS unusable for data warehouses. Consequently, the hierarchical database model remains firmly entrenched in OLTP applications.

The CODASYL Generation Of Database Management

Many of the problems associated with flat-file systems were partially addressed with the introduction of the IMS database product by IBM, but there remained no published standard for commercial database systems. In the late 1970s, an ANSI committee created the Committee on Development of Applied Symbolic Languages (CODASYL). The CODASYL committee formed a database task group (the DBTG) to address database standards and required some of the leading database theoreticians to participate in the development of the standard. The CODASYL DBTG was commissioned to develop a set of rules, or standards, for database management systems. The CODASYL DBTG developed what is called the *Network Model* for databases. Among other things, the CODASYL DBTG decided:

- *A framework for a Metadata Dictionary would be created.* The data dictionary was designed to store all metadata, including information about the database entities, relationships between entities, and information about how programs use the database.

- *To describe a standard architecture for network database systems.* This architecture was based on a combination of the BDAM (direct access) and linked-list data structures.

- *A method for separation of the logical data structure of the data from the physical access methods.* For example, a programmer could state **obtain calc customer where cust-id='IBM'**, without having to worry about where the record was physically stored on the disk.

- *A process for database recovery.* Databases would manage record locks, preventing information overlaying, and databases could be rolled-forward or rolled-back, thereby ensuring data integrity. (See Figure 1.6.)

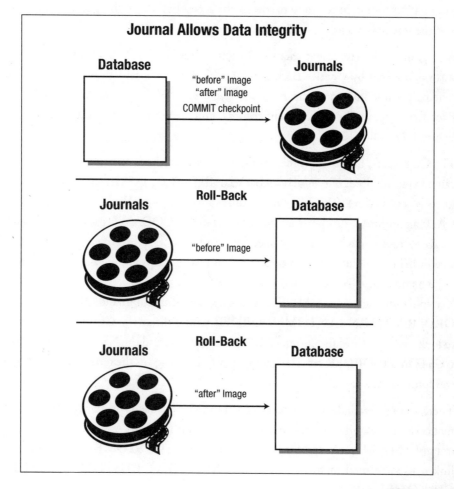

Figure 1.6
The use of database recovery mechanisms.

The CODASYL model became the framework for new commercial database systems, such as the IDMS database from Cullinet Software (now Computer Associates) and the MDBS2 database.

While the CODASYL Network Model was very good at representing complex data relationships, it had one major drawback: Internal data structures were not transparent to programmers, so programmers were required to *navigate* database structures to extract information. Unlike a declarative language like SQL, a network database programmer would be required to specify the access path, describing all of the records and the sets that would be used to satisfy the request.

A diagram tool to represent the data structures required by the CODASYL model was popularized by Charles Bachman, and his graphical depiction of the database schema became known as the *Bachman diagram*, or *data structure diagram*. In the Bachman diagram, boxes represent records, and arrows represent relationships (see Figure 1.7).

The CODASYL model combines two data storage methods to create an engine that can process hundreds of transactions per second. The CODASYL model uses the basic direct access method (BDAM), which utilizes a hashing algorithm (sometimes called a CALC algorithm) to quickly store and retrieve records. CODASYL also employs linked-list data structures, which create embedded pointers in the prefix of each occurrence of a record. These pointers are used to establish relationships among data items. These pointers are called **NEXT**, **PRIOR**, and **OWNER** and are referenced in the Data Manipulation Language (DML). For example, the DML command **OBTAIN NEXT ORDER WITHIN CUSTOMER-ORDER** would direct the CODASYL database to look in the prefix of the current **ORDER** record and find the **NEXT** pointer for the **CUSTOMER-ORDER** set. The database would then access the record whose address was found at this location.

There were several advantages to the CODASYL approach, primarily with performance and the ability to represent complex data relationships. In the following example, BDAM is invoked for the **OBTAIN CALC CUSTOMER** statement, and linked lists are used in the statement **OBTAIN NEXT CUSTOMER WITHIN CUSTOMER-ORDER**.

For example, to navigate a one-to-many relationship, (e.g., to get all of the orders for a customer), a CODASYL programmer would enter the following code:

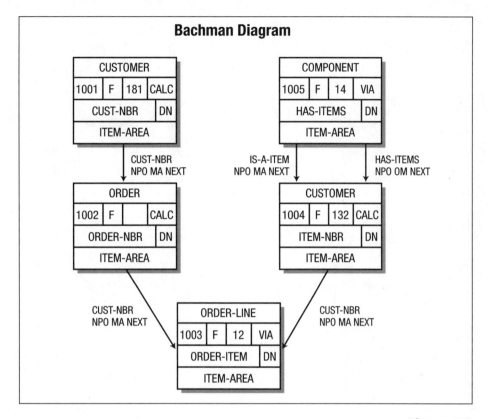

Figure 1.7
The Bachman diagram for describing data models.

```
MOVE 'IBM' to CUST-ID.
    OBTAIN CALC CUSTOMER.
    PERFORM ORDER-LOOP UNTIL END-OF-SET.

    ORDER-LOOP.
    OBTAIN NEXT ORDER WITHIN CUSTOMER-ORDER.
    MOVE ORDER-NO TO OUT-REC.
    WRITE OUT-REC.
```

As a visual tool, the set occurrence diagram, shown in Figure 1.8, has great potential for understanding internal data relationships. The relationships between the objects are readily apparent, and the programmer can easily visualize the navigation paths. For example, in the sample diagram, you can easily see that order 123 is for 19 pads, 3 pencils, and 12 pens. Cross over to the item side of the diagram, and you can easily

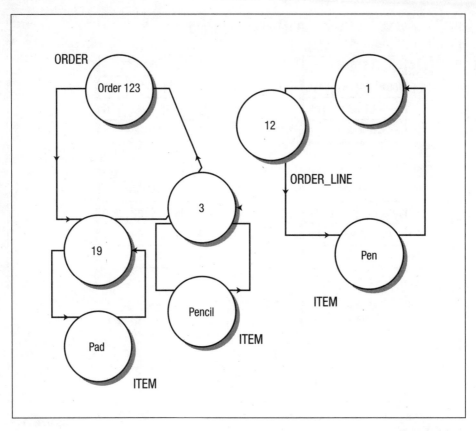

Figure 1.8
The set occurrence diagram.

see which orders include pens. For systems that physically link objects, the set occurrence diagram is an extremely useful visual tool.

Although the design of the CODASYL network model is very elegant, there were serious problems with the ongoing use of network databases. Network databases, much like hierarchical databases, are very difficult to navigate and administer. Learning the Data Manipulation Language (DML), especially for complex navigation, is a skill acquired through many months of training.

Structural changes are a nightmare with network databases. Because the data relationships are *hard linked* with embedded pointers, the addition of an index or a new relationship requires special utility programs to "sweep" each and every affected record in the database. As each record is located, the prefix is restructured to accommodate the new pointers. Object-oriented databases encounter this same problem when a class hierarchy requires modification.

CODASYL databases were still far superior to any other technology of the day, and thousands of corporations began to implement their mission-critical systems on IDMS platforms. Even the Air Force used the IDMS database at the North American Air Defense Command (NORAD) to track incoming Soviet missiles (and, of course, Santa Claus at Christmas time). However, as soon as relational databases became fast and stable enough to support mission-critical systems, the cumbersome and inflexible CODASYL systems were abandoned.

Today, we see that the new object-oriented databases are remarkably similar to the CODASYL model. However, a data warehouse relies on the introduction of data redundancy to achieve its speed, and the pointer-based architecture of the network databases makes them less flexible than relational databases for warehouses.

Overall, we see that the CODASYL model is a database architecture that has been optimized for online record retrieval, and it's not designed for data warehouse applications. While CODASYL records can be denormalized, the record location modes of **CALC** and **VIA** do not allow for contiguous storage of records. Consequently, we see that data warehouse applications are not very well suited to this database architecture.

Introduction Of The Relational Model

Dr. Ted Codd, a researcher from IBM, developed a model for a *relational database* in which the data resided in *pointerless* tables. Relational database tables can be navigated in a declarative fashion, without the need for any database navigation. Dr. Codd called these tables *relations*. Relations within his model are very simple to conceptualize, and they can be viewed as two-dimensional arrays of columns and rows. Codd's relational model contains a set of relational *criteria* that must be met before a database can be truly relational. It is interesting that Dr. Codd's model of relational characteristics is so stringent that no company has yet offered a commercial database that meets all of his criteria.

Relational databases provide the following improvements over earlier database architectures:

- *Data independence*—The data resides in freestanding tables, which are not hard-linked with other tables. Columns can be added to relational tables without any changes to application programs, and the addition of new data or data relationships to the data model seldom requires restructuring of the tables.

- *Declarative data access*—Queries are issued with SQL, and database navigation is hidden from the programmers. When compared to navigational languages such as CODASYL DML, in which the programmer was required to know the details of the access paths, relational access is handled with an SQL optimizer, which takes care of all navigation on behalf of the user. Relational data access is a *state space* approach, whereby the user specifies the boolean conditions for the retrieval, and the system returns the data that meets the selection criteria in the SQL statement.

- *Simple conceptual framework*—The relational database is very easy to describe, and even naive users can understand the concept of rows, columns, and tables. The complex network diagrams used to describe the structures of network and hierarchical databases are not needed to describe a relational database.

- *Referential integrity (RI)*—Because business rules are not enforced with pointers, relational databases allow for the control of business rules with *constraints*. These RI rules are used to ensure that one-to-many and many-to-many relationships are enforced within relational tables. Referential integrity is most useful when loading a data warehouse. RI is only checked when a row is added, updated, or deleted, so RI is of no importance during the period where the data warehouse is serving queries. (See Figure 1.9.)

- *Contiguous record storage*—While this was not an initial feature of the relational model, the ability of a relational database to store rows in physical sequential order on disk makes it very appealing for data warehouse applications. As you may know, most data warehouse queries retrieve many rows in a predefined order, and a relational database can aid in reducing physical I/O, because many rows are placed into the database buffer in a single physical I/O.

One of the greatest benefits of relational databases for data warehouses is the concept of *data independence*. Because data relationships are not hard-linked with pointers,

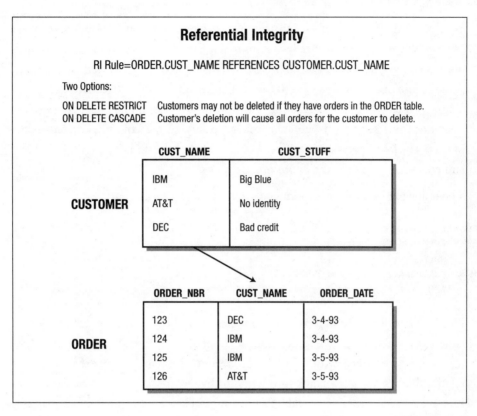

Figure 1.9
An example of referential integrity.

systems developers are able to quickly design warehouses based solely on business requirements.

As mentioned earlier, Codd's relations, or tables, consist of columns and rows. Dr. Codd chose to call a row a *tuple* (rhymes with *couple*), and he refers to many rows as *instantiations of tuples*. Personally, I believe that this obtuse terminology helped to ensure that the relational model gained respect as a legitimate offering, and many professionals began to use Dr. Codd's confusing terminology.

Dr. Codd also introduced the concept of the Structured Query Language (SQL). One should note that SQL is *not* a query language; SQL performs much more than queries (SQL allows updates, deletes, and inserts). SQL is also *not* a language (SQL is embedded within procedural languages such as COBOL or C). Consequently, the name of *Structured Query Language* seemed a logical name for Dr. Codd's new tool.

SQL offers three classes of operators: **select**, **project**, and **join**. The **select** operator serves to shrink the table vertically by eliminating unwanted rows (tuples). The **project** operator serves to shrink the table horizontally by removing unwanted columns. And the **join** operator allows the dynamic linking of two tables that share a common column value. Most commercial implementations of SQL do not support a **project** operation, and projections are achieved by specifying the columns desired in the output. The **join** operation is achieved by stating the selection criteria for two tables and equating them with their common columns.

The following example incorporates a **select**, a **project**, and a **join**:

```
SELECT cust_name, order_date            /* PROJECT  (choose columns)   */
   FROM CUSTOMER, ORDER
   WHERE
   CUSTOMER.cust_nbr = ORDER.cust_nbr   /* JOIN     (tables together) */
   AND cust_type = 'new';               /* SELECT   (specific rows)    */
```

Due to its flexible nature, relational databases are still the vehicle of choice for very large data warehouses. Unlike previous architectures, where all data relationships had to be hard-linked with pointers, the relational database allows for new data relationships to be added at any time with no changes to the physical database structure. All that is required is two tables with common key values, and the data relationship is established with a relational **join**. The relational model is also desirable for data warehouses because of the simplicity of SQL queries (at least, when compared to earlier data access methods). SQL for data retrieval has allowed for end-user query tools to be developed where a non–computer professional can state the data that they need, and the tools generate the SQL on behalf of the end-user. Because many data warehouse queries are ad hoc in nature, this is a very powerful feature.

Database Architectures For The 1990s

The next progression of database architecture is toward object-oriented databases. Early file managers stored data; network databases stored data and relationships; now, object-oriented databases store data, data relationships, and the behaviors of the data. (See Figure 1.10).

The object-oriented approach borrows heavily from the influence of object-oriented procedural languages such as C++ and Smalltalk. Both of these languages allow

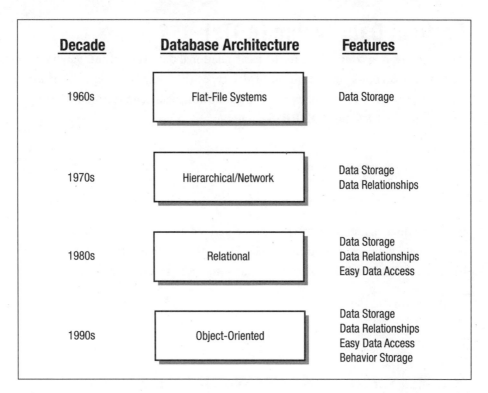

Decade	Database Architecture	Features
1960s	Flat-File Systems	Data Storage
1970s	Hierarchical/Network	Data Storage Data Relationships
1980s	Relational	Data Storage Data Relationships Easy Data Access
1990s	Object-Oriented	Data Storage Data Relationships Easy Data Access Behavior Storage

Figure 1.10
The database evolution toward object-orientation.

coupling behaviors with data. In object-oriented databases, the data and the programs that manipulate the data share common repositories.

With the properties of encapsulation, abstraction, and polymorphism, object technology systems are moving toward a unified data model that models the real world far more effectively than previous modeling techniques. Furthermore, a properly designed object-oriented model promises to be maintenance free, because all changes to data attributes and behaviors become a database task and not a programming task.

The distinguishing characteristic of the object-oriented database is its ability to store data behavior. But how is the behavior of the data incorporated into the database? At first glance, this may seem to be a method for moving application code from a program into a database. While it is true that an object-oriented database stores behaviors, these databases must also have the ability to manage many different objects, each with different data items.

Abstract Data Typing (ADTs)

Rather than being constrained to the basic relational datatypes of **int**, **varchar**, and **float**, Oracle8 allows the definition of datatypes that may be composed of many subtypes (see Figure 1.10). For example, the following data definition could be implemented in Oracle8 as an **ADDRESS** datatype:

```
03 ADDRESS.
          05 street-address              varchar(30).
          05 city-address                varchar(30).
          05 zip-code                    number(5).
```

In this manner, aggregate datatypes can be defined and addressed in a table definition just like any other relational datatype. In the following example, we see the **PHONE_NBR** and **ADDRESS** datatypes being used in a table definition:

```
create table CUSTOMER (
      cust_name           varchar(40),
      cust_phone          PHONE_NBR,
      cust_address        ADDRESS);
```

Here, we see that a single data *field* in a table may be a range of values or an entire table. This concept is called *complex*, or *unstructured*, data typing (see Figure 1.11). The domain of values for a specific field in a relational database may be defined with this approach. This ability to *nest* data tables allows for relationship data to be incorporated directly into the table structure. For example, the **occupations** field in the table establishes a one-to-many relationship between an employee and his or her valid occupations. Also, note the ability to nest the entire **SKILLS** table within a single field. In this example, only valid skills may reside in the **skills** field, and this implements the relational concept of *domain integrity*.

Definition Of Aggregate Objects

In Oracle8, aggregate objects can be defined and preassembled for fast retrieval. For example, a **report_card** may be defined for a university database. The **report_card** object may be defined such that it is assembled at runtime from its atomic components (similar to an Oracle view), or the **report_card** may be preassembled and stored in the database. These aggregate objects may have methods (such as stored procedures) attached to them, such that an Oracle object couples data and behavior together.

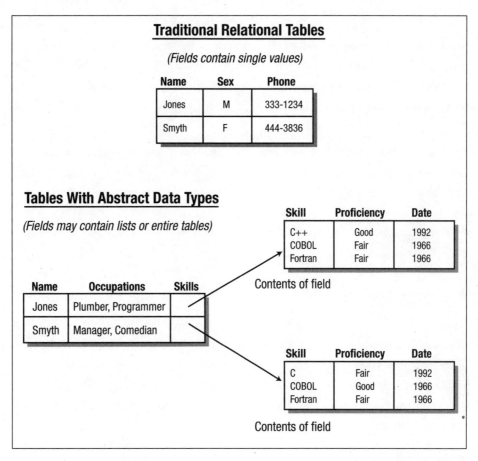

Figure 1.11
An example of abstract datatypes (ADTs).

Coupling Of Data And Behavior

The Oracle8 engine allows for the direct coupling of a database entity (a table or object) with a set of predefined behaviors. In this fashion, calls to Oracle will be made by specifying an object name and the method associated with the object. For example:

```
CUSTOMER.add_new("Jones", 123, "other parms");
```

This call tells Oracle to invoke the **add_new** procedure attached to the **CUSTOMER** object using the supplied parms. As you might expect, this new way of invoking database calls has important ramifications for the developers and DBA staff.

For developers, applications will become SQL-less and will consist of calls to stored procedures. Of course, this has the important benefit of making applications portable across platforms, while also making it very easy to find and reuse code. In addition, because each method is encapsulated and tested independently, the pre-tested methods can be assembled with other methods without worry of unintended side effects.

For DBAs, the coupling of data with behaviors will dramatically change the way DBAs perform database administration tasks. Instead of only managing data and tables, the Oracle8 DBA will also be responsible for managing objects and the methods associated with each object. These new *object administrator* functions will need to be defined so developers know the functions and parameters of each method.

Abstraction

Abstraction within Oracle8 is defined as the conceptual (not concrete) existence of classes within the database. For example, a database may have a class hierarchy that includes classes without objects. A military database may contain the conceptual entities of **division**, **battalion**, **squadron**, and **platoon**. The function of the database is to track the platoons, and the entity classes of **division**, **battalion**, and **squadron** may not have any associated objects. This is not to say that abstract classes have no purpose. When a class is defined, it is associated with behaviors, which in turn will be inherited by each object in the **platoon** class. From a database perspective, there will be no instances of any objects except **platoon**, but higher levels in the class hierarchy will contain behaviors that the **platoon** objects inherit.

Inheritance

Inheritance is defined as the ability of a lower-level object to inherit or access the data structures and behaviors associated with all classes above it in the class hierarchy. *Multiple inheritance* refers to the ability of an object to inherit data structures and behaviors from more than one *superclass*.

To illustrate, let's look at an application of this system for a vehicle dealership. Occurrences of items to a dealership are vehicles; beneath the **vehicle** class, we may find subclasses for cars and boats. The **car** class may be further partitioned into **truck**, **van**, and **sedan** classes. The **vehicle** class would contain the data items unique to vehicles, including the vehicle ID and the year of manufacture. The **car** class, because it **IS-A vehicle**, would inherit the data items of the **vehicle** class. The **car** class might contain data items, such as the number of axles and the gross weight of the vehicle. Because the **van** class **IS-A car**, which in turn **IS-A vehicle**, objects of the **van** class will inherit all data structures and behaviors relating to the **car** and **vehicle** classes.

Important Facts About Inheritance

It is critical to the understanding of inheritance to note that inheritance happens at different times during the life of an object.

- *Inheritance of data structures—At object creation time, inheritance is the mechanism whereby the initial data structure for the object is created. It is critical to note that only data structures are inherited never data. It is a common misconception that data is inherited, such that an order may inherit the data items for the customer that placed the order. We must understand that inheritance is only used to create the initial, empty data structures for the object. In our example, all vehicles would inherit data definitions in the **vehicle** class, while an object of a lower-level class (say, **sailboat**) would inherit data structures that only apply to sailboats—as in **sail_size**.*

- *Inheritance of methods—Inheritance also happens at runtime when a call to a method (stored procedure) is made. For example, assume that the following call is made to sailboat object:*

```
SAILBOAT.compute_rental_charges();
```

*The database will first search for the **compute_rental_charges** in the **sailboat** class; if it is not found, the database will search up the class hierarchy until **compute_rental_charges** is located.*

Not all classes within a generalization hierarchy will have objects associated with them. The object-oriented paradigm allows for abstraction, which means that a class may exist only for the purpose of passing inherited data and behaviors. The classes **vehicle** and **car** would probably not have any concrete objects, while objects within the **van** class would inherit from the abstract **vehicle** and **car** classes. Multiple inheritance is also demonstrated by the **amphibian_car** class. Any instances of this class will inherit data and behaviors from both the **car** and the **boat** classes.

It is important to note the tremendous difference between one-to-many relationships and IS-A relationships. In the previous example, this entire class hierarchy describes vehicles that are associated with the **item** entity in the overall database. Class hierarchies do not imply any data relationships between the classes. While one **customer** may place many **orders**, it is not true that one **car** may have many **sedans**.

Polymorphism

Polymorphism is the ability of different objects to receive the same message and behave in different ways. This concept has many parallels in the real world. An event such as a volcanic eruption may have many different effects on living things in the area. The poisonous gasses may kill all air-breathing animals while at the same time nourish small marine organisms. In this scenario, the single behavior of **eruption** has different effects on objects within the **animal** class. Another analogy can be found in the business world. For a personnel manager, the event of **promotion** will cause different behaviors depending on the class of **employee** that receives the **promotion**. **Management** objects will receive stock options and country club memberships, which are not offered to **staff** objects.

Ronald Popeil was a master of polymorphism. Many folks remember the heyday of Ronco and Popeil, where polymorphic products were advertised at the national level. Consider the statement: *It's a hair cream AND a floor wax.* If this is indeed true, the method **spread_it_on** would invoke very different processes depending upon whether we are applying the cream to a floor or a person's head.

The concept of polymorphism originally came from the programming concept of overloading. *Overloading* refers to the ability of a programming function to perform more than one type of operation depending on the context in which the function is used. For example, consider the following Basic program:

```
REM    Sample Basic program to show polymorphism
REM    Increment the counter
COUNTER = COUNTER + 1
REM Concatenate the String
N$ = "Mr. Burleson"
S$ = "Hello there, " + N$
END
```

In this example, the operator + is used to indicate addition in one context and concatenation in another context. But what determines the way the operator will function? Clearly, the Basic compiler knows that the + operator means addition when it is used in the context where a number is passed as an argument, and it knows that concatenation is required when character strings are passed as an argument to the operator.

The implications of polymorphism are that a standard interface may be created for a related group of objects. The specific action performed by the object will depend on the message passed to the interface. Because the programmer is no longer concerned with the internal constructs of the object, extremely complex programs can be created. The programmer only needs to understand the interface to use the object.

In the real world, polymorphism can be described by looking at standard interfaces. In most PC-based software, the F1 key has a special meaning. Pressing F1 will invoke a context-sensitive help function and explain the function to the user. These help functions have vastly different methods and different data storage techniques, but the standard interface (F1) is polymorphic and invokes different internal mechanisms depending on the software.

Another example are the controls on an automobile. While the internal workings of automobiles are vastly different, the steering wheels are usually round, and the gas pedal is usually to the right of the brake. These polymorphic interfaces make it possible for any person to drive a car without being concerned with the underlying structures of the vehicle.

All communication between objects and their behaviors is accomplished with *messages* that are passed as behaviors. For example, consider the two objects of **rush_order** and **cod_order** belonging to the **order** class (see Figure 1.12).

When a message such as **prepare_invoice** is called, it may contain sub-behaviors, such as **prepare_invoice** and **compute_charges**. The message **prepare_invoice** directs the system to compute the shipping charges. Different procedures will then be invoked depending on whether the receiving object is a **rush_order** object or a **cod_order** object—even though they are both objects within the **order** class. A rush order would include overnight mail calculations, while the COD order would contain additional computations for the total amount due.

Following is an illustration of the differences between an object-oriented procedure call (a message) and the procedural language equivalent:

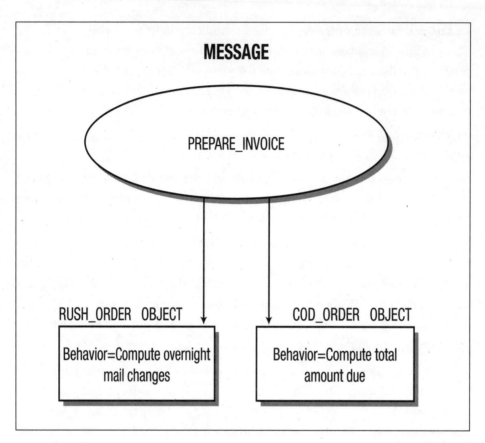

Figure 1.12
An example of polymorphism.

- Object-oriented call:

```
place_order(prepare_invoice(compute_charges))
```

- Procedural language equivalent:

```
if (rush_order)
        compute shipping = tot_amnt * .25
else
        compute shipping = tot_amnt * .10

if (cod_order)
        compute tot_due = tot_amnt + shipping
else
        compute tot_due = 0
```

Encapsulation

Encapsulation means that each object within the system has a well-defined interface with distinct borders. In plain English, encapsulation refers to the "localized" variables that may be used within an object behavior and cannot be referenced outside of that behavior. This closely parallels the concept of *information hiding*. Encapsulation also ensures that all updates to the database are performed by using (or by way of) the behaviors associated with the database objects.

Code and data can be enclosed together into a *black box*, and these "boxes" may then function independently of all other objects within the system. (See Figure 1.13.) From a programming perspective, an object is an encapsulated routine of data and behaviors. Objects may contain *public* variables, which are used to handle the interfaces to the object, and *private* variables, which are known only to the object. Once created, an object is treated as a variable of its own type. For example, an object of class **car** is

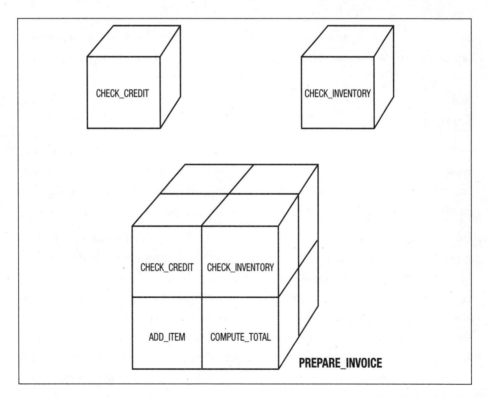

Figure 1.13
An example of encapsulation.

created as a routine with a datatype called **CAR** and is treated as a compound variable by the program.

Encapsulation is used in non-database object-oriented applications to ensure that all operations are performed through the programmer-defined interface, and that data will never be modified outside of the application shell. But what about ad hoc queries and updates? It appears that any declarative database language, such as SQL, that allows external retrieval and update does not follow the dictates of encapsulation and is, therefore, inconsistent with object-oriented database management.

For example, a relational database could be defined to have a behavior called **add_line_item**, which serves to check inventory levels for an item and add an item to an order only if sufficient stock is available. This behavior ensures that orders are not entered for out-of-stock items. However, with a language such as SQL, the object-oriented behavior could be bypassed, and **line_item** records could be added without any regard for inventory levels.

Because encapsulation and SQL are clearly incompatible, the only conclusion that can be reached is that encapsulation may be violated in Oracle8 by using ad hoc tools such as SQL*Plus.

Extensibility

Extensibility is the ability of the Oracle8 engine to add new behaviors to an existing application, without affecting the existing application shell. This is an especially powerful concept and will allow Oracle8 to extend existing classes, guaranteeing that no unintended side effects from the introduction of a new object class will occur.

For example, consider a company that provides payroll services for businesses in many states. Some payroll computations are global (for example **gross_pay** = **hours_worked** * **payrate**), while others are specific to a municipality or state. Using Oracle8, an existing object class definition can be extended, such that the new object behaves exactly like its superclass definition, with whatever exceptions are specified. For example, if New York City instituted a new payroll rule for New York City residents, then the general definition for New York payroll customers could be extended with a new class definition for New York City payroll customers. The only method that would be attached to this class definition would be the code specific to New York City; all other methods would be inherited from the existing superclasses.

The IS-A Construct

Oracle is planning to introduce an extension to their Designer/2000 product to allow for the modeling of class hierarchies. This new extension, tentatively dubbed Designer/2001, should allow for object-oriented constructs to be described and modeled.

Here is a vision of how it might work. After establishing a class hierarchy with the Entity/Relation model (E/R model), the principle of generalization is used to identify the class hierarchy and the level of abstraction associated with each class. Generalization implies a successive refinement of the class, allowing superclasses of objects to inherit the data attributes and behaviors that apply to the lower levels of the class. Generalization establishes *taxonomy hierarchies*, organizing the classes according to their characteristics—usually in increasing levels of detail. Generalization begins at a very general level and proceeds to a specific level, with each sublevel having its own unique data attributes and behaviors.

The IS-A relationship is used to create a hierarchy within the object class, and all of the lower-level classes will inherit the behaviors. The IS-A relationship is used to model the hierarchy created as the class entity is decomposed into its logical subcomponents. Customers may be **preferred_customers** or **new_customers**, and orders may be **cod_orders** or **prepaid_orders**—each with their own data items and behaviors.

The creation of these types of class hierarchies are vitally important for Oracle data warehouses. See Chapter 3, *Data Warehouse Analysis*, for a complete description of creating class hierarchies for Oracle data warehouses.

While the object-oriented data model as defined by ODMG appears to be more rigid than the relational data model, it still has some compelling features for data warehousing. The main drawback to object-oriented databases is their use of embedded pointers to establish data relationships. This means that new relationships cannot be easily added to a data warehouse model. In an object-oriented database, when a new relationship is added, each object in the database must be visited and restructured to make room for the new pointer that establishes the new relationship. Once the objects have restructured to make room for the pointer, a program must be written to add the physical pointers to the pointer fields. This is a very complex and time-consuming operation. In short, the object-oriented data model requires much more careful up-front analysis to ensure that all of the data relationships have been identified before the database schema is compiled.

On the positive side, object-oriented databases have some very useful features for data warehousing. The ability to tightly couple data with behavior makes it very easy to locate warehouse queries. In addition, we can also quickly overload existing behaviors to create new methods. Finally, encapsulation helps ensure that changes to methods only affect their target object type—we never see any unintended side effects from code changes.

Now that we have reviewed the basic database architectures, we should address some of the issues that will arise when extracting data for Oracle warehouses. Remember, many of the data sources for your Oracle warehouse will come from non-relational database architectures, and the savvy warehouse designer must understand how data extraction will function.

To understand the types of applications that Oracle warehouses will be expected to support, let's move on to discuss the basics of decision support systems and expert systems.

Decision Support Systems And Expert Systems

If you look at the evolution of data management platforms, you can see a clear pattern of their use in complex data warehouses. The one factor that has changed is the speed at which questions are being answered. From 1975 through 1990, it was not uncommon for strategic planning managers to have to wait overnight before receiving answers to questions. Today, decision support warehouses require that end users receive query answers in sub-second response times. This fast response time is required primarily because of the nature of the problems being solved. As the user of the warehouse constructs a simulation or develops a what-if scenario, the answer to one question will often generate new questions. Fast response times from databases are indispensable and allow decision makers to develop new questions in response to prior answers.

Expert Systems And Data Warehouses

Expert system is a term used very loosely in the computer community regarding anything from a spreadsheet program to any program containing an **if** statement. In general terms, an expert system models the well-structured decision process of the human mind and applies that reasoning process to a real-world situation. Any decision-making process with quantifiable rules can have the rules stored in an *inference engine*. An inference engine is used to drive the information-gathering component of a system, which eventually arrives at the solution to the problem.

It has been said that an expert system makes a decision *for* the user, while a decision support system makes a decision *with* the user. This distinction is essentially true, because an expert system makes no provision for human intuition in the decision-making process. Many real-world management decisions do not require human intuition, and the data warehouse can provide answers without end-user input. For example, one of the crucial jobs of a retail manager is the choice of what goods to order, the quantity, and the ordering time frame. These decisions can be represented by a model called *economic order quantity* (EOQ). If the EOQ equation knows the speed at which the goods are leaving the retail store, the delivery time on reorders, the average time goods remain on the shelf, and the cost of the goods, the computer can confidently produce automatic daily reports specifying which goods to order and the appropriate quantity. Also, a DSS pre-summarizes data so the manager can quickly take a high-level look at the relevant figures (see Figure 1.14).

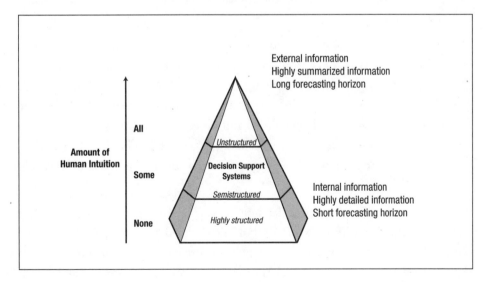

Figure 1.14
Defining different levels of aggregation.

Decision Support Systems And Data Warehouses

Decision support systems (DSS) are generally defined as the class of warehouse system that deals with solving a semistructured problem. In other words, the task has a structured component as well as an unstructured component. In short, the unstructured component involves human intuition and requires human interaction with the DSS. The well-structured components of a DSS are the decision rules stored as the problem-processing system. The intuitive, or creative, component is left to the user.

The following represent some examples of semistructured problems:

- *Choosing a spouse.* While there are many structured rules (I want someone of my religion, who is shorter than me), there is still the unstructured, unquantifiable component to the process of choosing a spouse.

- *Choosing a site for a factory.* This is a nonrecurring problem that has some structured components (cost of land, availability of workers, and so on), but there are many other unstructured components in this decision (e.g., quality of life).

- *Choosing a stock portfolio.* Here the structured rules are the amount of risk and the performance of stocks, but the choice of stocks for a portfolio requires human intuition.

Decision support technology recognizes that many tasks require human intuition. For example, the process of choosing a stock portfolio is a task that has both structured and intuitive components. Certainly, rules are associated with choosing a stock portfolio, such as diversification of the stocks and choosing an acceptable level of risk. These factors can be easily quantified and stored in a database system, allowing the user of the system to create what-if scenarios. However, just because a system has well-structured components does not guarantee that the entire decision process is well-structured.

One of the best ways to tell if a decision process is semistructured is to ask the question, Do people with the same level of knowledge demonstrate different levels of skill? For example, it's possible for many stockbrokers to have the same level of knowledge about the stock market. However, these brokers will clearly demonstrate different levels of skill when assembling stock portfolios.

Computer simulation is one area used heavily within the modeling components of decision support systems. In fact, one of the first object-oriented languages was SIMULA. SIMULA was used as a driver for these what-if scenarios and was incorporated into decision support systems so that users could model a particular situation. The user would create a scenario with objects subjected to a set of predefined behaviors.

In order to be a DSS, a system must have the following characteristics:

- *A nonrecurring problem needs to be solved.* DSS technology is used primarily for novel and unique modeling situations that require the user to simulate the behavior of some real-world problem.

- *Human input is required.* A DSS makes decisions *with* users, unlike an expert system, which makes decisions *for* users.

- *A method is available for testing hypotheses.* A true DSS allows the end user to develop models and simulate changes to the model. For example, the end user could ask questions like, "What will happen to my net return if I exchanged my IBM stock for Microsoft stock?" or "How much faster would I be able to service my customers if I add two more checkout registers?"

- *Users must have knowledge of the problem being solved.* Unlike an expert system that provides the user with answers to well-structured questions, decision support systems require the user to thoroughly understand the problem being solved. For example, a financial decision support system, such as the DSSF product, would require the user to understand the concept of a stock Beta. *Beta* is the term used to measure the covariance of an individual stock against the behavior of the market as a whole. Without an understanding of the concepts, a user would be unable to effectively use a decision support system.

- *Ad hoc data queries are allowed.* As users gather information for their decision, they make repeated requests to the online database, with one query answer stimulating another query. Because the purpose of ad hoc query is to allow free-form queries to decision information, response time is critical.

- *More than one acceptable answer may be produced.* Unlike an expert system, which usually produces a single, finite answer to a problem, a decision support system deals with problems that have a domain or range of acceptable solutions. For example, a user of DSSF may discover that many acceptable stock portfolios match the selection criteria of the user. Another good example is a manager who needs to place production machines onto an empty warehouse floor. The goal would be to maximize the throughput of work in process from raw materials to finished goods. Clearly, he or she could choose from a number of acceptable ways of placing the machines on the warehouse floor in order to achieve this goal. This is called the *state space* approach to problem-solving—first a solution domain is specified, then the user works to create models to achieve the desired goal state.

- *External data sources are used.* For example, a DSS may require classification of customers by Standard Industry Code (SIC) or customer addresses by Standard Metropolitan Statistical Area (SMSA). Many warehouse managers load this external data into the central warehouse.

Decision support systems also allow the user to create what-if scenarios. These are essentially modeling tools that allow the user to define an environment and simulate the behavior of that environment under changing conditions. For example, the user of a DSS for finance could create a hypothetical stock portfolio and then direct the DSS to model the behavior of that stock portfolio under different market conditions. Once these behaviors are specified, the user may vary the contents of the portfolio and view the results.

The types of output from decision support systems include:

- *Management information systems (MIS)*—Standard reports and forecasts of sales.

- *Hypothesis testing*—Did sales decrease in the Eastern region last month because of changes in buying habits? This involves iterative questioning, with one answer leading to another question.

- *Model building*—Creating a sales model, and validating its behavior against the historical data in the warehouse. Predictive modeling is often used to forecast behaviors based on historical factors.

- *Discovery of unknown trends*—For example, why are sales up in the Eastern region? Data mining tools answer questions in those instances where you may not even know what specific questions to ask.

The role of human intuition in this type of problem solving has stirred great debate. Decision support systems allow the user to control the decision-making process, applying his or her own decision-making rules and intuition to the process.

However, the arguments for and against using artificial intelligence to manage the intuitive component of these systems has strong proponents on both sides.

Now that expert systems and decision support systems have been described, let's take a look at how databases are used to develop these systems.

Data Warehouses And Multidimensional Databases

Multidimensional databases are approaching the DSS market through two methods. The first approach is though *niche* servers that use proprietary architecture to model multidimensional databases. Examples of niche servers include Arbor and IRI. The second approach is to provide multidimensional front ends that manage the mapping between the RDBMS and the dimensional representation of the data. Figure 1.15 offers an overview of the various multidimensional databases.

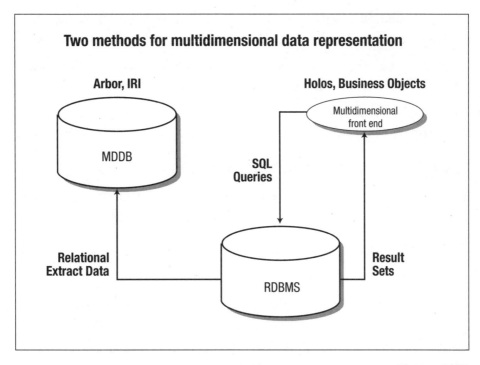

Figure 1.15
The major types of multidimensional databases.

In general, the following definitions apply to data warehouses:

- *Subject-oriented data*—Unlike an online transaction processing application that is focused on a finite business transaction, a data warehouse attempts to collect all that is known about a subject area (e.g., sales volume, interest earned) from all data sources within the organization.

- *Read-only during queries*—Data warehouses are loaded during off-hours and are used for read-only requests during day hours.

- *Highly denormalized data structures*—Unlike an OLTP system with many "narrow" tables, data warehouses pre-join tables, creating *fat* tables with highly redundant columns.

- *Data is pre-aggregated*—Unlike OLTP, data warehouses pre-calculate totals to improve runtime performance. Note that pre-aggregation is anti-relational, meaning that the relational model advocates building aggregate objects at runtime, only allowing for the storing of atomic data components.

- *Features interactive, ad hoc query*—Data warehouses must be flexible enough to handle spontaneous queries by users. Consequently, a flexible design is imperative.

When we contrast the data warehouse with a transaction-oriented, online system, the differences become apparent. These differences are shown in Table 1.1.

Aside from the different uses for data warehouses, many developers are using relational databases to build their data warehouses and simulate multiple dimensions. Design

Table 1.1 Differences between OLTP and data warehouses.

OLTP	Data	Warehouse
Normalization	High (3NF)	Low (1NF)
Table sizes	Small	Large
Number of rows/table	Small	Large
Size/duration of transactions	Small	Large
Number of online users	High (1,000s)	Low (< 100)
Updates	Frequent	Nightly
Full-table scans	Rarely	Frequently
Historical data	< 90 days	Years

techniques are being used for the simulations. This push toward STAR schema design has been somewhat successful, especially because designers do not have to buy a multidimensional database or invest in an expensive front-end tool. In general, using a relational database for OLAP is achieved by any combination of the following techniques:

- *Pre-joining tables together*—This is an obtuse way of saying that a denormalized table is created from a normalized online database. A large pre-join of several tables is sometimes called a *fact table* in a STAR schema.

- *Pre-summarization*—This prepares the data for any drill-down requests that may come from an end user. Essentially, the different levels of aggregation are identified, and aggregate tables are computed and populated when the data is loaded.

- *Massive denormalization*—The side effect of very inexpensive disks has been the rethinking of the merits of third normal form. Today, redundancy is widely accepted, as seen by the popularity of replication tools, snapshot utilities, and non-first-normal-form databases. If you can pre-create every possible result table at load time, your end user will enjoy excellent response time when making queries. The STAR schema is an example of massive denormalization.

- *Controlled periodic batch updating*—New detail data is rolled into the aggregate table on a periodic basis while the online system is down, with all summarization recalculated as the new data is introduced into the database. While data loading is important, it is only one component of the tools for loading a warehouse. There are several categories of tools that can be used to populate warehouses, including:

  - *Data extraction tools*—Different hardware and databases.

  - *Metadata repository*—Holds common definitions.

  - *Data cleaning tools*—Tools for ensuring uniform data quality.

  - *Data sequencing tools*—RI rules for the warehouse.

  - *Warehouse loading tools*—Tools for populating the data warehouse.

Data Extraction For The Oracle Warehouse

As we know, most data warehouses are loaded in batch mode after the online system has been shut down. In this sense, a data warehouse is bimodal, with a highly intensive loading window, and an intensive read-only window during the day. Because many data warehouses collect data from non-relational databases such as IMS or CA-IDMS, no standard methods for extracting data are available for loading into a warehouse. However, there are a few common techniques for extracting and loading data, including:

- *Log "sniffing"*—Applying archived redo logs from the OLTP system to a data warehouse.

- *Using update, insert, and delete triggers*—Firing-off a distributed update to a data warehouse.

- *Using snapshot logs to populate the data warehouse*—Using log files to update replicated table changes.

- *Running nightly extract/load programs*—Using extracts to retrieve operational data and load it into a warehouse.

For details about data extraction and loading of Oracle warehouses, see Chapter 10, *Oracle Data Warehouse Utilities*.

Data Aggregation

Several methods can be used to aggregate data within OLAP servers. As you can see in Figure 1.16, this method extracts data from the relational engine and summarizes the data for display. Another popular method pre-aggregates the data and keeps the summarized data ready for retrieval.

Economic Factors

Two major changes have occurred over the past several years that have driven the movement toward data warehousing. These changes are:

- *Disk space became inexpensive*—One gigabyte of disk carried a price tag of $100,000 in 1988. Today, one gigabyte is less than $1,000. To support large data warehouses, it is not uncommon to require terabytes of disk storage.

- *The movement into open systems*—The migration away from centralized processors has led to data residing on a plethora of different computer and database architectures.

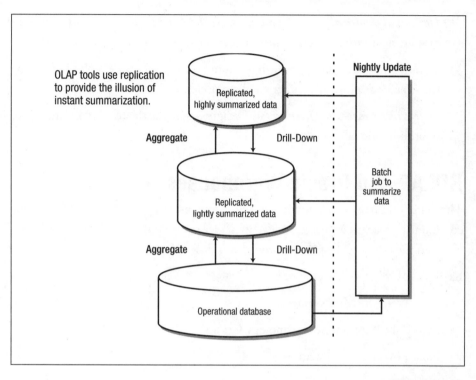

Figure 1.16
Aggregation and OLAP servers.

Metadata And The Oracle Warehouse

Because data is collected from a variety of sources, many warehouse installations find it necessary to create a metadata repository. But what is the role of a metadata repository? When data is consolidated from a variety of diverse systems, many intrasystem problems can arise, such as:

- *Homonyms*—Different columns with the same name.

- *Synonyms*—The same column with different names.

- *Unit incompatibilities*—Inches versus centimeters, dollars versus yen, and so on.

- *Enterprise referential integrity*—Business rules that span operational systems.

- *The warehouse design rules*—Determine how the tables will be built.

- *Horizontal denormalization (chunking tables based on time periods)*—The process of splitting a very large table into smaller sub-tables.

- *Vertical denormalization*— Splitting columns out of very wide tables and storing the separated columns in other database nodes.

- *Using multidimensional front ends*—Designed to make the relational data appear multidimensional.

ROLAP And Oracle Warehouses

There are alternatives to using a pure multidimensional database (MDDB). One common approach is to insert a metadata server between the OLTP relational database and the query tool, as shown in Figure 1.17.

Examples of this approach include:

- DSS Agent, by MicroStrategy

- MetaCube, by Stanford Technology Group

- Holos, by Holistic Systems

Problem Solving For The Oracle Warehouse

If we presume that the main goal of an Oracle data warehouse is to help management answer business questions, then we will need to have some insight into the types of questions that management may ask. For classification purposes, all of the queries against a data warehouse will fall into one of the following categories:

- *Statistical analysis*— Computation of sums, averages, and correlations.

- *Multivariate analysis*—Comparing classes of database objects with each other to analyze patterns.

- *Simulation and modeling*—Using the data warehouse to validate a hypothesis.

- *Forecasting*—Using the warehouse to predict future values.

- *Aggregation*—Composing new objects from existing data structures.

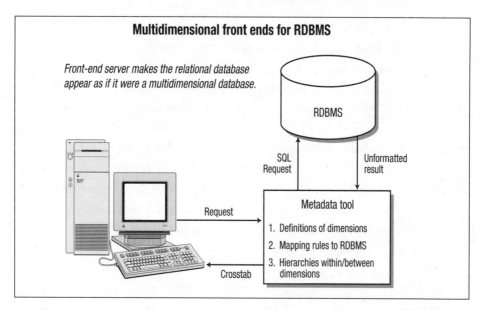

Figure 1.17
Using metadata repositories for multidimensional databases.

Statistical Analysis And Oracle

In general, statistical analysis is one of the easiest end-user vehicles to deliver. Standard Oracle SQL can be used to calculate sums, averages, and aggregate values, and front-end statistical packages such as SAS and SPSS are also commonly used for this purpose. Statistical requests may include multivariate analysis, simulation and modeling, forecasting (linear regression), and aggregation.

Multivariate Analysis

This type of analysis includes comparing various classifications of database objects. Multivariate analysis involves the use of chi-square statistical techniques to compare ranges of values among different classifications of objects. For example, a supermarket may keep a data warehouse of each customer transaction. Multivariate techniques are used to search for correlations among items, so the supermarket management can place these correlated items nearby on the shelves. One supermarket found that whenever males purchased diapers, they were also likely to buy a six-pack of beer! As a consequence, the supermarket was able increase sales of beer by placing a beer display between the diaper displays and the checkout lines.

Multivariate analysis is normally used when the answers to the query are unknown and is commonly associated with data mining and neural networks. For example, whereas a statistical analysis may query to see what the correlation is between customer age and probability of diaper purchases when the end user suspects a correlation, multivariate analysis is used when the end user does not know what correlation may exist in the data. A perfect example of multivariate analysis can be seen in the analysis of the Minnesota Multiphasic Personality Inventory (MMPI) database. MMPI is one of the most popular psychological tests in America, and millions of Americans have taken this exam. By comparing psychological profiles of subjects with diagnosed disorders to their responses to the exam questions, psychologists have been able to generate unobtrusive questions that are very highly correlated with a specific mental illness. One example question relates to a subject's preference to take showers versus baths. Answers to this question are very highly correlated with the MMPI's measure for self-esteem. (It turns out that the correlation showed that shower-takers tend to have statistically higher self-esteems than bath-takers.)

Note that the users of this warehouse do not seek answers about why the two factors are correlated; they simply look for statistically valid correlations. This approach has made the MMPI one of the most intriguing psychological tests in use today; by answering the seemingly innocuous 500 True/False questions, psychologists can gain an incredible insight into the personality of a respondent.

Simulation And Modeling

Simulation modeling is not new for data warehouses. In fact, one of the first object-oriented languages, called SIMULA, dates from the late 1960s. Simulation and modeling are generally used with decision support warehouses where the end user develops a hypothesis and uses the data warehouse to test it. For example, the end user of a shipping warehouse might ask, "What would happen to my total costs if we change from shipper A to shipper B?" Modeling involves taking the data warehouse as input to a model for testing the validity of the model. For instance, a model may have been developed to predict the propensity of a particular type of customer to purchase a particular class of product. This model can be validated against the data warehouse.

Forecasting

Forecasting involves using a data warehouse to predict future values of data items. While forecasting is not new to computer processing, the use of massive data warehouses can create a new vehicle for validating long-term forecasts.

Forecasting has long suffered from a statistical reality called the *trumpet of doom* (see Figure 1.18). While it is very easy to generate a forecast for a short-term future value within an alpha of .05 (*alpha* is a measure of the "confidence interval" for a forecast), a long-term forecast will see the confidence interval widening as time passes.

Following are the four methods for nonlinear regression forecasting:

- Sum of the least squares.
- Single exponential smoothing.
- Double exponential smoothing.
- Triple exponential smoothing.

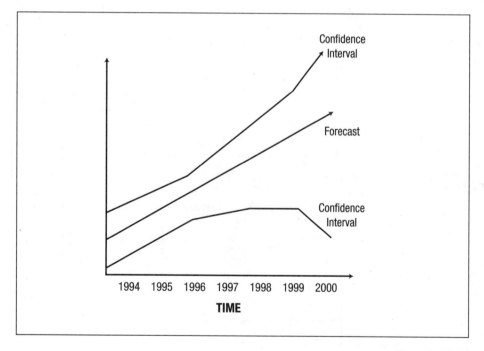

Figure 1.18
The trumpet of doom.

These techniques are applied based upon the nature of the curve exhibited in the baseline data. These forecasting methods are well known to computerized statistical packages, and many tools such as the SAS system hide the smoothing method from the end user. Today's data warehouse tools enable the query system to choose the most appropriate forecasting method based on the characteristics of the historical data. This relieves the end user from the cumbersome task of applying different smoothing methods to each forecast. These smoothing methods are described in detail in any advanced statistics textbook that explains linear regression techniques.

Aggregation

Another common use for statistical analysis is the recomposition of data into new forms. As we know from the relational database model, data is stored in tables at the atomic level. That is, many composite objects must be constructed from their pieces (see Figure 1.19).

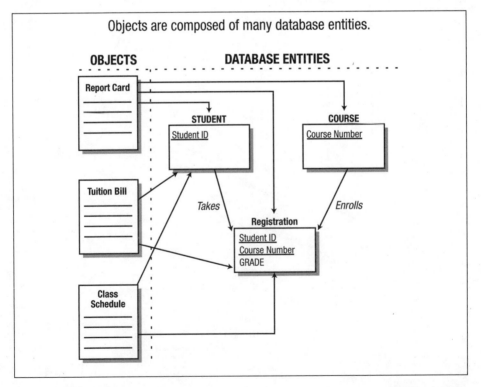

Figure 1.19
Composition of new database objects.

In Figure 1.19, you can see that the data warehouse user desires to model an aggregate object so that the behavior of the artificial aggregate can be compared with the behavior of other aggregate objects. In other words, the data warehouse manager may wish to analyze the nature of tuition bills, class schedules, and report cards, even though these entities are composed, or created, from different components in the OLTP database. This type of aggregation is often achieved through massive denormalization of the data structures when the data warehouse is designed.

Summary

Now that you have a high-level understanding of database architectures and basic types of applications used with data warehouses, we are ready to discuss the details about using Oracle as a vehicle for your data warehouse. The material in this text will become increasingly Oracle-specific, and this book is designed to provide increasing insight into the applications of the Oracle engine for data warehouses. The next chapter will provide an overview of the data warehouse system's development life cycle and describe the importance of project planning in a warehouse development effort.

The Data Warehouse Development Life Cycle

CHAPTER

2

The Data Warehouse Development Life Cycle

In order to fully appreciate the differences between developing an Oracle data warehouse and a traditional online system, we need to concentrate on the major differences in focus and fully understand how data warehouse analysis is unique.

The Evolution Of Database Development

In the early 1960s, corporations began to change their attitudes about information. Prior to this time, corporate information was considered a burden, a thing to be managed and controlled. However, the widespread availability of commercial database management caused corporations to rethink their attitudes about information. Corporations began to consider their information to be an asset, an asset that could be exploited to make better and faster decisions. As most companies adopted database systems, reaction time to changes in the marketplace dropped significantly, and companies had to be able to consult their databases quickly to stay ahead of their competition. By the 1970s, corporate databases were firmly entrenched, and companies struggled to collect and disseminate their information.

One of the main goals of database management systems was the concept of the "central repository," which would store all of a corporation's information and allow information to be accessed and distributed to all areas in the corporation. Many companies underwent expensive conversion efforts and established megadatabases

49

containing many gigabytes of corporate information. The centralized repository promised to allow complete control and sharing of information for all areas within the organization.

As the idea of the corporate repository matured, companies discovered that many of the promises of database technology were not being fulfilled. Even though the data was stored in a central repository, the managers complained that some information was not being provided to them, or the information was not in a form that the managers could use. Many areas within the company also felt that they were hostages of their information systems department. In order to make changes to their systems, they were forced to work with a team of programmers who they felt were unresponsive to their needs. Often, simple changes could take many months and cost thousands of dollars.

The promise of computer systems with a perpetual life span has also proved to be a fallacy. Systems designed to have a useful life of several decades were literally falling apart as a result of the constant maintenance required to keep up with changing demands. Systems delivered with complete documentation and well-structured code soon became unmanageable conglomerations of "spaghetti." An excellent example is the social security system. When the social security system was first implemented, the programs were well-structured and completely documented. The system processed hundreds of thousands of social security checks each month. This very same system received Senator Proxmire's "Golden Fleece" award several years later, when the system was paying social security benefits to many people who were not entitled to benefits. The system, once pristine and well-structured, had become so unmanageable that even the programming staff had trouble describing the functions of each program. The system had to be scrapped and redesigned.

Even with centralized databases, users still faced the problem of diverse data platforms. Many companies embarked on "downsizing" or "rightsizing" their system to take advantage of cheaper processing on minicomputers and PC platforms. In the process, many users abandoned the idea of a central repository of data and attempted to build "bridges" between the applications. Unfortunately, these bridges were often quite complex and difficult to manage. For example, establishing communications between a PC relational database and a CODASYL mainframe database is very cumbersome.

Many companies found that frequent reorganizations and corporate acquisitions led to many diverse platforms for their information. Most large companies have many different database management systems and perhaps dozens of hardware platforms. These market conditions have led many information systems managers to develop systems in a reactive mode, focusing on the immediate need for these systems to communicate, rather than on a common, centralized access method.

In the 1980s, IBM introduced the concept of enterprise modeling, whereby the entire organization's information was modeled, and the overall system was composed of a large client/server environment. This model was based on the idea that data should become independent of its source and that information can be accessed regardless of the type of database manager and hardware platform.

Today, many companies adopt the posture that their systems should exploit the "right" database systems, and it is acceptable to have many different database systems on many different platforms. A relational database, for example, is ideal for a marketing system, while an object-oriented database is well-suited for a CAD system.

Friendly application interfaces also helped to foster downsizing. As end users were exposed to windowing systems on PC networks, they began to view the block-mode systems on the mainframe as unacceptable and began to be more demanding on the information systems staff to produce friendlier and more intuitive systems.

The goal of a centralized data repository could never materialize, especially for dynamic companies. Acquisitions of new companies, mergers, and reorganizations helped to ensure that managers always faced diverse information systems. Ironically, the reason for many acquisitions was to take advantage of the synergy that would materialize from the sharing of information. Consequently, information systems managers became the agents of achieving this synergy, and they faced complex problems associated with establishing communications among diverse platforms.

Data Warehouse Development Methods

Now that we have reviewed the life cycle of a traditional system, let's take a look at how a data warehouse systems development is different from traditional systems. When we examine the differences between a traditional systems development project and a data warehouse project, we need to start at a very high level and examine the major steps that are undertaken in the project. If we compare the development life cycle of a data warehouse with the development of a traditional MIS system, we see some parallels and some surprising differences.

In general, all projects consist of five main phases: feasibility study, systems analysis, systems design, implementation, and ongoing maintenance. Data warehouse projects also have these phases, but there are some differences in the goals in each phase.

In traditional development, the greatest share of effort is generally spent in the implementation phase. In addition, the benefits from the project do not begin until the complete system is delivered (see Figure 2.1).

To understand all of the steps that occur between the inception of a warehouse project and the delivery of the finished system, let's take a quick look at the overall phases of a data warehouse development project. Later in this chapter, we'll take a more in-depth look at each phase.

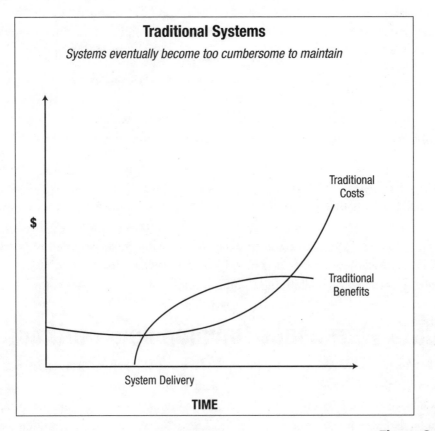

Figure 2.1
The traditional systems development life cycle.

Phase 1: Feasibility Study

A *feasibility study* is a cost/benefit analysis for a proposed system, quantifying all tangible costs and benefits for the warehouse, as well as describing intangible costs and benefits. Essentially, the goal of this study is to provide a go/no go decision about whether to proceed with the data warehouse project. Activities involve an analysis of technological and economic feasibility with a focus on understanding all of the costs and benefits that will accrue from the data warehouse.

Phase 2: Systems Analysis

A *systems analysis* is a logical description of the data sources for the warehouse, data extraction analysis, data cleansing analysis, and data loading analysis. Unlike a traditional system, the warehouse analysis is heavily data-centric and not concerned with defining the system interfaces.

When compared to implementation, the systems analysis phase requires a relatively small amount of effort. This is often due to an impatience with management, as well as a reflection of the power of the new CASE tools. It is no longer necessary to devote a huge amount of effort into a systems analysis before undertaking systems design. The inherent flexibility of the Oracle architecture makes it very easy to alter the database structure if some data item was missed during the analysis phase. For more information on this topic, see Chapter 3, *Data Warehouse Analysis*.

Phase 3: Systems Design

The *systems design* phase is the physical implementation of the logical data model that was developed in the systems analysis phase. This includes the design of the warehouse, specifications for data extraction tools, data loading processes, and warehouse access methods. At this phase, a working prototype should be created for the end user.

The system design phase is also where the logical documentation is transformed into a physical structure. For database design, this involves the creation of the entity/relation model, and the determination of appropriate data storage techniques and index usage. This phase is where a thorough understanding of Oracle architecture will pay off. For more information on this topic, see Chapter 4, *Oracle Data Warehouse Design*.

Phase 4: Implementation

The *implementation* phase is the phase in which the warehouse is constructed and the software is written and tested.

The implementation phase normally consumes as much effort as all of the other steps combined. Advocates of object-oriented development claim that this is a direct result of a failure of the team to do a thorough job in the analysis and design phases. They argue that this phase is time consuming because hidden anomalies are discovered and code must be revised constantly to accommodate new insights into the nuances of the system. Regardless of the reason why, it remains true that the implementation phase is by far the most time-consuming phase in the creation of a warehouse system.

Oracle also has some very specific rules and techniques that can be used to ensure maximum performance. There are several chapters devoted entirely to Oracle-specific topics, but the text will first concentrate on providing a firm conceptual understanding of data warehouse design for relational databases.

Phase 5: Ongoing Maintenance

Ongoing maintenance is the final phase of the creation of a warehouse. The ongoing maintenance of the warehouse generally involves the constant loading of new data and addressing the changing analysis requirements of end users.

If a development team has done a good job of analyzing, designing, and coding a new system, you might suspect that the programming team would disband immediately after coding is completed. But this is not the case. The cost curve continues to grow after a system has been delivered. This can be attributed to the dynamic nature of systems requirements. Almost by definition, most long-term development efforts will deliver an obsolete system to their end users. The end users often lament, "You gave me the system that I needed two years ago when you began the project! Many requirements have changed, even while you were creating the system." Of course, this is a very common complaint, and it is not surprising to see that the programming staff immediately begins addressing the maintenance requests that have been stacking up while they were initially creating the system. Of course, a traditional computer system will continually become more and more expensive to maintain, until the cumulative costs exceed the benefits of the system. A goal of a savvy systems manager is to foresee this dilemma and to start rewriting the system so that a new system is ready to replace the aging system when the costs become too cumbersome.

Here, you will begin to see some of the major differences between a warehouse project and the type of project that you may have worked on in the past. As noted earlier, systems analysis and design phases are very data-centric as opposed to process-centric. In the early stages of warehouse development, designers are very concerned about collecting all of the data from the legacy data feeds and not at all concerned with how end users may use the data.

Warehouse End-User Requirements

Not concerned about end-user analysis? Yes! When you approach your end-user community, especially those who have not used a data warehouse before, you will be met with blank stares when you begin to gather data analysis requirements. Many experienced warehouse developers attest that the end users become increasingly sophisticated in their use of the data warehouse, largely as a function of becoming familiar with the power of the system. Initially, all the warehouse designer needs to address is getting the data into the warehouse. The uses for the data will follow when the end-user community becomes familiar with the data delivery vehicle and recognizes the potential types of data analysis that can be delivered by your warehouse.

When a data warehouse system is delivered, end users initially tend to make simple queries, followed by an ongoing cycle of more and more complex types of data analysis. In general, the following progression of usage takes place for a brand-new data warehouse.

1. *Basic analysis*—Calculation of averages and sums across salient subject areas. This phase is characterized by a reliance on heuristic analysis methods.

2. *Correlation analysis*—End users begin to see the value of their warehouse, and they develop models for correlating facts across data dimensions. This stage marks the beginning of stochastic data analysis.

3. *Multivariate data analysis*—End users begin to perform correlations on groups of related facts, and they become more sophisticated in their use of analytical statistics.

4. *Forecasting*—End users begin to use statistical packages (SAS, SPSS) to generate forecasts from their data warehouses.

5. *Modeling*—End users begin to recognize that they can test hypotheses against their data warehouse, and they begin to construct simple what-if scenarios.

6. *Simulation*—End users are now intimate with their data, and they begin to construct sophisticated simulation models. This is the phase where previously unknown data relationships (correlations) are often discovered.

7. *Data mining*—End users begin to extract aggregates from their warehouses, and feed them into neural network programs to discover unobtrusive correlations.

The time required for end users to go from simple analysis to data mining may take years! Hence, there is no way that a data warehouse designer can predict the types of analysis that end users may someday request from the warehouse.

Most warehouse developers concentrate their efforts into providing an *n*-way interface into the warehouse, such that the end user is able to extract cross-aggregates by any two data items they choose. See Chapter 4, *Oracle Data Warehouse Design*, for details on this method.

Now that we've taken a broad look at data warehouses, let's narrow our focus and examine some of the main features of a typical data warehouse project.

The Feasibility Study

The feasibility study is the phase of a data warehouse project with the smallest amount of overall effort. This is to be expected because the cost/benefit analysis for a proposed system can be done fairly quickly by a few qualified analysts. However, the speed of the delivery of a feasibility study should not minimize the importance of this phase. All computer systems must deliver a benefit relative to their costs, and this phase determines the payback period for the effort. The first phase of any warehouse development project is the assessment of feasibility. In general, a feasibility study addresses the following two components:

- *Technological Feasibility Analysis*—Answers the question, "Are the requirements for the system achievable with current technology?"

- *Economic Feasibility Analysis*—Answers the question, "Will the return on investment warrant the development of the warehouse?"

Technological Feasibility

Technological feasibility is an analysis process that is always changing, and data warehousing is no exception. Companies have always wanted the ability to store and analyze vast quantities of historical data, but the cost of disk storage was prohibitive. For example, in 1985, a 2 GB IBM 3380 disk drive cost more than $100,000. Given this cost disparity, it is not surprising that end-user requirements for sub-second response times were technologically feasible but prohibitively expensive. Therefore, data continued to be stored on magnetic tape, and end users were forced to wait overnight for their answers.

Today, a 2 GB disk drive (with faster access speed) can be purchased for less than $300, but it is still not uncommon to see requirements that are not feasible with today's technology. Ever since Arthur Clark's movie *2001* made its debut, people have had a misconception about the power of computers. The HAL computer in *2001* gave many viewers the impression of a higher level of computer sophistication than is really possible, and this misconception remains today.

The end-user management for a legal publishing system once stated that they required a display format screen that would replicate the shape of an $8^1/_2 \times 11$ sheet of paper. Another manager wanted to create an OLTP system that was capable of processing 5,000 requests per second.

While these examples may seem extreme, the savvy warehouse developer must ensure that the end-user community does not hold any misconceptions about the functions of their new data warehouse. It is imperative to clearly state to the end users what functions their new warehouse can and cannot perform. While end users may appreciate that their data warehouse will evolve, becoming increasingly more sophisticated, they must clearly understand what types of analysis will be possible after the initial delivery of the data warehouse.

Economic Feasibility

Just as any computer system must be justified in financial terms, the data warehouse project must also demonstrate an ability to add a positive cash flow to the company that is creating the warehouse. Economic feasibility considerations include (but are not limited to) development costs, warehouse benefits, and ROI (return on investment).

Development Costs

As we know, it's fairly simple to calculate the hardware and software costs for creating the data warehouse. All of a data warehouse's basic costs, such as the cost of the processor and disk, are known in advance and are fully quantifiable. But there are other hidden, intangible costs that may be quite real, but are more difficult to quantify. For example, using a nascent technology may provide a competitive advantage, but there is a very real cost associated with the risk in using a new technology. Some managers have resorted to a probabilistic method for attempting to quantify the costs of risk, just as actuaries have developed very sophisticated methods for assessing the costs associated with risks. However, risk costs are rarely factored into the development costs of a data warehouse project because they cannot be precisely measured. But does this mean that the cost does not exist? Of course not. The costs associated with risk will become tangible during the development of the data warehouse, when increasing human and technical resources are required to fix problems that crop up during the implementation phase of the warehouse. While development costs may not be factored into development costs, the costs should not catch developers by surprise. Developers should keep hidden risk costs in mind, especially when conducting a feasibility study.

Warehouse Benefits

The benefits from a data warehouse are far less easy to measure than development costs. Benefits for a data warehouse project fall into two categories: tangible benefits and intangible benefits. Of course, it is important to have a very concrete idea about the benefits that will accrue from a data warehouse project, especially because the expenditures of human resources and computer equipment is a substantial investment.

A *tangible benefit* is a benefit that can be accurately measured. For example, a data warehouse that allows for more direct targeting of promotional mailings could be said to have a tangible benefit of reducing mailing costs by $300,000 per year.

An *intangible benefit* is recognized as a value that clearly exists but is not quantifiable. For example, goodwill is often listed as an intangible benefit. A company may have achieved a loyal customer base due to goodwill. Customer loyalty translates directly to increased sales, but goodwill remains intangible because goodwill sales can't accurately be separated from total sales. According to generally accepted accounting principles, an intangible benefit becomes tangible only when a dollar amount can be fixed to the benefit. For example, let's say that a business with an intangible benefit of goodwill is sold for an amount greater than the value of the company's property, plant, and equipment. If the property, plant, and equipment of the company is only valued at, say, $30 million, yet a buyer is willing to pay $40 million, the accountant must assume that the $10 million difference is due to the intangible benefit of goodwill. At this point, goodwill becomes a tangible benefit because a precise dollar amount has been assigned to it. The point is, intangible benefits are very real, and they should not be ignored even though it is difficult to place a dollar amount on the benefit. Other examples of intangible benefits include:

- Worker productivity

- Quantity of information

- Confidence in management

- Fast delivery of information/products

- High quality of information/products

Computing Return On Investment (ROI)

Return on investment is the financial method most commonly used by organizations to determine which projects should be undertaken. In simple terms, *ROI* is the payback period for a project. For a data warehouse project, ROI analysis begins by looking at the business areas that will be changed by the implementation of the warehouse.

ROI is only one of several methods that a company might use to make an investment decision about a project. Other techniques, such as the Net Present Value method, the Internal Rate of Return method, and the Payback period method, may also be utilized for the calculations.

ROI is not restricted to data warehouse investment decisions. Often ROI is used to make financial decisions such as deciding whether to acquire new property, choosing to downsize operations, and determining whether to lease or to buy assets.

To illustrate ROI, let's look at a simple example. Assume that you are an antique dealer, and you see a Maxfield Parrish print at a yard sale for $20. You purchase the print and immediately run home to look up the book value of the print. You see that this print has a full retail value of $250, and you are delighted with your investment. Now, however, you are immediately faced with another decision. You can price your print at full retail of $250, knowing that it will probably take a year to sell the print, or you could price the print at $200 and sell it immediately.

The ROI on an immediate sale for $200 can be quickly computed using the following formula:

```
ROI = Present Value Of Benefits / Present Value Of Costs
```

Using the formula, you can determine that an immediate sale would yield an ROI of ((200-20)/20), or a 800 percent return on your $20 investment. Not too shabby, but what about waiting a while to see if you get $250 for the print?

Here, you enter the realm of the time value of money. Because you will have to wait a year to acquire the additional $50 in benefit, you need to consider your opportunity cost of capital. That is, if you freed up your $20 investment by an immediate sale, how much additional revenue could you generate by having that $20 to invest in other antiques? To know the answer, you must compute your opportunity costs and determine the relative merits of each option. In corporations, the opportunity cost of capital has been carefully computed, and the answer can be determined by applying the discounting factor associated with the opportunity cost of capital to the future revenues.

The discounting factor must take into account more than just the opportunity cost of capital. For example, if our current inflation rate is 10 percent, then you must also factor this into your decision. The intangible costs of risk are also sometimes factored into a discounting rate. Remember, you are dealing with the probability that your Parrish print will take one year to sell for $250, and your confidence in this estimate must also be taken into account. If you are 95 percent certain that the print will sell within one year, then there is a 5 percent possibility that the print will remain in the store for a period longer than one year, and you must factor this risk into your equation.

Applying the discount rate to future costs and benefits is not as simple as subtracting the future amount by the percentage discount rate. When computing the net present value of a cost or benefit, you must recognize that the discount rate is applied in an iterative fashion according to specific time periods. For example, your opportunity cost of capital might be the rate of return that you could earn from a certificate of deposit that pays 8 percent compounded yearly. If this were the case, then you would reapply your discount rate on a yearly basis. However, matters get more complicated when opportunity costs are compounded more frequently. Some financial institutions pay interest compounded monthly, daily, and even continuously. In our picture example, the opportunity costs might be the inability to purchase other antiques that may sell faster, or at a higher profit margin.

Usually, the data warehouse manager can call the accounting department and ask for the discount rate for the company and the periods for the rates. Then, it is a simple matter of using net present value techniques to compute the present values of costs and benefits.

Regardless of the method, all of the return-on-investment calculations should result in a net dollar value. Remember, when doing a cost-benefit analysis you must take into account the total accrued future costs and benefits, all the while expressing the terms in net present value dollars. Quantitatively, this involves using calculus to determine the space under the cost and benefit curves.

To illustrate how costs and benefits are quantified and discounted for a data warehouse project, let's consider the data warehouse project estimates for Project alpha. Table 2.1 shows Project alpha's costs, and Table 2.2 shows Project alpha's tangible and intangible benefits.

The first thing to note is that Project alpha's costs and benefits do not occur within the same spans of time. In order to compare apples with apples, both the costs and the benefits in the project need to be expressed in net present value dollars. This involves discounting the cashflows according to the opportunity cost that the company possesses. Not all opportunity costs are the same. A securities investment firm

Table 2.1 Project alpha's costs.

Cost	Amount	Time Frame
Ongoing Costs		
Cost of analysis and design team	$40,000/month	Immediate
Costs of programming team	$60,000/month	6 Months
One-Time Costs		
Cost of CPU and DASD	$15,000,000	10 months
Costs for data extraction and loading	$10,000,000	12 months
Costs for client hardware/software	$10,000,000	15 months

Table 2.2   Project alpha's benefits.

Benefits	Amount	Time Frame
Tangible		
Reduced direct mail costs	$3,000,000/year	24 months
Reduced inventory costs	$2,000,000/year	24 months
Intangible		
Improved quality of information	unknown	24 months
Improved response time to market changes	unknown	24 months

that commonly realizes a 24 percent return on investments will have much higher opportunity costs than a conservative organization that realizes an average 12 percent return on investment.

Regardless of the discounting method, both future costs and future benefits must be expressed in today's dollars. Ten years ago, President Reagan had a favorite joke about the Russian million-dollar lottery, where the winner was paid at the rate of one dollar a year for a million years. This joke illustrates that a future amount of money can radically change in value depending upon the rate at which that the money is received. Clearly, in a fair economic analysis all cashflows must be summed and expressed in present value dollars. Graphically, this involves computing the areas under the cost curve and the benefit curve over the useful life of the data warehouse.

In most cases, a project's costs and benefits reach a point when cumulative benefits exceed the costs of the project. But this doesn't mean that every project whose benefits outweigh the cost should be undertaken. Most companies have limited capital resources and can only afford to choose those projects that have the fastest return on investment. As such, a company needs to weigh its options and invest in the projects that show the most promise for a fast payback, with an ongoing revenue stream.

However, it is a very common mistake for an organization to rely too heavily on quantitative methods for choosing projects, ignoring intangible benefits that may accrue from investment in a data warehouse. Many intangibles, such as the ability to remain competitive in an aggressive market, are enormously important to a company, even though they cannot be expressed in dollars. It is for this very reason that many data warehouse projects are driven by top management without regard for the costs, simply because it has become a requirement for doing business. Whether the company is a banking institution, a supermarket chain, or a manufacturer, companies in a competitive marketplace are beginning to realize that the proper use of information resources is imperative to the ongoing success of a company.

Data Warehouses And ROI

A data warehouse project should never begin unless management feels that the benefits of a data warehouse outweigh the cost. With that basic assumption under our belts, let's look at some of the differences between how the ROI for a data warehouse compares to the ROI for other information systems development projects.

The International Data Corporation (IDC) conducted a survey in 1996 that studied ROI for data warehouse projects. IDC found the following trends in data warehouse projects:

- *Very fast payback*—The average ROI for a data warehouse is far above the industry average. Corporations with complex organizational and customer environments benefit the most. IDC found that more than 60 percent of data warehouse projects have a payback period of less than two years.

- *Large ROI variance*—The variance of ROI among organizations ranges from 3 percent to 1,800 percent. The low ROI values are attributed to very expensive data warehouse projects that take several years to develop and have a small amount of usage.

- *Higher ROI for data marts*—IDC found that databases larger than 200 GB had smaller ROI values than smaller data warehouses. This difference is attributed to the extra work required to integrate and maintain the diverse data sources.

- *Application area differences*—There are differences among data warehouse ROIs based on the type of organization that develops the data warehouse. Data warehouses designed to support engineering and operations tend to have the highest ROI. This makes sense because, historically, manufacturing organizations have been among the first to embrace data warehousing. The IDC study also shows that European companies developing data warehouses lag behind American companies by a 100 percent margin of ROI, with European companies averaging 340 percent ROI and American companies averaging 440 percent ROI.

The overall finding in the IDC study showed that data warehouses are popular primarily because of the fast payback period for the dollar investment. Interestingly, the payback period most likely will become even shorter as data warehouse developers create more intelligent queries against their data and become more adept at locating and analyzing trend information.

Warehouse Project Management

When embarking on a data warehousing project, many pitfalls can cripple the project. Characteristics of successful data warehouse projects generally include the following aspects:

- *Clear business justification for the project*—Measurable benefits must be defined for a warehouse project (e.g., sales will increase by 10 percent, customer retention will increase by 15 percent). Warehouses are expensive, and the project must be able to measure the benefits.

- *Staff is properly trained*—Warehousing involves many new technologies, including SMP, MPP, and MDDB. The staff must be trained and comfortable with the new tools.

- *Ensuring data quality and consistency*—Warehouses deal with historical data from a variety of sources, so care must be taken to create a metadata manager that ensures common data definitions and records changes of historical data definitions.

- *Ensuring subject privacy*—Gathering data from many sources can lead to privacy violations. A good example of privacy violation is the hotel chain that targeted frequent hotel customers and sent a frequent-user coupon to their home addresses. Some spouses intercepted these mailings, leading to numerous divorces.

- *Allow the warehouse to start small and evolve*—Some projects fail by defining too broad of a scope for the project. Successful projects consider their first effort as a prototype and continue to evolve from that point.

- *Ensure intimate end-user involvement*—Data warehouses cannot be developed in a vacuum. The system must be flexible to address changing end-user requirements, and the end users must understand the architecture so they are aware of the limitations of their warehouse.

- *Properly plan the infrastructure*—A new infrastructure must be designed to handle communications among data sources. Parallel computers must be evaluated and installed, and staff must be appropriately educated.

- *Perform proper data modeling and stress testing*—The data model must be validated and stress tested so that the finished system performs at acceptable levels. A model that works great at 10 GB may not function as the warehouse grows to 100 GB.

- *Choose the right tools*—Many projects are led astray because of vendor hype. Unfortunately, many vendors inappropriately label their products as "warehouse" applications, or they exaggerate the functionality of their tools.

Basic Project Management

As a general definition, a *project* is any set of tasks with a specific objective to be completed within certain specifications (including defined start and end dates) that consumes capital resources. Given this simplistic definition of a project, let's define what *project management* is and how it applies to a data warehouse project.

For every large data warehouse project, traditional management must be replaced by a new type of management that is temporary and very flexible, with a fast reaction time, and able to respond rapidly to both internal and external changes. With this type of management in place, data warehouse project management encompasses the following activities:

- Defining work requirements
- Defining the quantity of work
- Defining the resources needed
- Monitoring the project by:
    - Tracking progress (dates and milestones)
    - Comparing actual figures to predicted figures
    - Analyzing the impact of changes
    - Making adjustments to the project

While these tasks may seem mundane, effective project management is critical to the success of a data warehouse. Successful project management is defined as meeting the objectives of a project within project and cost constraints, while maintaining a desired level of performance and fully utilizing the proper technology.

To effectively fulfill the project management functions listed previously, data warehouse project managers must be able to:

- Identify function responsibilities and ensure that all activities are accounted for.

- Minimize the need for continuous reporting.

- Identify the time limits for scheduling.

- Identify a methodology for tradeoff analysis (shifting resources).

- Measure the project accomplishments against the plans.

- Identify and resolve problems quickly.

- Improve estimation capabilities for future planning.

- Keep track of meeting project objectives.

Data warehouse project management is different from traditional management in several ways. First, while the evolution of data warehouse queries may be perpetual, the initial creation of the warehouse is a finite activity, and the project manager must be able to deal with this temporary authority because other managers are performing the staffing functions, supplying members of the data warehouse team. To further confound matters, the data warehouse project manager does not have direct control over the financial resources.

Effective Project Management

In general, there are two levels of project management: top-level project management, which controls the overall warehouse project, and functional management, which incorporates everyone involved in the operational details associated with each specific milestone of the project.

The size of a warehouse project does not really impact how the project is modeled and controlled. While there are numerous tools, such as PERT (Project Evaluation and Review Technique), that can be used for very large data warehouse projects, all warehouse projects are fundamentally the same; the only variables are the number of sub-projects and the complexity of integrating the sub-projects.

A very large warehouse project, such as building an enterprise wide data model for a large corporation, may involve thousands of milestones and man-centuries of effort, but they still maintain the fundamental nature of a warehouse project. (A man-century is equivalent to 100 people working full time for a year.) The issues are purely a matter of scale. However, it is comforting to see that a data warehouse project, even with a man-century of effort, is relatively small when compared to other projects such as building an aircraft carrier, which could consume the full-time efforts of thousands of people for several years. Table 2.3 shows three levels of project size. As you can see, a data warehouse project is generally classified as a medium-size project.

The management of an organization must not underestimate the importance of effective project management, and effective project management includes troubleshooting. Troubleshooting usually involves at least one of the following three categories:

- *High Costs*—Cost overruns stemming primarily from improper allocation of human resources.

- *Project Delays*—Project delays are often a result of wasted resources (i.e., materials, people, and so forth), which can cause the premature or late delivery of project resources.

- *Poor Quality*—Poor quality occurs when a project does not meet performance or functionality objectives.

In any case, special care must be taken to ensure that project management avoids as many unforeseen problems as possible. One of the best ways to ensure that a data warehouse project is created soundly is for the warehouse team to prepare a complete description of the project, clearly stating all project requirements and expectations up front. This description is called a *scope of work agreement.*

The Scope Of Work Agreement

Once the basic requirements for a warehouse have been determined, the next step is to codify the project with a *scope of work (SOW)* agreement. Simply put, a data warehouse

Table 2.3   Levels of project size.

Project Size	Number Of Tasks	Project Duration
Small	Hundreds	Months
Medium	Thousands	Years
Large	Millions	Decades

SOW is a contract between end-user management and systems development management that states the functions of the data warehouse, costs for the warehouse, and expected benefits from the warehouse.

Unlike an ordinary SOW, there are some specific issues that need to be addressed when creating a data warehouse SOW contract. First, notice that end-user *management* is involved in a data warehouse SOW, as opposed to the end-user *community* normally involved in an information system SOW.

End-user management for a data warehouse project usually consists of *top-level managers*. Unlike line and staff managers who deal with information systems on a regular basis, top-level management may be somewhat detached from the actual use of information systems. Also, top-level management may not be used to using decision support warehouses because much of their decision making has traditionally relied heavily on "human intuition." The introduction of an information warehouse can be both exciting and frightening for top-level managers, especially when a data warehouse may provide counterintuitive information or may be regarded as threatening by some managers.

Another consideration in an SOW is the dynamic nature of the data warehouse. It's practically guaranteed that system requirements are going to change as the data warehouse develops, both as a function of changing needs from the end-user community as well as from additional insight into the uses of the data warehouse. Therefore, it is imperative that the SOW spells out as much detail as is known at this phase of the project (see Figure 2.2).

Of course, developers are not going to know all of the details about a proposed warehouse until system analysis has been completed, but developers need to carefully document the details that *are* known at this point. For example, details may include:

- *A description of the data sources for loading the warehouse*. This may specify that the data sources reside in IMS hierarchical databases, DB2 mainframe relational databases, Oracle Unix databases, ISAM flat files, or any other data sources. Legacy and OLTP data sources need to be identified as a part of the SOW, as well, so the project can justify any human resources needed for data extraction tasks. For example, data extraction from an IMS database requires an IMS programmer with DL1 skills, while extraction from an IDMS database requires the services of an MVS systems programmer and an application

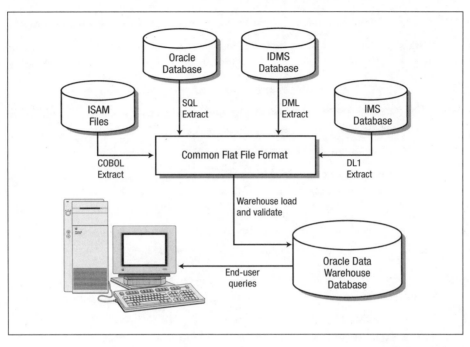

Figure 2.2
The overall development for a data warehouse project.

programmer who understands JCL, IBM mainframe utilities, and CODASYL DML programming.

- *A description of the basic data elements of interest to the warehouse users.* This description incorporates the facts that will constitute the data warehouse and consist of the definitions of numeric items, such as sales amounts, inventory levels, and net revenue. Even for a warehouse that consumes terabytes of disk storage, there may only be a small handful of these facts that are being tracked. The size of the warehouse comes from the wholesale denormalization of the facts with their data attributes.

- *A description of the "dimension" attributes.* Dimension attributes are non-fact items that lend value to a fact, such as a date, an item type classification, or a sales district. The dimension attributes for facts are critical to the implementation of the data warehouse. The SOW must describe each of these attributes and how attributes may be nested within other attributes. (For example, end-user management may want to see summary sales of states within districts, within regions.) Many warehouse development managers include classification hierarchies in the SOW to clearly identify the nature of the attributes relation to other data attributes.

- *A determination of the amount of aggregation and summarization for each fact.* This is sometimes called the *level of data granularity.* For example, the SOW might state that monthly sales will be tracked against sales district, inventory class, item category, and so on, until each and every aggregation has been identified. The level of summarization varies from system to system, but it needs to be clear what levels of summarization will be available to end users and whether they will be able to drill-down into increasing levels of detail. For example, most Oracle warehouses do not allow end users to drill-down into the lowest level of transaction detail because this data is often stored in a non-Oracle database system.

- *The choices for hardware and software platforms.* While designers may not know the exact types and model numbers of disks, CPUs, and software programs, they should be able to specify broad categories of hardware and software elements. For example, at this point, designers should know what processors are required, and they should be able to estimate the necessary amount of disk space and the cost of the Oracle engine and any other client software and statistical packages that will be used. (Many experienced managers have remarkable success in making disk space estimations by using a SWAG—a scientific wild-assed guess! A SWAG should apply proven statistical estimation techniques to educated guesses. Fortunately, experienced designers often prove to be remarkably accurate when their SWAG is later compared to actual figures.)

- *A listing of the functional deliverables.* This list is a functional description of the analytical capabilities that end users expect from the data warehouse. For example, the listing might state that end-users require a multidimensional presentation of Oracle data and that they desire simulation, modeling, decision support, forecasting, data mining, and so on. The listing should be a broad description of functional requirements, without delving into technical or product-specific details. Often, the details will not become apparent until the warehouse design phase. At this point, designers merely specify the type of end-user delivery metaphor that will be used. For example, multidimensional data analysis commonly uses a spreadsheet metaphor—this can be stated without actually picking a spreadsheet product.

- *A detailed cost-benefit analysis.* As discussed earlier in the chapter, a detailed cost-benefit analysis includes a complete description of the costs and benefits of the data warehouse, both tangible and intangible, expressed in net present value dollars. This analysis may also include an estimate of the payback period for the project, which was also discussed earlier in this chapter.

- *A current project plan.* A project plan is where the high-level project plan and work breakdown structure is documented. Project plans should include rough estimates of the number of project participants and their desired skill requirements, as well as a Gantt chart showing the progression of the major phases of the project.

In addition to specifying as much detail as possible, the SOW should spell out the function that the data warehouse will *not* be able to perform. The data warehouse development staff must take every precaution against any misconceptions from the end-user community, and it is far better for the end user to have low expectations that are exceeded by the Oracle warehouse, than it is to have the end users excited with grandiose and unrealistic expectations, only to have them disappointed during the implementation phase of the project.

The SOW should be regarded as a binding agreement between the end-user management and the data warehouse management, and it should be as formal as possible, spelling out realistic scope and delivery schedules for each phase of the project. There have been numerous data warehouse projects that have collapsed after the data warehouse management has spent several million dollars on hardware and software, only to become mired in issues of scale. And while most savvy data warehouse managers create rough prototypes to demonstrate the data warehouse to end-user managers, this sometimes creates difficulties because end-user management may not understand why a project is taking so long if they've already seen a working prototype, leading them to believe that you have already done much of the work!

Misunderstandings are common, but they can be minimized if data warehouse management can help end-user managers understand the technical issues involved in the creation of the warehouse. No mater how well-designed a data warehouse might be, it is imperative to keep the lines of communication open between end-user management and the data warehouse management in each and every phase of warehouse development. In short, the SOW makes or breaks the success of a data warehouse development, and it should be treated very formally.

The Data Warehouse Team

Unlike a traditional systems development project, planning for a data warehouse project involves a very different type of staff, including programmers from each legacy data source and managers who understand the architectures of each database supplying input to the data warehouse. Very specific sets of skills are often required for the development of any Oracle warehouse project, and these skills are simple to identify, even before the minute details are fleshed out. In general, a data warehouse team uses a *matrix organization*. In a matrix organization, data warehouse team members are given data warehouse development assignments while they continue to report to their traditional line managers. In other words, managers continue to maintain authority over their personnel, while the data warehouse project manager holds authority over the data warehouse *project*, using data warehouse team members only within their capacity for the development effort (see Figure 2.3).

While the size of a data warehouse team may vary from a handful of participants to more than 100 full-time developers, all data warehouse teams should consist of a

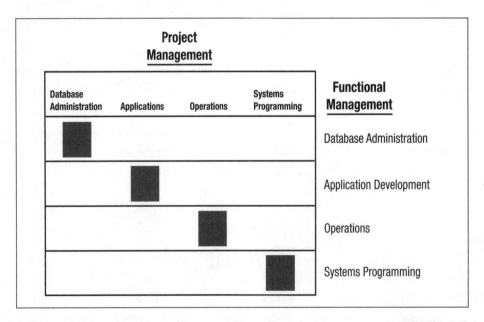

Figure 2.3
A matrix organization for a data warehouse development team.

project sponsor, project manager, warehouse architect, systems administrator, legacy database experts, data warehouse DBA, operations manager, metadata specialist, end-user interface specialist, network administrator, Oracle developers, and a statistician. The roles for each participant are as follows:

- *Project Sponsor*—The project sponsor for a data warehouse should be a senior vice president who truly believes in the necessity of the data warehouse and is zealous in his or her conviction about developing a first-rate data warehouse.

  The relationship between the project sponsor and the project manager is defined such that the sponsor exists solely for the purpose of facilitating communications among the end-user management and the data warehouse management. Because the project sponsor is a figurehead—in the sense that he or she is not directly involved in the data warehouse project as a full-time occupation—it is desirable to find a project sponsor from the highest ranks of management because end-user managers are often highly placed within most organizations. Ideally, the project sponsor is at the vice president level or Chief Information Officer (CIO), the top person in an information systems organization. This ensures that the project sponsor is able to facilitate the needs of the data warehouse project from the highest levels of the organization. The right placement of the project sponsor can also be invaluable when a project is delayed, and the sponsor can remind end-user management about the value of the data warehouse and obtain any additional staffing or capital required to overcome the hurdle.

- *Project Manager*—Project managers must have superior organizational, communication, and technical skills. As discussed earlier, data warehouse project management generally involves millions of dollars and dozens of participants. Consequently, a data warehouse project manager must be well-versed in quantitative project management techniques, such as PERT and CPM. Project managers must always be up-to-date on warehouse development activities, and they should be able to efficiently allocate resources to ensure a timely and cost-effective project completion.

- *Warehouse Architect*—A warehouse architect is usually a senior Oracle database administrator who has an extensive background in data modeling and data design. For organizations that are new to data warehousing, an outside consultant is often used to train an in-house architect in the nuances of data warehouse design. The idea of massive denormalization and data redundancy may sometimes seem abhorrent to data architects for OLTP systems, and it can be a wise investment to augment the architect with an outsider who has a proven record in effective Oracle data warehouse design.

- *Systems Administrator*—A systems administrator is in charge of low-level operating system software. The systems administrator should understand the technical ramifications of the data warehouse hardware, including parallel processing, RAID, and system access security. Many of these technologies will be foreign to systems administrators, and it is usually a good idea to hire data warehouse consultants to review the hardware operations and computer configurations.

- *Legacy Database Experts*—Legacy database experts are the DBAs, SAs, and programmers who can assist in the analysis and extraction of data from the legacy systems. Members of this sub-team are usually chosen for their expertise in understanding their OLTP applications, especially in the areas of data extraction and data formatting. Dealing with members of the legacy team can sometime be challenging because legacy team members may feel "trapped" in ancient technology. Consequently, it is often helpful to orient the legacy staff to the "big picture" relating to the data extraction, cleansing, and loading processes of the data warehouse.

- *Data Warehouse DBA*—A data warehouse DBA is often a senior Oracle database administrator who has the technical skills required to ensure that the data warehouse is fast and efficient. The DBA will be responsible for developing backup and recovery strategies as they directly apply to the data warehouse, horizontally partitioning the fact tables into manageable pieces, and creating the Oracle SGA and ensuring optimal data warehouse performance. If an Oracle parallel server is chosen as part of the software configuration, the Oracle DBA should be trained in the use of Oracle with SMP or MPP processors. Again, it is often wise for organizations to hire outside Oracle DBA consultants to conduct a review of existing Oracle database architectures, and this cost should be incorporated into the project estimates.

- *Operations Manager*—The operations manager controls the hardware and the machine room. The operations manager will be challenged with devising methods for enforcing physical data security, backup and recovery systems, disaster recovery systems, and capacity planning. The area of backup and recovery is especially challenging to an operations manager when many terabytes of data must be kept recoverable. The operations manager should develop a close working relationship with the Oracle DBA and the systems administrators in developing a strategy for operations functions.

- *Metadata Specialist*—The metadata specialist is usually a senior data administrator who, ideally, has an intimate knowledge of the data in the operational systems, whether the systems are legacy databases such as IMS or OLTP Oracle databases. In addition to understanding the data structures and data relationships, the metadata specialist must also be well-versed in SQL and understand the ramifications of **not null** data characteristics. The metadata specialist will work closely with the legacy data extraction team to develop a common data format for the extraction and to devise a method for cleansing and validating the data.

- *End-User Interface Specialist*—The end-user interface specialist is the PC guru who will be charged with determining client-side requirements. This includes the end-user interface software, any client-side statistical packages, and ad hoc Oracle query tools. End-user interface specialists work concurrently with the development of the data warehouse, and they polish the end-user interfaces using small-scale prototypes of the data warehouse. Interpersonal skills are imperative for this specialist because they will be working directly with the end-user managers to meet their data requirements.

- *Network Administrator*—A network administrator is usually a network engineer whose job is to ensure that data is cleanly transported from the Oracle servers to the client platforms. For many distributed Oracle data warehouses, the scope of the data transport network may be worldwide and may also involve Web-based data delivery techniques. As such, a network administrator must be familiar with cross-domain data transport (i.e., LU6.2 with TCP/IP), and they must be able to ensure that the network does not become a bottleneck, especially when large amounts of data are transported to the clients.

- *Oracle Developers*—Oracle developers are the programmers who assist in the project by developing the data aggregation and data summarization programs for the data warehouse. These programmers should be well-versed in all aspects of the Oracle database, as well as Oracle parallel query techniques. In addition, these programmers should be intimate with operating system language interfaces, including Tcl, Perl, OraPerl, C, and so on.

- *Statistician*—A statistician is the one member of the data warehouse development team that is assigned the task of translating the end-user data analysis requirements into an operational method. The statistician must be fluent in all areas of quantitative data analysis techniques, including multivariate analysis (chi square), forecasting, simulation, and hypothesis testing, as well as having an intimate knowledge of computer-based statistical packages, such as the Statistical Analysis System (SAS) or the Statistical Package for the Social Sciences (SPSS). The statistician will work closely with the data warehouse programmers to ensure that all data analysis requirements are met.

The Organizational Framework

The first step in organizing an Oracle data warehouse project is to have the warehouse sponsor inform the line managers of their needs for staff within each functional area. As each functional area becomes staffed, inter-area communication is very important for the effective development of the system. Many developers must be familiar with concepts that are outside their functional areas, and they must have the freedom to get the external information that they require. For example, the Oracle developer may need DBA information from the Oracle DBA, and the Oracle DBA may need systems information from the SAs. In general, the organizational hierarchy for the project involves a traditional reporting structure, as shown in Figure 2.4.

Note the relationship between the project manager and the project sponsor in Figure 2.4. The project sponsor's job is to facilitate communications with all operational areas to ensure that the project manager gets the resources they require in a timely fashion.

The Project Delivery Schedule

Unlike many traditional information system projects, where a new system is being developed to replace a legacy system, the data warehouse project does not need to have a firm delivery date. In fact, most successful data warehouse projects follow an iterative delivery schedule, where small pieces of the data warehouse are delivered, one at a time, widening in scope, until the completed warehouse is delivered (see Figure 2.5).

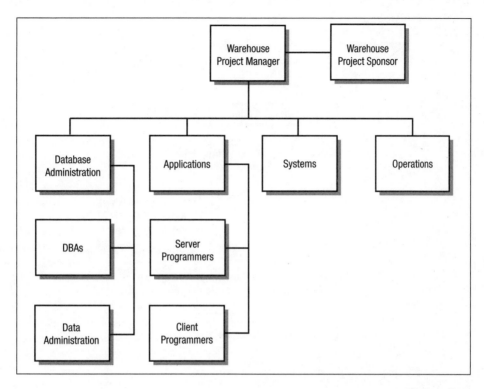

Figure 2.4
A sample reporting structure for a data warehouse development team.

As you can see in Figure 2.5, small pieces of the data warehouse can be delivered independently from other pieces. In general, the slices of the data warehouse fall into two categories: data slices and function slices. For example, a data warehouse manager may be able to deliver the sales data for 1995 through 1997 to end-user managers within six months, and then, while the end users use the 1995-97 data, the 1993-94 data can be extracted and loaded into the data warehouse. In addition, functional delivery partitioning is common for the data warehouse. Cross-tabulations of summary data (multidimensional displays) can be delivered quickly so that end users can use this functionality, while the warehouse team completes the simulation and modeling components of the data warehouse system.

When the overall project delivery schedule is examined, designers often notice many opportunities for concurrent development exist, as shown in Figure 2.6. In this Gantt chart, you can see how the development of the end-user interface can proceed at the

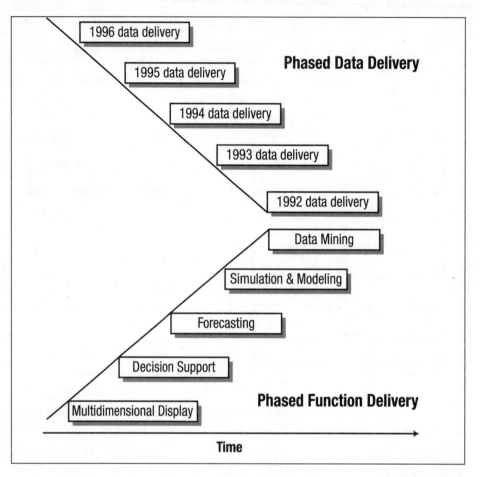

1996 data delivery

Phased Data Delivery

1995 data delivery

1994 data delivery

1993 data delivery

1992 data delivery

Data Mining

Simulation & Modeling

Forecasting

Decision Support

Phased Function Delivery

Multidimensional Display

Time

Figure 2.5
A phased delivery schedule for a data warehouse.

same time as the data extraction and cleaning processes are performed. The effective application of human resources to these types of concurrent tasks is called *crashing* a project, and it has been demonstrated that data warehouse projects have many opportunities to accelerate the delivery times.

In order to accelerate the delivery times for a data warehouse project, a Project Evaluation and Review Technique (PERT) chart or a Critical Path Method (CPM) chart must be developed to identify those tasks that fall onto the critical path for the system. PERT was developed in the 1960s by the U.S. Navy to manage their Polaris submarine projects. Both PERT and CPM involve identifying tasks that fall onto

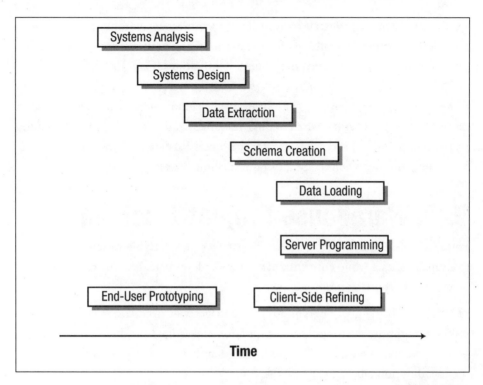

Figure 2.6
Gantt chart for a data warehouse project.

the critical path for a system. A *critical path task* is a task for which there is no slack time. Hence, if the critical path task is delayed, the delivery time for the entire project is delayed. Conversely, if the delivery time for the critical path task is accelerated, then the delivery of the entire project is faster. It is a critical management skill for the data warehouse project manager to constantly identify those task that lie on the critical path.

As time is reported after development is underway, data warehouse managers may see that the critical path changes. It is not uncommon to misjudge time estimates for tasks, especially when the project involves a new technology. A project manager must be diligent in identifying tasks on the critical path. The second component involves identifying the necessary skill sets for each task. Remember, at any given time, there will only be a few tasks that lie on the critical path. The rest of the tasks have slack time and can be delayed without affecting the overall project delivery time.

Consequently, managers can usually reallocate resources away from noncritical tasks to critical tasks, thereby crashing the task on the critical path and speeding the delivery of the overall system. Of course, there are limitations. Consider the old adage: *If one woman can have a baby in nine months, nine women should be able to have a baby in one month*. There comes a time in every development project where we see a diminishing rate of return when adding resources, and it is indeed true that "too many cooks spoil the broth." The key for the successful data warehouse project manager is determining when the point of diminishing return has been reached.

Data Warehouse Project Tracking

For a data warehouse project, the savvy manager must be able to track the project from many angles while ensuring that the lower-level management produces complete project reporting information.

Let's start with the obvious. The project manager will need to identify the major tasks that comprise the project implementation and assign time durations, resources, and completion criteria (quality checks) to each major task. For example, consider the task duration table shown in Table 2.4.

Here, you can see how this collection of tasks, resources, times, and dependencies can be collected and graphically displayed. As mentioned earlier, there are two major ways to display project information: PERT and CPM.

Warehouse Project Model

As mentioned, the critical path is a task(s), which, if delayed, puts the delivery of the finished project behind schedule. While both PERT and CPM allow for critical paths to be identified and tracked as the status of the projects are updated, these techniques also allow for modeling how human resources can be reallocated among the tasks. The reallocation of human resources enables managers to shift time requirements and recompute the critical paths. Both PERT and CPM allow crashing techniques used to accelerate delivery times.

Contingency modeling is another popular feature, whereby the manager may create artificial scenarios and use their model to predict the overall impact on the project.

Table 2.4 A task duration table.

TASK ID	TASK_NAME	Duration	Dependencies	Skill Required
101	Extract Program	79 hours	98, 100	C++ Proficient
102	Load Program	28 hours	101, 95	VB Proficient
103	Report Menu Program	19 hours	37	HTML
104	Report Program	49 hours	98, 101	C++ Proficient

The most effective project management tools contain the following features:

- A central data repository that can be accessed and updated by remote sub-project managers. Ideally, the software includes the ability to notify the top manager of any sub-managers who have failed to update their current project status.

- A time-based "versioning" facility, whereby the status of a project at any given time can be created.

- The ability to "drill-down" into increasing levels of detail regarding task and status information.

- The ability to "roll-up" to the highest level of summarization for the purpose of identifying tasks that are on the critical path for the entire project. (Remember, while each sub-manager must deal with their own critical paths, the top-level project manager must recognize that *some* of these critical tasks will also appear on the critical path for the overall project.)

- The ability to tie human capabilities to tasks while weighing the relative skills of the human resources. For example, a "guru" level C++ programmer can write a program four times faster than a "standard" level C++ programmer, who, in turn, writes code two times faster than a "newbie" level C++ programmer.

- A modeling facility that can be used to create and test what-if scenarios. There are three categories of modeling:

  1. Additional resources are applied to a project to accelerate delivery dates (crashing the project).

  2. Human resources are reallocated to tasks, and the expected delivery dates for all sub-tasks are recomputed.

3. Delivery times for major milestones can be quickly recomputed from current delivery estimates, providing the top management with the most critical in-process subtasks.

There are several project management software packages in the marketplace to assist with managing a data warehouse project. The most popular software for very large projects include Project Management by Primavera, P2, and Artemis. For smaller projects, Table 2.5 provides a list of popular tools for small- to medium-size projects.

Risk Management And Data Warehouse Projects

Data managers must always be cognizant that estimates of resources for a data warehouse project are only *estimates*, and that a certain element of risk is involved in any estimation. In the following example, you can see that the addition of human resources to a specific programming task has been estimated. You know, of course, that each marginal resource assigned to a project will increase the costs, and you can also safely assume that at some point, adding another resource will increase costs, without necessarily improving delivery dates (see Figure 2.7).

As you can see from Table 2.6, the data warehouse project manager must understand how to add additional human resources to a task in order to maximize delivery time. Just about any task that falls in the critical path of a project can be crashed by adding

Table 2.5 Popular project management software for smaller projects.

SOFTWARE TOOL	VENDOR
Project	Microsoft
CA-SuperProject	Computer Associates
Time Line	Time Line Solutions
Insta Plan	Micro Planning International
FlowCharting	Patton & Patton
MacProject	Claris
Project	Scitoc
Project Management	Primavera Systems

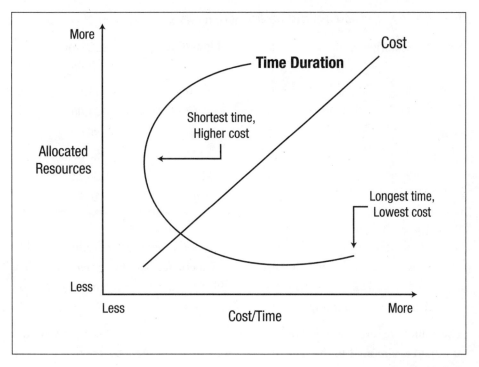

Figure 2.7
Risk and project management.

more resources, but, as mentioned earlier, there is a point of diminishing returns. This concept is especially true for data warehouse development, because many programming tasks cannot easily be partitioned into pieces that can be concurrently developed.

The project manager must also be able to make conscious tradeoffs when assigning programming resources to data warehouse tasks. As you can see in Table 2.7, there is

Table 2.6   A comparison of resources to assign to a specific task.

Resources	Time	Cost
Joe	7 days	$700 (Best for a noncritical task)
Joe and Francis	5 days	$800
Joe and Sam	4 days	$900 (Maximum crash point)
Joe, Sam, and Francis	4 days	$800

Table 2.7   A comparison of cost per line of computer code.

Years Of Experience	Rate	Lines/Day	Cost/Line
1	$20	10	$2.00
3	$30	20	$1.50
5	$40	40	$1.00
7	$50	80	$0.62
10	$60	160	$0.38
12	$70	300	$0.23
15	$80	400	$0.20

often a tradeoff between programmer experience and programmer productivity. The real test is to weigh the additional costs for experienced programmers with their productivity. Table 2.7 demonstrates that while experienced programmers may cost more than naive programmers, they are often a better investment.

The point here is very simple; the duration of a task is a function of both the amount of resources allocated to the task and the productivity of the resource that has been assigned to the task.

Summary

Now that we have covered the basic areas of project planning for our data warehouse, we are ready to proceed with the formal analysis of warehouses. The subsequent chapters will follow the data warehouse development cycle presented in this chapter in approximate the same order. First, we'll look at warehouse analysis, followed by warehouse design, and then warehouse implementation. As the chapters proceed, the material will become increasingly Oracle-centric and technical in nature.

HIGH PERFORMANCE

Data Warehouse Analysis

CHAPTER

3

HIGH PERFORMANCE

Data Warehouse Analysis

There are many differences between traditional systems analysis and Oracle warehouse systems analysis. In a traditional systems analysis, the goal is to document all of the logical processes, describing data transformations, data stores, and external inputs and outputs from an existing system and a proposed system. Figure 3.1 displays a traditional systems development project.

In contrast, a data warehouse systems analysis focuses on determining the data requirements and data sources of a system, and documents how to extract and package data for end users. Figure 3.2 displays an Oracle data warehouse development project.

Another major difference between analysis for OLTP systems and data warehouse systems lies in the descriptions of the user interface. In a traditional analysis, careful attention is given to the method the end user will implement when interacting with the system. In a data warehouse analysis, developers expect that most, if not all, queries against the warehouse will be ad hoc. As such, data warehouse developers have more interest in specifying the data for the warehouse than for specifying the data access methods.

Do not confuse the analysis of data access methods with the analysis of data query requirements. While you may not care what *tool* is used to extract queries from your warehouse, you should care very much about what *types of queries* will be executed against your warehouse. We will discuss this issue later in this chapter.

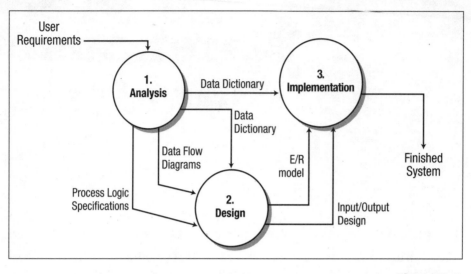

Figure 3.1
A traditional systems development project.

Another analysis issue comes into play because Oracle warehouse developers know in advance that they are using an Oracle database to implement the warehouse. Oracle, by virtue of being relational, is inherently flexible, and it is relatively easy to drop or add data columns to table structures. A consequence of this reality is that

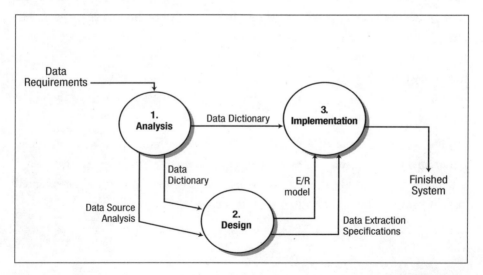

Figure 3.2
A data warehouse development project.

developers can often begin prototyping the data warehouse before a complete analysis of data sources has been completed. To demonstrate this flexibility, consider the following code where we quickly alter our fact table to drop one column and add another:

```
SQL > ALTER TABLE FACT DROP COLUMN customer_type;
column dropped
SQL > ALTER TABLE FACT ADD COLUMN total_sale INT;
column added.
```

Of course, the flexibility of the relational architecture is only useful when prototyping the warehouse. The final data items should be carefully considered before the initial rollout of the system because altering a very large table can cause a huge amount of table fragmentation in a production warehouse. To fully appreciate the differences between traditional systems analysis and data warehouse analysis, let's review the analysis steps for both traditional data processing systems and data warehouses.

Traditional Systems Analysis

There are three commonly accepted methods for systems analysis: the Gane & Sarson method, the Ed Yourdon method, and the Tom DeMarco method. Recently, we have seen a new interest in systems analysis methodologies using object orientation, with new methodologies being introduced by Jim Rumbaugh, Peter Coad, Grady Booch, and Schaller & Mellor. Regardless of the individual theory, all systems analysis models share some common goals and activities. For example, all the theories state that before any physical construction of a system may begin, the new system must be completely analyzed to determine all of the process logic involved in the system. In addition, all the methodologies require identification of the functional primitive processes and documentation of all data stores and data flows among the processes.

The output of a system analysis is logical because no physical constructs are introduced into the model. Physical constructs are added in the design phase. For example, the analysis phase may document a customer file, but developers are concerned only with defining the data characteristics and not at all concerned about how this file will be represented physically. Whether the customer file is stored on Rolodex cards, an ISAM file, a BDAM file, or an Oracle database is irrelevant in data analysis. Remember, it is the *logical* specification that is used as the input in systems design. But how does the systems analysis change when a data warehouse system is being developed?

Regardless of the type of system being created, a logical analysis must always precede the start of systems design, and the design must be completed before programming can begin. In an effort to consolidate the systems development methodologies, research papers have been published about the proper way to incorporate data warehouse development into existing analysis and design methodologies.

Fundamentally, the purpose of any systems analysis is to logically identify the processes and the data moving between the processes, and to describe the processing rules and data items. Only after these items are defined can design begin, regardless of the physical implementation of the system. To meet these goals, a data warehouse analysis should begin with the creation of a structured specification. A *structured specification* is a document that describes all of the data, data storage, external entities, and processes for a system. This document is then used in the design phase for the creation of the behaviors, entity/relation model, and class hierarchy.

The Structured Specification

Most of the system analysis methodologies provide a method for documenting logical processes, data items, and data stores. These components generally include:

- *Data Flow Diagrams*—A set of top-down diagrams that depict all processes within a system, the data flow among the processes, and the data stores. Figure 3.3 depicts a sample data flow diagram. The data flow diagrams (DFDs) begin at a very general level and become progressively more detailed. The lowest level of processing is called the *functional primitive* level, and this primitive level has been traditionally used as the starting point for systems design.

- *Data Dictionary*—A description of all of the logical data items, including all data flows and data stores (files). The data dictionary describes how all of the data items are stored and how they have been transformed by the processes. The data dictionary file specifications also become the foundation for the relational tables that will comprise the Oracle warehouse.

- *Process Logic Specifications (mini-specs)*—A description of all functional primitive processes. A process is defined as an operation that modifies a data flow. The tools used to describe processes include pseudocode, procedure flowcharts, decision trees, and decision tables.

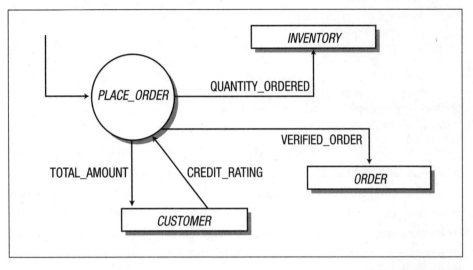

Figure 3.3
A sample data flow diagram.

In a traditional systems analysis, the DFD does not stand by itself. Rather, the DFD is augmented by a data dictionary that describes all of the data flows and files, and a set of process logic specifications that describe how each process transforms data flows. A process logic specification (sometimes called a *mini-spec*) can be expressed as structured English, decision trees, or any of the many other techniques used to describe how data flows are being changed. Listing 3.1 shows a sample process logic specification using structured English.

Listing 3.1   A Level 1 DFD process logic specification for the **place_order** behavior.

```
Mini-spec for PLACE_ORDER:

IF TOTAL_AMT > 1000
   CHECK credit_rating in CUSTOMER
   IF credit_rating = 'BAD' THEN reject order
   ELSE store order record
END IF

FOR  (each item on the order)

   -- Compare qty_ordered in order with qty_on_hand in item.
   IF qty_on_hand < qty_ordered
```

```
    Remove item from order
    Prepare backorder slip
ELSE

-- Add the item to the order.
Subtract qty_ordered from qty_on_hand
Move qty_ordered to qty in line_item
Store line_item record.
NEXT ITEM
```

In traditional systems analysis, data dictionary definitions for all data items are *normalized*, or grouped, into database entities, which become entity/relational models in systems design. Eventually, the E/R models become relational tables during system implementation. The identification and grouping of data items constitutes the entities that will establish the basic entity/relation model for the database engine. For example, consider the interaction between the **place_order** process and the data files in Figure 3.3. The process **place_order** uses the data flow **total_amt** to check the credit rating in the **CUSTOMER** file. It also uses **qty_ordered** to check the inventory level for the item, then moves **qty_ordered** to the **line_item** record, and finally stores this record in the file.

The Role Of Functional Decomposition

The principles of top-down analysis tells us to begin our data flow diagram (DFD) at a very general level. The entire system is viewed as a single process, and this view is called a *context-level* DFD. Next, the DFD is decomposed, and levels of detail are added to the model. Any process that can be identified can probably be subdivided into smaller processes, and it is possible to decompose a DFD to the level where each process represents a single statement. An extreme example of functional decomposition would be showing a statement such as **ADD 1 TO counter** as a separate process on the data flow diagram. The pivotal question is: *At what point should the developer stop decomposing the processes?*

Theoreticians such as Gane and Sarson tell us that a DFD should be decomposed to the functional primitive level, where each process bubble performs one granular function. Under this definition, one could consider that the **place_order** behavior performs only one function and is therefore a functional primitive process. A good rule of thumb for data warehouse analysis, especially when the warehouse is intended to be used with a relational database, is that a DFD should be decomposed to the level where each process corresponds to an SQL operation. This allows the use of triggers within a relational database and greatly simplifies the data warehouse design.

As you are probably beginning to see, the level of partitioning is critical for a successful data warehouse systems analysis. Let's explore this concept of partitioning a little further. In a traditional systems analysis, the **place_order** behavior is sufficiently partitioned, whereby the **place_order** process would become a single computer program. This program would perform all of the data manipulation and would have many DML verbs embedded within the code (see Figure 3.4). Following is what the mini-spec might look like for a **place_order** process:

```
place_order (
    check_credit(SELECT ON CUSTOMER)
    add_order(INSERT ON ORDER)
    check_inventory_level(SELECT ON ITEM)
    decrement_inventory(UPDATE ON ITEM)
    add_line_item(INSERT ON LINE_ITEM)
)
```

While this level of decomposing is fine for traditional systems analysis, it is better to continue to decompose the **place_order** behavior in relational data warehouses. In a relational data warehouse, **place_order** would be divided into its sub-processes, namely

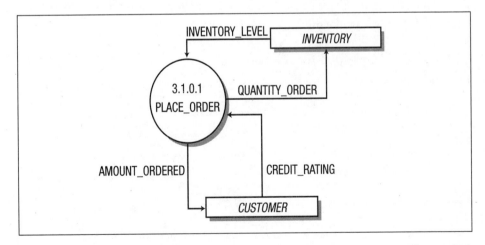

Figure 3.4
A Level 1 data flow diagram.

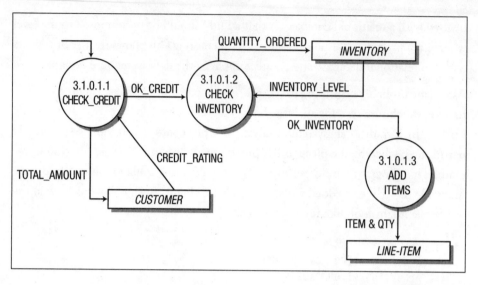

Figure 3.5
A decomposed data flow diagram.

check_credit, add_order, check_inventory_level, decrement_inventory, and add_line_item (see Figure 3.5).

Each of the sub-processes within the place_order behavior will have its own process logic specifications, and each sub-process can be encapsulated into an Oracle stored procedure or trigger. The behavior place_order is now decomposed into its sub-behaviors, as shown by the mini-spec in Listing 3.2.

Listing 3.2 Mini-spec for a Level 2 DFD.

```
IF TOTAL_AMT > 1000
    CHECK credit_rating IN CUSTOMER
    IF credit_rating = 'BAD' THEN reject order
    ELSE store order record
END IF

MINI-SPEC for CHECK_INVENTORY

FOR (each item on the order)

    -- Compare qty_ordered in order with qty_on_hand in item.
    IF qty_on_hand < qty_ordered
        Remove item from order
        Prepare backorder slip
```

```
NEXT ITEM

MINI-SPEC for ADD_LINE_ITEM

FOR (each item on the order which is in stock)

    -- Add the item to the order.
    Subtract qty_ordered from qty_on_hand.
    Move qty_ordered to qty in line_item.
    Store line_item record.

NEXT ITEM
```

As you can see, each behavior within the database now corresponds with a single database update operation. The insert on the **line_item** record is associated with the **add_item** behavior. This one-to-one partitioning is only important for database updates, as **SELECT** operations may still access many records within the database.

There is still a great deal of controversy about the best way to approach database analysis for data warehouse systems. Architecturally, some theoreticians state that the relational model is better suited for use in an online transaction processing environment and multidimensional architectures are better suited to data warehouses. Oracle Corporation has stated that they will incorporate a user-defined datatype in their future release of Oracle8. Some argue that a database must be able to have datatypes that are lists rather than finite values, and some databases, such as UniSQL, allow for single datatypes (fields) to contain lists of values or even another table.

Developers must remember that the main difference between traditional systems analysis and data warehouse analysis is the focus on the data sources. Because a data warehouse will never have data coming from an online data input screen and all of the end-user interfaces will be ad hoc in nature, the data identification, loading, and query processing is of foremost importance.

Data Warehouse Analysis

Another basic distinction between traditional systems and data warehouse systems is the goal of the analysis phase. Data warehouse analyses are data-driven, unlike traditional systems where process logic is the central focus. But, how does an analyst shift from thinking about systems in the traditional way to thinking about systems as a collection of integrated data items?

As discussed earlier, traditional analysis is focused on understanding the process logic and documenting the data behind each process. Data warehouse analysis differs in that the source databases that already exist have been clearly defined. Therefore, the goal of data warehouse analysis is to understand which data items are of interest to the warehouse users, how to extract these data items from the operational databases, how to load and package the new warehouse, and how to deliver the information to the end users. In short, data warehouse analysis involves the following processes:

- *Process Analysis*—Defines the data loading and extraction processes.

- *Data Source Analysis*—Describes the data items that will be of interest to end users. This phase also describes how the data will be edited, cleansed, aggregated, and summarized.

- *Data Loading Analysis*—Concentrates on describing how data will be loaded into a data warehouse.

- *Data Query Analysis*—Focuses on how end users will use the data.

Let's take a look at each of these processes.

Data Warehouse Process Analysis

As mentioned in the previous list, the goal of data warehouse process analysis is to define the data loading and extraction processes. In an operational sense, all processing takes place at either data loading time or at data query time. Also, processes in a data warehouse analysis seldom store data outputs, unless they are aggregations or summaries of existing data warehouse information.

Data Warehouse Source Analysis

In this phase of warehouse analysis, developers identify end-user data requirements and legacy data sources. This process begins by understanding the types of queries that the end-user community desires from their new database. Data source analysis always begins by soliciting the data warehouse user community. Unlike other systems where the end users may be semiskilled workers, the end-users of a data warehouse are generally highly trained statisticians whose job is to identify and exploit trends within their functional area. Examples of this type of end user would be a financial manager or a marketing analyst. It is only by interrogating the end users that the data warehouse analyst can understand how source data will be captured from external systems. Remember, a data warehouse always begins as a *tabula rasa*, and the data is loaded and transformed from numerous external sources.

Analyzing Source Document Input

Because the data for a data warehouse already exists in a database, it is very tempting for the data warehouse analyst to gloss over an analysis of the source documents for the organization. However, a thorough source document analysis will provide insight into both the internal structure of the data as well as management's uses for the data. Consequently, we will begin with the first step in data analysis for a data warehouse—analyzing the source documents that comprise the values in the existing OLTP databases.

To review basic systems analysis, you need to be familiar with the following notations used to describe values in the data dictionary:

- *Optional Item*—An item that is not required is placed in parentheses. Optional items are any data items that may exist in the Oracle database with a **NULL** value. For example:

```
customer_date = name, (age), address,  (social_security_number)
```

- *Repeating Item*—An item that repeats is placed in curly braces. The range of values for the repeating group is noted with numbers, with the lower bound on top of the curly braces and the upper bound on the bottom of the curly braces. Items with an unlimited number of repetitions use an *n* for the upper bound. The following code shows some examples of a repeating item:

```
       5
hand = {fingers}
       5


               0
job_history = {employer_name, dates_of_employment, ending_salary}
               6
```

- *Choose One Item*—An item selection with a specific range of values is indicated with vertical bars. This type of data description indicates a range of valid values for a data item as follows:

```
sex  = | Male    |
       | Female  |
       | Unknown |

payment_method = | cash        |
                 | check       |
                 | credit_card |
                 | food_stamps |
```

These data descriptions will be used later in this chapter as we create the source documents for our sample data warehouse.

Guttbaum's Grocery Stores

For many future examples in this text, we will be using a fictional grocery store chain called *Guttbaum's Grocery*. Guttbaum's has been using computers to record sales for about 10 years but has only recently decided to put their transaction data online. As we begin our review of Guttbaum's data system, we see that transactions are captured at the point of sales and summarized on a monthly basis for the OLTP system and individuals. Transactions are archived using tape storage. The use of tape storage was chosen because it was deemed to be the most efficient method for storing the massive quantities of data captured by Guttbaum's system.

Inside Guttbaum's data structures, one row of the transaction table is used for each purchased item within a grocery purchase. For example, if a customer checks out with a grocery cart holding 100 items, 100 rows are added to the fact table at the time the transaction is completed. Guttbaum's Grocery chain has 50 supermarkets with an average of 3,000 customers each day per supermarket. Each customer averages 10 items per transaction. If we do the math, we can see that 1,500,000 rows are added to Guttbaum's database each day. 1.5 million rows continue to be added each day until the monthly aggregation summarizes the data and archives the original transactions to tape. Each transaction row is 100 bytes, meaning that 150 MB of storage is used each day, in addition to the 50 MB necessary for indexes. Therefore, Guttbaum's data structure, which requires 200 MB per day of disk storage, requires a monthly total of disk space equaling 200 MB × 30 days, or about 6 GB. Figure 3.6 displays Guttbaum's existing OLTP environment.

Until recently, Guttbaum's was only able to track purchases at the point of sale with their scanners. This didn't allow any understanding about the type of

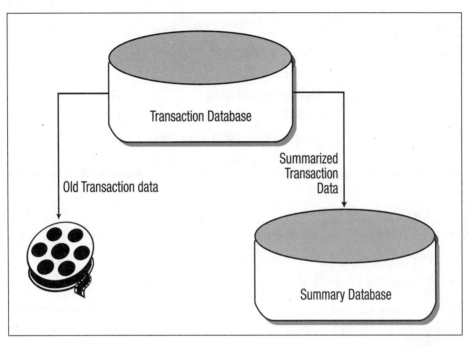

Figure 3.6
An overview of Guttbaum's existing OLTP environment.

customer making the purchase. However, the introduction of the data warehouse provides an opportunity for this to change.

Guttbaum's Grocery Club Card

In order to capture information about each customer at the point of sale, it is necessary for each customer to identify themselves to the system. But how can Guttbaum's identify their customers? To create an information base, the Information Systems analysts sponsored a survey of characteristics among Guttbaum's customers. The results of the survey are shown in Table 3.1.

So, if we examine the characteristics in Table 3.1, it becomes apparent that Guttbaum's could identify 80 percent of their customers if they required customers to use a special card when paying by check or credit card. In addition, more of the cash customers could be identified if Guttbaum's encouraged customers to use a card to take advantage of in-store price specials. Guttbaum's estimates that capturing customer information at the point of sale will add millions of dollars in additional revenue by providing opportunities to:

Table 3.1 Results of Guttbaum's customer survey.

Characteristic	Customer Response
Payment method	Pay by check (50%)
	Pay by credit card (30%)
	Pay with cash (20%)
Coupon usage	Use in-store sales promotions (75%)
	Use manufacturer's coupons (5%)

- Target coupon mailings to specific customers.

- Analyze customer spending patterns, thereby enabling each store to stock according its particular customer base.

- Eliminate the need to place store coupons in newspaper advertisements.

Because of these compelling benefits, a new club was formed called the *Grocery Club*. Starting on a specific date, a Grocery Club Card would be required for a customer to pay for purchases by check or credit card. The Grocery Club Card would look just like a credit card, and it would be "swiped" at the checkout counter. In addition, all in-store promotions would be exclusively for Grocery Club members, thereby providing an incentive for casual shoppers to get a Grocery Club Card to take advantage of in-store sales.

Grocery Club Application Form

Figure 3.7 shows an application form for a Grocery Club Card. As you can see, this form captures some very useful customer information. As data warehouse analysts, our job will be to describe this document using standard data dictionary descriptions. Then, our description will be used in the next chapter as input for the normalization process, and it will eventually provide input about the structure of the Oracle tables that comprise Guttbaum's warehouse.

From this application, we can create the following data dictionary description:

```
Grocery_club_application =

last_name, first_name, middle_name,
home_address, (apartment_number), city_state_zip,
(date_of_birth),
```

```
(social_security_number),
home_phone,
(employer_name),
(work_phone)
(age_group = |1 through 5|)
(education_level = |1 through 20|)
(number_in_family = |1 through 20|)
(number_of_children = |1 through 20|)
own_or_rent_flag = | O |
                   | R |,
mort_or_rent_amount,
household_income = | A |
                   | B |
                   | C |
                   | D |,
date_of_application
```

Product Description Sheet

As purchases are made by Guttbaum's buyers, product description sheets are gathered from each vendor. Unfortunately, these product description forms contain vastly different information depending on the type of product. Figures 3.8 and 3.9 show product descriptions for two sample products.

As we can see, product descriptions vary dramatically. For example, shelf life applies to the meat but not the bleach, and the products' units of measurement differ. Also, meat products require a USDA inspection date and is graded (Grade A, choice), while bleach has no such grade scale or inspection requirement.

Now, given that each product may have many different characteristics, including units of weight and measurements, how can we develop a standard description that will work for all of Guttbaum's products? The answer lies in the creation of a classification hierarchy, and we'll describe this process in detail later in this chapter. However, the common details for product descriptions can be listed as follows:

```
product_description =

product_ID,
product_name,
supplier_name,
shipment_terms,
minimum_order_amount;
```

Guttbaum's Groceries   Grocery Club Application

General Information:

Last name:_____ First:_____ Middle:_____

Home address:_____ Apt No.:_____

City:_____ State:_____ Zip:_____

Date of Birth:_____ Social Security number:_____ Home phone: (___)_____

Driver's license number :_____ State:_____

Employer:_____ Work phone: (___)_____

Check your age group: _____ 20–35
                             _____ 36–50
                             _____ 51–65
                             _____ over 65

Circle highest level of education: 1 2 3 4 5 6 7 8 9 10 11 12 13 14 15 16 17 18 19 20

Circle size of immediate family: 1 2 3 4 5 6 7 8 9 10 11 12 13 14 15 16 17 18 19 20

Circle number of children: 1 2 3 4 5 6 7 8 9 10 11 12 13 14 15 16 17 18 19 20

Do you own: _____ or rent: _____ your residence?

Check approximate yearly household income:

_____ $10,000–$30,000

_____ $30,001–$60,000

_____ $60,001 –$99,000

_____ Over $99,000

Signature   Date of notification
_____   _____

Figure 3.7
An application form for a grocery club card.

Product Invoice

The product invoice contains all of the information necessary to describe the products being sold and their relative prices. These fields include the product description, sizes, ship-to address, manufacturer's location, quantity purchased, unit price, delivery date, and cost. Note that the cost may vary with each purchase because prices are determined by time, quantity, and other market factors.

CARL'S
Product Description Sheet

Carl's delivers the finest meats right to your market. All cuts are available in the following grades:

- Prime
- Choice
- Grade A
- Better eat it quick

Carl's offers the following types of meats for your customer:

- Pork
- Beef
- Chicken

Carl's delivers either whole meats of specific parts. The parts include:

- Legs
- Lips
- Rennet

Shipping terms are 2/10 net 30 with a minimum order of $1,000. For a 5% fee, we can ship your order via overnight delivery.

Figure 3.8
A product description for a meat product provider.

From this invoice, we can create the following data dictionary description:

```
product_invoice =

ship_to_address,
   1
   { product_ID, product_name, unit, quantity, unit_price,
     total_price},
   20


   1
   total_amount_due = { total_price}
   20
```

Blotto Bleach
The finest bleach for clothing and hair.

Our product is available in the following sizes:

SIZE	WHOLESALE PRICE	SUGGESTED RETAIL PRICE
Quart	$1.49	$3.99
Half Gallon	$2.50	$4.99
Gallon	$4.99	$7.99

We also feature a 50-gallon drum with a convenient spigot for use in the generic product aisle for only $39.95.

Minimum order is $2,000. Product has an infinite shelf life and is shipped in cartons of 30 packages per crate. Shipping terms are 5/30 net 60.

Figure 3.9

A product description for a bleach product provider.

Note that the line items on the invoice are defined to repeat from 1 through 20 times. Also, note that the **total_amount_due** is listed in the description even though it is derived from the values of the sum of **total_price**.

CARL'S
INVOICE
Ship to:_____

ID	Description	Unit	Quantity	Unit Price	Total Price
463	Beef lips	lbs.	300	2.00/lb.	$600
987	Rennet	each	200	3.00 each	$600
5456	Rooster fries	lbs.	500	1.00/lb.	$500
				Total Due	$1,700

Figure 3.10

A product invoice.

Customer Transaction

The heart of our data warehouse is the measurement of customer transactions. This document is embodied in the sales receipt that a customer receives when they pass through the check-out register, which is shown in Figure 3.11. However, we must note that our point-of-sale register will be recording more information than will be displayed on the receipt.

From Figure 3.11, we can create the following data dictionary description:

```
customer_transaction =

store_location,
date,
time_of_day,
cashier ID,
(grocery_club_ID),
payment_method = | 1 = cash            |
                 | 2 = VISA            |
                 | 3 = MC              |
                 | 4 = check           |
                 | 5 = Food stamps     |
store_id,
   1
   { trans_type = | GC  |, quantity_sold, product_description,
     total_price },
   999            | WT  |
                  | N/A |
   1
   total_sale_amount =  { total_price },
   999


   1
   grocery_club_discount = { trans_type = | GC |, quantity_sold,
   product_description, total_discount },
   999


   1
   total_discount_amount = {total_discount},
   999

sale_price_before_tax = total_sale_amount + total_discount_amount,
sales_tax_amount = sale_price_before_tax * .08
net_amount_collected = sale_price_before_tax - sales_tax_amount
```

Guttbaum's Groceries

Welcome to Guttbaum's in Santa Monica

date: 01/21/97   time: 18:03   cashier ID: 61
grocery club ID: 99   payment method: 16   store: 56

Trans Type	Quantity	Description	Total Price
GC	3	Depends	$ 9.37
WT	3 lbs.	Bananas	$ 4.19
N/A	1	Delmont Peaches	$ 1.59
N/A	3	Toilet paper	$ 4.73
GC	4	Eggs	$ 3.49
		TOTAL	$23.37

Grocery Club Discounts:

GC	3	Depends	$ 1.59
GC	4	Eggs	$ 0.40
		TOTAL Discount	$ 1.99
		New Total	$ 19.39
		Tax	$ 1.71
		TOTAL Due	$21.10

Figure 3.11
A customer transaction.

Note that the price for each discount amount may vary by the current date because grocery club discounts are offered within specific time periods.

Advertising Data Sources

As we discussed, Guttbaum's will now require shoppers to have a Grocery Club Card if they want to take advantage of in-store sales. Figure 3.12 shows a typical in-store special for Guttbaum's.

Also as we discussed, Guttbaum's will no longer issue coupons in its newspaper advertisements—a substantial savings in costs for Guttbaum's. However, Guttbaum's continues to advertise Grocery Club specials in the local newspaper, as shown in Figure 3.13.

From the in-store advertisement and the newspaper advertisement, we can derive the following data dictionary entry:

```
newspaper_ad =

product_name,
sale_price,
size_requirement,
start_date,
end_date
```

Now that we have created data descriptions for each source document, you might think we are prepared to take these logical data descriptions into the data warehouse design phase. But are we done with data analysis? Not quite yet. Let's investigate the

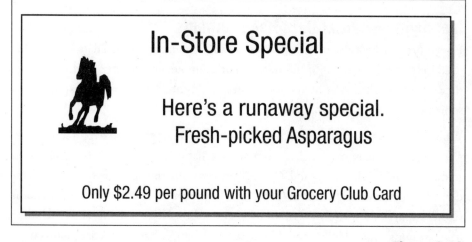

Figure 3.12
An in-store advertisement.

Guttbaum's Grocery

Patty O. Furniture
Gourmet Coffee

$3.00 off a five pound bag.

Discount valid from 6/1/97 through 6/31/97.
Not good with other promotions or coupon.

Good only with your Guttbaum's Grocery Club Card.

Figure 3.13
A sample newspaper advertisement.

need to capture external information for our new data warehouse. By external information, I'm talking about data that resides outside of Guttbaum's databases.

Identifying External Data Requirements

Data source analysis also means developers should identify external data sources that need to be incorporated into the system. For example, an end user might state that they want to analyze sales by metropolitan area. Figure 3.14 shows an external data source analysis for a data warehouse.

While the request to measure sales by geographic region might seem to be a straightforward request, it may require data from an external database. For example, if a sales transaction only includes city and ZIP code information, then information about Standard Metropolitan Statistical Areas (SMSA) may be required. In other words, Guttbaum's Grocery may want a study of sales in the entire Los Angeles metro area, including Santa Monica, Watts, Hollywood, Mar Vista, and Venice. The SMSA data allows these suburbs to be logically grouped by ZIP code into a geographically related area.

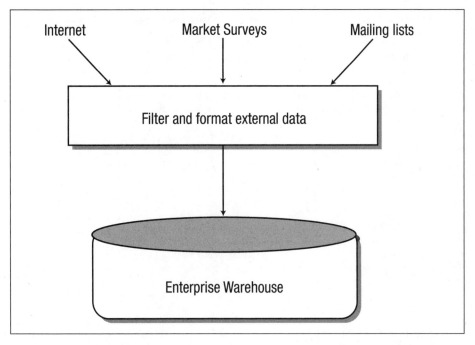

Figure 3.14
External data source analysis for a data warehouse.

Legacy Data Analysis

Another source of external data consists of legacy data systems. It is not uncommon for analysts to discover that one class of data resides in different database formats. For example, sales data from 1980 through 1990 may reside on an IMS database, while transactions from 1991 to present are stored in a DB2 database. The data analyst must be able to deal with the problem of translating data archive tapes in varying formats.

In some cases, developers find it fortunate that a data source is stored in an OLTP Oracle database and believe that the data extraction and loading will be easier because the source and target data sources reside within Oracle. However, it must be noted that many of the standard Oracle utilities for data extraction and loading (**export-import**) are of no use with Oracle data warehouse loading. This is because of the data transformation that takes place as a part of data extraction and loading. For example, the denormalized format of the data warehouse makes it impossible to export an OLTP Oracle database that uses five tables to represent a sales transaction.

As a general rule, data extraction involves formatting legacy data for loading into the warehouse. For example, data could be extracted directly from an Oracle OLTP system into the denormalized Oracle warehouse as shown in Listing 3.3.

Listing 3.3   One-step data extraction and load between Oracle databases.

```
CREATE TABLE FACT
AS
SELECT customer_name,
   customer_address,
   sales_date,
     to_char(sales_date,'YYYY'),
     to_char(sales_date,'MM'),
     to_char(sales_date,'DD'),
   sale_amount,
   quantity_sold,
   total_price,
FROM

   CUSTOMER@oltp cust,
   SALES@oltp sale,
   LINE_item@oltp li,
   ITEM@oltp item

WHERE
   CUST.cust_num = SALE.cust_num
AND
   SALE.sales_num = LI.sales_num
AND
   LI.item_num = ITEM.item_num;
```

Here, you can see that the data is pulled from the Oracle OLTP database using Oracle's SQL*Net facility. For details on this distributed SQL technique, see Chapter 9, *Distributed Oracle Data Warehouses*. Also, note the dissection of the **sales_date** column. Rather than store the **sales_date** as a single column of the **DATE** datatype, the Oracle data warehouse transformation stores the **sales_date** in three columns: one for the day, another for the month, and a third column for the year. The reason for this **DATE** breakout will become clear later in this chapter when we discuss data query analysis.

Data Warehouse Loading Analysis

The third process involved in data warehouse analysis is the analysis of loading data into the data warehouse. Analysis of data loading involves understanding how the data is going to be extracted from the target system, how the data will be cleansed and validated, and how the data will be loaded, aggregated, and summarized at warehouse load time. Most Oracle professionals use Oracle's referential integrity to validate incoming warehouse data. Referential integrity can be used to check for valid data values and ensure that all data relationships are maintained. Because referential integrity is only used at load and purge time, it causes no performance problems to the Oracle data warehouse, especially since loading is generally done during off-hours. For more information on using Oracle utilities with referential integrity, see Chapter 10, *Oracle Data Warehouse Utilities*. Figure 3.15 displays methods for cleansing, validating, and loading Oracle data into a data warehouse.

Data Warehouse Query Analysis

The fourth and final process of the data warehouse analysis is the analysis of data warehouse queries. From Chapter 1, you should have a very general idea about the types of queries that data warehouses can address. We can now take a look at how the data can be logically stored to optimize query speed. In this phase of analysis, developers need to take a close look at the types of queries that end users plan to use. Query analysis assists in warehouse design. Developers also need to look at how to model the access requirements within Oracle. In addition, this analysis aids in determining the types of front ends required for the warehouse. Front ends include multidimensional front ends such as Oracle Express, a data mining tool report, or any of a number of ad hoc query front ends used for Oracle warehouses. Unlike an OLTP system, which may have hundreds of types of queries, all of the queries against a data warehouse fall into the following four categories:

- *Statistical Analysis*—Computing sums, averages, and so forth.

- *Multivariate Analysis*—Comparing classes of database objects with each other to analyze patterns.

- *Simulation And Modeling*—Using the data warehouse to validate a hypothesis.

- *Forecasting*—Using the warehouse to predict future values.

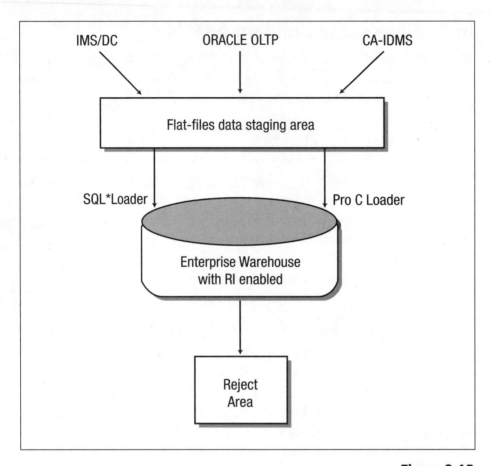

Figure 3.15
Methods for cleansing, validating, and loading Oracle data.

Why is the type of query important to warehouse analysis? Most data warehouse queries rely on a classification taxonomy, and these taxonomies create the foundation for the data warehouse query model. Just as class hierarchies in an object-oriented database describe different flavors of an object, a classification taxonomy creates categories of database objects.

Ad Hoc Classification

One common mistake in data warehouse analysis is the failure to plan for new classifications of data warehouse attributes. These classifications are not always known in advance, and it is not uncommon to see that the delivery of the data warehouse provides end users with a mechanism for identifying new classifications.

In our example for Guttbaum's Grocery, we might see arbitrary, or ad hoc, groupings of data attributes. These ad hoc groupings of existing data attributes might be used to perform what-if analyses for decision support. Some examples of ad hoc classification might include:

- A *"yuppie" (young urban professional)*—This is an individual in age category two or three, with an income greater than $50,000 a year, who owns his or her home and has less than four children. Show me a breakdown by product category for all yuppie expenditures on non-food items.

- A *"dink" (dual-income, no kids)*—This is a family unit where there are two wage earners with a combined yearly income greater than $60,000. Show me the buying habits of dinks for dairy products.

- A *"cheapskate"*—This is an individual who uses coupons for more than 50 percent of their purchases. Show me the buying habits of cheapskates for all non-coupon purchases.

As you can see, the ability of the data warehouse to develop arbitrary classifications can greatly improve the usefulness of a data warehouse. Note that these classifications do not always form a hierarchy, and that they may sometimes be required for the pre-calculation of aggregate values. For example, we may need our data warehouse to pre-summarize sales by product classes and brands for yuppies, dinks, and cheapskates.

Warehouse developers often see that the ability to reclassify data attributes may lead to new "facts" within a data warehouse. As in our example, Guttbaum's has two facts: **sale_amount** and **quantity_sold**. However, the ability to reclassify according to data attribute may lead to derivations from these base facts. These derivations might include:

- The average number of items per transaction.

- Total dollars spent per product and brand name category.

- Total dollars spent, grouped by customer category.

- The correlation quotient between attribute X and attribute Y (e.g., compare the propensity of a customer to purchase beer with diapers with the propensity of all customers to purchase beer with cigarettes).

If we accept the premise that there are n! possible combinations of possible data attributes that can be combined into a classification, then how can we possibly plan for all of the possible combinations? As it turns out, when developers build an Oracle warehouse to be flexible in nature, the base architecture can be easily extended to accommodate new classifications. Building a flexible warehouse involves planning for the ability to define new aggregate summary tables and creating an application front end that allows easy query classification. Some of these flexibility techniques will be discussed in Chapter 4, *Oracle Data Warehouse Design*.

An Example Of Ad Hoc Classification

Let's illustrate this concept with an example from Guttbaum's Grocery. One of management's requirements is to be able to compute the demand curve for each item category. As you may remember from Economics class, the demand curve for an item is a downward sloping curve that measures the propensity of a customer to pay for a product as the price changes. Obviously, the smaller the price the greater the sales, but it is the slope of the curve that is of interest to Guttbaum's management. For example, Guttbaum's management needs to be able to compute the demand curve for all brands of coffee to make an intelligent decision about which product to offer at a sale price. In Figure 3.16, you can see the computed demand curve for all customers for all brand names within a specific product category, in this case, coffee.

Here, you can see that there are different demand curves depending on the brand name. Essentially, this is a measure of product loyalty, and this type of information is very useful when management decides which product to advertise at a discounted price. In this example, a $1 per pound price reduction will have drastically different effects on various brands of coffee. For instance, a price reduction will not affect the demand for Java Joe's Coffee, indicating that consumers of Java Joe's have a high product loyalty, as evidenced by the inelastic demand curve. Peak Coffee, on the other hand, shows a very large increase in demand when the price is reduced by $1 per pound. If the goal of a sale is to get customers into the supermarket, then it appears that the brand name with the most elastic demand curve would be the best choice for an advertised price reduction. Guttbaum's wants to offer specials on those products that demonstrate a high elasticity—the products that will substantially increase sales volume with a small drop in price.

Now, the question from the developer's corner is: *How will our data warehouse gather the necessary data to plot these demand curves?* Because this type of analysis is required

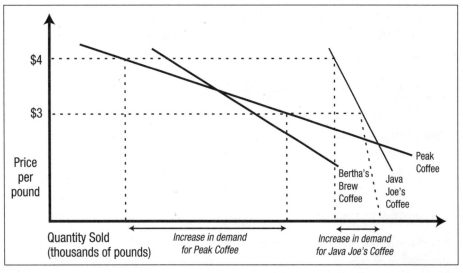

Figure 3.16
The demand curves for different brands of coffee.

by the marketing department, we must be able to plan for the ability to plot the demand curves for each brand name within a specific product or product line.

If we examine the data required for this function, we'll find that the data warehouse will need to track the total dollar amount spent for each and every brand name that Guttbaum's sells, and group the total sales figures according to the prices of the products at the time each product is sold. In addition, we also need to group these averages by product line. Operationally, this type of data function is implemented by keeping arrays of accumulators for each price/sales grouping. The array is three-dimensional, and each slice of the cube would be for a specific product. For example, a slice for Bob's Bleach might appear as shown in Table 3.2.

Table 3.2   A slice of a data array showing statistics for Bob's Bleach.

Price ($)	Sales
2.00	$167,000
2.10	$150,000
2.20	$145,000
2.30	$130,000

The data aggregations shown in Table 3.2 will need to be included in the data analysis of summarized and aggregated data for the data warehouse. As you can see from this example, the aggregations required for data analysis are not always obvious.

Data Transformation Analysis

When performing data query analysis, it is critical to note how the data will need to be transformed in order to meet the needs of end users. Data transformation analysis involves two specific tasks: data classification and data dissection. *Data classification* involves taking a data entity and classifying all permutations of the data entity, while *data dissection* is breaking a single data value into derivative components. Both of these activities are essential for a valid and complete warehouse analysis.

Data classification falls into two categories: single-valued classification and multi-valued classification. We may encounter a data entity that has many permutations, and each permutation may have its own unique data values. For example, we may be designing a data warehouse for a vehicle rental organization. A rental vehicle may be a sailboat, a car, or an airplane. While each of these entities will be represented in our warehouse as a vehicle, each entity type has distinct data attributes that do not apply to the other entities. A query that references average hull length would not apply to airplanes and cars. These are called *single-valued* classifications, in that there are distinct data values that apply to each class of entities. *Multi-valued* data classification applies to mutually exclusive values between data items. For example, we could track the sex of a customer with a multivalued flag that would be set to M, F, or U.

> *Note: The U value is for unknown sex, as in the case with customers with unisex names like Pat, Chris, or Shelby.*

To illustrate the importance of class hierarchies in a data warehouse analysis, let's take a look at how data classification may aid data warehouse queries. To illustrate the principle of data classification, let's return to the Guttbaum's example. Recall that customer information is collected at the time a customer obtains a Grocery Club Card, and transaction information is obtained at the time a customer "swipes" the Grocery Club Card at the checkout counter.

Also recall that Guttbaum's has a fact table in which each item appears as a separate row in the table. In this way, correlational analysis can be used to determine associations between grocery items. However, even though the database stores a row for each item in a transaction, there is no direct information about the different categories in which each item participates. A transaction may record the sale of two pounds of calf livers, but it does not record the fact that calf liver is a part of the beef category, that beef is a part of the meat category, and that meat is a part of the food category. Guttbaum's classification hierarchy might look something like the hierarchy shown in Figure 3.17.

In practice, just about every "object" in a data warehouse could become a part of a classification hierarchy, and because a data warehouse is subject-oriented, it is usually the subject that is classified. Another example would be a data warehouse for a bookstore where sales of books would need to be classified into fiction, nonfiction, and so on. The identification of these classification hierarchies is critical to warehouse analysis because a method must be designed to allow the subjects to be categorized for queries.

As noted earlier, the idea of classification hierarchies in a data warehouse analysis has parallels in the object-oriented world. In a C++ program, class hierarchies can be created to distinguish between different types of an object, where each type has its own data items and behaviors. The same principle applies to the data warehouse.

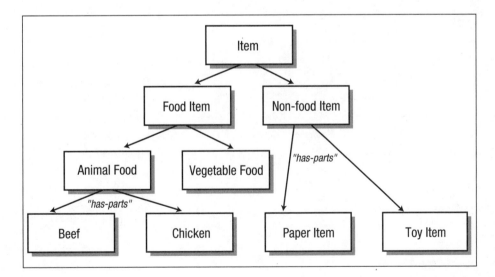

Figure 3.17
A classification hierarchy for Guttbaum's Grocery.

The end user may want to query, *How many paper products were sold last week?* Unless our warehouse knows which items participate in the paper products categories, the warehouse will not be able to easily answer this query.

As we will discuss in the next chapter, classification hierarchies are added to basic entity/relation models so that the data warehouse analyst can describe each type of item. In Figure 3.18, you can see that a bill-of-material's entity for an item has been extended to allow for different types of items. We'll take a closer look at extending entity/relation models in the next chapter, when we begin to apply physical techniques to our logical systems analysis.

In the next chapter, we'll also discuss data warehouse design where physical techniques are used to store unique data attributes within data warehouse tables. For example, some grocery attributes are specific to a class of items, such as the shelf life data attribute that applies to calf livers, but not to paper towels. These are just some of the types of data issues that must be addressed in a data warehouse design.

This leads us to the second task in data transformation analysis—data dissection. Let's start with an example. Your end users state that they want to analyze sales by date. Armed with this knowledge, you note that a date column is necessary, and you don't give the issue another thought. However, what if your end users want to compare sales for the same months, except in different years? What if an end user wants

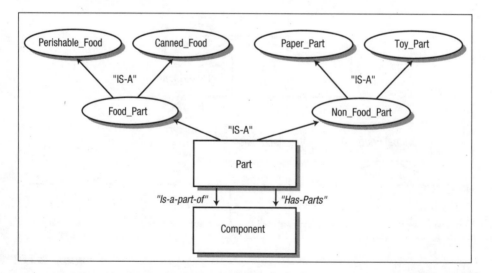

Figure 3.18
An extension of an entity/relation model.

to compare sales by quarter? In order to quickly service these queries, you'll want to decompose the date component into its component parts. With some thought, you may be able to identify many other data items that need to be decomposed for representation in your data warehouse.

Data dissection implies that the data has a functional dependency upon the derived components. As you may recall from basic data normalization theory, full functional dependence is required for data models to participate in second normal form (2NF) and third normal form (3NF) relations. Functional dependence implies that one "key" value will be the determinant for another "non-key" value. For example, if we know the date, we also know the day, month, quarter, and year. If we know a ZIP code, we therefore could know the state, city, and metropolitan area.

While this analysis may seem obvious, the decomposition of these types of column values can greatly aid the query speed for Oracle databases. Let's consider a simple example using a **DATE** column. As you may know, a **DATE** column datatype contains the century, year, day, month, and time. However, getting these values out of a **DATE** datatype is not always easy, especially when groupings such as the quarter of a year are desired. This type of date transformation also has a nasty side effect of invalidating the use of date indexes in Oracle, causing painful full-table scans. However, if we break out the **DATE** datatype into its component **year**, **month**, and **quarter** values, we see that SQL queries can be greatly simplified, as shown in Table 3.3.

This gets even more obvious when we try to compare sales for the same month in two different years. Listing 3.4 compares sales using SQL code implementing the **DATE** datatype, and Listing 3.5 compares sales using SQL code that breaks **DATE** out into three columns.

Table 3.3   DATE datatype predicates.

Type	With DATE Datatype	With DATE Breakout
year	to_char(sales_date,'YYYY') = '1997'	sales_year = 1997
month	to_char(sales_date,'MM') = 'MAR'	sales_month = 'MAR'
quarter	sales_date between '01-JAN-97' and '31-MAR-97'	quarter = 'SPRING'

Listing 3.4 SQL using the **DATE** datatype.

```
SELECT SUM(SALES)
WHERE
sales_date =
to_char(sales_date,'MM-YY') = 'MAR-96'
AND
to_char(sales_date,'MM-YY') = 'MAR-97'
GROUP BY to_char(sales_date,'MM-YY') = 'MAR-97';
```

Listing 3.5 SQL breaking **DATE** out into three columns.

```
SELECT SUM(SALES)
WHERE sales_month = 'MAR'
AND sales_year IN (96,97)
GROUP BY sales_year;
```

Here, you can clearly see that avoiding the use of the **to_char** built-in functions (and any date functions) within Oracle can greatly simplify complex data warehouse SQL queries. For details on breakouts of datatypes for data warehouses see Chapter 12, *Tuning Oracle SQL*.

Summary

Now that we have covered the basic tasks involved in the logical analysis of data warehouses, we are ready to proceed into a discussion of the physical design phase. In the next chapter, we'll apply physical constructs to our logical data model, and we will begin to look at Oracle-specific design techniques for fast data loading and retrieval.

HIGH PERFORMANCE

Oracle Data Warehouse Design

CHAPTER

4

Oracle Data Warehouse Design

This chapter focuses on data warehouse design techniques for creating high-performance Oracle warehouses. While traditional online systems design involves the design of the input screens, data structures, and output reports, data warehouse design places the focus on designing flexibility into the Oracle table structures and the creation of flexible query input software. Without an effective database design, no amount of tuning will allow the Oracle warehouse to achieve optimal performance. Hence, it is critical to a database design that we properly design the Oracle table structures and the data input screens.

Normalization And Modeling Theory

Let's begin by briefly reviewing data modeling theory from a normalization perspective. It is interesting to note that Dr. Codd coined the term *normalization* in reference to current events of the day. At the time Dr. Codd was developing his mathematical rules for data redundancy, President Nixon was normalizing relations with China. Because Nixon was normalizing relations, Dr. Codd decided that he would also normalize relations as he refined his rules. (I'm not making this up!)

For database systems, a systems developer begins by taking raw, unnormalized relations from a systems analysis. Then, the developer takes the relations to third normal form and looks at the introduction of redundancy for improved performance. Of course, data redundancy becomes even more important for an Oracle warehouse developer than for a traditional OLTP designer, so we will carefully explore the options of table denormalization in this chapter. In addition, we will also design a method for storing the precalculated data summaries that were defined in our systems analysis. Finally, as pointed out in the last chapter, we cannot always predict all the possible combinations of data attributes that will compose aggregate fact tables, so we must design a method for allowing our end users to dynamically define aggregation criteria and store the aggregate values into Oracle tables.

This text does not attempt to fully explore data normalization because dozens of texts are available for that purpose. Instead, this text offers a brief discussion of the normalization process as it applies to our example from Guttbaum's Grocery. The processes of normalization was originally intended to be a method for decomposing data structures into their smallest components. The process begins with the original data structures, which are called unnormalized relations, and progresses through first, second, and third normal forms. At this stage the data structures are completely free of redundancy and are at their most decomposed level. To fully appreciate the process, let's take a look at the successive levels of normalization.

Unnormalized Form

Essentially, an *unnormalized relation* is a relation that contains repeating values. An unnormalized relation can also contain relations nested within other relations, as well as all kinds of transitive dependencies. Sometimes unnormalized relations are signified by 0NF. An unnormalized relation is not to be confused with a denormalized relation. An unnormalized relation is any relation in its raw state, and commonly contains repeating values and other characteristics that are not found in denormalized relations. The process of denormalization is a very deliberate attempt to introduce controlled redundant items into an already normalized form.

Today, only a handful of database management systems support repeating values, including UniSQL and some object databases. The relational database model requires that each column within a table contain atomic values, and there is no facility for indexing multiple occurrences of a data item within a table. The idea of repeating groups was first made popular with the use of the COBOL language with ISAM files. For example, a COBOL working storage definition could allow for repeating occurrences of items, as follows:

```
03 order_form.
   05 customer_name    pic x(80).
```

```
05 customer_address   pic x(80);
05 ordered_items occurs from 1 to 10 times depending on number-
   ordered.
   07 item_number        pic s9(8) comp3.
   07 item_description    pic x(80).
   07 quantity_ordered    pic 9(4).
```

In any case, relations with repeating groups are not supported by Oracle, and they must be moved into new relations. Here are some relations from Chapter 3 that have repeating groups:

```
Transaction =
1
{ trans_type = | GC  |, quantity_sold, product_description,
                         total_price },
999             | WT |
                | N/A |
1
total_sale_amount =  { total_price },
999


1
grocery_club_discount =
    { trans_type = | GC |, quantity_sold, product_description,
                          total_discount },
999


1
total_discount_amount =   {total_discount },
999
```

In this case, you can see that a customer transaction consists of many repeating groups, and each of these groups will be moved from the transaction relation. Also, notice that some of the repeating groups, such as **total_discount_amount**, are derived from the sum of other values in the transaction relation. In those cases, we must make a conscious decision whether to redundantly store these summations or have Oracle compute them at runtime.

First Normal Form

In essence, a relation is in first normal form if it does not contain any repeating values. Here, we have taken our relations with repeating values and moved them to separate relations. When the new relations are created, we carry the primary key of the original relation into the new relation.

Second Normal Form

The purpose of the second normal form (2NF) test is to check for partial key dependencies. *Partial key dependencies* are created when we break off an unnormalized relation into first normal form by carrying the key, thereby creating a *concatenated key* with several data items. The formal definition of second normal form is as follows:

A relation is in second normal form if and only if the relation is in first normal form and each non-key attribute is fully functionally dependent on the entire concatenated key.

However, I prefer the following definition:

A relation is in second normal form if each attribute depends on the key, the whole key, and nothing but the key, so help me Codd.

It should be apparent that the second normal form test only applies to relations that have more than one key field. A relation in first normal form that only has one key is automatically in second normal form if each attribute is functionally dependent on the key.

In the following example, we see *partial dependencies*, where an attribute is functionally dependent on only one key field. In this type of situation, the partial dependency is moved to another relation.

```
Report_card = Student_num, course_num, course_name, grade
```

In this case, we see that **grade** depends on both **Student_num** and **course_num**, because you must know both the student and the course to know the grade. **course_name**, on the other hand, is fully functionally dependent only on the **course_num** key and does not require **Student_num**.

Third Normal Form

The third normal form (3NF) test refers to transitive dependencies. A *transitive dependency* is a circumstance where one non-key attribute is functionally dependent on another non-key attribute. Whereas the 2NF test serves to check for dependencies between key fields and attribute fields, the 3NF test serves to check for dependencies between non-key attributes.

Entity/Relation Modeling

If we have followed the process for normalization through third normal form, we will be able to derive an entity/relation model that is essentially free of redundant information (see Figure 4.1). The entity/relation model was first introduced by Professor Emeritus Peter Chen from the University of Louisiana, and it is sometimes called a *Chen diagram*. In the 15 years since the introduction of this model, many permutations have been created, but the basic principles of entity/relations (E/R) modeling remain intact.

But is the E/R model for Guttbaum's Grocery truly free from data redundancy? While the model is free of redundant information, it is impossible to implement the

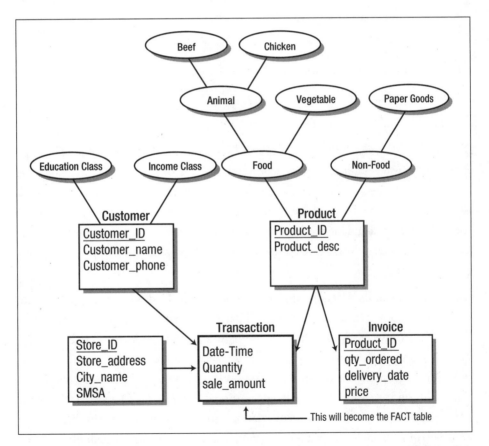

Figure 4.1

An entity/relation model for Guttbaum's Grocery.

model in a relational database without introducing redundancy to support the data relationships. For example, if Guttbaum's model was implemented using a pointer-based DBMS, such as IMS, pointers would be used to establish relationships between entities. For relational databases, data columns must be copied as foreign keys to establish data relationships, thereby introducing redundancy.

Introducing Redundancy Into An Entity/Relation Model

As we know, five types of data relationships must be considered when designing any Oracle database:

- One-to-one relationship
- One-to-many relationship
- Many-to-many relationship
- Recursive many-to-many relationship
- The IS-A relationship (class hierarchies)

The effective data warehouse designer's role is to represent these types of relationships in a sensible way and ensure acceptable warehouse performance. In a hierarchical or CODASYL (Network) database, it is possible to define and implement a database design that contains absolutely no redundant information (such as pure third normal form). Hierarchical and Network databases can be truly free of redundant information because all data relationships are represented through pointers and not through duplicated foreign keys.

The complete elimination of redundancy requires embedded pointers to establish the data relationships. Therefore, no relational database can ever be totally free of redundant data because relational databases use redundant foreign keys to establish SQL **JOIN** columns for one-to-many data relationships. In a sense, the requirement for non-redundant models absolves the theoretical purist perspective, which states that normalization is the only way to design relational systems. An Oracle database with either one-to-many or many-to-many relationships must have redundant foreign keys embedded in the tables to establish logical relationships. Redundant duplication of foreign keys in the subordinate tables creates the data relationships, making it possible to join tables together and relate the contents of the data items in the tables.

As the size of the database increases, redundancy can become a major problem. Today, many users create very large databases, many of which contain trillions of bytes. For databases of this size, a single table can contain more than a billion rows, and the introduction of a single new column to a table can represent thousands of dollars in additional disk expense. Data redundancy is detrimental for two reasons. First and foremost, duplicating redundant material consumes disk storage space. Second and more ominous, updating redundant data requires extra processing. Redundant duplication of very large and highly volatile data items can cause huge processing bottlenecks.

However, the overhead associated with data redundancy does not imply that redundancy is always undesirable. Performance is still an overriding factor in most systems. Proper control of redundant information implies that redundant information can be introduced into any structure as long as the performance improvements outweigh the additional disk costs and update problems.

Since the first publication of Dr. Codd's 1993 research paper, *Providing OLAP (Online Analytical Processing) to User-Analysts: An IT Mandate*, database designers have attempted to find an optimum way of structuring tables for low data redundancy. Codd's rules of normalization guide the designer to create a logically correct table structure with no redundancy, but performance rules often dictate the introduction of duplicated data to improve performance.

This is especially true for Oracle data warehouses. However, the warehouse designer does not have free reign to introduce redundancy anywhere in the model. Redundancy always carries a price, whether it is the cost of the disk storage or the cost of maintaining a parallel update scheme. Figure 4.2 shows a strategy for analyzing the consequences of data redundancy.

In Figure 4.2, a boundary line lies within a range between the size of a redundant data item and the frequency of update of the data item. The size of the data item relates to the disk costs associated with storing the item, and the frequency of update is associated with the cost of keeping the redundant data current, whether by replication techniques or by two-phase commit updates. Because the relative costs are different for each hardware configuration and for each application, this boundary may be quite different depending on the type of application. The rapid decrease in disk storage costs designates that the size boundary is only important for very large-scale redundancy. A large, frequently changing item (for example, **street_address**) is not a

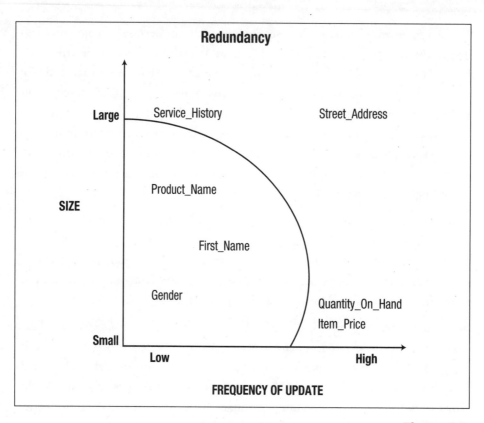

Figure 4.2

A comparison of size versus volatility for redundant data.

good candidate for redundancy. But large static items (for example, **service_history**) or small, frequently changing items (for example, **item_price**) are acceptable for redundancy. Small static items (for example, **gender**) represent ideal candidates for redundant duplication. Because most Oracle data warehouse designs are static in the sense that data is seldom modified after it is loaded, the only consideration in the introduction of redundancy is the disk storage costs of the redundant item.

Denormalizing One-To-Many Data Relationships

One-to-many relationships exist in many real-world situations. Many entities that possess one-to-many relationships can be removed from the data model, eliminating some join operations. The basic principle here is simple: Redundant information avoids expensive SQL joins and yields faster processing. But remember, we must deal with the issue of additional disk storage and the problems associated with

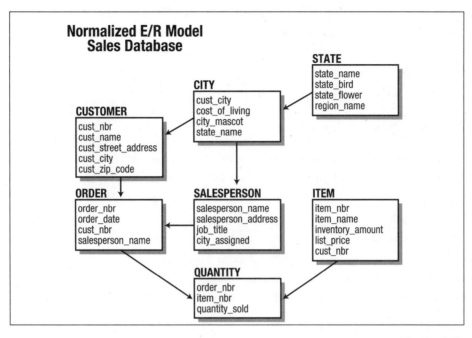

Figure 4.3

A fully normalized E/R model sales database.

updating the redundant data. For example, consider the entity/relation (E/R) model shown in Figure 4.3.

Here, we see that the structure is in pure third normal form. Note that the **CITY** and **STATE** tables exist because each state has many cities and each city has many customers. This model works for most transactions on an online transaction processing (OLTP) system. However, this high degree of normalization would require the joining of the **CITY** and **STATE** tables each time address information is requested, forcing some SQL requests to perform very slowly.

Consider a query to display the **state_bird** for all orders that have been placed for bird seed. This is a cumbersome query that requires the joining of six tables, as follows:

```
SELECT state_bird
FROM STATE, CITY, CUSTOMER, ORDER, QUANTITY, ITEM
WHERE
item_name = 'BIRDSEED'
AND
ITEM.item_nbr = QUANTITY.item_nbr
```

```
AND
QUANTITY.order_nbr = ORDER.order_nbr
AND
ORDER.cust_nbr = CUSTOMER.cust_nbr
AND
CUSTOMER.cust_city = CITY.cust_city
AND
CITY.state_name = STATE.state_name;
```

With Oracle and the rule-based optimizer, this type of complex join guarantees that at least one table is read front to back using a full-table scan. This is a shortcoming of Oracle's rule-based optimizer because an SQL optimizer should always avoid a full-table scan whenever indexes are present—and full-table scans are very expensive. This situation might be avoided by using Oracle hints with the cost-based optimizer to determine the optimal path to this data. A *hint* is an extension of Oracle's SQL that directs the SQL optimizer to change its normal access path. For more detailed information on optimizing full-table scans and using hints, refer to Chapter 12, *Tuning Oracle SQL.*

What if your goal is to simplify the data structure by removing several of the one-to-many relationships? Adding redundancy imposes two requirements: You need additional space for the redundant item, and you need a technique to update the redundant item if it changes. One solution is to build a table of columns that rolls the **CITY** and **STATE** tables into the **CUSTOMER** table. For example, Table 4.1 assumes that the **STATE** table contains 50 rows, the **CITY** table contains 2,000 rows, and the **CUSTOMER** table contains 10,000 rows.

In Table 4.1, you can see that the **CITY** and **STATE** tables can be removed entirely for a total savings of 400,000 bytes (see Figure 4.4).

Table 4.1 Redundancy matrix to determine optimal normalization.

Column	Size	Duplication	Total Space	Change
state_bird	10	10,000	100,000	Rare
state_flower	10	10,000	100,000	Rare
region_name	2	10,000	20,000	Never
cost_of_living	8	10,000	80,000	Quarterly
city_mascot	10	10,000	100,000	Rare

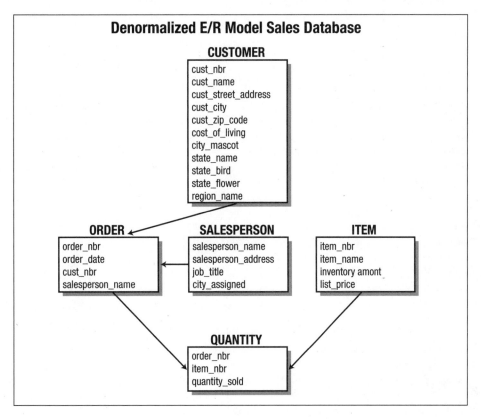

Figure 4.4

Denormalized E/R model sales database.

What about the **cost_of_living** field? If we choose to eliminate the **CITY** table and duplicate **cost_of_living** in every **CUSTOMER** row, it would be necessary to visit each and every **customer** row—which means changing **cost_of_living** 10,000 times. Before making this change, the following SQL should be used to update each **CITY** table:

```
UPDATE CITY SET cost_of_living = :var1
WHERE CITY = :var2;
2000 ROWS UPDATED
```

While the management of redundancy seems a formidable challenge, the following SQL **UPDATE** statement makes this change easily, and we can make the change to all affected rows as follows:

```
UPDATE CUSTOMER SET cost_of_living = :var1
WHERE CITY = :var2;
100,000 ROWS UPDATED
```

Using the same **state_bird** query as before, we can see how it is simplified by removing the extra tables, as follows:

```
SELECT state_bird
FROM CUSTOMER, ORDER, QUANTITY, ITEM
WHERE
item_name = 'BIRDSEED'
AND
ITEM.item_nbr = QUANTITY.item_nbr
AND
QUANTITY.order_nbr = ORDER.order_nbr
AND
ORDER.customer_nbr = CUSTOMER.customer_nbr;
```

It is still necessary to join all four tables together, but this results in a much faster, simpler query than the original five-way table join. You can carry this concept to the point where this model is condensed into a single, highly redundant table.

Denormalizing 3NF Relationships

When creating an E/R model, it is often tempting to look at the data model from a purely logical perspective, disregarding the physical implications of the model. The designer strives to recognize and establish all of the logical relationships in the model while sometimes finding that the relationships are misleading. A relationship can be misleading when the relationship actually exists, but the application may have no need to reference this relationship. Consider the E/R model for a university shown in Figure 4.5.

Consider the association of the **hair_color** attribute to the **student** entity. Does a many-to-many data relationship really exist between **hair_color** and **student**? Let's think about this for a minute. Many students have blonde hair, and blonde hair is common to many students. Why not create a many-to-many relationship between **student** and **hair_color**? The solution depends on whether any other non-key data items exist within the **hair_color** entity.

If many other data items relating to hair color are present, then it is perfectly appropriate to create another entity called **hair_color**. But in this case, even though a

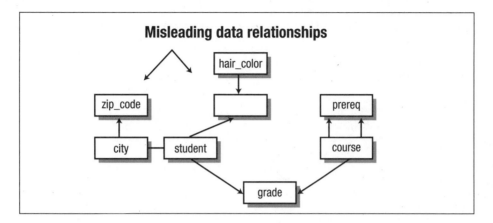

Figure 4.5
An example of unnecessary data relationships.

many-to-many relationship exists between **hair_color** and **student**, **hair_color** is a standalone data attribute, so it is unnecessary to create an additional data structure.

Another example is the **zip_code** attribute in the **student** entity. At first glance, it appears that a violation of third normal form (that is, a transitive dependency) has occurred between **city** and **zip_code**. In other words, it appears that a **zip_code** is paired with each student's city of residence. Since each **city** has many **zip_code**s, and each **zip_code** refers only to one **city**, it makes sense to model this as a one-to-many data relationship. The presence of this data relationship requires creating a separate entity called *zip* with attached **student** entities. However, this is another case where an entity (**zip**, in this case) lacks key attributes. It would be impractical to make **zip** an entity. In other words, **zip_code** has no associated data items. Creating a database table with only one data column would be nonsense, and the model would finally appear as shown in Figure 4.6.

This example demonstrates that it is not enough to group "like" items and then identify the data relationships. A practical test must be made regarding the presence of non-key attributes within an entity class. If an entity has no attributes (that is, the table has only one field), the presence of the entity is nothing more than an index to the foreign key in the member entity, which means that it can be removed from the E/R model. This technique not only simplifies the number of entities, but it creates a better environment for a client/server architecture. More data is logically grouped together, resulting in less data access effort.

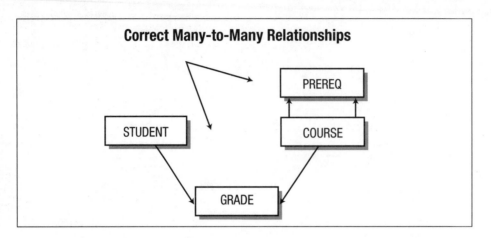

Figure 4.6

An example of correct many-to-many relationships.

Denormalizing Many-To-Many Data Relationships

In many cases, a many-to-many relationship can be condensed into a more efficient structure to improve the speed of data retrieval. After all, fewer tables will need to be joined to get the desired information. Using the relationship between a course and a student as an example, Figure 4.7 shows how a many-to-many relationship can be collapsed into a more compact structure.

A student takes many courses, and each course has many students. This is a classic many-to-many relationship and requires us to define a junction table between the base entities to establish the foreign keys necessary to join them together. Note that

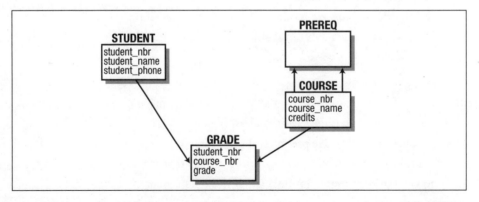

Figure 4.7

Collapsing a many-to-many relationship into a more compact structure.

the **GRADE** is the junction table, and it contains the following contents: **course_nbr**, the primary key for the **COURSE** table; **student_nbr**, the primary key for the **STUDENT** table; and **grade**, which is a non-key attribute for both foreign keys. Next, consider the following: *In what context does a grade have meaning?* Simply stating that *The grade is A in CS-101* is insufficient, and stating *Joe earned an A* makes no sense, either. Only when both the student number and the course number are associated does the grade column have meaning. Stating *Joe earned an A in CS-101* makes sense.

Dealing With Recursive Data Relationships

Recursive many-to-many relationships contain a database object that has a many-to-many relationship with other occurrences of the same object. These relationships are often termed *Bill-of-Materials* (BOM) *relationships*, and the graphical representation of the recursive relationship is sometimes termed a *Bill-of-Materials explosion*. These relationships are termed recursive because a single query makes many sub-passes through the tables to arrive at the solution (see Figure 4.8).

Bill-of-materials relationships are very common in data warehouses, and they present a difficult problem with system performance. For example, a part may consist of other parts, but at the same time, it is a component in a larger assembly. A class at a university may have many prerequisites, but at the same time, the class is a prerequisite for another class. In the legal arena, a court case may cite other cases, but at the same time, it is being cited by later cases.

To illustrate, a BOM request for components of a Big Meal shows that it consists of a hamburger, fries, and soda. Yet a hamburger consists of a meat patty, bun, and pickles—and a meat patty consists of meat and filler, and so on. Another example of a BOM relationship would be the division of a carburetor into subparts, although the carburetor itself is a subpart in a larger unit (the engine, which is a subpart of the car).

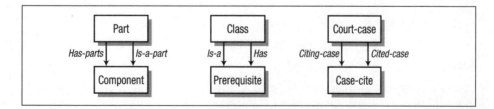

Figure 4.8

An example of recursive many-to-many relationships.

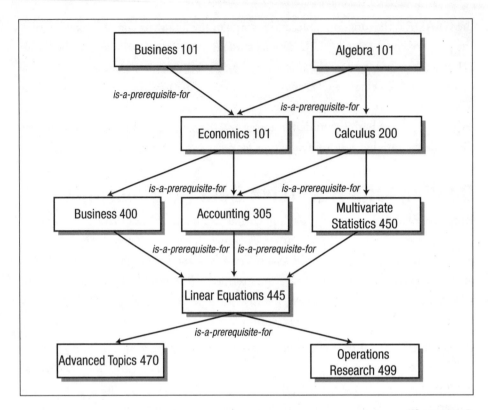

Figure 4.9

A recursive data relationship for course prerequisites.

Figure 4.9 describes the course-prerequisite hierarchy for a university. Note that the IS-A prerequisite relationships are relatively straightforward, indicating which courses are required to be completed before taking other courses. For example, the prerequisites for Linear Equations 445 are Business 400, Accounting 305, and Multivariate Statistics 450. These courses all have prerequisites of their own, which may also have prerequisites, and so on.

Each occurrence of a **course** object has different topics, and a complete implementation must iterate through all courses until reaching terminus, the point where the course has no further prerequisites.

Unfortunately, the recursive many-to-many relationship is very confusing and almost impossible to understand without the aid of a graphical representation. Visualize the recursive many-to-many relationship as an ordinary many-to-many

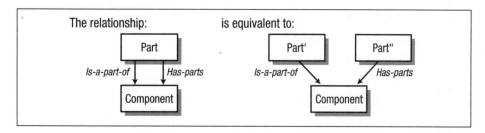

Figure 4.10

Viewing a recursive many-to-many relationship as a many-to-many relationship.

relationship with the **owner** entity "pulled apart" into **owner1** and **owner2**. Figure 4.10 shows how the junction entity establishes the relationship.

The best way to conceptualize a recursive many-to-many relationship in a CODASYL model is through *set occurrence diagrams*. These diagrams show the pointer chains that link the relationships (see Figure 4.11). Table sketches show junction tables contain both implosion and explosion columns in relational databases.

In Figure 4.11, we can navigate the database, determining the components for a **Big_Meal**. To navigate this diagram, start at the object **Big_Meal** and follow the **Has_parts** link to the bubble containing the number 1. This is the quantity for the

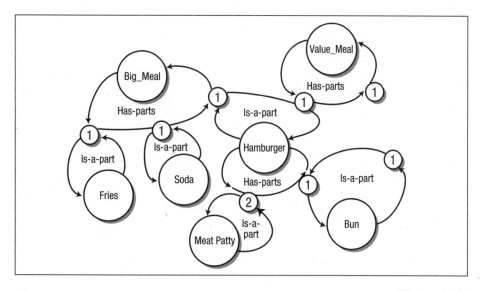

Figure 4.11

A set occurrence diagram for a recursive relationship.

item. We now follow these bubbles to the **Is-a-part** link, which shows that one order of fries is included in a **Big_Meal**. We return to the **Has-parts** link for **Big_Meal** and find the next bubble. The **Is-a-part** link shows that one soda is included in a **Big_Meal**. We then continue this process until no further entities can be found in the **Has-parts** relationship. In sum, the **Has-parts** relationships indicate that a **Big_Meal** consists of one order of fries, one soda, and one hamburger. In addition, the hamburger consists of two meat patties and one bun.

Here, we can see how the database is navigated to determine which parts use a specific component. For example, if you start at the **Hamburger** bubble and navigate through the **Is-a-part** relationships, you see that one hamburger participates in the **Value_Meal** and also in the **Big_Meal**.

Recursive relationships can now be generated from the structure. For example, when listing the components of a **Big_Meal**, all components appear as shown in Table 4.2.

Conversely, the recursive association can be applied to any item to see its participation in other items. For example, the uses of **grease** can be seen by running an implosive query, as shown in Table 4.3.

Clearly, we compound the problem of recursive relationships by adding this additional construct—namely, a class hierarchy (see Figure 4.12). Unfortunately, these

Table 4.2 BOM Explosion for **Big_Meal**.

Part 1	Part 2	Part 3	Quantity
Hamburger			1
	Meat Patty		2
		Oatmeal	4 oz.
		Beef	3 oz.
	Bun		1
Fries			1 order
	Potato		1
	Grease		1 cup
Soda			1
	Ice		1/2 cup
	Drink		1/3 cup

Table 4.3 BOM implosion for **grease**.

Part 1	Part 2	Part 3
Fries		
		Big Meal
		Value Meal
Meat Patty		
	Hamburger	
		Big Meal
		Value Meal
	Cheeseburger	
	Big Beefy	
Fried Pies		
		Value Meal

types of challenges are very common. While it is true that "parts are parts," the different parts have subtle variations, leading to different data items depending on part type. For example, a food-related part might have a **shelf_life** column, but that column does not apply to a nonfood-related part. The class hierarchy design in Oracle tables is covered later in this chapter.

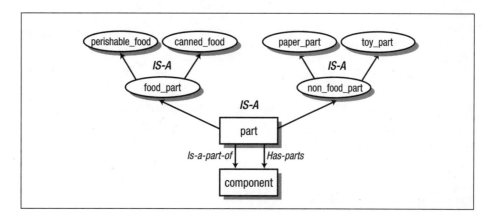

Figure 4.12

A recursive many-to-many relationship with the addition of an IS-A hierarchy.

With an understanding of the nature of recursive relationships, the question becomes one of implementation: What is the best way to represent a recursive relationship in Oracle and navigate the structure?

The following Oracle table definitions describe the tables for the part-component example:

```
CREATE TABLE PART(
    part_nbr      number,
    part_name     varchar2(10),
    part_desc     varchar2(10),
    qty_on_hand   number);

CREATE TABLE COMPONENT (
    Has_part      number,
    Is_a_part     number,
    qty           number);
```

Look closely at the **COMPONENT** example. Both the **Has_part** and **Is_a_part** fields are foreign keys for the **part_nbr** field in the **PART** table. Therefore, the component table is all keyed except for the **qty** field, which tells how many parts belong in an assembly. Look at the following SQL code that is required to display the components in a **Big_Meal**:

```
SELECT part_name
FROM PART, COMPONENT
WHERE
has_part = 'HAPPY MEAL'
AND
PART.part_nbr = COMPONENT.has_part;
```

This type of Oracle SQL query requires joining the table against itself. Unfortunately, because all items are of the same type (namely, **PART**), no real substitute exists for this type of data relationship.

Massive Denormalization: STAR Schema Design

The STAR schema design was first introduced by Dr. Ralph Kimball as an alternative database design for data warehouses. The name *STAR* comes directly from the design form, where a large fact table resides at the center of the model surrounded by various *points*, or reference tables. The basic principle behind the STAR query schema is the introduction of highly redundant data for high performance. With a STAR schema, the designer can simulate the functions of a multidimensional database without having to purchase expensive third-party software. Kimball describes denormalization as the pre-joining of tables, such that the runtime application does not have to join tables. At the heart of the STAR schema, the fact table is usually comprised entirely of key values and raw data. A fact table is generally very long and may have millions of rows.

Surrounding the fact table is a series of *dimension tables*, which serve to add value to the base information in the fact table. For example, consider the E/R model for the sales database shown earlier in the chapter in Figure 4.3.

There, we see a standard third normal form (3NF) database used to represent the sales of items. No redundant information is given; therefore, salient data such as the total for an order would have to be computed from the atomic items that comprise the order. In this 3NF database, a list of line items would need to be created, multiplying the quantity ordered by the price for all items that belong in order 123.

In the following example, an intermediate table called **TEMP** is created to hold the result list:

```
CREATE TABLE TEMP AS
SELECT (QUANTITY.quantity_sold * ITEM.list_price) line_total
FROM QUANTITY, ITEM
WHERE
QUANTITY.order_nbr = 123
AND
QUANTITY.item_nbr = ITEM.item_nbr;

SELECT sum(line_total) FROM TEMP;
```

Also, note that the **STATE-CITY** table hierarchy shown in Figure 4.3 is very deliberate. In order to be truly in third normal form, we do not allow any redundant information (except, of course, foreign keys). Given that this example has been fully normalized into five tables, a query that would appear very simple to the end user would have relatively complex SQL. For example, the SQL to calculate the sum of all orders in the Western region might look very complex, involving a five-way table join as follows:

```
CREATE TABLE TEMP AS
SELECT (QUANTITY.quantity_sold * ITEM.list_price) line_total
FROM QUANTITY, ITEM, CUSTOMER, CITY, STATE
WHERE
QUANTITY.item_nbr = ITEM.item_nbr          /* join QUANTITY and ITEM */
AND
ITEM.cust_nbr = CUSTOMER.cust_nbr          /* join ITEM and CUSTOMER */
AND
CUSTOMER.city_name = CITY.city_name        /* join CUSTOMER and CITY */
AND
CITY.state_name = STATE.state_name         /* join CITY and STATE */
AND
STATE.region_name = 'WEST';
```

In the real world, of course, we would introduce enough redundancy to eliminate the **CITY** and **STATE** tables. But, the point is clear: A manager who wants to analyze a series of complete order totals would need to do a huge amount of realtime computation. Here, we arrive at the basic tradeoff: If we want true freedom from redundant data, we must pay the price at query time.

Remember, the rules of database design have changed. Ten years ago, normalization theory emphasized the need to control redundancy and touted the benefits of a structure that was free of redundant data. Today, with disk prices at an all-time low, the attitude toward redundancy has changed radically. The relational vendors are offering a plethora of tools to allow snapshots and other methods for replicating data. Other vendors, such as UniSQL, are offering database products that allow for non–first normal form implementations. Today, it is perfectly acceptable to create first normal form implementations of normalized databases, which means prejoining tables to avoid the high performance costs of runtime SQL joins.

The basic principle behind the STAR query schema is to introduce highly redundant data for performance reasons. Let's evolve the 3NF database into a STAR schema by creating a fact table to hold the quantity for each item sold. Essentially, a fact table is a first normal form representation of the database, with a very high degree of redundancy being added into the tables. This unnormalized design (see Figure 4.13) greatly improves the simplicity of the design, but at the expense of redundant data.

At first glance, it is hard to believe that this representation contains the same data as the fully normalized database. The new fact table will contain one row for each item on each order, resulting in a tremendous amount of redundant key information. Of

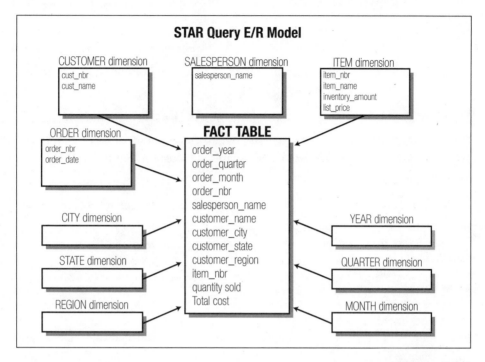

Figure 4.13
The completed STAR schema.

course, the STAR query schema is going to require far more disk space than the 3NF database. The STAR schema would most likely be a read-only database due to the widespread redundancy introduced into the model. Also, the widespread redundancy would make updating difficult, if not downright impossible.

Note the dimension tables surrounding the fact table. Some of the dimension tables contain data that can be added to queries with joins, while other dimensions such as **REGION** do not contain any data, and only serve as indexes to the data.

Considering the huge disk space consumption and read-only restriction, what does this STAR schema really buy for us? The greatest benefit of the STAR schema is the simplicity of data retrieval. Now that we have a STAR schema, we can formulate SQL queries to quickly get the information we desire. For example, we can use the following simple query to get the total cost for an order :

```
SELECT sum(total_cost) order_total
FROM FACT
```

```
WHERE
FACT.order_nbr = 123;
```

By doing some of the work up front, the realtime query becomes both faster and simpler.

Now, let's consider what would happen if the user of this schema wanted to analyze information by aggregate values. Assume our manager wants to know the breakdown of sales by region. The data is not organized by region, but the fact table can easily be queried to find the answer.

At this point, retrieving the sum of all orders for the Western region becomes trivial, as shown in the following snippet:

```
SELECT sum(total_cost)
FROM FACT
WHERE
region = 'WEST'
```

In addition to making the query simpler in structure, all of the table joining has been eliminated, so we can easily get the extracted information from our STAR schema.

> **Note**: A value such as **region** would be an ideal candidate for the use of Oracle 7.3 bitmapped indexes. Columns that have a small number of distinct values can see dramatic performance improvements by utilizing the bitmapped index technique. Bitmapped indexes are described in detail in Chapter 8, Oracle Features For The Data Warehouse.

The natural consequence of this approach is that many IS shops will keep two copies of their production databases: one in third normal form for online transaction processing and another denormalized version of the database for decision support and data warehouse applications.

Populating STAR Schemas With Distributed SQL

Although it is evident at this point that having several copies of the same database can sometimes be desirable, problems arise with this dual approach when attempting to keep the STAR schema in sync with the operational database. Fortunately, Oracle provides several mechanisms to assist in this synchronization. It is safe to assume that the STAR schema will be used by executives for long-range trend analysis, so it is probably not imperative that the STAR schema be completely up-to-date with the operational database. Consequently, we can develop an asynchronous method for updating the STAR schema.

If we make this assumption, then a single SQL statement can be used to extract the data from the operational database and populate the new rows in the STAR schema. In Listing 4.1, we assume that the STAR schema resides at our corporate headquarters in London, and we will use Oracle's SQL*Net with database links to directly reference the remote data warehouse directly from our OLTP database.

Listing 4.1 Updating the STAR schema.

```
INSERT INTO FACT_TABLE@london
VALUES
(SELECT
    order_year,
    order_quarter,
    order_month,
    order_nbr,
    salerperson_name,
    customer_name,
    customer_city,
    customer_state,
    customer_region,
    item_nbr,
    quantity_sold,
    price*quantity_sold
FROM QUANTITY, ITEM, CUSTOMER, CITY, STATE
WHERE
QUANTITY.item_nbr = ITEM.item_nbr      /* join QUANTITY and ITEM */
AND
ITEM.cust_nbr = CUSTOMER.cust_nbr      /* join ITEM and CUSTOMER */
AND
CUSTOMER.city_name = CITY.city_name    /* join CUSTOMER and CITY */
AND
CITY.state_name = STATE.state_name     /* join CITY and STATE */
AND
order_date = SYSDATE                   /* get only today's transactions */
);
```

This is a very simple method for achieving the extraction, normalization, and insertion of the operational data into the STAR schema. Note that we can even handle computed values such as **total_cost**, which is **price** times **quantity_sold**. By specifying the **SYSDATE** in the **WHERE** clause, we ensure that only the day's transactions are extracted and loaded into the STAR schema **FACT_TABLE**. Of course, we are still undertaking a very large five-way table join, but we would hope to run this extraction during off-hours when the retrieval would not impact the production users.

But what about rows that have been deleted? While uncommon, we still need to account for the possibility that some orders may be canceled. We need a mechanism for updating the STAR schema to reflect these deletions. The most obvious method for removing deleted orders from the STAR schema is to utilize Oracle triggers to create a **DELETE** trigger on the **ORDER** table of the operational system. This **DELETE** trigger will fire off a remote delete from the trigger to delete all rows from the STAR schema that are no longer valid, as follows:

```
CREATE TRIGGER delete_orders
    AFTER DELETE ON ORDER
AS
(DELETE FROM FACT_TABLE@london
    WHERE
    order_nbr = :del_ord
);
```

We now have a mechanism for keeping our data warehouse in relative synchronization with the operational database.

Table Partitioning

What are we going to do as the **FACT_TABLE** expands beyond normal table capacity? Let's assume that our organization processes 20,000 orders daily, leading to 7.3 million rows per year. With Oracle's efficient indexing, a table this large can create unique performance problems, primarily because the index must spawn many levels to properly index 7.3 million rows. Whereas a typical query might involve three index reads, a query against a 7 million row table might involve five index reads before the target row is fetched.

To alleviate this problem, many designers will use the concept of *horizontal partitioning* to split the tables into chunks by date. Here, we partition the table into smaller sub-tables, using the data as the distinguishing factor. As such, we may have a table for each month, with a name such as **FACT_TABLE_1_97**,

FACT_TABLE_2_97, and so on. For details on using automatic table and index partitioning, see Chapter 14, *Oracle8 For The Warehouse.*

Whenever we need to address multiple tables in a single operation, we can use the SQL **UNION ALL** statement to merge the tables together, as follows:

```
SELECT * FROM FACT_TABLE_1_97
UNION ALL
SELECT * FROM FACT_TABLE_2_97
UNION ALL
SELECT * FROM FACT_TABLE_3_97
ORDER BY order_year, order_month;
```

> **Note**: In addition to having the benefit of smaller table indexes, this type of table partitioning combined with the **UNION ALL** statement has the added benefit of allowing Oracle's parallel query engine to simultaneously perform full-table scans on each of the sub-tables. In this case, a separate process would be invoked to process each of the three table scans. Oracle query manager would then gather the result data and sort it according to the **ORDER BY** clause. In the previous example, we could expect a 50 percent performance improvement over a query against a single **FACT_TABLE**.

For more information on data warehouse table partitioning, see Chapter 9, *Distributed Oracle Data Warehouses.*

Denormalization And Data Warehouse Sizing

Now, let's apply these principles to the analysis we conducted on Guttbaum's Grocery. The first step is to start with our 3NF model from Figure 4.1 and locate the "facts," which are always numerical items at the bottom of the entity hierarchy. In our example, **quantity** and **sale_amount** in the transaction entity are the facts. Because these appear in the **TRANSACTION** table in our 3NF model for Guttbaum's Grocery, we can presume that the transaction table will form the basis for our fact table for our data warehouse.

However, here we return to an important point regarding data aggregation. Our 3NF model for Guttbaum's assumes that there will be one row for each item on each and every transaction. Because Guttbaum's Grocery chain has 50 supermarkets, and an average of 3,000 customers each day for each supermarket, with an average of 10 items per transaction, we see that 1.5 million rows are added to Guttbaum's database each day. Assuming that each transaction row is 20 bytes, we need 30 MB of disk space per day just to hold the transactions, which translates into 30,000,000 × 365 days = 1,100,000,000,000 bytes, or 1.1 terabytes per year! Even with the price of disk running at the relatively inexpensive rate of $100 per gigabyte or $10,000 per terabyte, we may decide that the cost of disk storage is prohibitively expensive to store this level of transaction detail. One alternative to keeping the lowest level of transaction detail would be to summarize the transaction data, either by total per customer transaction or total by product category. Of course, we may lose some information in this summarization, but we would save a substantial amount of disk storage expense. For details on the issues involved with data aggregation and summarization, refer to Chapter 10, *Oracle Data Warehouse Utilities*.

So, even if we can keep our transaction table rows to 20 bytes, the additional disk cost for adding another redundant data item to the fact table is rather substantial. Each additional 20 bytes of data will cost Guttbaum's $10,000 per year in additional disk expense, so we must carefully consider which redundant data items will appear in the fact table and which data items will reside in the adjacent tables of our STAR schema design. Remember the tradeoff—we are sacrificing disk costs for speed of data retrieval. Each attribute added to the fact table reduces the number of table joins that our Oracle warehouse must incur to service a transaction. Hence, only frequently referenced data items are candidates for inclusion in out fact table.

Handling Attribute Classification

One of the foremost problems in a data warehouse is the design of the non-fact data attributes. In all cases, attributes will either be choose-one, finite value, or hierarchical. Let's discuss each of these data attributes and the design techniques that can be used to implement them within a data warehouse.

- *Choose-One Attributes*—These are mutually exclusive attributes such as gender, level of education, category of income, and so on. In most cases, a flag column would be used to represent these data attributes, and Oracle check constraints would be used to enforce the valid values for the flag. The check constraint validates incoming columns at row insert time. For example, rather than having an application verify that all occurrences of **region** are North, South, East, or

West, a check constraint can be added to the table definition to ensure the validity of the **region** column.

- *Finite Value Attributes*—These attributes contain specific values that cannot be categorized by range values. Examples include **last_name**, **street_address**, and **phone_number**.

- *Hierarchical Attributes*—This is the most challenging to represent in a data warehouse. Within a classification tree, each branch may have many levels, and once an entity has been classified, it should automatically participate in all superclasses up the tree.

Choose-One And Finite Value Attributes

To illustrate the concept of Oracle constraints for choose-one and finite value attributes, consider the following Oracle table definition:

```
CREATE TABLE STUDENT (
   student_nbr             number
      CONSTRAINT stud_ukey
      PRIMARY KEY (student_nbr),
   major_name              char(10)
      CONSTRAINT major_fk REFERENCES DEPT ON DELETE CASCADE,

   region_name             char(1)
      CONSTRAINT region_check
         CHECK (region_name in ('N', S', 'E', 'W');
```

Here, we see the following attribute validation:

- The student number is defined as unique, such that no two **STUDENT** rows may have the same **student_nbr**. Oracle uses a unique index to enforce this primary key constraint.

- The major name is validated against the existing values in the **MAJOR** table when a row is inserted. Hence, only valid department names are allowed to be stored into the **major_name** column.

- The **region_name** column may only have the values of N, S, E, or W. Oracle will not allow any other values to be stored in this column.

Returning to our example from Guttbaum's Grocery, we remember that while the customer entity has many attributes, each attribute is distinct and can be represented independently of other attributes. The Oracle table definition for Guttbaum's fact table might include the following customer attributes:

```
CREATE TABLE FACT (
. . .
highest_education              number(2)
   CONSTRAINT highest_education_check
      CHECK (highest_education between 0 and 20);
size_of_immediate_family       number(2)
   CONSTRAINT family_check
      CHECK (size_of_immediate_family between 0 and 20);
number_of_children             number(2)
   CONSTRAINT children_check
      CHECK (number_of_children between 0 and 20);
own_or_rent                    char(1)
   CONSTRAINT own_check
      CHECK (own_or_rent in 'U','O','R');
yearly_income_class            number(1)
    CONSTRAINT income_check
       CHECK (yearly_income_class between 1 and 5);
```

Here, we see that a total of 8 bytes would be added to the fact table to provide fast reference to information about the type of customer who made the transaction. We also note that there are provisions for unknown values for the customer, as would be the case when a customer did not use their Grocery Club card, in this case, a "U" for unknown character values and a zero for unknown numeric values. Now, queries from end users desiring transaction information according to the type of customer are easy to respond to because the fact table does not need to be joined with the customer table. But what about the product classifications? Because the product classifications are hierarchical in nature, we need to develop another mechanism for representing them in our fact table.

Hierarchical Attribute Design

Hierarchies are especially difficult to maintain in a data warehouse. Unlike finite attributes, hierarchical classifications may assign many values when an item is added to an Oracle data warehouse. The hierarchical classification displayed in Figure 4.14 shows a hierarchical attribute classification for a product.

For example, when a transaction for the purchase of chicken wings is recorded, attributes made for the transaction need to include the sale of a chicken product, a

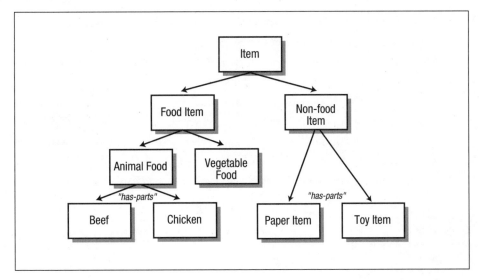

Figure 4.14

A classification hierarchy for a product.

meat product, and a food product. As such, a mechanism needs to be devised to store the hierarchy of attributes in a meaningful way and to insert the proper values each time a row is added to the fact table.

In our example, we have the following two methods for representing our hierarchy of product attributes:

1. *Assign an arbitrary level classification for each level in the hierarchy.* Because each level is mutually exclusive (for example, the product cannot be both food and nonfood), the following scheme would be the most efficient use of storage in the fact table:

```
level_one          char(1)
   CONSTRAINT level_one_check
      CHECK (level_one in ('F','N'));
level_two          char(1)
   CONSTRAINT level_two_check
      CHECK (level_two in ('A','V','P','T'));
level_three        char(1)
   CONSTRAINT level_three_check
      CHECK (level_three in ('U','B','C'));
```

In our over-simplified example, we see that **level_one** can be food or nonfood; **level_two** can be animal, vegetable, paper, or toy; and **level_three** can be beef, chicken, or "U" for unclassified (in cases where a level three classification does not apply). The advantage of this representation of the hierarchy is that this representation will only add 3 bytes to each fact row. The downside is that queries are cryptic for end users. End users will have to know the valid values for each classification level in their queries. For example, to query for the total sales of non-food items by customers who earn more than $50,000 per year would require that the end users know the proper flag values shown here:

```
SELECT sum(sale_amount) FROM FACT
WHERE
level_one = 'N'
AND
yearly_income_class > 3;
```

2. *Assign a descriptive name for each level in the hierarchy.* This method would assign descriptive values for each product class, thereby making it easier for the end users to query the fact table. For example:

```
food_flag                char(1)
   CONSTRAINT food_check
      CHECK (food_flag in ('Y','N'));
animal_or_vegetable_flag  char(1)
   CONSTRAINT animal_check
      CHECK (animal_or_vegetable_flag in ('A','V','U'));
type_of_meat_flag        char(1)
   CONSTRAINT meat_check
      CHECK (type_of_meat_flag in ('F','C','P','B'));
. . .
```

The benefit of this approach is that the queries can be made very descriptive, for example:

```
SELECT * FROM FACT
WHERE food_flag = 'N'
AND
yearly_income_class = 2;
```

The downside, of course, is that there will be many more flags in the fact table, and, because the values are mutually exclusive at each level, most of the flags will contain **NULL** values. There will also be far more indexes on the fact table, and they will slow down the nightly batch update process. As data warehouses grow into the terabyte range, even a few additional bytes can have a substantial disk cost. Also, the type of front end will also influence the decision about the type of flags. If your application hides the SQL behind a front-end query tool, then this type of approach has no real advantage.

Again, these physical attribute representation issues go to the very heart of the data warehouse, and intelligent up-front planning will ensure a sound, robust system.

Data Warehouse Input Screen Design

In addition to the design of the table structures, the design phase is a good time to take a look at how the end-user community will be accessing the table structures. One of the primary goals of the data warehouse designer is to provide a flexible method for the end-user to access all of the data that they could possibly desire without going to the IS department to have new input screens created.

Some designers address this issue by providing third-party tools or a spreadsheet metaphor tool for multidimensional queries, but simple design techniques exist for allowing access by custom-designed front ends. The "build versus buy" choices apply to this type of decision. On the one hand, many front ends such as multidimensional spreadsheets have built-in statistical capabilities that are very difficult to replicate with custom-written code. On the other hand, many data warehouses provide simple methods for extracting and downloading sets of data into PC files. In these cases, we see that customized front ends are often easier for the end user to use than off-the-shelf solutions.

Creating An SQL Generating Front End

One popular technique for allowing end users to query values in the data warehouse is to design a method that generates SQL according to a series of menu screen selections. The code example in Listing 4.2 allows end users to enter constraints in a simple and straightforward fashion.

The examples in this section were originally written for an IBM mainframe environment, using DB2 as the database and IBM REXX as the language for the SQL generator. The first end-user screen, shown in Figure 4.15, allows a user to choose a

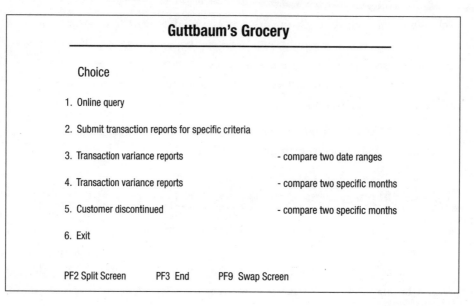

Guttbaum's Grocery

Choice

1. Online query

2. Submit transaction reports for specific criteria

3. Transaction variance reports   - compare two date ranges

4. Transaction variance reports   - compare two specific months

5. Customer discontinued   - compare two specific months

6. Exit

PF2 Split Screen   PF3 End   PF9 Swap Screen

Figure 4.15

A screen to choose a report type.

type of query. The end user is presented with a list of predefined reports. In this fashion, end users may choose from a set of report templates.

After choosing the type of report desired, the next screen appears. This screen allows the entry of variance criteria (see Figure 4.16). The selected variance is used in the **WHERE** clause of the SQL **SELECT** statement, and this screen will be interrogated by the routine to generate the SQL. Note that the warehouse allows queries that compare one specific month with another specific month. This makes it very easy to compare two periods of time.

Figure 4.16 shows a sample data selection screen as it could be filled out by a user. The next screen, shown in Figure 4.17, allows end users to choose specific data attributes to limit a query. The end user may select a specific store, all stores in a city, or all stores within a standard metropolitan statistical area (SMSA). This screen also allows end users to constrain a query by a range of ZIP codes or a number of transactions during a chosen period. Each constraint is added to the **WHERE** clause with an **AND** condition.

After setting the constraints, the user selects which fields will be displayed in the query results. The next screen, shown in Figure 4.18, adds a tremendous amount of

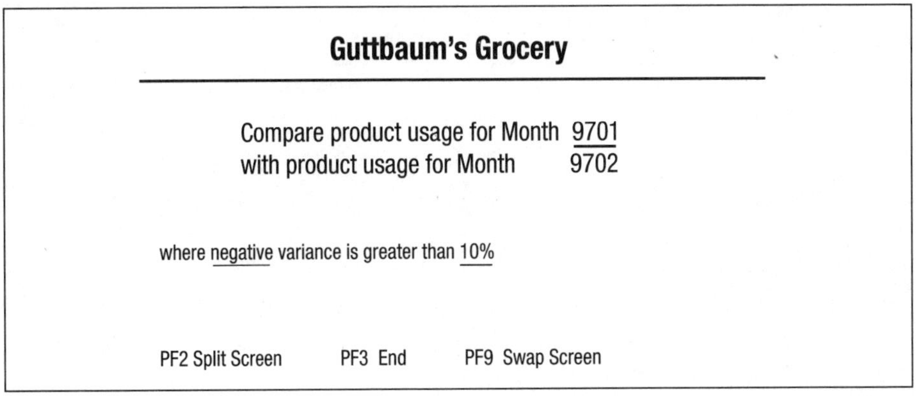

Figure 4.16

A screen used to choose variance criteria.

flexibility to the front end, allowing end users to create an almost infinite variety of custom reports. The screen determines the objects of the SQL **SELECT** and **ORDER BY** statements.

By interrogating the values from the screen, the appropriate mainframe Job Control Language (JCL) and SQL are created and shipped to the internal reader of the IBM

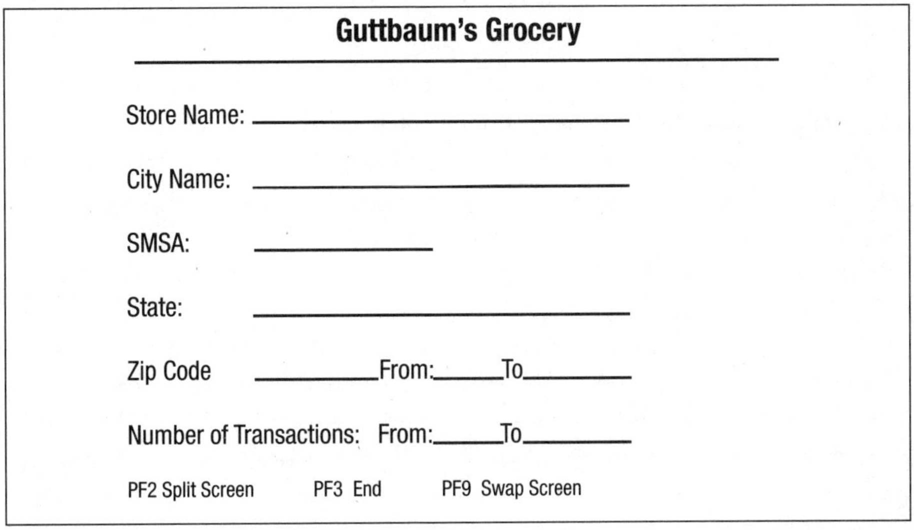

Figure 4.17

Additional selection criteria.

Guttbaum's Grocery

Select Field	Sort Order	Field Name
X	3	Percentage of Variance. <Variance Reports Only>
		Name Of Store
		Number Of Transactions. <descending order>
		Customer Type
		Full Street Address
X	2	City
		State
X	1	Zip Code
		Total Quantity Purchased

| PF2 Split Screen | PF3 End | PF9 Swap Screen |

Figure 4.18

Choosing the display values and sort order.

mainframe. Users are notified that *JOB xxx HAS BEEN SUBMITTED*, and they are notified of the completion by using the **NOTIFY** JCL statement. Users are then free to browse or print the results of their SQL statement. As is true with most decision support systems, the answer to one query often stimulates additional questions. Users can swap screens, thereby viewing output on one screen while creating a new query on another.

REXX routines are very simple to generate, and an understanding of the structure of SQL allows for very quick development of an SQL generator that can display any of the data items in the desired form or sequence. The screens are generated very quickly with SDF in ISPF, and, as mentioned, the REXX routines are very straightforward.

It is not enough to have SQL used only as an access tool. End users demand simple, check-the-box access to their data, and they are often unwilling to use ad hoc SQL tools such as QBE. By creating this simple front end for SQL, the best possible outcome for the IS project is achieved. Listing 4.2 shows the REXX code used to generate the SQL. It is in three sections: the **SELECT** portion, the **FROM** portion, and the **WHERE** clause. Note that this system has two levels of aggregate details, and the SQL generator points to either detail or summary tables depending on the type of end-user query.

Listing 4.2   A REXX routine to generate SQL from screen values.

```
/* ————————————————
Add SQL command to input stream...
———————————————— */
sql_write:

queue "SET CURRENT SQLID = 'AUTOC';"

if XBILL = ' ' &,
   XSNUM = ' ' &,
   XDATE = ' ' &,
   XSITE = ' ' &,
   XADDR = ' ' &,
   XCITY = ' ' &,
   XSTATE = ' ' &,
   XZIP  = ' ' &,
   XACCT = ' ' &,
   XACTIVE = ' ' &,
   XREQ  = ' ' &,
   XTIME = ' ' &,
   XTYPE = ' ' then
queue "SELECT *                    "
else
   queue "SELECT                    "

COMMA = ' '

if SUMMARY ^= ' ' then
do

/* add summary stuff here     */

    if XACCT ^= ' ' then
    do
       queue "   TOT_USER_SITES"
       COMMA = ','
    end

    if XACTIVE ^= ' ' then
    do
       queue COMMA    "   ACTIVE_USER_SITES"
       COMMA = ','
    end
```

```
end

if XDATE    ^= ' ' then
do
   queue COMMA    "    DATE_YYMM"
   COMMA = ','
end

if XSITE    ^= ' ' then
do
   queue COMMA    "    NAME_LINE_1"
   COMMA = ','
end

if XADDR    ^= " " then
do
   queue COMMA    "    NAME_LINE_2"
   COMMA = ','
   queue COMMA    "    NAME_LINE_3"
   queue COMMA    "    NAME_LINE_4"
   queue COMMA    "    NAME_LINE_5"
end

if XCITY    ^= ' ' then
do
   queue COMMA    "    CITY_NAME"
   COMMA = ','
end

if XSTATE   ^= ' ' then
do
   queue COMMA    "    STATE_ABBR"
   COMMA = ','
end

if XZIP    ^= ' ' then
do
   queue COMMA    "    ZIP"
   COMMA = ','
end

if XTYPE    ^= ' ' then
do
   queue COMMA    "    CUST_TYPE_DESC"
   COMMA = ','
end
```

```
if DETAIL  ^= ' ' then queue "FROM FACT_TABLE"
if SUMMARY ^= ' ' then queue "FROM FACT_TABLE_SUMMARY"

WHERE = 'WHERE'

AND = '   '

if SUMMARY ^= ' ' then
do
/* add summary stuff here    */

    /* do the number of active users  ************ */
    if SUSER ^= ' ' & EUSER  ^= ' ' then
    do
     temp = " ACTIVE_USER_SITES > " SUSER
     temp = temp     " AND ACTIVE_USER_SITES < "    EUSER
     temp = AND    WHERE    temp
     AND = "AND"
     WHERE = ""
     queue temp
    end
    else
     if SUSER  ^= ' ' then
     do
      temp = " ACTIVE_USER_SITES > "    SUSER
      temp = WHERE    AND    temp
      WHERE = ""
      AND = "AND"
      queue temp
     end
     else
      if EUSER    ^= ' ' then
      do
        temp = " ACTIVE_USER_SITES < "    EUSER
        temp = WHERE    AND    temp
        AND = "AND"
        WHERE = ""
        queue temp
      end
end
/*  add a "like" parm here   */
if CNAME    ^= ' ' then
do
  temp = WHERE  AND  "  NAME_LINE_1 LIKE '%" CNAME    "%'"
  AND = "AND"
  WHERE = ""
```

```
   queue temp
end

if STATE     ^= ' ' then
do
  temp = WHERE  AND " STATE_ABBR = '"  STATE     "'"
  WHERE = ""
  AND = "AND"
  queue temp
end

if METRO     ^= ' ' then
do
  temp = WHERE  AND "  CITY_NAME = '"  METRO     "'"
  WHERE = ""
  AND = "AND"
  queue temp
end

if CTYPE     ^= ' ' then
do
 temp = WHERE AND "  CUST_TYPE_DESC = '" CTYPE   "'"
  WHERE = ""
  AND = "AND"
  queue temp
end

/* do the dates ****************************** */

if SDATE ^= ' ' & EDATE ^= ' ' then
do
temp1 = " (DATE_YYMM >= "    SDATE
temp2 =  " AND DATE_YYMM <= "    EDATE    ")"
temp = WHERE    AND    temp1    temp2
  WHERE = ""
  AND = "AND"
  queue temp
end
else
   if EDATE     ^= ' ' then
   do
      temp = WHERE AND " DATE_YYMM <= "    EDATE
      AND = "AND"
      WHERE = ""
      queue temp
   end
   else
```

```
     if SDATE     ^= ' ' then
     do
       temp = WHERE  AND "  DATE_YYMM >= "  SDATE
       WHERE = ""
       AND = "AND"
       queue temp
     end


/* do the zips  **************************** */
if SZIP      ^= ' ' & EZIP  ^= ' ' then
do
 temp = "  ZIP  > "   SZIP " AND ZIP  < "    EZIP
 temp = AND    WHERE    temp
 AND = "AND"
 WHERE = ""
 queue temp
end
else
  if SZIP       ^= ' ' then
   do
     temp = WHERE  AND  "  ZIP       > "    SZIP
     WHERE = ""
     AND = "AND"
     queue temp
   end
   else
     if EZIP      ^= ' ' then
     do
       temp = WHERE  AND  "  ZIP   < "    EZIP
       AND = "AND"
       WHERE = ""
       queue temp
     end

/* now, order the fields as specified by the user....    */
ORDER = 'ORDER BY'
COMMA = ' '

DO counter = 1 to 12

    if SUMMARY ^= ' ' then
    do
    /* add summary stuff here    */

      if TACCT    = counter then
      do
         queue ORDER  COMMA  "   TOT_USER_SITES ASC"
```

```
          ORDER = ""
          COMMA = ','
      end

   end


   if TDATE    = counter then
   do
      queue ORDER    COMMA    "   DATE_YYMM ASC"
      ORDER = ""
      COMMA = ','
   end

   if TSITE    = counter then
   do
      queue ORDER    COMMA    "  NAME_LINE_1 ASC"
      ORDER = ""
      COMMA = ','
   end

   if TADDR    = counter then
   do
      queue ORDER    COMMA    "  NAME_LINE_2 ASC"
      ORDER = ""
      COMMA = ','
      queue ORDER    COMMA    "  NAME_LINE_3 ASC"
      ORDER = ""
      COMMA = ','
      queue ORDER    COMMA    "  NAME_LINE_4 ASC"
      ORDER = ""
      COMMA = ','
      queue ORDER    COMMA    "  NAME_LINE_5 ASC"
      ORDER = ""
      COMMA = ','
   end

   if TCITY    = counter then
   do
      queue ORDER    COMMA    "  CITY_NAME ASC"
      ORDER = ""
      COMMA = ','
   end

   if TSTATE   = counter then
   do
      queue ORDER    COMMA    "  STATE_ABBR ASC"
```

```
      ORDER = ""
      COMMA = ','
   end

   if TZIP    = counter then
   do
      queue ORDER    COMMA    "   ZIP ASC"
      ORDER = ""
      COMMA = ','
   end

   if TTYPE   = counter then
   do
      queue ORDER    COMMA    "   CUST_TYPE_DESC ASC"
      ORDER = ""
      COMMA = ','
   end
end

queue ';'

return 0

end
```

As we can see from this example, it is relatively trivial to write a system that generates SQL. Also, Oracle allows SQL to be generated and executed in a dynamic fashion.

Summary

This chapter has demonstrated how a proper design can be critical for good performance. While far from being an exhaustive description of all relational design techniques, the text has focused on the basic principles that will help to ensure that your Oracle database functions as quickly as possible. Now, we are ready to look into the details of the Oracle architecture and how the Oracle database can be exploited to make fast data warehouses.

Many experts believe that response time is one of the most critical factors in the success of any database, especially a data warehouse. Regardless of how well a system is analyzed and implemented—no matter now flashy the GUI interface—if a system fails to deliver data in a timely fashion, the project is doomed. Now that we have reviewed logical database design, let's move on to the physical implementation of Oracle databases.

Online
Analytical
Processing
And Oracle

CHAPTER

5

HIGH PERFORMANCE

Online Analytical Processing And Oracle

Dr. E. F. (Ted) Codd coined the phrase *online analytical processing (OLAP)* in a 1993 white paper called *Providing OLAP (Online Analytical Processing) to User-Analysts: An IT Mandate*. Soon after the publication of this paper, OLAP became the latest buzzword in the database arena and every IS professional struggled to understand OLAP and how it fit into the paradigm of decision support system (DSS) applications. In addition to defining OLAP, Dr. Codd also went on to create 12 rules for OLAP that are similar in form to Codd's 12 rules for relational databases. Given the recent popularity of OLAP, it is very easy to view OLAP as a nascent technology. However, OLAP, as defined by Codd, is not a new technology, and some products, such as the IRI Express OLAP engine, have been available for more than 20 years.

As more companies embrace the concept of creating a historical data repository for OLAP and DSS applications, new client/server issues are emerging as developers struggle to create Oracle-based client/server applications. This chapter reviews OLAP with a focus on the various techniques used to interface OLAP applications with Oracle databases.

A great deal of interest has surfaced in the application of data warehousing and multidimensional databases for advanced systems. Advanced systems, such as expert systems and decision support systems, have been used for decades to solve semi-structured and even unstructured problems. Traditionally, these types of systems combine inference engines and relational databases in order to store the knowledge-processing components, without the benefit of having a huge data warehouse.

OLAP News

The explosive interest in OLAP has fueled the creation of a popular new Internet newsgroup dedicated to OLAP issues. You can find the newsgroup at comp.database.olap.

OLAP Fundamentals

Essentially, an OLAP system is any system that captures summarized information and allows the summaries to be displayed as cross-tabulations between two variables. In the following example, we explore OLAP using the Excel spreadsheet pivot table feature.

The terms *OLAP* and *multidimensional database* have become synonymous, thus adding to the confusion surrounding the two terms. Essentially, a multidimensional database is a database architecture that stores summarized information such that all salient data items (called *dimensions*) are cross-referenced with each other (see Figure 5.1). For example, a multidimensional database might store sales totals cross-referenced by month, product line, territory, and salesperson. The multidimensional database could then display the sales totals according to the possible combinations of cross-referenced tables, as shown in Table 5.1.

So, if this is a multidimensional database, then what is OLAP? OLAP is a presentation front end that allows end users to choose the dimensions and facts that will be cross-referenced. The data does not necessarily have to come directly from a multidimensional database. The possible data sources for an OLAP application include:

Sum of QTY-Sold	YEAR 1994	QTY	1994 Total	1995		1995 Total	Grand Total
Customer	Q1	Q2		Q1	Q2		
ABC Corp.	110	0	110	388	0	388	498
AT&T	60	0	60	22	0	22	82
IBM	37	0	37	38	0	38	75
Oracle	0	18	18	0	21	21	39
XYZ Inc.	71	0	71	122	0	122	193
Grand Total	278	18	296	570	21	591	887

Figure 5.1

A sample multidimensional database display.

Table 5.1   Possible plots of facts and dimensions.

Fact	Dimensions
Total Sales	Month by product line
Total Sales	Month by territory
Total Sales	Month by salesperson
Total Sales	Product line by territory
Total Sales	Product line by salesperson

- Multidimensional databases

- Relational databases (via ROLAP tools)

- Spreadsheet data (extracted from any database architecture)

To illustrate, let's take a close look at a simple OLAP application. Note that while the following example may seem overly simplistic, many Oracle shops are using this very technique to deliver OLAP applications to their end users. Excel spreadsheets can hold very large datasets, and in many cases, managers can get their data loaded entirely into their spreadsheet, thereby alleviating the need to create a client/server Oracle application. Instead of using a client/server application, the summary data for a spreadsheet is refreshed from Oracle each day, ensuring that the manager has current data for the OLAP application.

Using Excel Pivot Tables For OLAP

The Microsoft Excel spreadsheet product is an excellent way to demonstrate the capabilities of an OLAP application. Many companies extract denormalized information from their Oracle databases, FTP the data to a PC LAN, and load the file into a very large Excel spreadsheet on a client PC (see Figure 5.2). The manager can then use Excel's PivotTable Wizard to analyze the data, just as if they were using a multidimensional database. Of course, this approach requires a very powerful PC, but it is a fast, simple, and straightforward approach to simulating a multidimensional database with an OLAP application.

The Oracle data extraction is usually invoked from a Unix **crontab** task, which invokes an SQL script to extract the summarized data from Oracle, format the data,

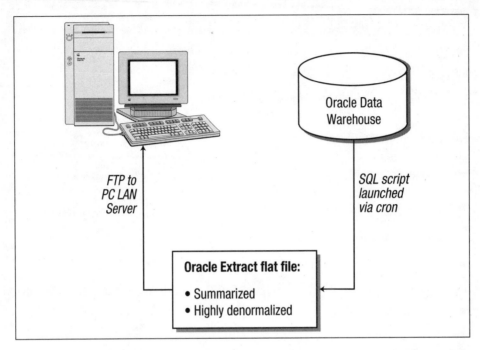

Figure 5.2

Extraction of summarized data for PC-based OLAP.

and pipe it to a flat file. Using NFS, a mount on a PC LAN can be created so that the extracted data is transferred directly to the PC disk. The data can then be easily loaded into a spreadsheet, where the wizard will allow the manager to perform complex cross-tabulations and decision support queries.

> *Note: To get the maximum benefit from this exercise, I recommend that you follow along on your PC. This short exercise will only take about ten minutes, and it has proven to be the best method for understanding multidimensional databases.*

Step 1: Load The Sample Spreadsheet

The first step of this exercise is to load the sample spreadsheet named *pivot.xls*, which can be found on the CD-ROM included with this book.

Please note that the input data provided in pivot.xls is highly denormalized and ready to use. Each row represents a line item within an order, and there is a high degree of duplicated data. Also, note that every field is a potential key except for **QTY-sold** and **Tot-cost**. Getting this file onto a PC platform involves writing an SQL statement that will extract the required columns while joining the salient Oracle tables (see Figure 5.3). The SQL is generally executed by invoking Oracle's SQL*Plus from a **cron** task on Unix. The resulting flat file will then be transferred to a PC LAN by using FTP, where it will be loaded into the Excel spreadsheet. Figure 5.3 shows what the spreadsheet should look like.

Step 2: Invoke The PivotTable Wizard

The second step in this exercise is to invoke the PivotTable Wizard. To accomplish this, choose Data|Pivot Table. The wizard should appear, and it will enable you to define the fact and dimension columns for the pivot table. Perform the following steps:

1. In the first wizard screen, choose Data From Excel List, and press Next.

2. Verify the data range (a1:l47), then press Next.

	YEAR	QTR	MONTH	ORDER #	Salesperson	Customer	Cust-city	Cust-State	cust-region	item#	QTY-Sold	Tot-cost
1	YEAR	QTR	MONTH	ORDER #	Salesperson	Customer	Cust-city	Cust-State	cust-region	item#	QTY-Sold	Tot-cost
2	1994	Q1	Jan	112	Jones	AT&T	Chicago	IL	NORTH	400	2	$14
3	1994	Q1	Jan	112	Jones	AT&T	Chicago	IL	NORTH	300	44	$2,300
4	1994	Q1	Jan	112	Jones	AT&T	Chicago	IL	NORTH	200	2	$352
5	1994	Q1	Jan	112	Jones	AT&T	Chicago	IL	NORTH	600	12	$7,453
6	1994	Q1	Feb	343	Smith	IBM	Miami	FL	SOUTH	300	11	$3,427
7	1994	Q1	Feb	343	Smith	IBM	Miami	FL	SOUTH	400	8	$14
8	1994	Q1	Feb	343	Smith	IBM	Miami	FL	SOUTH	700	18	$4,536
9	1994	Q1	Feb	343	Smith	ABC Corp	Atlanta	GA	SOUTH	600	14	$3,456
10	1994	Q1	Feb	343	Smith	ABC Corp	Atlanta	GA	SOUTH	500	22	$13,276
11	1994	Q1	Feb	343	Smith	ABC Corp	Atlanta	GA	SOUTH	700	34	$65,748
12	1994	Q1	Feb	343	Smith	ABC Corp	Atlanta	GA	SOUTH	600	12	$4,637
13	1994	Q1	Feb	343	Smith	ABC Corp	Atlanta	GA	SOUTH	400	11	$3,456
14	1994	Q1	Feb	343	Smith	ABC Corp	Atlanta	GA	SOUTH	300	17	$6,593
15	1994	Q1	Feb	411	Bradley	XYZ Inc.	Fresno	CA	WEST	100	21	$4,565
16	1994	Q1	Feb	411	Bradley	XYZ Inc.	Fresno	CA	WEST	200	22	$35
17	1994	Q1	Feb	411	Bradley	XYZ Inc.	Fresno	CA	WEST	600	1	$665
18	1994	Q1	Feb	411	Bradley	XYZ Inc.	Fresno	CA	WEST	700	5	$45
19	1994	Q1	Feb	411	Bradley	XYZ Inc.	Fresno	CA	WEST	100	13	$342
20	1994	Q1	Feb	411	Bradley	XYZ Inc.	Fresno	CA	WEST	300	9	$876
21	1994	Q2	May	666	Jones	Oracle	Rockwood	WI	NORTH	100	6	$342
22	1994	Q2	May	666	Jones	Oracle	Rockwood	WI	NORTH	200	1	$6,352
23	1994	Q2	May	666	Jones	Oracle	Rockwood	WI	NORTH	400	5	$7,362
24	1994	Q2	May	666	Jones	Oracle	Rockwood	WI	NORTH	700	6	$772

Figure 5.3

Denormalized Oracle data after transfer into Excel spreadsheet.

3.   Finally, specify the axis names by highlighting your choice, and then dragging and dropping them onto the pivot table axis, as shown in Figure 5.4. Press Finish when you're done.

Now, you should have a pivot table defined and displayed on your screen that looks similar to the one shown earlier in Figure 5.1.

Because the entire table is in addressable memory, it is very simple to change the axis of the pivot table and completely recompute the table. To accomplish this, simply press the PivotTable Wizard button, which appears immediately above the pivot table. You can now redefine the dimensions of the pivot table and create a new representation of your data, as shown in Figures 5.5 and 5.6.

Note that we can nest dimensions to create a hierarchy of dimensions. This is a very powerful feature of multidimensional databases and relates to our discussion of attribute hierarchies presented in Chapter 4, *Oracle Data Warehouse Design*. Figure 5.7 shows an example of nested dimensions, with the **Cust-State** dimension nested within the **Cust-Region** dimension. It is also possible to quickly change a displayed fact. For example, in Figure 5.8, the fact is changed from **Tot-sales** to **Tot-cost**.

Figures 5.9 and 5.10 show how you can quickly rotate dimensions to display **Tot-sales** against the **Customer** and **item#** dimensions. It should be obvious that there is incredible power in this ability to change dimensions and quickly recompute facts.

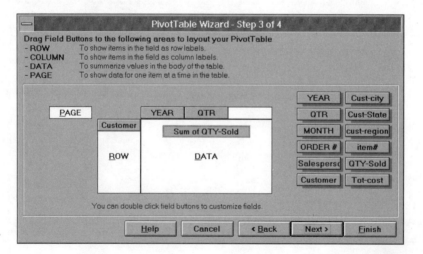

Figure 5.4

Specifying the axis for a pivot table.

Sum of QTY-Sold	YEAR 1994	QTR	1994 Total	1995		1995 Total	Grand Total
Cust-Region	Q1	Q2		Q1	Q2		
NORTH	60	0	78	22	0	43	121
SOUTH	147	0	147	426	0	426	573
WEST	71	0	71	122	0	122	193
Grand Total	278	18	296	570	21	591	887

Figure 5.5

QTY-Sold with YEAR/QTR against Cust-Region.

Sum of QTY-Sold	Cust-Region			
QTR	NORTH	SOUTH	WEST	Grand Total
Q1	82	573	193	849
Q2	39	0	0	39
Grand Total	121	573	193	887

Figure 5.6

QTY-Sold with Cust-Region against QTR.

Sum of QTY-Sold		Cust-Region NORTH	Cust-State	NORTH Total	SOUTH	
YEAR	QTR	IL	WI		FL	GA
1994	Q1	60	0	60	37	110
	Q2	0	18	18	0	0
1994 Total		60	18	78	37	110
1995	Q1	22	0	22	38	388
	Q2	0	21	21	0	0
1995 Total		22	21	43	38	388

Figure 5.7

QTY-Sold with Cust-Region/Cust-State against YEAR.

Sum Of Total Cost	Cust-Region		
Salesperson	NORTH	SOUTH	WEST
Bradley	0.00	0.00	13056.00
Jones	49,894.08	0.00	0.00
Smith	0.00	210,286.08	0.00

Figure 5.8

Tot-cost with Cust-Region against Salesperson.

As you can see, a pivot table gives a manager the ability to analyze information in any conceivable combination.

Even data that does not appear directly can be displayed. For example, let's say that normally we only display the **SUM of cost** or the **SUM of sales**, but today, we want to drag a dimension into the fact area of the pivot table. Dragging a non-numeric data attribute into the computation area of a pivot changes the fact from a **SUM** to a **COUNT**. As you can see in Figure 5.11, the number of orders that have been placed within each city are now counted and displayed by month. In this fashion, a data attribute can be counted without having to include only numerical items in the body of the pivot table. It is possible to count the number of any data attribute,

Sum Of Total Sales	MONTH		
Customer	Jan	Feb	May
ABC Corp.	0.00	194,332.00	0.00
AT&T	20,238.08	0.00	0.00
IBM	0.00	15,954.08	0.00
Oracle	0.00	0.00	29,656.00
XYZ Inc.	0.00	13,056.00	0.00

Figure 5.9

Tot-sales with MONTH against Customer.

Sum of Tot-sales	MONTH		
item#	Jan	Feb	May
100	0.00	9,814.00	684.00
200	704.00	70.00	12,704.00
300	4,600.00	21,792.00	0.00
400	28.08	6,940.08	14,724.00
500	0.00	26,552.00	0.00
600	14,906.00	17,516.00	0.00
700	0.00	14,0658.00	1,544.00

Figure 5.10

Tot-sales with **MONTH** against **item#**.

including the number of salespersons and customers. For example, we might want to count the number of customers, plotting this count by region and by month.

Now that you understand how multidimensional database front ends function for decision support applications, let's take a look at how data warehouses fit into multidimensional database frameworks.

Count of ORDER #	MONTH			
Customer-City	Jan	Feb	May	Grand Total
Atlanta	0	12	0	12
Chicago	8	0	0	8
Fresno	0	12	0	12
Miami	0	6	0	6
Rockwood	0	0	8	8
Grand Total	8	30	8	46

Figure 5.11

The resulting pivot table of order counts.

## CHAPTER 5

Data Warehouses And Multidimensional Databases

Multidimensional databases are approaching the DSS market through two methods. The first approach is though *niche* servers that use a proprietary architecture to model multidimensional databases. Examples of niche servers include Arbor and IRI. The second approach is to provide multidimensional front ends that manage the mapping between the RDBMS and the dimensional representation of data. Figure 5.12 offers an overview of various multidimensional databases.

In general, the following features apply to data warehouses:

- *Subject-oriented data*—Unlike an online transaction processing application focused on a finite business transaction, a data warehouse attempts to collect all known data about a subject area (e.g., sales volume, interest earned, and so forth) from all data sources within an organization.

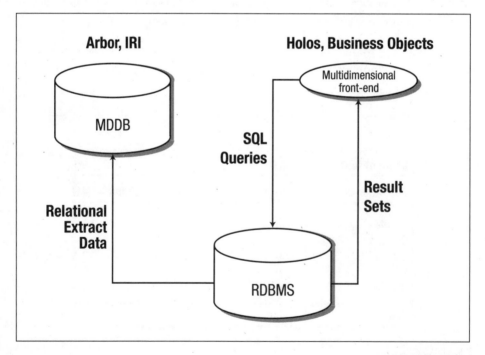

Figure 5.12

Major types of multidimensional databases.

- *Read-only during queries*—Data warehouses are loaded during off-hours and are used for read-only requests during day hours.

- *Highly denormalized data structures*—Unlike an OLTP system with many narrow tables, data warehouses pre-join tables, creating fat tables with highly redundant columns.

- *Data is pre-aggregated*—Unlike OLTP, data warehouses pre-calculate totals to improve runtime performance. Note that pre-aggregation is antirelational, meaning that the relational model advocates building aggregate objects at runtime, only allowing for the storing of atomic data components.

- *Features interactive, ad hoc query*—Data warehouses must be flexible enough to handle spontaneous queries by users. Consequently, a flexible design is imperative.

When we contrast the data warehouse with a transaction-oriented online system, the differences become apparent. These differences are shown in Table 5.2.

Aside from the different uses for data warehouses, many developers are using relational databases to build their data warehouses and simulate multiple dimensions. Design techniques are being used for the simulations. This push towards STAR schema design has been somewhat successful, especially because designers do not have to buy multidimensional databases or invest in expensive front-end tools. In general, using a relational database for OLAP is achieved by any combination of the following techniques:

Table 5.2 Differences between OLTP and data warehouse systems.

Feature	OLTP	Data Warehouse
Normalization	High (3NF)	Low (1NF)
Table sizes	Small	Large
Number of rows in table	Small	Large
Size and duration of transactions	Small	Large
Number of online users	High (1,000s)	Low (< 100)
Updates	Frequent	Nightly
Full-table scans	Rarely	Frequently
Historical data	< 90 days	Years

- *Pre-joining tables together*—This is an obtuse way of saying that a denormalized table is created from the normalized online database. A large pre-join of several tables is sometimes called a *fact table* in a STAR schema.

- *Pre-summarization*—This prepares the data for any drill-down requests that may come from the end user. Essentially, the different levels of aggregation are identified, and the aggregate tables are computed and populated when the data is loaded.

- *Massive denormalization*—The side effect of very inexpensive disks has been the rethinking of the merits of third normal form (3NF). Today, redundancy is widely accepted, as seen by the popularity of replication tools, snapshot utilities, and non-3NF databases. If you can pre-create every possible result table at load time, your end user will enjoy excellent response time when making queries. The STAR schema is an example of massive denormalization.

- *Controlled periodic batch updating*—New detail data is rolled into the aggregate table on a periodic basis while the online system is down, with all summarization recalculated as the new data is introduced into the database. While data loading is important, it is only one component of the tools for loading a warehouse. There are several categories of tools used to populate the warehouse, including:

  - *Data extraction tools*—Tools to retrieve information from different hardware and database platforms, resulting in flat files in a common format.

  - *Metadata repository*—Holds common data definitions, and data definitions that have changed over time.

  - *Data cleaning tools*—Tools for ensuring uniform data quality, and converting non-uniform data, such as international currencies to dollars.

  - *Data sequencing tools*—RI rules for the warehouse that enforce business rules.

  - *Warehouse loading tools*—Tools for populating the data warehouse, such as SQL*Loader.

There is also a difference between the presentation style of OLAP systems and multidimensional databases. OLAP engines generally have an SQL-like interface that allows ad hoc queries to be processed against the warehouse data, using SQL SELECT operations, and producing output lists of query results. Multidimensional databases use a spreadsheet metaphor as the front-end, and the end-user models the dimensions and views the resulting summary as a cross-tabulation in the spreadsheet. Table 5.3 shows the differences between the presentation and display styles for OLAP and MDDB servers.

The base rule is simple: If the data looks like it will fit well into a spreadsheet, it is probably well-suited to an MDDB—or at least an MDDB representation. However, it is not always best to apply this general rule to data warehouse architectures. Many techniques exist for allowing Oracle databases to appear to be OLAP servers or multidimensional databases.

Simulation Of Cubic Databases (Dimensionality)

For an illustrative example, consider the sample customer table in Table 5.4.

Let's take this data structure and assume that the table is physically stored in data order. We can imagine how this data might look as a cubic table by reviewing Figure 5.13.

Of course, the cubic representation would require data to be loaded into a multidimensional database or a spreadsheet that supports pivot tables. When considering an

Table 5.3   Differences between OLAP and MDDB presentations.

Feature	OLAP	MDDB
Presentation display	List	Crosstab
Extraction	Select	Compare
Series variable dimensions	Columns	User-defined

Table 5.4   A sample customer table.

Customer Name	# Sales	YY-MM	City	State
Bob Papaj & Assoc.	300	97-01	NY	NY
Mark Reulbach Inc.	400	97-01	San Fran	CA
Rick Willoughby Co.	120	97-02	NY	NY
Kelvin Connor Co.	300	97-02	San Fran	CA
Jame Gaston Inc.	145	97-03	NY	NY
Linda O'Dell Assoc.	337	97-03	Fairport	NY
Rick Wahl & Assoc.	134	97-03	San Fran	CA

MDDB, two arguments emerge. Relational database vendors point out that MDDBs are proprietary, and they feel that more *open* relational databases should be used. The MDDB vendors point out some serious inadequacies with SQL that make it very difficult to use a relational database.

Keep in mind that dimensions may be hierarchical in nature, adding further confusion. A time dimension, for example, may be represented as a hierarchy with **year**, **quarter**, **month**, and **day**. Each of these levels in the dimension hierarchy may have its own values. In other words, a cubic representation with **time** as a dimension may be viewed in the following two ways:

- A series of cubes—one for **year**, another for **quarter**, and another for **full_date**.

- A five-dimension table.

MDDBs are most commonly used with data that is a natural fit for pivot tables, and it should come as no surprise that most MDDB sites are used with finance and marketing applications. Unfortunately, most multidimensional databases do not scale

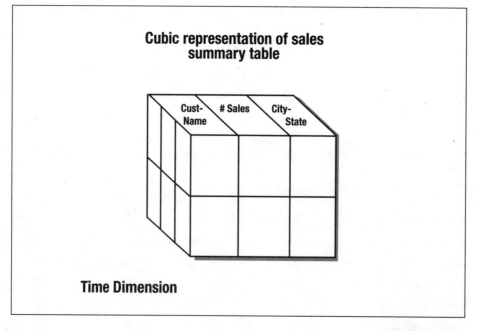

Figure 5.13

Cubic representation of relational data.

up well for warehouse applications. For example, the largest supported database for Essbase is about 20 GB, whereas data warehouses with sizes measured in terabytes are not uncommon.

It is important to note that defining aggregation of a multidimensional database is no different than defining aggregate tables for a relational database. At load time, the database will still need to compute the aggregate values. MDDBs also employ the concept of sparse data. Because data is aggregated and pre-sliced, some cells on a cube may not contain data. For example, consider a cube that tracks sales of items across a large company. The cells representing sales of thermal underwear would be null for Hawaii, and the sales of surfboards in Wyoming would also be null. Nearly all of the product offerings are able to maintain a mechanism for compressing out these types of null values.

OLAP, ROLAP, And MOLAP

Now that we understand that OLAP is a tool that displays summarized data, plotting one dimension against another, let's look at the vendor implementations of this technology. As you saw in the previous section, pivot tables are an excellent way to display multidimensional data, but OLAP involves more than just the multidimensional display of information. OLAP tools also must be able to extract and summarize requested data according to the needs of an end user, and there are two approaches for this data extraction that need to be discussed.

When multidimensional OLAP was first introduced, data was extracted from the relational engine and loaded into a proprietary architecture called a multidimensional database. The data was displayed quickly by accessing the pre-summarized data. This type of OLAP utilizes a multidimensional database, which has become known as *MOLAP*, or *multidimensional OLAP*. The other approach to data extraction uses a mapping facility and extracts the raw data from an operational relational database at runtime, summarizing and displaying the data. Because this approach does not require a multidimensional database, it has become known as *ROLAP*, or *relational OLAP*.

There are many different types of ROLAP and MDDB products on the market today. As shown in Table 5.5, OLAP and MDDB have their own relative advantages and disadvantages, and they are both fighting to achieve recognition for their strengths.

Table 5.5   OLAP versus MDDB.

Trait	OLAP	MDDB
Speed	Slow	Fast
Queries	Flexible	Fixed
Disk cost	Low	High

Speed Vs. Flexibility

To the end user, ROLAP and MOLAP are transparent. The front ends for these tools are similar, and the types of decision support activities are roughly the same. There are, however, significant differences between the operational details of ROLAP and MOLAP that are of primary concern to the data warehouse designer. The biggest difference between ROLAP and MOLAP involves the tradeoff between speed and flexibility (see Figure 5.14). MOLAP engines, by virtue of their pre-summarization and loading, have the data ready to display and give the end user incredibly fast response times. ROLAP engines, by virtue of their ad hoc data extraction and summarization, give end users incredible flexibility in their choices of queries. This is the very heart of the difference between ROLAP and MOLAP— speed versus flexibility.

There is also the issue of economics. For non-relational shops, such as IMS installations, MOLAP can be far less expensive than ROLAP solutions. Whereas a MOLAP database can be purchased and configured for as little as $200,000, ROLAP solutions have a much higher expense in terms of human resources for setup and configuration, as well as increased processing demands on the computer hardware.

On the other hand, shops that already have a relational database such as Oracle can quickly extract denormalized data from their operational databases for downloading into MS-Excel pivot tables. This is by far the cheapest approach to OLAP because there is no investment in either hardware or software. Table 5.6 gives a listing of the most popular ROLAP/MOLAP products.

Over the past 10 years, there have been significant advances in ROLAP and MOLAP, but there remains a chasm between these technologies. Let's take a look at the most salient differences between the technologies.

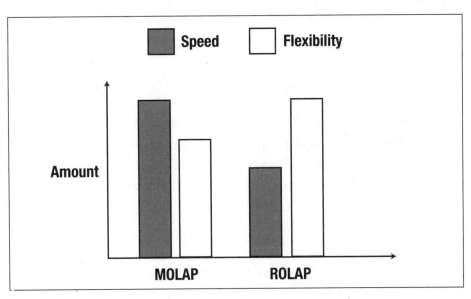

Figure 5.14

MOLAP speed versus ROLAP flexibility.

Multidimensional OLAP (MOLAP)

Multidimensional OLAP is generally thought of as the traditional multidimensional database (MDDB), and many of the early offerings advertised themselves as "pure"

Table 5.6 ROLAP/MOLAP product information.

Vendor	Tool	Description
Oracle	Express	Excel spreadsheet extension, true OO
Oracle	Oracle 7.3	STAR query hints, parallel query, bitmap indexes
MicroStrategy	DSS Agent	MDDB queries against RDBMS
D&B	Pilot LightShip	OLAP with custom and spreadsheet GUI
IBI	FOCUS Fusion	MDDB engine
VMARK	UniVerse	NT-based MDDB engine
Kenan	Acumate ES	MDDB with PC-OLAP GUI
Arbor	OLAP Builder	Extracts data from DW for Essbase
Arbor	Essbase	MDDB engine with Excel spreadsheet GUI
Think Systems	FYI Planner	PC-GUI, with MDDB and OLAP server

multidimensional databases. As we have discussed, a multidimensional database is a database structure optimized for storing facts categorized along many dimensions. The MDDBs are far more effective for storing OLAP data than relational databases because they were designed exclusively with this purpose in mind. The other major consideration with multidimensional OLAP is the fact that all of the data is loaded, summarized, and stored in the MDDB prior to making the database available to end users. Because all the calculations have already been performed, multidimensional OLAP offers astounding response times. For these reasons, multidimensional OLAP is the best choice for applications with the following characteristics:

- *Impatient end users*—MOLAP engines offer end users fast and predictable response times for their queries. In some cases, end users need to be able to quickly create new queries based on the responses from previous queries without losing their train of thought. This speed differential is getting smaller as the speed of relational databases improves, but there remains a dramatic difference between the retrieval of pre-summarized data from an MDDB and the runtime extraction and summarization from a relational back end. It is not uncommon for an end user to report a system outage when the ROLAP tool takes several hours to roll up summaries from a relational database extract.

- *Sophisticated data analysis*—MOLAP engines provide a more robust analysis environment than ROLAP tools. MOLAP engines support budgeting and forecasting functions and tend to have a much more advanced statistical toolkit than their ROLAP cousins. ROLAP, on the other hand, has the ability to provide ad hoc groupings while MOLAP cannot aggregate on the fly.

- *Ease of use*—MOLAP engines are very easy for end users to configure and use to set up scenarios for decision support systems. Because the data is pre-summarized and stored in the multidimensional database, all an end user needs to do is specify the dimensions and groupings within dimensions. ROLAP, on the other hand, requires an end user to understand the mapping of the operational databases, and it is much more difficult to configure.

Relational OLAP (ROLAP)

The advent of the multidimensional database led to an effort by tools vendors to create a method where data could be extracted from a relational database and presented to end users as if it were from a multidimensional database (see Figure 5.15). There are several methods for accessing a relational database and presenting aggregated data as if it were from a multidimensional database. These alternatives include ROLAP middleware tools and downloading pre-aggregated data to local pivot tables. Another common approach is to insert a metadata server between the OLTP relational database and the query tool.

In order to be considered a ROLAP product, a tool must extract runtime data from a relational database, present summarized data in cross-tabular format, and possess a mechanism for translating the relational design into a multidimensional format. Examples of popular ROLAP products include:

- DSS Agent by MicroStrategy

- MetaCube by Stanford Technology Group

- Holos by Holistic Systems

- AXSYS Suite by Information Advantage

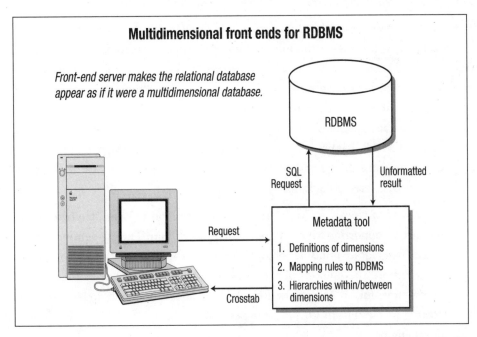

Figure 5.15

Overview of a ROLAP system.

- Red Brick Warehouse by Red Brick Systems

- Prodea Beacon by Platinum Technology

ROLAP systems provide extremely flexible query engines by making any number of operational data stores available to end users. These back-end databases are usually relational databases, but ROLAP tools can also extract from a variety of different relational database.

ROLAP tools require the definition of the mapping between the OLAP model and the relational database, and generate SQL to extract the required data from the operational databases in a very similar fashion to the SQL generators described in Chapter 4.

Because the entire enterprise can be made available to a ROLAP tool, it is not surprising that ROLAP is far more flexible than its MOLAP cousin. Any data, on any platform or database, can be mapped into a multidimensional format; the ROLAP engine will obediently extract and summarize the data according to the extraction specifications. Because ROLAP is far more robust in this sense, it is the OLAP tool of choice for data warehouses that support the following features:

- *Data changes frequently*—In a data warehouse where data is very dynamic and end users require up-to-the-minute summarizations, ROLAP is the only choice. MOLAP tools must extract and summarize data offline for loading into their multidimensional databases. To make matters worse, most multidimensional databases require recalculation of the entire database when a new dimension is added, an aggregation scheme changes, or data is added. These overhead factors make MOLAP inappropriate for decision support systems with highly volatile data sources. Examples of these types of applications include stock market DSS and weather forecasting tools.

- *Large data volumes*—For very large database warehouses in the terabyte range, the cost of supporting MOLAP tools can be exorbitant. The pre-summarization of data can require hundreds of gigabytes of disk storage, and many companies cannot afford the millions of extra dollars required to provide sub-second response times for OLAP queries. ROLAP tools allow companies to leverage their existing investment in OLTP databases without having to buy a multidimensional engine.

- *Unpredictable types of queries*—Because ROLAP engines can allow virtually any operational data source to be queried and summarized, ROLAP has a clear advantage for the decision support application that cannot predefine its query requirements. Of course, this flexibility comes at the cost of ease-of-use, because the IS department must often get involved to assist end users in creating the mappings to the operational databases.

Today, many developers are using relational databases to build their data warehouses and simulate multiple dimensions, and specific design techniques are being used for this. The push toward STAR schema design has been somewhat successful, especially because designers do not have to buy multidimensional databases or invest in expensive front-end tools.

Several methods can be used to aggregate data within OLAP servers. As you can see in Figure 5.16, one method extracts data from the relational engine and summarizes the data for display. Another popular method pre-aggregates the data and keeps the summarized data ready for retrieval.

OLAP Hybrids

It is interesting to note that many products are beginning to create hybrid technologies that use both ROLAP and MOLAP. Oracle Express, for example, was originally implemented with an internal multidimensional database and required data to be pre-summarized and loaded. Today, Oracle Express has been extended to allow ROLAP functionality, and an Express user may query either from the multidimensional database or directly from Oracle relational tables. Oracle Express stores both the definition of the multidimensional data model as well as the mapping between the OLAP model and the relational data. Unfortunately, the mapping between the OLAP model and the relational database is still difficult and usually requires the assistance of an IS professional to use Oracle's Express 4GL tool to manually maintain the mappings. Oracle is addressing this problem by creating a graphical mapping interface that will make it easier for end users to map their OLAP requirements to the Oracle RDBMS engine.

There are upper limits on the size of multidimensional databases, and Express is suitable for storing summarized data up to about 50 GB. These types of hybrid tools are popular for applications where there are small standard summarizations that can be pre-summarized and stored in the multidimensional engine, while very large summarizations use the ROLAP component of Express. Also, the

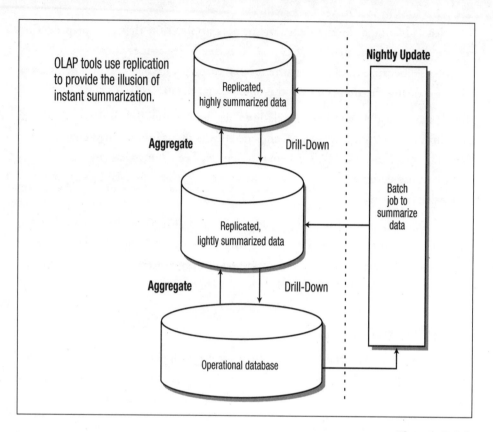

Figure 5.16

Aggregation and OLAP servers.

availability of Oracle's parallel server has allowed SMP and MPP technology to be applied to operational Oracle databases, greatly improving the speed of ROLAP extracts and summarization.

Alternatives To OLAP Data Representation

Many traditional database designs can be used to simulate a data cube. One alternative to the cubic representation would be to leave the table in linear form, using SQL to join the table against itself to produce a result, as shown in Figure 5.17.

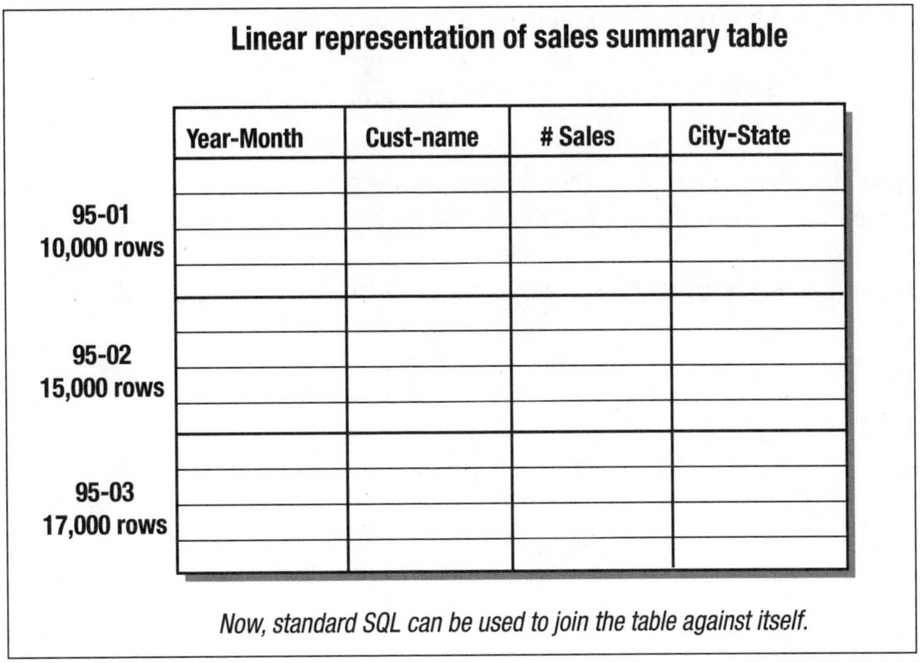

Linear representation of sales summary table

	Year-Month	Cust-name	# Sales	City-State
95-01 **10,000 rows**				
95-02 **15,000 rows**				
95-03 **17,000 rows**				

Now, standard SQL can be used to join the table against itself.

Figure 5.17

Joining a relational table against itself.

Let's take a look at some queries that might require the self-joining of a table. For example:

- Show all customers in Hawaii who purchased our product more than 500 times.

- Show all customers in Los Angeles who purchase less than 10 times per month.

- Show all large customers (buying more than 100 items per month) in Alaska whose usage has dropped more than 10 percent in 1995.

- Show all customers in New York whose usage in March of 1990 deviated more than 20 percent from their usage in March of 1995.

- Show all customers in California where the company name contains *Widget* and usage has dropped more than 20 percent in 1995.

Figure 5.17 shows how a large sales summary table can be logically partitioned into pieces by extracting rows according to the year and month. With a single table such as this one, we can issue SQL that will join the table against itself to compare two date ranges. This is a very powerful SQL technique for sophisticated variance analysis without buying expensive tools. Listing 5.1 shows that a subset of this data can be extracted such that only California sites with more than 100 uses per month are displayed. For display, we chose percentage variance, number of requests, site number, ZIP code, and city. Note the sort order of the report in Listing 5.1; it is sorted first by ZIP, followed by city, and then by percentage variance within city.

Listing 5.1 Sophisticated variance analysis with Oracle SQL.

```
SELECT INTEGER
(((e.number_of_sales - s.number_of_sales) / s.number_of_sales) * 100) ,
e.customer_name , e.city_name , e.zip , s.number_of_sales ,
e.number_of_sales

FROM DETAIL S , DETAIL E

WHERE
s.customer_name = e.customer_name
 AND
e.state_abbr = 'CA'
 AND
e.date_yymm = 9601
 AND
s.date_yymm = 9701
 AND
e.number_of_sales < s.number_of_sales - (.05 * s.number_of_sales)

ORDER BY e.zip ASC , e.city_name ASC , 1 ;
```

Note that the variance analysis in Listing 5.1 is done directly in the SQL statement. This case displays California users whose usage has dropped by more than 5 percent (comparing January 1996 to January 1997).

But, what if the user wants to compare one full year with another year? The table is structured for simple comparison of two specific month dates, but the SQL query could be modified slightly to aggregate the data, offering a comparison of two ranges of dates.

The query shown in Listing 5.2 will aggregate all sales for an entire year and compare 1996 with 1997. Here, we meet the request *show me all customers in California whose sales have dropped by more than 5 percent between 1996 and 1997.*

Listing 5.2   Aggregating sales for an entire year.

```
SELECT INTEGER
(((e.number_of_sales - s.number_of_sales) / s.number_of_sales) * 100) ,
e.customer_name , e.city_name , e.zip , s.number_of_sales ,
e.number_of_sales

FROM Detail S , Detail E

WHERE
s.customer_name = e.customer_name
 AND
e.state_abbr = 'CA'
 AND
substr(e.date_yymm,1,2) = "96"
 AND
substr(s.date_yymm,1,2) = "97"
 AND
e.number_of_sales < s.number_of_sales - (.05 * s.number_of_sales)

ORDER BY e.zip ASC , e.city_name ASC , 1 ;
```

On the surface, it appears that SQL can be used against two-dimensional tables to handle three-dimensional time-series problems. It also appears that SQL can be used to roll up aggregations at runtime, alleviating the need to do a roll up at load time, as with a traditional database. While this implementation does not require any special multidimensional databases, two important issues remain unresolved:

- *Performance*—Joining a table against itself—especially when comparing ranges of dates—may create many levels of nesting in the SQL optimization and poor response time.

- *Ability*—Most end users would not be capable of formulating this type of sophisticated SQL query.

If you strip away all of the marketing hype and industry jargon, you can see that a data warehouse and a multidimensional database can be easily simulated by pre-creating many redundant tables, each with pre-calculated roll-up information. In fact, the base issue is clear—complex aggregation needs to be computed at runtime or data load time.

Summary

Now that you understand the history and evolution of OLAP and multidimensional database technology, we can proceed to take a look at how OLAP and MDDB can be simulated, by developing techniques for pre-aggregating summary information within Oracle tables. It is through these techniques that you, as an Oracle warehouse designer, can form the foundation for your robust decision support systems.

HIGH PERFORMANCE

Aggregating Data For The Oracle Warehouse

CHAPTER

6

HIGH PERFORMANCE

Aggregating Data For The Oracle Warehouse

In order to create the illusion of fast calculation time, most data warehouses are loaded in batch mode after the online system has been shut down and all the common aggregate values are rolled up into summary tables. In this sense, a data warehouse is bimodal, with a highly intensive loading window during off-hours and an intensive query window during the day. Because many data warehouses collect data from nonrelational databases such as IMS or CA-IDMS, no standard methods for extracting data are available for loading into a warehouse and pre-aggregating summary data. Even when the warehouse is fed from an OLTP Oracle database, there are numerous techniques for loading in new data. However, we do have a few common techniques for extracting and loading a data warehouse from operational Oracle databases:

- *Log "sniffing"*—Applies the archived redo logs from the OLTP system to the data warehouse.

- *Update, insert, and delete triggers*—Fires off a distributed update to the data warehouse.

- *Snapshot logs used to populate the data warehouse*—Updates the replicated table changes.

- *Nightly extract/load programs*—Extracts and retrieves the operational data, and loads it into the warehouse.

Note: For more information on using triggers and snapshots to update your Oracle data warehouse, see Chapter 9, Distributed Oracle Data Warehouses.

Once the extraction and loading details have been determined, we need to take a look at the levels of summarization for our aggregate tables. Several methods can be used to aggregate data within OLAP servers. As you can see in Figure 6.1, the ROLAP method extracts data from the relational engine, summarizing the data for display. The other popular method manually pre-aggregates the data and keeps the summarized data ready for retrieval. This chapter focuses on those techniques.

It is important to remember that aggregation is a form of data redundancy, because the aggregations are computed from other warehouse values. As such, we must always keep in mind that some pre-calculated averages may need to be recomputed as new data is loaded into our warehouse.

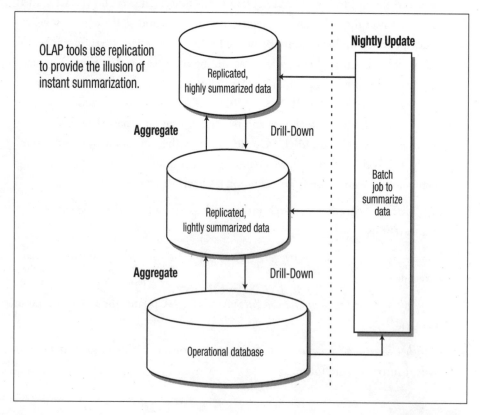

Figure 6.1
Aggregation and OLAP servers.

Data Aggregation And Drill-Down

One of the most fundamental principles of the multidimensional database is the idea of aggregation. As we know, managers at different levels require different levels of summarization to make intelligent decisions. To allow the manager to choose the level of aggregation, most warehouse offerings have a "drill-down" feature, allowing the user to adjust the level of detail, eventually reaching the original transaction data. For obvious performance reasons, the aggregations are pre-calculated and loaded into the warehouse during off-hours. (See Figure 6.2.)

Of the several types of aggregation, the most common is called a *roll-up aggregation*. An example of this type of aggregation would be taking daily sales totals and rolling them up into a monthly sales table. These types of summaries are easily computed from the base data warehouse by using the SQL **SUM** operator.

The more difficult type is the aggregation of boolean and comparative operators. For example, assume that a salesperson table contains a boolean column called **turkey**. A salesperson is a turkey if his or her individual sales are below the group average for

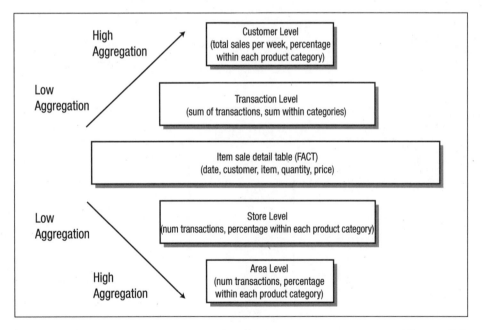

Figure 6.2
Levels of pre-aggregation of summary data.

the day. A salesperson may be a turkey on 15 percent of the individual days; however, when the data is rolled up into a monthly summary, a salesperson may become a turkey even if they only had a few (albeit very bad) sales days.

Aggregation, Roll-Ups, And STAR Schemas

Let's illustrate some methods for pre-calculating aggregate tables by looking at a sample STAR schema design. In Figure 6.3, you can see that our base data warehouse consists of a highly denormalized fact table and numerous dimension tables.

Now, let's assume that we have already defined and populated our STAR schema that contains the **Total_cost** for each order for each day. While it is now easy to see the total for each order, rarely do the users of a decision support system require this level of detail. Most managers would be more interested in knowing the sum of sales or units sold—aggregated by month, quarter, region, and so on. Even with a STAR schema, these types of aggregations would be hard to compute at runtime from our Oracle warehouse with an acceptable response time.

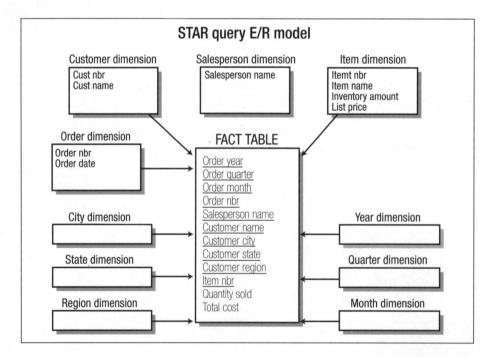

Figure 6.3
A sample STAR schema.

Essentially, we can either aggregate at runtime using ROLAP technology or pre-aggregate the data offline, thus making the totals available without realtime computation. While realtime data aggregation may provide up-to-the-minute detail, the expense of purchasing a ROLAP engine and the slow response time may make the data warehouse designer look for other methods of providing summary data. One simple alternative to realtime aggregation is to write SQL to pre-aggregate data according to the dimensions that end users may want to see. In our example, let's assume management wants to aggregate total cost by region, state, item type, and salesperson. Because we have four possible dimensions, we can generate a list of the following six aggregate tables to pre-create. Assume that all of the tables would have a **month_year** field as their primary key.

- *Region by state*—This table would have **region_name**, **state_name** for dimensions, and **total_cost** as the fact column.

- *Region by item type*—This table would have **region_name**, **item_type** as dimensions, and **total_cost** as the fact column.

- *Region by salesperson*—This table would have **region_name**, **salesperson_name** as dimensions, and **total_cost** as the fact column.

- *State by item type*—This table would have **state_name**, **item_type** as dimensions, and **total_cost** as the fact column.

- *State by salesperson*—This table would have **state_name**, **salesperson_name** as dimensions, and **total_cost** as the fact column.

- *Item type by salesperson*—This table would have **item_type**, **salesperson_name** as dimensions, and **total_cost** as the fact column.

The SQL to produce these table can be easily run as a batch task during your end-of-month processing. For example, we can use the following SQL to create the **REGION_ITEM_TYPE** summary table for March 1997:

```
INSERT INTO REGION_ITEM_TYPE
VALUES
(SELECT "3", "1997", region_name, item_type, SUM(total_cost)
FROM FACT_TABLE
WHERE
    year=1997
    AND month=3
GROUP BY region_name, item_type
);
```

Table 6.1 A sample **REGION_ITEM_TYPE** table.

Date	Region	Type	Monthly Sales
3/97	West	Clothes	$113,999
3/97	West	Hardware	$ 56,335
3/97	West	Food	$ 23,574
3/97	East	Clothes	$ 45,234
3/97	East	Hardware	$ 66,182
3/97	East	Food	$835,342
3/97	South	Clothes	$ 1,223
3/97	South	Hardware	$ 56,392
3/97	South	Food	$ 9,281
3/97	North	Clothes	$826,463
3/97	North	Hardware	$ 77,261
3/97	North	Food	$ 43,383

The resulting **REGION_ITEM_TYPE** table might look like Table 6.1.

While this technique provides summaries for March 1997, what if we want to keep a rolling average of regions and items regardless of the date? In this case, we can use the same SQL that we used earlier, without the SQL **WHERE** clause. Because the values will change each time the warehouse is updated, new aggregate tables can be built in the middle of the night if need be—right after the master fact tables have been populated with the day's sales. The next morning, the prior day's sales will have been rolled up into these summaries, giving management an accurate, fast, and easy-to-use tool for decision support.

> **Note**: PARALLEL CREATE TABLE AS SELECT (PCTAS) can be very useful in an Oracle data warehouse environment where tables are replicated across numerous servers or when pre-aggregating roll-up summary tables. PARALLEL CREATE TABLE AS SELECT is also very useful when performing roll-up activities against your Oracle warehouse. For details on PCTAS, see Chapter 7, Parallelism And Oracle Data Warehousing.

Alternate Summary Data Formats

Of course, the other tables are two-dimensional—comparing one dimension against the other—but these table definitions can easily be massaged by an application to provide a tabular representation of several dimension attributes. Table 6.2 presents a tabular display of **item_type** against **region**, much as a multidimensional database would present these summaries.

But what if management wants to look at quarterly summaries instead of monthly summaries? What about yearly summaries? Of course, this same technique can be used to roll up the monthly summary tables into quarterly summaries, yearly summaries, and so on, according to the demands of end users.

Just as the fact table is time based, aggregate tables can be time based, and the ranges of times can be specified, as shown in the following code:

```
SELECT SUM(cost*qty), store_id
FROM SALE_FACT
WHERE DATE > '31-DEC-96'
AND
DATE < '01-JAN-97'
GROUP BY store_id;
```

Remember, data warehouse fact tables are usually ordered by some type of date, and it makes sense that aggregate tables will also be ordered by a date.

Data Aggregation And Data Redundancy

As we have emphasized, the pre-aggregation of data to achieve fast response times is a form of redundancy, and we must always be careful to recompute any summary data when new information is loaded into our Oracle warehouse. To use a very

Table 6.2   region versus **item_type**.

Region	Clothes	Food	Hardware
West	$113,999	$23,574	$56,335
East	$45,234	$835,342	$66,182
North	$826,463	$43,383	$77,261
South	$1,223	$9,281	$56,392

simple example, the computation **gross_pay = hrs_worked * payrate** computes a **gross_pay** value that could be stored in an Oracle table. Because **gross_pay** is computed from the values of other data columns, it is redundant and must be recomputed each time a component values changes.

Pre-calculation of aggregates speeds up the query, and because data is static, there is no need to update the aggregate table. But there can be a problem with increased system overhead when overall averages need to be recomputed, since overall averages will change with each new entry into the detailed fact table. This problem of having to recompute running averages can be easily overcome by keeping total values and doing the division to get the average at runtime. For example, an average sales amount computation uses two other summary values: **number_of_sales** and **total_sales_amount**. Because the calculation of average sales amount involves a quick division of the other factors, it would make more sense to keep the parts of the average and compute the average sales amount at runtime.

A Method For Pre-Calculating And Storing Summary Data

If we are using a vanilla Oracle database without a multidimensional engine, we can create a method for determining new tables that will contain summary data. Then, we can come up with a method for keeping these summary tables correct. Let's start by examining the table structure of our existing data warehouse. As you saw in Figure 6.3, the fact table is highly denormalized and there are two facts: **Quantity_sold** and **Total_cost** (the facts are usually listed last in the fact table, after all of the key columns). You also saw that there are dimensions of attributes relating to customers, salespersons, and items. Now, let's take a look at how we might create aggregate tables from this model.

Determining The Number Of Aggregate Tables

The first step in creating summary data tables is to identify all the possible dimensions that our Oracle warehouse will use. Let's start by listing the dimension attributes that might be used in our summary tables, such as:

- Month

- Quarter

- Year

- Customer_name

- Customer_city

- Customer_state

- Customer_region

- Item_name

- Item_price

- Salesperson_name

Now that we have listed the data attributes that might become dimensions in pre-summarized tables, it becomes apparent that pre-calculating all of the possible dimensions would involve many possible combinations. But how many summary tables? Let's start with a simple example. Assume that we have four attributes: A, B, C, and D. We would have six possible combinations of attributes, namely, A-B, A-C, A-D, B-C, B-D, and C-D. As it turns out, the following formula can be used to determine the number of possible tables:

*Number of dimension summary tables = (n)! / (n-2)! * 2*

where *n* equals the number of dimension attributes.

For four dimensions, we can quickly compute that there are six summary tables that can be built against the database, as follows:

*Number of dimension summary tables = (4)! / (4-2)! * 2*

Number of dimension summary tables = 24 / 4

Number of dimension summary tables = 6

However, in our example, we have 10 dimensions. We can compute the number of possible combinations of these attribute tables, as follows:

*Number of dimension summary tables = (10)! / (10-2)! * 2*

*Number of dimension summary tables = 3,628,800 / 40,320 * 2*

Number of dimension summary tables = 3,628,800 / 80,640

Number of dimension summary tables = 45

> **Note**: *The number of combinations for each table equals 45, so the real number of tables we need is 90, because we have to perform the calculations twice—once to summarize the **Total_cost** fact and again for the **Quantity_sold** fact.*

Also, we will not be able to create summary hierarchies like our Excel pivot table did in Chapter 5, so each aggregate table will be isolated and referenced by some permutation of the dimension names. If we are going to create 45 tables for each fact, we need to provide meaningful names to our tables. Sample table names might include **MONTH_BY_YEAR**, **MONTH_BY_QUARTER**, and **MONTH_BY_CUSTOMER_NAME**.

Using SQL To Create Summary Tables

If we keep our summary tables in the same database as our data warehouse, it becomes easy to create the summary tables. In the following example, you can see how we can easily use Oracle SQL to create our tables:

```
CREATE TABLE MONTH_BY_CUSTOMER_NAME
AS
SELECT month, customer_name, SUM(total_sales)
FROM FACT
GROUP BY customer_name;

CREATE TABLE REGION_BY_ITEM
AS
SELECT region, item_number, SUM(total_sales)
FROM FACT
GROUP BY item_number;
```

> **Note**: *These summary calculations may invoke full-table scans against your data warehouse and may also use a very large sort area, requiring sorting to disk. Because of the intense nature of these queries, you will want to ensure that these summary tables are created during off-hours. For more information about tuning the creation of summary tables, see Chapter 12, Tuning Oracle SQL.*

Now that you see how easy it is to create summary tables, note that it would be very easy to parameterize the Oracle SQL to allow the dimension names to be replaced by symbolic variables. For example:

```
CREATE TABLE &1_BY_&2
AS
SELECT &1, &2, SUM(total_sales)
GROUP BY &2;
```

If we created a metadata table that contained each possible dimension, it would be easy to write a PL/SQL routine to dynamically re-create and populate the 45 summary tables that are required. The pseudocode for such a routine might look something like this:

```
DECLARE CURSOR c1 AS
    SELECT dimension_name FROM DIMENSIONS ORDER BY dimension_name;
FOR EACH outer_dimension
REPEAT
   OPEN CURSOR c1;
   FETCH c1 INTO dimension_one;
   DECLARE CURSOR c2 AS
       SELECT dimension_name FROM DIMENSIONS ORDER BY dimension_name;
   FOR EACH inner_dimension
   REPEAT;
      OPEN CURSOR c2;
      FETCH c2 INTO dimension_two;
      CALL create_SQL (dimension_one, dimension_two);
   NEXT inner_dimension
NEXT outer_dimension
```

In this fashion, we could create all 45 summary tables each night immediately after our new values have been loaded. But will all of these tables be needed by our end users? Because a complete pre-calculation of 45 tables is not an overwhelming task, we may decide that we can afford to have all possible summary table combinations available to our end users.

On the surface, it appears that SQL can be used against two-dimensional tables to handle three-dimensional time-series problems. It also appears that SQL can be used to roll up aggregations at runtime, alleviating the need to do a roll up at load time, as with a traditional database. While this implementation does not require any special multidimensional databases, the following two important issues remain to be resolved:

- *Performance*—Joining a table against itself (especially when comparing ranges of dates) may create many levels of nesting in the SQL optimization resulting in poor response time.

- *Ability*—No end user would be capable of formulating this type of sophisticated SQL query.

If you strip away all of the marketing hype and industry jargon, you can see that a data warehouse and a multidimensional database can be easily simulated by pre-creating many redundant tables, each with pre-calculated roll-up information. In fact, the base issue is clear—complex aggregation needs to be computed at runtime or when data is loaded.

Summary

Now that you have a fundamental understanding of OLAP and do-it-yourself data aggregation techniques, we are ready to dive into the internals of the Oracle database. Subsequent chapters will take a close look at how to tune the Oracle architecture for data warehousing and the issues involved with managing Oracle locks and tuning Oracle SQL. Even if you are an experienced Oracle professional, I suggest that you take the time to read these chapters. The information is directly related to data warehousing, and some of the tuning tips are not intuitive.

Parallelism And Oracle Data Warehousing

CHAPTER

7

Parallelism And Oracle Data Warehousing

The widespread acceptance of parallel processing and multitasking operating systems has heralded a new mode of designing and implementing data warehouses. Instead of the traditional *linear* warehouse design where queries are single-threaded, today's state-of-the-art Oracle warehouses incorporate massively parallel processors. Indeed, this new processing paradigm is not limited to data warehouses. The corporate information resource has been expanded in definition to include all sources of information, not just relational databases. Corporate information resides within email, Lotus Notes, and many other nontraditional sources, and many companies are collecting information without fully exploiting its value. Oracle universal server, in conjunction with Oracle parallel server, provides an ideal technique for searching the huge amounts of free-form corporate information.

Parallel Processing

Before we get too deep into our discussion of parallel processing, a distinction needs to be made between multitasking and multiprocessing. *Multitasking* refers to the ability of a software package to manage multiple concurrent processes, thereby allowing parallel processing. OS/2 and Windows NT are examples of this technology, but multitasking is found within all midrange and mainframe databases. *Multiprocessing*, on the other hand, refers to the use of multiple CPUs within a distributed environment where a master program directs parallel operations against numerous machines. There are two areas of multiprocessing: hardware and software. At the hardware level, arrays of CPUs are offered, and at the software level, a single CPU is partitioned into separate "logical" processors. The Prism software in the IBM mainframe environment is an example of multiprocessing technology.

In any case, programming for multiprocessors is quite different from programming for linear systems. Multiprocessing programming falls into two arenas: data parallel programming and control parallel programming. In *data parallel programming*, the data is partitioned into discrete pieces and the same program is run in parallel against each piece (see Figure 7.1). Data parallel can be used in any type of Oracle environment, including uniprocessor, symmetric multiprocessor (SMP), or massively parallel processor (MPP) environments. With *control parallel programming*, independent functions are identified and independent CPUs are used to simultaneously solve each independent function. Control parallel is generally associated with MPP environments.

One of the greatest problems faced by developers when implementing parallel processing systems is the identification of parallelism. *Parallelism* refers to the ability of a computer system to perform processing on two data sources at the same time. Whereas many of the traditional database applications were linear in nature, today's systems have ample opportunities for parallel processing.

For the most part, parallelism is an issue of scale—not of speed. Some think that if a linear process can solve a problem in one hour, then a parallel system with 60 processors should be able to solve the problem in one minute. This is analogous to stating

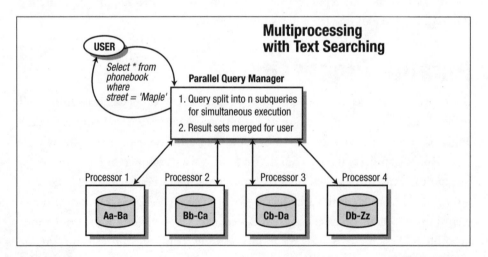

Figure 7.1

An example of data parallel processing.

that because it takes nine months to have a baby, then nine women should be able to produce a baby in one month. Clearly, while there are many separate processes in having a baby (zygote, fetus, infant), each of these tasks requires the completion of the previous task. Traditional linear systems (systems in which one process may not begin until the preceding one ends) will not benefit from parallel processing.

On the other hand, parallel processing can return enormous benefits for large databases that are not designed as traditional linear systems. In other words, a query against a very large database can be dramatically improved if the data is partitioned and, simultaneously, each partition is accessed by a process. For example, if a query against a text database takes one minute to scan a terabyte, the partitioning of the data and processing into 60 pieces will result in a retrieval time of one second. There is also the issue of balancing the CPU processing with the I/O processing. In a traditional data processing environment, the systems are not computationally intensive, and most of the elapsed time is spent waiting on I/O. However, this does not automatically exclude business systems from taking advantage of multiprocessing.

Parallelism is especially effective in scientific applications that can benefit from having hundreds or even thousands of processors working together to solve a problem. Basically, parallelism can dramatically reduce the response time for any query that can be split into sub-queries and each sub-query assigned to a processor (see Figure 7.2).

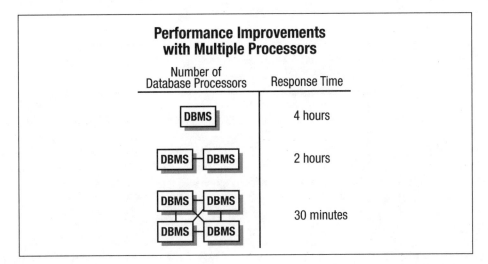

Figure 7.2

Speed reduction with parallel processors.

A continuum of processing architecture exists for parallel processing. On one end of the spectrum, we find a few loosely connected powerful CPUs, while on the other end, we see a large amount of tightly coupled small processors. Parallel tasks can be easily identified in an Oracle data warehouse environment. For the database administrator, routine maintenance tasks, such as export/import operations, can be run in parallel, thereby reducing the overall time required for system maintenance. Also, tasks such as index rebuilding can be run in parallel mode.

In an open systems environment, parallelism may be easily simulated by using a remote mount facility. With a remote mount, a data file may be directly addressed from another processor, even though the data file physically resides on another machine. This can be an especially useful technique for speeding up table replication on remote sites, as shown in Figure 7.3.

As we can see in Figure 7.3, parallelism is used to speed up table replication. To speed up the replication of two tables, a Unix shell script directs CPU-A to begin the copy of Table A as a background task. The script then directs CPU-B to issue a remote mount to Table B, making Table B addressable as if it were a local disk to CPU-B. The script then issues a copy of Table B, and the tables are copied simultaneously, reducing the overall processing time (see Figure 7.4).

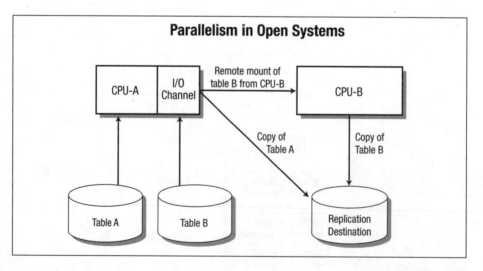

Figure 7.3
Parallelism across multiple CPUs.

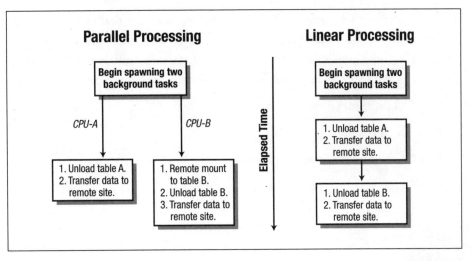

Figure 7.4

Linear versus parallel processing.

Of course, the overall elapsed time will not be half of the time required for a linear process—the remote mount still requires the database on CPU-A to manage the I/O against Table B. The benefit lies in having the second processor (CPU-B) handle all of the processing for the unload of Table B.

SMP And MPP Processing

SMP, or symmetrical multiprocessing, describes an architecture where many CPUs share a common memory area and I/O buffer. This type of architecture is not scaleable, as additional processors must compete for the shared memory and I/O resources. On the other hand, MPP, or massively parallel processors, describes an architecture where many independent processors share nothing, operating via a common I/O bus. An MPP system can add processors without impeding performance, and performance will actually increase as processors are added.

Some tasks are naturally suited for parallel execution. But more common are tasks that have components that can be parallelized while also containing some serial operations. One of the most common examples of highly parallel operations is the text search of a very large database. In this case, thousands of concurrent processes can search portions of the data, and when all processes have completed, the query manager can merge and sort the results for presentation.

The most confounding tasks for parallel processing are those that have many steps that rely on the output from previous steps. But even with these types of processes, we can find some tasks that have components that can be run in parallel. For example, consider the tasks involved in placing an order for a product:

1. Check customer profile.

2. Check customer credit rating.

3. Check customer payment history.

4. Check inventory levels.

5. Calculate the costs for the items.

6. Add sales tax.

7. Decrement the inventory on hand.

8. Prepare a shipping order.

9. Print customer bill.

Now, which of these processes can be parallelized? It appears that there are some operations that can be parallel while others must be serial (see Figure 7.5).

Here, we can see that there are three phases to the process, where the output of one phase serves as input to the next phase. Within each phase, we can see a number of tasks that can be run in parallel. In essence, the process of parallelism requires the restructuring of linear tasks to identify those tasks that can run concurrently, while preserving the sequence of tasks that must be serialized.

Coordination Of Concurrent Tasks

For an Oracle warehouse to function properly, Oracle needs to manage concurrent tasks, as well as serial tasks. One of the most common bottlenecks to the management of parallel processes is the need to synchronize certain tasks. Let's return to our previous scenario where a customer places an order for a product. While we can concurrently check a customer's credit rating and payment history, both of these tasks, as well as the check inventory task, must be completed *before* the next processing phase begins. In Oracle parallel server, the synchronization of concurrent tasks is maintained by the Distributed Lock Manager (the DLM). In some cases, the benefits of parallelism can be lost if the DLM spends too much time waiting for a single process to complete.

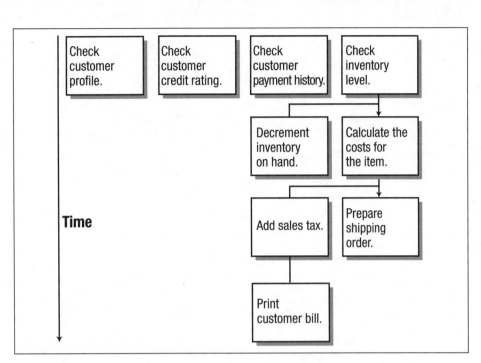

Figure 7.5
Parallelism of dependent tasks.

Oracle Parallel Database And Server

In general, a parallel database is defined as a database that has several memory regions that share a common disk drive. Within Oracle, several Oracle instances run within RAM memory, and each independent instance shares access to the same Oracle tables. Within the Oracle parallel server, this is called the *shared-nothing parallel server configuration*. Figure 7.6 shows a shared-nothing parallel server configuration.

Oracle also supports symmetric multiprocessing (SMP) configurations where a single host contains multiple processors (see Figure 7.7). In SMP configurations, we see that the multiple processors will provide concurrent processing, but that all of the processors must share a common buffer pool. In short, a symmetric multiprocessor configuration is one where a number of processors share common memory and disk resources.

There is a great deal of confusion about the difference between Oracle's parallel server and parallel query. While Oracle's parallel query can be used with any computer configuration, including standalone processors, SMP, or MPP, Oracle's parallel

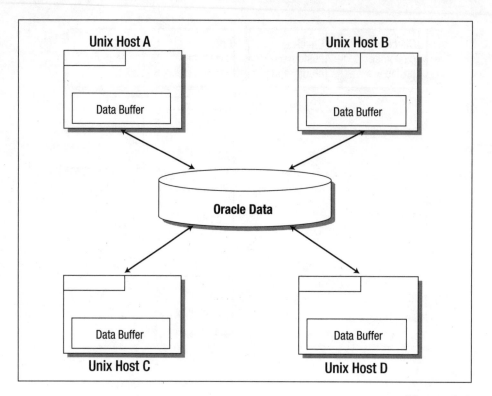

Figure 7.6

A shared-nothing parallel server configuration.

server can only be used on MPP systems. As stated earlier, MPPs are systems where a number of independent nodes, each with its own memory, share a common disk resource. As such, SMP is sometimes called shared memory multiprocessing and MPP is called shared-nothing multiprocessing. Examples of SMP processors include IBM SP2 and the IBM SP3, which contains eight processors. In parallel server parlance, a processor is called a *node*.

Oracle parallel server only works with MPP because each node on the host box requires its own memory area for the Oracle SGA. To illustrate, consider the shared-nothing example shown in Figure 7.6. Here, we see that a four-processor system has been configured to share a common data resource. As such, any user, on any node, will get a complete view of the entire database. For example, user **Scott** could login to node 1 and create a public access table called **TIGER**. Immediately after creation, another user on node 4 could also access that table.

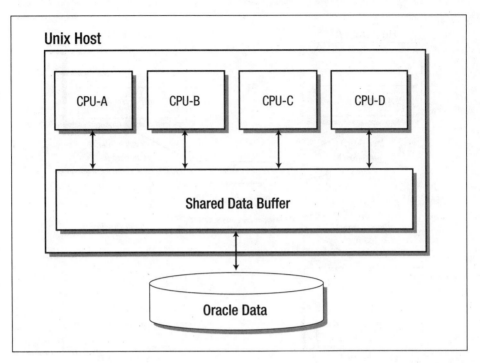

Figure 7.7
A shared memory SMP configuration.

In parallel server, careful consideration must be given to the uses of parallelism, because the resulting system could often perform slower than a single node system. For example, in parallel server, the DLM may force the Oracle database writer to write transactions to the database more frequently than a standalone Oracle database.

When planning for parallel server tasks, it is a good idea to segregate specific types of tasks to specific nodes (see Figure 7.8). As you can see in this figure, queries against the **ITEM** table are launched from Host A, queries against the **INVOICE** table use Host B, queries against the **CUSTOMER** table are managed against Host C, while queries against the **ORDER** table are managed on Host D. For example, common update routines against tablespace A could be segregated onto node 1, while queries against tablespace B could be segregated onto node 2. Because each Oracle instance has its own complete SGA, a full-table scan on one node will not flush any data out of the buffer pool of another node.

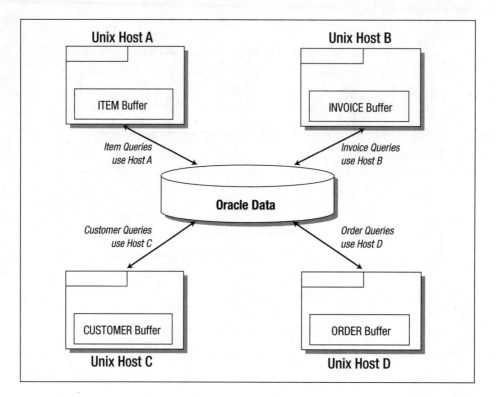

Figure 7.8
Buffer pool segregation in Oracle parallel server.

Of course, it is not always possible to segregate all data into separate buffer pools, especially with a highly denormalized data warehouse. The Oracle designer will be able to partition the Oracle instances such that similar data queries are launched from the same instance, thereby improving the probability that the data will be waiting in the buffer.

Note: It is possible to run Oracle parallel query on an Oracle parallel server system. In this case, the MPP system would allocate the sub-queries evenly across the nodes, and the concurrency manager would coordinate the receipt of data from each sub-query. Of course, this type of parallel query would run faster than a parallel query on an SMP box because the MPP box has isolated buffer pools. With SMP, the concurrent queries read their data into a common buffer pool.

Parallel processing is ideal for the Oracle data warehouse. Warehouse requests generally involve some type of aggregation (sum, average) and also require full-table scans. As such, parallelism can be used to dramatically reduce the execution time for these types of queries.

The parallel query option behaves the same regardless of whether the Oracle parallel server option has been installed. For more information, see the *Oracle Parallel Query* section later in this chapter.

The Distributed Lock Manager

Many parallel server novices are confused by the Distributed Lock Manager (DLM) and believe that the DLM is a component of the Oracle manufactured software. In reality, the DLM is a non-Oracle locking facility that is used in conjunction with the Oracle parallel server to synchronize concurrent processes. The DLMs are operating-system specific, and there are numerous DLM vendors for Solaris, AIX, and HP-UX implementations of Unix. At the most basic level, the DLM keeps track of the concurrent Oracle tasks executing on each CPU and keeps track of lock requests for resources.

With Oracle parallel server, the limitation of one instance to one database has been lifted. You can now configure many Oracle instances to share the same data warehouse. Of course, all of the Oracle instances are running in the same shared memory, and the DLM is used to provide locking between instances.

> **Note:** You can tell if your system is running the DLM by checking for the LCK process. Just as the RECO process indicates that distributed transactions are enabled, the presence of an LCK process indicates that the DLM is active. Traditional distributed systems do not have a DLM because they are not sharing the same databases.

Tuning The Parallel Server

To fully appreciate the facilities of the Oracle parallel server, we need to take a look at the two types of parallelism: internal and external.

- *Internal parallelism*—Oracle takes an SQL query and fires off concurrently executing processes to service the SQL request.

- *External parallelism*—The operating system parallelizes the query.

Oracle recommends that data warehouse applications use parallel server if the hardware is clustered or arranged in an MPP environment. For SMP, parallel query may be used, but in SMP cases, the data is usually loaded into Oracle at night, and the warehouse is read-only during the daytime hours.

To understand the difference between tuning an Oracle warehouse on a single instance versus tuning a warehouse mapped to multiple servers, we need to take a look at the differences between these two approaches.

In a warehouse mapped to a single Oracle instance, we tend to look for those resources that appear to be the most active. This could be a "hot" data file on a disk, excessive paging of the buffer cache (buffer hit ratio), or any number of other factors. As we have discussed, in a parallel server configuration, we have many independent Oracle instances sharing the same database.

In a sense, we can think of the shared-nothing configuration as having numerous, independent Oracle instances, and we can expect to tune each instance as if it were an independent entity. However, we must always bear in mind that each Oracle instance is competing for the same data resources. This competition is directly measured by the DLM.

Oracle parallel server only achieves a high degree of parallelism when careful planning has partitioned the tasks onto each instance in such a way that no two instances are constantly competing for data resources. If we find evidence that two Oracle instances are frequently accessing the same data blocks, the first remedy is to move common tasks into the same instance, where they can share the same buffer cache and eliminate calls to the DLM.

Indeed, tuning of the parallel server is all about DLM lock contention. Our goal should be to independently tune each Oracle instance and to keep a careful eye on how these instances interact with each other to manage inter-node locks. As DLM lock contention is identified, we have numerous options, including repartitioning the application to move tasks to other instances, adding multiple free lists to frequently accessed blocks, or using table replication techniques to alleviate I/O contention.

Here is a very simple approach to the tuning of a parallel server warehouse:

- *Monitor statistics independently for each Oracle instance.* The goal should be to minimize physical I/O by tuning the buffer cache and providing input into an overall load plan. For example, if we discover one instance is heavily loaded when compared to other instances, we can take a look at the partitioning of tasks and rebalance the load by moving tasks onto other instances.

- *Monitor each instance's buffer cache, looking for common data blocks.* If the same data blocks show up in multiple buffer caches, move one of the tasks into a common Oracle instance. Remember, the idea of tuning parallel server is to segregate common tasks into common instances.

- *Monitor for multiple tasks that modify rows on the same block.* When multiple tasks contend for the updating of rows on the same data block, adding free lists or free list groups may relieve the bottleneck.

- *Monitor the DLM for lock conversions.* If the maximum lock convert rate for your DLM has been reached, you will need to repartition the application to balance "alike" transactions into common instances.

It should be apparent that the inherent complexity of parallel processing makes it very difficult to come up with generic tuning techniques. Every parallel system is unique, and the Oracle professional must analyze each system carefully, considering its unique structure and behavior.

Free Lists And Oracle Parallel Server Contention

Free lists are especially important for Oracle data warehouses that experience a high volume of localized update activity. A free list is the parameter used when more than one concurrent process is expected to access a table. Oracle keeps one free list for each table in memory, and uses the free list in order to determine what database block to use when an SQL **INSERT** occurs. When a row is added, the free list is locked. If more than one concurrent process is attempting to insert into your table, one of the processes may need to wait until the free list has been released by the previous task. To see if adding a free list to a table will improve performance, you will need to evaluate how often Oracle has to wait for a free list. Fortunately, Oracle keeps a **V$** table called **V$WAITSTAT** for this purpose. The following query example tells you how many times Oracle has waited for a free list to become available. As you can see from the following query, Oracle does not tell you which free lists are experiencing the contention problems:

```
SELECT CLASS, COUNT
FROM V$WAITSTAT
    WHERE CLASS = 'free list';
```

CLASS	COUNT
free list	83

Here, we see that Oracle had to wait 83 times for a table free list to become available. This could represent a wait of 83 times on the same table or perhaps a single wait for 83 separate tables. We have no idea. While 83 may seem to be a large number, remember that Oracle may perform hundreds of I/Os each second, so 83 may be quite insignificant to the overall system. In any case, if you suspect that you know which table's free list is having the contention, the table can be exported, dropped, and redefined to have more free list. While an extra free list consumes more of Oracle's memory, additional free lists can help the throughput on tables that have lots of inserts. Generally, you should define extra free lists only on those tables that have many concurrent update operations. Now, let's take a look at some table definitions and see if we can infer the type of activity that will be taking place against the tables. Listings 7.1 and 7.2 each present a table definition.

Listing 7.1 Table definition—Example 1.

```
CREATE TABLE ORDER (
    order_nbr        number,
    order_date       date)
STORAGE ( PCTFREE  10 PCTUSED  40 FREE LISTS 3);
```

Here, we can infer that the table has very few updates that cause the row length to increase because **PCTFREE** is only 10 percent. We can also infer that this table will have a great deal of delete activity, because **PCTUSED** is at 40 percent, thereby preventing immediate reuse of database blocks as rows are deleted. This table must also have a lot of insert activity, because **FREE LISTS** is set to three, indicating that up to three concurrent processes will be inserting into the table.

Listing 7.2   Table definition—Example 2.

```
CREATE TABLE ITEM (
    item_nbr                    number,
    item_name                   varchar(20),
    item_description            varchar(50),
    current_item_status         varchar(200) )
STORAGE ( PCTFREE  40 PCTUSED  60 FREE LISTS 1);
```

Here, we can infer that update operations are frequent and will probably increase the size of the **varchar** columns, because **PCTFREE** is set to reserve 40 percent of each block for row expansion. We can also infer that this table has few deletes, because **PCTUSED** is set to 60, making efficient use of the database blocks. Assuming that there will not be very many deletes, these blocks would become constantly re-added to the free list.

The V$LOCK_ACTIVITY View

The **V$LOCK_ACTIVITY** view is a very good way to determine if you have reached the maximum lock convert rate for your DLM. Because the maximum lock convert rate is unique to each vendor's DLM, you need to compare the results from **V$LOCK_ACTIVITY** with the maximum values in your OS vendor's documentation for their DLM. Regardless, if the maximum lock convert rate has been reached, you will need to repartition the application to balance alike transactions into common instances.

The V$SYSSTAT View

The **V$SYSSTAT** view can be used to determine whether lock converts are being performed too often. Excessive lock convert rates usually mean there is contention for a common resource within the database. This resource may be a commonly updated table. For example, inventory management systems often utilize one-of-a-kind (OOAK) rows. An OOAK row may be used to keep the order number of the last order, and all application tasks must increment this row when a new order is placed. This type of architecture forces each parallel instance to single-thread all requests for this resource. But how do we identify these types of database resources?

Just as the buffer hit ratio measures contention for data blocks, the lock hit ratio can be used to identify excessive lock conversion by the DLM. The lock hit ratio should generally be above 90 percent, and if it falls below 90 percent, you should look for sources of data contention. Here is the SQL to determine the lock hit ratio for Oracle parallel server:

```
SELECT
   (a.value - b.value)/(a.value)
FROM
   V$SYSSTAT a, V$SYSSTAT B
WHERE
   a.name = 'consistent gets'
AND
   b.name = 'global lock converts (async)';
```

If you suspect that there may be data contention, there are several remedies. For example:

- If you identify a specific table as a source of contention, try increasing the free lists for the table.

- If you identify an index as the source of contention, try localizing all access to the index on a single instance.

But how can we identify the source of contention? Oracle parallel server provides a view called **V$PING** to show lock conversions. We start by querying the **V$PING** view to see if there are any data files experiencing a high degree on lock conversions, as follows:

```
SELECT
   substr(name,1,10),
   file#,
   class#,
   max(xnc)
FROM
   V$PING
GROUP BY 1, 2, 3
ORDER BY 1, 2, 3;
```

You will receive an output that looks similar to Table 7.1.

Here, we see that File 16 may have a problem with excessive lock conversions. To further investigate, return to **V$PING**, and get the sums for File 16, as follows:

Table 7.1   Querying the **V$PING** view.

Name	File #	Class #	Max (XNC)
Customer	13	1	556
Customer	13	4	32
Item	6	1	11
Item	3	4	32
Order	16	1	33456

```
SELECT *
FROM
   V$PING
WHERE
   file#=16
ORDER BY block#;
```

Now, we can see additional detail about the contents of File 16, as shown in Table 7.2.

From this output, we can clearly see that Block 12 is the source of our contention.

The following query against the **ORDER** table will reveal the contents of the rows in the data block, as shown in Table 7.3. Remember, data blocks are numbered in hex, so we convert Block 12 to a hex(c).

```
SELECT
   ROWID,
   order_number,
   customer_number
FROM
   ORDER
WHERE
chattorowid(ROWID) LIKE '0000000C%';
```

Table 7.2   Viewing additional file details.

File #	Block #	Stat	XNC	Class #	Name	Kind
16	11	XCUR	5	1	ORDER	Table
16	12	XCUR	33456	1	ORDER	Table
16	13	XCUR	12	1	ORDER	Table

Table 7.3 Viewing row contents.

ROWID	ORDER_NUMBER	CUSTOMER_NUMBER
0000000C.0000.0008	1212	73
0000000C.0000.0008	1213	73
0000000C.0000.0008	1214	73

In Table 7.3, we see that the lock conversion relates to orders placed by customer number 73. Other than a random coincidence, we can assume that there may be free list contention in the **ORDER** table as new orders are added to the database. Adding new free lists will allow more concurrency during SQL **INSERT** operations, and the value for free lists should be reset to the maximum number of end users who are expected to be inserting an **ORDER** row at any given time. Unfortunately, Oracle does not allow the dynamic modification of free lists, because they are physically stored in each data block. So, the only alternative is to drop and re-create the table with more free lists in each block header. Following is the SQL used to drop and re-create the **ORDER** table:

```
CREATE TABLE ORDER_DUMMY
STORAGE (free lists 10)
AS
SELECT * FROM ORDER;

DROP TABLE ORDER;

RENAME ORDER_DUMMY TO ORDER;
```

Oracle Parallel Query

One of the most exciting performance features of Oracle version 7.3 and above is the ability to partition an SQL query into sub-queries and dedicate separate processors to concurrently service each sub-query. At this time, parallel query is only useful for queries that perform full-table scans on long tables, but the performance improvements can be dramatic.

Parallel queries are most useful in distributed databases where a single logical table has been partitioned into smaller tables at each remote node. For example, a customer table ordered by customer name may be partitioned into a customer table at each remote database, such that we have a **PHOENIX_CUSTOMER**, a **LOS_ANGELES_CUSTOMER**, and so on. This approach is very common with distributed databases where local autonomy of processing is important. However, what about the needs of those in corporate headquarters? How can they query all of these remote tables as a single unit and treat the logical customer table as a single entity? For large queries that may span many logical tables, the isolated tables can be easily reassembled using Oracle's parallel query facility, as follows:

```
CREATE VIEW ALL_CUSTOMER AS
   SELECT * FROM PHOENIX_CUSTOMER@phoenix
   UNION ALL
   SELECT * FROM LOS_ANGELES_CUSTOMER@los_angeles
   UNION ALL
   SELECT * FROM ROCHESTER_CUSTOMER@rochester;
```

> **NOTE:** the @ references refer to SQL*Net service names for the remote hosts. For details on distributed Oracle communications, see Chapter 9, Distributed Oracle Data Warehouses.

We can now query the **ALL_CUSTOMER** view as if it were a single database table, and Oracle parallel query will automatically recognize the **UNION ALL** parameter, firing off simultaneous queries against each of the three base tables. It is important to note that the distributed database manager will direct each query to be processed at the remote location, while the query manager waits until each remote node has returned its result set. For example, the following query will assemble the requested data from three table segments in parallel, with each query optimized separately. The result set from each sub-query is then merged by the query manager.

```
SELECT customer_name
FROM ALL_CUSTOMER
WHERE
total_purchases > 5000;
```

Instead of having a single query server manage the I/O against the table, parallel query allows the Oracle query server to dedicate many processors to simultaneously access data.

In order to be most effective, the table should be partitioned onto separate disk devices, such that each process can do I/O against its segment of the table without interfering with the other simultaneous query processes. However, the client/server environment of the 1990s relies on RAID or a logical volume manager (LVM), which scrambles data files across disk packs in order to balance the I/O load. Consequently, full utilization of parallel query involves *striping* a table across numerous data files, each on a separate device.

Parallel Create Table As Select

Parallel Create Table As Select (PCTAS) can be very useful in an Oracle data warehouse environment where tables are replicated across numerous servers or when pre-aggregating roll-up summary tables. Parallel Create Table As Select is also very useful when performing roll-up activities against your Oracle warehouse. For example, we could specify the number of parallel processes to compute the monthly summary values from our fact table. In the following example, we assign five processes to simultaneously read the blocks from the customer table.

```
CREATE TABLE REGION_SALESPERSON_SUMMARY_03_97
PARALLEL (degree 5)
AS
SELECT region, salesperson, sum(sale_amount)
FROM FACT
WHERE
    month = 3
AND
    year = 1997;
```

Here, we dedicate five query servers to extract the data from the fact table and three query servers to populate the new summary table (see Figure 7.9).

Again, we must remember that it is not necessary to have SMP or MPP hardware to benefit from parallel query techniques. Even a single-processor Unix system will experience some improvement from using parallel processes, even though all of the processes are running on the same CPU.

Parallel Index Building

Parallel index builds are often useful to the Oracle database administrator who needs to rebuild indexes that have either spawned too many levels or contain too many deleted leaf rows. Parallel index creation is also useful when importing Oracle data

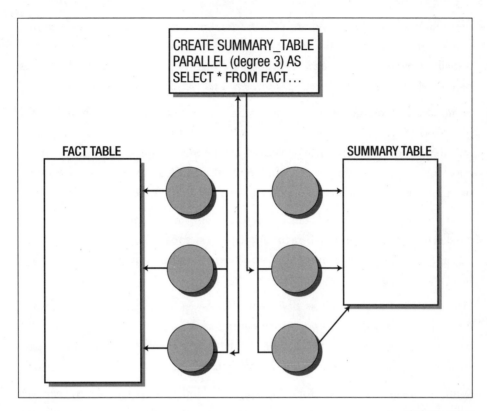

Figure 7.9
Parallel Create Table As Select.

warehouse tables. Because data warehouses are so large, Oracle exports should be configured to exclude the indexes and only export the row values. If a recovery of a table becomes necessary, the Oracle DBA can use **PARALLEL CREATE** to speed up the index re-creation. Parallel index creation takes place by allowing the degree of parallelism to be specified in the create index statement. For example:

```
ALTER INDEX customer_pk
REBUILD PARALLEL 10;
```

Because this type of index creation always involves reading the old index structure and a large sort operation, Oracle is able to dedicate numerous, independent processes to simultaneously read the base index and collect the keys for the new index structure. Just like parallel query, each sub-query task returns **ROWID** and key values to the concurrency manager. The concurrency manager collects this information for input in the key sorting phase of the index rebuild. For very large data warehouse tables, parallel index creation can greatly reduce the amount of time required to initially create or rebuild indexes. For more information about when Oracle indexes require rebuilding, see Chapter 8, *Oracle Features For The Data Warehouse*.

Some Oracle professionals mistakenly believe that it is necessary to have parallel processors (SMP or MPP) in order to use and benefit from parallel processing. Even on the same processor, multiple processes can be used to speed up queries. Oracle parallel query option can be used with any SQL **SELECT** statement—the only restriction being that the query performs a full-table scan on the target table.

Even if your system uses RAID or LVM, some performance gains are available with parallel query. In addition to using multiple processes to retrieve the table, the query manager will also dedicate numerous processes to simultaneously sort the result sets from a large query. (See Figure 7.10.)

However, parallel query works best with SMP boxes, which have more than one internal CPU. Also, it is important to configure the system to maximize the I/O bandwidth, either through disk striping or high-speed channels. Because of the parallel sorting feature, it is also a good idea to beef up the memory on the processor.

While sorting is no substitute for using a presorted index, the parallel query manager will service requests far faster than a single process. While the data retrieval will not be significantly faster because all of the retrieval processes are competing for a

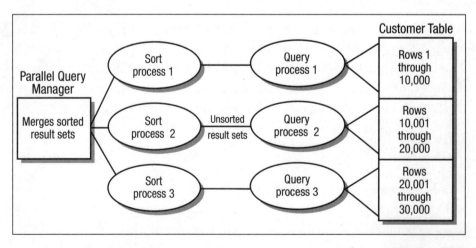

Figure 7.10

A sample parallel sort.

channel on the same disk, each sort process has its own sort area (as determined by the **SORT_AREA_SIZE** init.ora parameter), which speeds along the sorting of the result set. In addition to full-table scans and sorting, the parallel query option allows for parallel processes for merge joins and nested loops.

Invoking the parallel query option requires all indexing to be bypassed. And, most important, the explain plan for the query should specify a full-table scan. If the output of the explain plan does not indicate a full-table scan, the query can be forced to ignore the index by using query hints.

The number of processors dedicated to servicing an SQL request is ultimately determined by the Oracle query manager, but the programmer can specify the upper limit on the number of simultaneous processes. When using the cost-based optimizer, the **PARALLEL** hint can be embedded into the SQL to specify the number of processes. For example:

```
SELECT /*+ FULL(EMPLOYEE_TABLE) PARALLEL(EMPLOYEE_TABLE, 4) */
   employee_name
   FROM
   EMPLOYEE_TABLE
   WHERE
   emp_type = 'SALARIED';
```

If you are using SMP with many CPUs, you can issue a parallel request and leave it up to each Oracle instance to use its default degree of parallelism, as follows:

```
SELECT /*+ FULL(EMPLOYEE_TABLE) PARALLEL(EMPLOYEE_TABLE, DEFAULT,
DEFAULT) */
   employee_name
   FROM
   EMPLOYEE_TABLE
   WHERE
   emp_type = 'SALARIED';
```

The following several important init.ora parameters have a direct impact on parallel query:

- **SORT_AREA_SIZE**—The higher the value, the more memory available for individual sorts on each parallel process. Note that the **SORT_AREA_SIZE** parameter allocates memory for every query on the system that invokes a sort. For example, if a single query needs more memory and you increase the

SORT_AREA_SIZE, all Oracle tasks will allocate the new amount of sort area, regardless of whether they will use all of the space.

- PARALLEL_MIN_SERVERS—The minimum number of query servers that will be active on the instance. System resources are involved in starting a query server, so having the query server started and waiting for requests will speed up processing. Note that if the actual number of required servers is less than the value of PARALLEL_MIN_SERVERS, the idle query servers will be consuming unnecessary overhead, and the value should be decreased.

- PARALLEL_MAX_SERVERS—The maximum number of query servers allowed on the instance. This parameter will prevent Oracle from starting so many query servers that the instance is unable to service all of them properly.

To see how many parallel query servers are busy at any given time, the following query can be issued against the V$PQ_SYSSTAT table:

```
SELECT * FROM V$PQ_SYSSTAT
    WHERE STATISTIC = 'Servers Busy';

STATISTIC                 VALUE
- - - - - - - - - - -      - - - - - - - -
Servers Busy               30
```

In this case, we see that 30 parallel servers are busy at this moment in time. Do not be misled by this number. Parallel query servers are constantly accepting work or returning to idle status, so it is a good idea to issue the query many times over a one-hour period. Only then will you have a realistic measure of how many parallel query servers are being used.

Summary

Now that you can appreciate how parallelism can be used within the Oracle data warehouses, let's move on to take an in-depth look into the internal mechanisms of the Oracle architecture. It is only through an in-depth understanding of the internal details that an Oracle developer maximizes the performance of a very large Oracle warehouse. The following chapters will serve as a guide into the Oracle internals from a data warehouse perspective.

Oracle Features For The Data Warehouse

HIGH PERFORMANCE

CHAPTER

8

Oracle Features For The Data Warehouse

While Oracle markets itself as a generic database management system, there are several features that greatly assist in the creation of fast and useful data warehouses (which, of course, is the point of this book!). In this chapter, we'll focus on some Oracle features designed specifically for data warehouses. This chapter includes topics such as managing tables, indexes, and tablespaces in a data warehouse. In addition, bitmapped indexes, the table cache option, and other indispensable concepts for the Oracle data warehouse developer are discussed.

Oracle Tables In The Data Warehouse

One of the biggest problems in data warehousing is the issue of planning for growth and ensuring that your data warehouse continues to perform at an acceptable level. As you probably know, databases run within a well-defined domain of system resources, and a shortage of these system resources can lead to performance degradation. The trick is to design a data warehouse architecture with the ability to add resources on an as-needed basis, without interrupting processing.

Growth of a database can occur in several areas. As the physical size of the database increases, so does the need for disk storage. As the volume of users increases, so does the need for increased buffer and lock pool storage. As network traffic increases, an increasing demand falls on the routers and bandwidth may need to be increased. While the act of allocating Oracle tables is very straightforward, there are some specific issues that arise when creating a very large table for an Oracle data warehouse. To understand these issues, let's take a look at the allocation of Oracle tables and how the allocation parameters affect system performance.

Table Maintenance

Extended tables are not a concern for an Oracle data warehouse, provided the tables do not approach their values for maximum extents. Several benchmark studies have shown that extended tables do not impede performance, and they may actually perform faster than a table in a single extent, because the data is spread across the disk device. However, we must always be on the lookout for row chaining, which sometimes accompanies table extension. *Row chaining* occurs when a row within an Oracle table is updated, and a previously null column has data added. This will cause the row to physically expand in size, and if there is not enough room on the data block (as defined by the **PCTFREE** table creation parameter), then the row will fragment, causing a portion of the row to be stored on another block.

> **Note**: *For SQL utilities to detect and correct row chaining, see Chapter 10, Oracle Data Warehouse Utilities.*

Oracle's Table Cache Option

The table cache option is a major benefit of the Oracle architecture for data warehouses, and it deserves warehouse designers' complete attention. While the term *cache* is a misnomer in the sense that an Oracle table is not permanently stored in memory, the table cache option dramatically improves the buffer hit ratio for small, frequently accessed warehouse tables. When a request is made for Oracle to retrieve a row from a table, Oracle performs several steps.

First, Oracle checks the data buffer to see if the database block that contains the row already resides in Oracle's data buffer (see Figure 8.1).

This scan is made from the most-recently used end to the least-recently used end of the buffer, and because this buffer is in the SGA as RAM memory, the check happens very quickly. Only after Oracle has determined that the database block is not already in the buffer does Oracle move on to the second step, performing a physical I/O to fetch the data block. Finally, Oracle transfers the data block from the Unix buffer into the Oracle buffer.

> **Note**: *The Unix operating system is configured to check the cache area for physical RAM before Unix issues a physical I/O against a disk. Therefore, all*

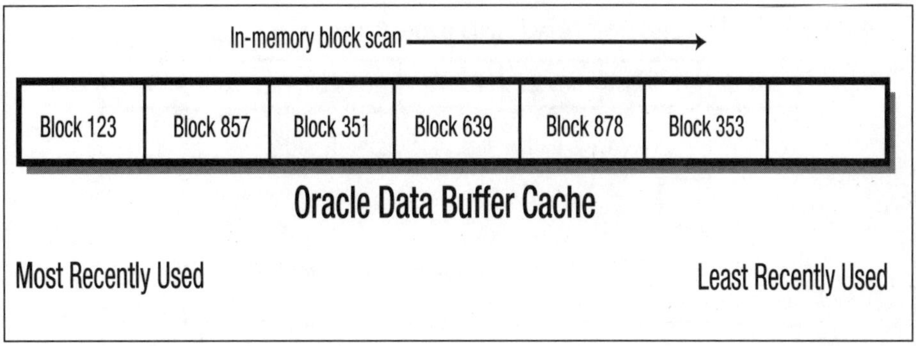

Figure 8.1
The Oracle data buffer.

I/O requests from Oracle do not always result in a disk I/O because it is possible that an Oracle data block is in Unix RAM even when it is not in the Oracle buffer cache.

When Oracle manages I/O against the database, it uses different rules to place new data blocks in the buffer cache. For all I/Os except full-table scans, rows are read into the most-recently used section of the Oracle buffer pool. As new data blocks are fetched, the older blocks work their way down to the least-recently used end of the buffer, where they are eventually erased from the buffer to make room for newly acquired data blocks (see Figure 8.2).

The exception to this rule involves data blocks acquired by using full-table scans. As data blocks are read into the buffer during a full-table scan, blocks are placed on the opposite end of the buffer, in the least-recently used section. In this fashion, full-table scans will not interfere with buffers on the most-recently used end of the buffer (i.e., rows from non–full-table-scan transactions). Because these rows are already at the least-recently used end of the buffer, they will be flushed quickly as new rows are fetched as part of the full-table scan (see Figure 8.3). Full-table scan data blocks are physically read into Oracle's buffer in chunk sizes specified by the init.ora parameter **db_file_multiblock_read_count**. For example, assume that the **db_block_size** is set to 8,192 bytes (8 K) and the **db_file_multiblock_read_count** is set to 8. When Oracle detects a full-table scan, Oracle will perform reads of four physical blocks at a time, pulling in 64 K with each I/O. Remember, physical I/O is very time consuming, and anything that can be done to reduce I/O will improve Oracle performance.

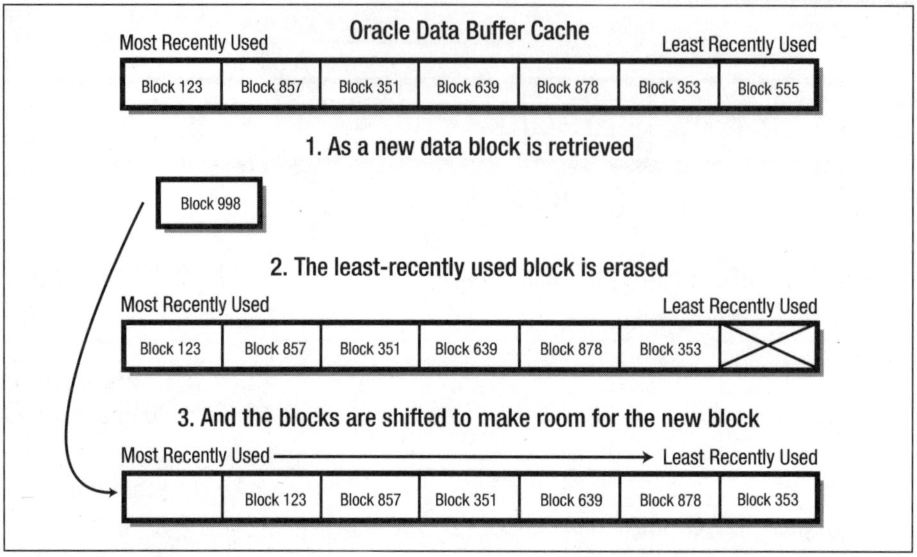

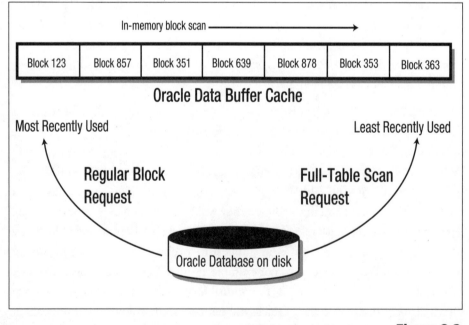

Figure 8 2
Aging blocks from the Oracle buffers.

Figure 8.3
Different ends of the buffer cache may be used for different tables.

The table cache option was introduced with Oracle 7.2 to change the behavior of full-table scan reads. When a table is created using the cache option, full-table scan fetches against a table are treated as if they are not full-table scans, and they are placed at the most-recently used end of the data buffer. Once the data blocks have been read to the buffer cache, they "age-out" and move toward the least-recently used side of the buffer, just like any other data block in Oracle.

In this sense, the term *cache* is somewhat misleading (as I hinted at earlier). For example, when Oracle packages are cached in the library cache, they are *pinned* (ineligible for being aged-out), and the packages remain in the library cache for the life of the Oracle instance. Data blocks, on the other hand, are not pinned into the data buffer with the cache option, and the data blocks age-out of the buffer at the same rate as other data blocks. Of course, the data blocks remain in the buffer for a much longer period than data blocks fetched with full-table scans, but they do not stay in the buffer indefinitely. At this time, the only way to pin a data block in an Oracle buffer is to utilize Oracle parallel server to dedicate an Oracle instance for a particular table and make the buffer large enough to hold the entire contents of the table.

Table Caching Setup

*The **cache_size_threshold** init.ora parameter must be set to use the table cache option. This parameter controls the space in the buffer cache that is used exclusively for full-table scans. The Oracle documentation falsely implies that the **cache_size_threshold** parameter is used exclusively with Oracle parallel server. In reality, this parameter applies to all Oracle databases.*

*Also, note that the cache_size_threshold parameter must be smaller than the table size. The default for this value is (.10 x **db_block_buffers**), such that any table larger than 10 percent of the buffer pool will not be affected by the cache option.*

Turning On The Table Cache Option

There are two ways to activate the table cache option. The option can be specified permanently with a **CREATE TABLE** or **ALTER TABLE** command, or a cache hint can be used with the cost-based SQL optimizer to direct the data blocks. A **CREATE** and **ALTER TABLE** example follows:

```
SQL> CREATE TABLE CUSTOMER
   > STORAGE (NEXT . . . )
```

```
> CACHE;

Table Created.


SQL > ALTER TABLE ORDERS CACHE;

Table Altered.
```

The second method of invoking table caching is accomplished by adding cache hints. A cache hint is generally used in conjunction with a full hint to ensure that a full-table scan is being performed against the target table. In the following example, a reference table called **ZIP_CODE** is cached into the buffer.

```
SELECT /*+ FULL(ZIP_CODE) CACHE(ZIP_CODE) */
zip_code, city_name, county_name, state_name
FROM
    ZIP_CODE;
```

The main purpose of the cache option is to allow small tables that are always read from front to back to remain in the data buffer. These types of tables might include small reference tables or any tables intended to be read by using a full-table scan. Remember, the cache option requires a table to be:

- Defined as cached (**ALTER TABLE CUSTOMER CACHE;**).

- Smaller than the value of **cache_size_threshold**.

- Accessed with a full-table scan.

In summary, the table cache option is useful in cases where a small, frequently referenced table needs to remain in the buffer cache for a longer period than traditional table scans. This occurs when the table is frequently reread by many transactions. It is implemented with **ALTER TABLE** and **CREATE TABLE** commands or cache hints, and it only works when the table is small and read with a full-table scan.

Now that we understand the basic dynamics of tables in an Oracle environment, let's take a look at how indexes can improve data warehouse performance. Of all the techniques available to the data warehouse administrator, indexes are the most powerful tool in the arsenal, and a topic that warrants careful attention.

Understanding Oracle Indexes

Most programmers do not realize that database deadlocks occur frequently within database indexes. It is important to note that a **SELECT** of a single row from a database can cause more than one lock entry to be placed in the storage pool, as all affected index rows are also locked. In other words, when an individual row receives a lock, each index node containing the value for that row will also have locks assigned (see Figure 8.4). If the "last" entry in a sorted index is retrieved, the database will lock all index nodes that reference the indexed value in case the user changes that value. Because many indexing schemes always carry the high-order key in multiple index nodes, an entire branch of an index tree can be locked—all the way up to the root node of the index. While each database's indexing scheme is different, some relational database vendors recommend that tables with ascending keys be loaded in descending order, so that the rows are loaded from Z to A on an alphabetic key field. Other databases, such as Oracle, recommend that indexes be dropped and re-created after rows have been loaded into an empty table.

Oracle indexes are basically B-tree structures, whereby each node in the index tree contains many pointers to other index nodes, as shown in Figure 8.5.

An Oracle index looks like a tree in concept, but in physical storage, index nodes reside in Oracle data blocks, similar to how table rows are stored in data blocks. As such, many index nodes may be read into memory in a single physical I/O.

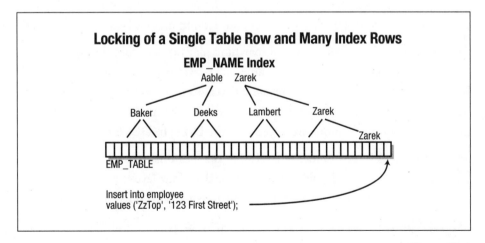

Figure 8.4
An overview of Oracle locking.

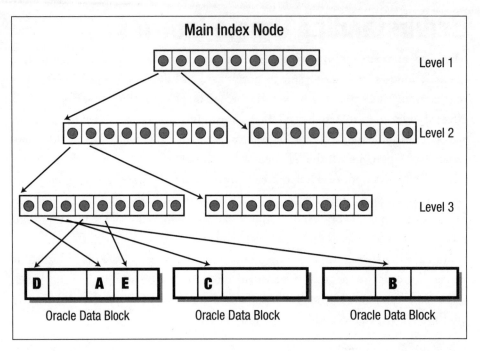

Figure 8.5
The basic structure of an Oracle index.

If we accept the conventional wisdom that database reorganizations (export/import) are not necessary solely for performance reasons, then the next issue that comes to mind is determining when an index needs to be reorganized (dropped and re-created). We'll review how to determine when to rebuild indexes later in this chapter.

As Oracle indexes grow, splitting and spawning may occur within the index. A *split* is where a new node is created at the same index level as the existing node. As each level becomes full, the index may *spawn,* or create a new level to accommodate the new rows. For indexes that have been analyzed with the **ANALYZE INDEX** command, the following columns are added into the **DBA_INDEXES** view:

- **blevel**—This is the number of levels that the index has spawned. Even for very large indexes, there should never be more than four levels. Each **blevel** represents an additional I/O that must be performed against the index tree.

- **leaf_blocks**—This is a reference to the total number of leaf blocks.

- **distinct_keys**—This is a reference to the cardinality of the index. If this value is less than 10, you may want to consider redefining the index as a bitmapped index.

- **avg_data_blocks_per_key**—This is a measure of the size of the index and the cardinality of the index. A low cardinality index (e.g.., sex or region) will have high values, as will very large indexes.

- **clustering_factor**—This is the most important measure in this report because it measures how balanced the index is, relative to the table. If the clustering factor is near the number of blocks in the table, then the table is said to be clustered within the index. This is good for data retrieval with the index because there will be less physical I/O. If the clustering factor approaches the number of rows in the table, then the index is said to be random. That is, the index keys are not in the same physical order as the rows in the table. Of course, only one index on a table will have a high clustering factor because the rows can only be physically ordered to match one index key value.

- **avg_leaf_blocks_per_key**—This value is always 1, with the exception of non-unique indexes.

These statistics give Oracle's cost-based optimizer clues about which indexes are best suited to service each query.

If you are collecting index statistics (i.e., your Oracle system utilizes the cost-based optimizer), you can see additional internal details for an index by running the report shown in Listing 8.1.

Listing 8.1   index.sql shows the details for indexes.

```
REM © 1997 by Donald K. Burleson
SET PAGESIZE 999;
SET LINESIZE 100;

COLUMN c1 HEADING 'Index'     FORMAT a19;
COLUMN c3 HEADING 'S'         FORMAT a1;
COLUMN c4 HEADING 'Level'     FORMAT 999;
COLUMN c5 HEADING 'Leaf Blks' FORMAT 999,999;
COLUMN c6 HEADING 'dist. Keys' FORMAT 99,999,999;
COLUMN c7 HEADING 'Bks/Key'   FORMAT 99,999;
COLUMN c8 HEADING 'Clust Ftr' FORMAT 9,999,999;
COLUMN c9 HEADING 'Lf/Key'    FORMAT 99,999;
```

```
SPOOL index.lst;

SELECT
   owner||'.'||index_name      c1,
   substr(status,1,1)          c3,
   blevel                      c4,
   leaf_blocks                 c5,
   distinct_keys               c6,
   avg_data_blocks_per_key     c7,
   clustering_factor           c8,
   avg_leaf_blocks_per_key     c9
FROM DBA_INDEXES
WHERE
owner NOT IN ('SYS','SYSTEM')
ORDER BY blevel desc, leaf_blocks desc;

SPOOL OFF;
```

Listing 8.2 shows the output of index.sql.

Listing 8.2   Output of index.sql.

Index	S	Level	Leaf Blks	dist. Keys	Bks/Key	Clust Ftr	Lf/Key
DON.LOB_FACT1_PK	V	2	25,816	3,511,938	1	455,343	1
DON.DON_EK_CUST_INV	V	2	23,977	2,544,132	1	1,764,915	1
DON.DON_FK_GLO_DEST	V	2	23,944	22,186	112	2,493,095	1
DON.JEN_FK_SHP	V	2	22,650	1,661,576	1	339,031	1
DON.DON_FK_ORL_ORIG	V	2	21,449	404	806	325,675	53
DON.PAT_FK_JEN	V	2	21,181	2,347,812	1	996,641	1
DON.JEN_FK_LOB	V	2	19,989	187	4,796	896,870	106
DON.FACT1_PK	V	2	19,716	3,098,063	1	1,674,264	1
DON.DON_FK_CAR	V	2	18,513	689	390	268,859	26
DON.DON_EK_ROLE	V	2	17,847	10	24,613	246,134	1,784
DON.DON_FK_SPT	V	2	16,442	4	46,872	187,489	4,110

```
DON.INV_EK_INV_NUM  V  2  16,407  2,014,268      1   518,206      1

DON.DON_FK_ORL_DEST V  2  15,863        385     692   266,656     41

DON.DON_FK_SRC      V  2  15,827         10  17,469   174,694  1,582

DON.INV_LINE_ITEM   V  2  14,731  2,362,216      1   102,226      1
```

One of the primary responsibilities of the Oracle DBA is to ensure that Oracle indexes are present when they are needed to avoid full-table scans. In order to achieve this goal, the Oracle DBA needs to understand the types of indexes that Oracle provides as well as the proper time to create a table index.

Unfortunately, the Oracle dictionary does not gather statistics about how many times an index is used, so the DBA must rely on the application developers to provide guidance regarding index placement. As Oracle moves toward Oracle8, this reliance on the application developers may change because most of the SQL will be stored within the Oracle dictionary where the DBA can analyze the explain plan output. However, until that time, the best an Oracle DBA can hope for is to keep the existing indexes clean and functioning optimally.

Clustered Indexes

Before we can take a look at the I/O path to data, we need to consider two factors: the logical I/O (calls) versus the physical I/Os required to service the request. As Oracle scans an index, we know that each node of the index tree is read before we access the data row. To illustrate, let's look at the simple example shown in Table 8.1.

Table 8.1 Table and index sizes.

Object	Customer Table	last_name_idx
ROWS	1,000,000	100,000
ROW LENGTH	160	
BLOCK SIZE	16K	16K
DATA BLOCKS	10,000	4,000

Note: This example has been oversimplified to illustrate the principle of clustered tables, and it does not consider other data block overhead, such as block headers and space management pages.

Now, we can run an index report from the Oracle data dictionary to see the following characteristics of **last_name_idx**:

```
SQL> @idx_list
```

Index	Level	Clust Ftr	# rows	reorg	dist. Keys
LAST_NAME_IDX	3	788,934	1,105,458	0.713	1,105,458

This is a typical index for an Oracle data warehouse. We see that the index has a three-level index tree with a tad over one million rows and distinct keys. This means that Oracle would perform four logical I/Os (three through the index and one to the data block) to retrieve each row when the index is scanned. Therefore, a 1,000,000 row table would require 4,000,000 logical I/Os to sweep the table in index order.

As you may know, performance is impeded by physical I/Os, not logical I/Os. But, how do we translate 4,000,000 logical I/Os into a number of physical I/Os? Let's assume the index requires 4,000 data blocks and resides in contiguous data blocks, but the **CUSTOMER** table is not stored in **last_name** sequence. This means that as we read each bottom-level node of the index, we are unlikely to find that the data block is already in our buffer because the table is ordered in a different sequence than our index (see Figure 8.6).

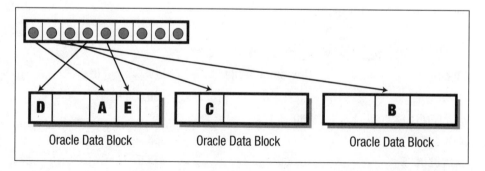

Figure 8.6
Physical I/O for a non-clustered index.

Now, let's examine the difference when the data table is stored in the same sequence as the index. Assume you have an index that is used more frequently than your other indexes. For example, let's say you have indexed on your **customer_last_name (last_name_idx)**, and this index is used for more than 90 percent of your database queries.

If it were possible to physically order the customer table in last name sequence, then we could save a considerable amount of physical I/O against the table. Using the same example, if the index data blocks are stored in the same sequence as the data table blocks, a full sweep of the table still requires 4,000,000 logical I/Os, but a much smaller number of physical I/Os (see Figure 8.7).

Here, we see that we still need to read all 4,000 index blocks to scan the index, but because 100 rows reside on each data block (160 byte rows in 16 K blocks), we only need to read 10,000 data blocks to scan the entire table. The difference in physical I/Os is dramatic, and the reduction in physical I/Os dramatically reduces the execution time for a full-index scan. Also note that if it could guarantee that the data is in the proper physical order, Oracle could perform a full-table scan and would not need

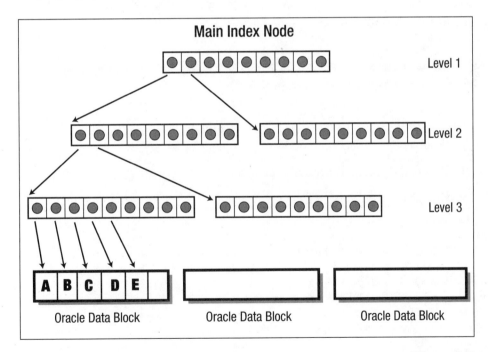

Figure 8.7
Physical I/O for a clustered table index.

to use the index at all. Unfortunately, we cannot guarantee the physical order; we can only approximate it.

How To Create A Clustered Index

For each table, there can only be one clustered index because only one index will be stored in the same physical order as the table. Unfortunately, Oracle does not give the DBA a simple method for ensuring the physical ordering of rows within a table. There are, however, some tricks that can be used to re-sequence a table to give it a different physical order. Beware, however, that the index may quickly be out of physical sequence as new rows are added to the end of the table and key values are updated to change the logical sequence in the index.

For Oracle data warehouses, updates are usually done on a time-based formula, so the issue becomes one of re-sequencing the index and ensuring that additions to the index are managed. In most cases, the obvious key for an Oracle data warehouse is the date column. Oracle data warehouses are updated in batch mode periodically, so the physical sequence of the data with the index could be maintained if we ensure that the new records are presorted in date order.

> **Note**: A date sequence for a clustered index is only beneficial if your system performs a lot of range scans by date.

Here are the options for appending new rows onto the end of a physically sequenced Oracle table:

- Presort the extract files in index key order, and load with SQL*Loader.

- Extract the data directly from an Oracle OLTP system using date predicates, as follows:

```
INSERT INTO WAREHOUSE_TABLE
   SELECT *
   FROM
       OLTP_TABLE@remote_instance
   WHERE
       trans_date > '01-JAN-1998'
   ORDER BY
       trans_date;
```

Note: Oracle export/import utilities have no mechanism for changing the physical sequence of tables, and they cannot be used to cluster an index.

Now, let's look at a dictionary query that will tell us the structure of our indexes (Listing 8.3). Note that the query shown in Listing 8.3 assumes that the Oracle database is using the cost-based optimizer and the tables have been analyzed with the **ANALYZE TABLE** command. Here, you can see that the indexes are grouped according to the tables they are built on. You can also see that the clustering factor for each index is computed as a percentage of the number of rows in the index.

Listing 8.3   An SQL*Plus routine to locate clustered indexes.

```
REM idx_bad1.sql, © 1997 by Donald K. Burleson
SET PAGESIZE 60;
SET LINESIZE 100;

COLUMN c0 HEADING 'Table'      FORMAT a8;
COLUMN c1 HEADING 'Index'      FORMAT a18;
COLUMN c2 HEADING 'Level'      FORMAT 999;
COLUMN c3 HEADING 'Clust Ftr'  FORMAT 9,999,999;
COLUMN c4 HEADING '# rows'     FORMAT 99,999,999;
COLUMN c5 HEADING 'Clust Pct'  FORMAT 999.9999;
COLUMN c6 HEADING 'dist. Keys' FORMAT 99,999,999;

SPOOL idx_bad1.lst;

BREAK ON c0 SKIP 1;

SELECT
  DBA_INDEXES.table_name                              c0,
  index_name                                          c1,
  blevel                                              c2,
  clustering_factor                                   c3,
  num_rows                                            c4,
  decode(clustering_factor,0,1,clustering_factor)/
  decode(num_rows,0,1,num_rows)                       c5,
  distinct_keys                                       c6
FROM DBA_INDEXES, DBA_TABLES
WHERE
DBA_INDEXES.owner NOT IN ('SYS','SYSTEM')
AND
DBA_TABLES.table_name = DBA_INDEXES.table_name
AND c5 < .25
ORDER BY c0, c5 desc;
SPOOL OFF;
```

Listing 8.4 shows a sample listing from idx_bad1.sql.

Listing 8.4   A sample listing from idx_bad1.sql.

```
SQL> @idx_bad1

Table     Index            Level Clust Ftr    # rows  reorg dist. Keys
--------  ---------------- ----- ---------- --------- ----- ----------
INV_LINE  INV_LINE_ITEM_PK   2      62,107  1,910,034 .0325  1,912,644
          ILI_FK_INV         2     164,757  1,910,034 .0339  1,659,625
          ILI_FK_ACT         2     283,343  1,910,034 .0436         47
          ILI_EK_CCHS_ACCT   3   1,276,987  1,910,034 .1450     25,041
```

Now, let's inspect this listing to see the clustering status of our indexes. The indexes are listed within each table heading in descending order of their clustering factor, with the most clustered indexes at the bottom of the list. The listing shows the **INV_LINE_ITEM_PK** index with a clustering factor of 62,107, indicating that the **INV_LINE** table has been loaded in nearly the same physical order as the index.

If the value for the clustering factor approaches the number of blocks in the base table, then the index is said to be clustered. If the clustering factor is greater than the number of blocks in the base table and approaches the number of rows in the base table, then the index is unclustered.

Determining When To Rebuild Indexes

One of the problems with Oracle data warehouses is their huge size. For very large database warehouses, performing a database reorganization is impractical because of the amount of time required to export the data warehouse to tape, drop the Oracle database, and re-create the warehouse using Oracle's **import** utility. Because of this time issue, the data warehouse manager must find alternative methods for ensuring that the Oracle data warehouse remains well-tuned from a physical data perspective.

In an Oracle data warehouse, a large index may take a long time to rebuild, and the prudent data warehouse administrator must carefully choose the right conditions that warrant an index rebuild. If very large database tables have been horizontally partitioned—where a large table is split into sub-tables according to date—there will be several smaller indexes to replace a single, very large index. For details on using index partitioning, see Chapter 14, *Oracle8 For The Warehouse*.

In general, indexes seldom require rebuilding in an Oracle data warehouse unless there has been a high amount of update or delete activity against the index columns. SQL **INSERT** operations, which are common for loads of new warehouse data, do not cause structural problems within the Oracle index structure.

So, how can you tell when an index will benefit from being rebuilt? There are two Oracle views that provide index statistics: **DBA_INDEXES** and **INDEX_STATS**. The **DBA_INDEXES** view contains statistical information that is placed into the view when the **ANALYZE INDEX xxx** command is issued. Unfortunately, the **DBA_INDEXES** view was designed to provide information to the cost-based SQL optimizer, and it does not keep statistics about the internal status of Oracle indexes.

To see the internal structure for an Oracle index, you must use the **ANALYZE INDEX xxx VALIDATE STRUCTURE** SQL command to validate the structure for the index. This command creates a single row in a view called **INDEX_STATS**. The **INDEX_STATS** view is a table that contains columns that describe the internals of the index. Here is a sample session:

```
SQL> ANALYZE INDEX DON.DON_FK_PLT VALIDATE STRUCTURE;

Index analyzed.

SQL> SELECT * FROM INDEX_STATS;



HEIGHT                      3
BLOCKS                   5635
NAME             DON_FK_PART
LF_ROWS
LF_BLKS                196103
LF_ROWS_LEN              2382
LF_BLK_LEN            3137648
BR_ROWS                 3900
BR_BLKS  BR_ROWS_LEN     2381
BR_BLK_LEN                18
DEL_LF_ROWS            41031
DEL_LF_ROWS_LEN         3956
DISTINCT_KEYS              7
MOST_REPEATED_KEY       112
BTREE_SPACE             125
```

```
USED_SPACE                56220
PCT_USED                9361008
ROWS_PER_KEY            3178679
BLKS_GETS_PER_ACCESS    787.912
```

Note: *The Oracle **INDEX_STATS** view will never contain more than one row. Therefore, you must perform the **ANALYZE INDEX xxx VALIDATE STRUCTURE** command and **SELECT * FROM INDEX_STATS** before issuing the next **ANALYZE INDEX** command. The script id1.sql on the CD-ROM found in the back of this book provides a method for getting a complete report for all indexes.*

Oracle's version of B-tree indexing uses an algorithm in which each index node may contain many index keys. As new key values are added to the index, Oracle must manage the configuration of each index node. Oracle index nodes are managed with two operations: splitting and spawning:

- *Splitting*—Describes what happens when an index node is filled with keys and a new index node is created at the same level as the full node. Splitting widens the B-tree horizontally.

- *Spawning*—Describes the process of adding a new level to an index. As a new index is populated, it begins life as a single-level index. As keys are added, a spawn takes place, and the first-level node reconfigures itself to have pointers to lower-level nodes. It is important to understand that spawning takes place at specific points within the index and not for the entire index. For example, a three-level index may have a node that experiences heavy insert activity. This node may spawn a fourth level without all of the other level-three nodes spawning new levels.

The **INDEX_STATS** view contains information about the internal structure of the B-tree index that can be useful when determining whether to rebuild the index. The following columns of **INDEX_STATS** are especially useful:

- **height**—Refers to the maximum number of levels encountered within the index. An index may have 90 percent of the nodes at three levels, but excessive splitting and spawning in one area of the index may cause some nodes to have more then three levels. Whenever the value of height is more than three, you may benefit from dropping and re-creating the index. Oracle indexing will not spawn a fourth level on a clean rebuild until about 10 million nodes have been added to the index.

- **del_lf_rows**—Refers to the number of leaf rows that have been deleted from the index. This occurs when heavy index update activity occurs within the index tree and indicates that the index will benefit from being dropped and re-created.

- **distinct_keys**—Indicates the number of distinct key values in the index. This is called the cardinality of the index, and values less than 20 are candidates for being re-created as bitmapped indexes.

- **most_repeated_key**—Counts the number of times the most frequent key value in a non-unique index appears in the B-tree.

Because the **INDEX_STATS** view will only hold one row at a time, it is not easy to create an SQL*Plus routine that will produce an **INDEX_STATS** report for all of the indexes on a system. The SQL presented in Listing 8.3 will perform an **ANA-LYZE INDEX xxx VALIDATE STRUCTURE** for each index in the schema and report the resulting values in **INDEX_STATS**.

> **Note**: *Running id1.sql on the CD-ROM included with this book will invoke id2.sql through id5.sql, automatically producing the unbalanced index report. Just be sure that id1.sql through id5.sql are present in a common directory when starting id1.sql.*

Despite the complexity of dealing with a one-row **INDEX_STATS** table, it is easy to use the script presented in Listings 8.5 through 8.10 to get **INDEX_STATS** for all warehouse indexes. In operational use, the unbalanced index report should be run whenever a DBA suspects update activity has unbalanced the indexes.

Listing 8.5 The SQL*Plus script to generate the report for INDEX_STATS.

```
REM id1.sql   The main driver routine for reporting index_stats
REM © 1997 by Donald K. Burleson
REM id1.sql
SET PAGES 9999;
SET HEADING OFF;
SET FEEDBACK OFF;
SET ECHO OFF;

SPOOL id4.sql;

SELECT '@id2.sql' FROM DUAL;
```

```
SELECT 'analyze index '||owner||'.'||index_name||
       'VALIDATE STRUCTURE;','@id3.sql;'
FROM DBA_INDEXES
WHERE
owner NOT IN ('SYS','SYSTEM');

SPOOL OFF;

SET HEADING ON;
SET FEEDBACK ON;
SET ECHO ON;

@id4.sql
@id5.sql
```

Listing 8.6   The SQL to create a temporary table for the **INDEX_STATS** report.

```
REM © 1997 by Donald K. Burleson
REM id2.sql
SELECT
  name                    ,
  most_repeated_key       ,
  distinct_keys           ,
  del_lf_rows             ,
  height                  ,
  blks_gets_per_access
FROM INDEX_STATS;
```

Listing 8.7   The SQL to insert the data from **INDEX_STATS** into the temporary table.

```
REM © 1997 by Donald K. Burleson
REM id3.sql
INSERT INTO TEMP_STATS
(SELECT
  name                    ,
  most_repeated_key       ,
  distinct_keys           ,
  del_lf_rows             ,
  height                  ,
  blks_gets_per_access
FROM INDEX_STATS
);
```

Listing 8.8   The SQL generated from running id1.sql.

```
REM © 1997 by Donald K. Burleson
REM id4.sql


ANALYZE INDEX DON.SHL_EK_TRUCK_LINK_NUM VALIDATE STRUCTURE;

@id3.sql;



ANALYZE INDEX DON.SHL_UK_FACT1_ID_SRC_CD_LOB VALIDATE STRUCTURE;

@id3.sql;



ANALYZE INDEX DON.PURCH_UNIT_PK VALIDATE STRUCTURE;

@id3.sql;
```

Listing 8.9   SQL*Plus script that generates the clustering report.

```
REM © 1997 by Donald K. Burleson
REM id5.sql - This creates the unbalanced index report
REM and the rebuild syntax
SET PAGESIZE 60;
SET LINESIZE 100;
SET ECHO OFF;
SET FEEDBACK OFF;
SET HEADING OFF;

COLUMN c1 FORMAT a18;
COLUMN c2 FORMAT 9,999,999;
COLUMN c3 FORMAT 9,999,999;
COLUMN c4 FORMAT 999,999;
COLUMN c5 FORMAT 99,999;
COLUMN c6 FORMAT 9,999;

SPOOL idx_report.lst;

PROMPT
PROMPT
```

```
PROMPT '                       # rep      dist.     # deleted              blk gets
PROMPT Index                   keys      keys      leaf rows  Height per access
PROMPT --------------         ------     ----      --------   ------ ----------

SELECT DISTINCT
  name                  c1,
  most_repeated_key     c2,
  distinct_keys         c3,
  del_lf_Rows           c4,
  height                c5,
  blks_gets_per_access  c6
FROM TEMP_STATS
WHERE
  height > 3
  OR
  del_lf_rows > 10
ORDER BY name;

SPOOL OFF;

SPOOL id6.sql;

SELECT 'alter index '||owner||'.'||name||' rebuild tablespace'||
         tablespace_name'
FROM TEMP_STATS, DBA_INDEXES
WHERE
  TEMP_STATS.name = DBA_INDEXES.index_name
  AND
  (height > 3
  OR
  del_lf_rows > 10);

SELECT 'analyze index '||owner||'.'||name||' compute statistics;'
FROM TEMP_STATS, DBA_INDEXES
WHERE
  TEMP_STATS.name = DBA_INDEXES.index_name
  AND
  (height > 3
  OR
  del_lf_rows > 10);

SPOOL OFF;
```

Listing 8.10 Completed unbalanced index report.

Index	# rep keys	dist. keys	# deleted leaf rows	Height	blk gets per access
DON_EK	159,450	25,420	934	4	41
DON_FK_ACT	1,009,808	542	101	3	1,705
INV_EK_INV_NUM	4	1,586,880	122	3	4
INV_FK_CAR	546,366	1,109	315	3	725
INV_FK_SRC	1,041,696	309	31	3	2,591
LOB_FACT1_PK	1	3,778,981	66,918	4	5
PAT_FK_JEN	37	2,736,262	436,880	3	4
PAT_FK_JEN	37	2,736,262	436,880	3	4
PAT_FK_JEN	37	2,736,262	436,880	3	4
PAT_FK_JEN	37	2,736,262	436,880	3	4
JEN_FK_SHP	88	1,464,282	97,473	4	6
JEN_FK_SHP	88	1,464,282	97,473	4	6
DON_FK_LEG	342,290	1,350	301	4	933
DON_FK_LEG	342,290	1,350	301	4	933
DON_FK_LEG	342,290	1,350	301	4	933
DON_FK_LEG	342,290	1,350	301	4	933

Dropping and re-creating an index has inherent problems and is not the best way to rebuild an Oracle index. The most common problem occurs when an extended index is dropped and then fails to re-create, failing due to a lack of space in the index tablespace (tablespace management is discussed in more detail later in this chapter).

For example, if you have an index with an initial size of 100 megabytes with 20 extents of 5 megabytes, you can drop the index, re-define the index with an initial extent of 200 megabytes, and re-create the index. Of course, first, you will need to ensure that there are 200 megabytes of free space within the index before you try this operation. Also, you may need to coalesce free index extents in the tablespace to make more contiguous space.

Index Tablespace Issues

When a large data warehouse has been created, it is not uncommon to see yearly aggregate values purged and recomputed on a scheduled basis. When this happens, the table and index extending will not be a problem because the tablespace will coalesce all free extents within the tablespace.

But what about the indexes? After a large purge, the indexes can become out of balance, and additional I/O may be required to access particular records. The logical remedy for an out-of-balance index would be to drop and rebuild all of the Oracle indexes. However, this poses another problem. To understand this process, let's examine a snapshot of an index tablespace prior to dropping all indexes in the tablespace (see Figure 8.8).

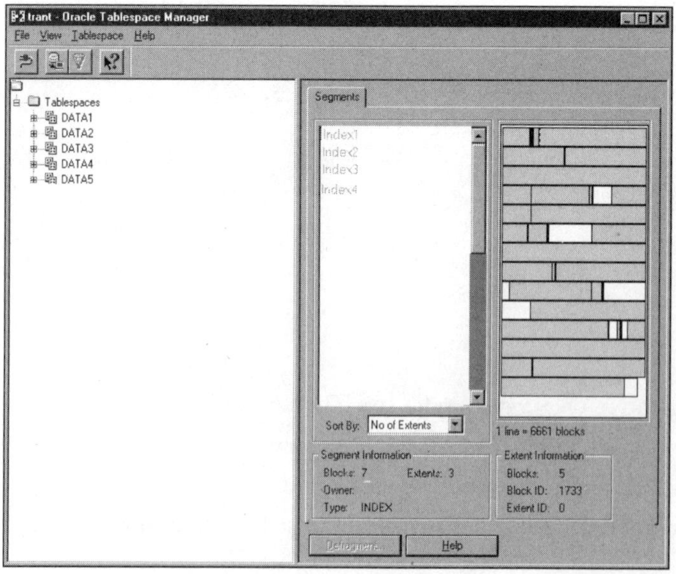

Figure 8.8
An Oracle index tablespace as seen by Oracle Tablespace Manager.

Figure 8.9
An Oracle index tablespace after dropping an index.

Now, let's drop the indexes, and look at the tablespace after the drop (see Figure 8.9).

Here, you can see that there are lots of empty extents in the tablespace because the empty storage has not been coalesced. Now, if you use Oracle 7.2 or above, you can issue the **ALTER TABLESPACE xxx COALESCE** command (see Figure 8.10). With the tablespace clear, the index can easily be re-created to reside in a single extent.

Rebuilding Unbalanced Indexes

So, what's the solution to rebuilding an unbalanced index? Oracle version 7.2 and above provide a facility that rebuilds an index in place without having to drop and re-create the index. This is done by issuing an **ALTER INDEX** command, as follows:

```
ALTER INDEX xxx REBUILD TABLESPACE yyy;
```

In-Place Index Rebuilding

You must specify the tablespace name when using the ALTER INDEX command. If the tablespace name is not present, Oracle will attempt to rebuild the index in the default tablespace name of the connected user who is issuing the command.

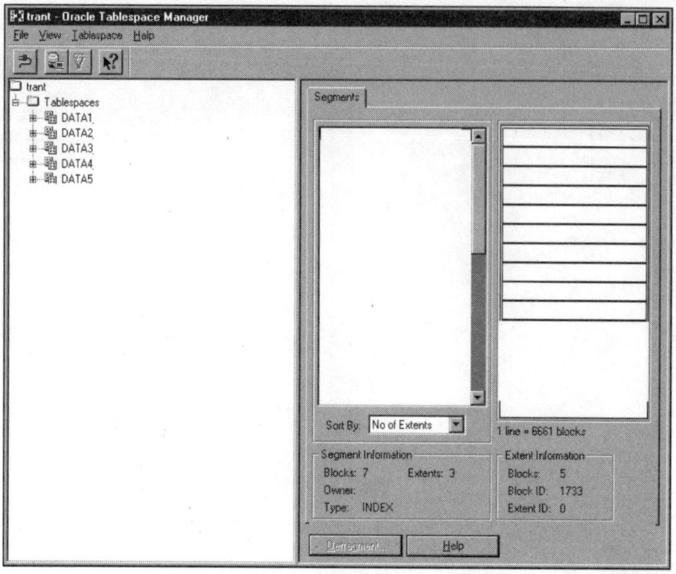

Figure 8.10
An Oracle index tablespace after coalescing the tablespace.

Let's take a look at what happens in an in-place rebuild of an Oracle index. An index rebuilt in place has the same number of extents as the original index. Hence, this command is not useful for reorganizing an index into a single extent. Each index node will be rebuilt in place, and the excessive levels and deleted leaf rows will be fixed. The goal of a data warehouse manager is to rebuild only those indexes that have more than three levels or lots of deleted leaf rows, so DBAs can use the id5.sql script to generate the rebuild commands directly from the **TEMP_STAT** table and store the output as id6.sql.

Using The Index REBUILD Command

While Oracle does not publish how the REBUILD command works internally, you must have extra space, equal to the index size, in each tablespace in order to issue the rebuild command. If Oracle cannot get enough scratch space in the target tablespace, the existing index will remain intact, and you will receive the message FAILED TO ALLOCATE AN EXTENT OF SIZE xxx IN TABLESPACE yyy.

As you can see, Listing 8.11 shows a list of indexes to be rebuilt, specifying the tablespace names. Please note that Oracle's index **REBUILD** command is very fast when compared to dropping and recreating an index. Using internal benchmarks of the **REBUILD** command, a one gigabyte index can be completely rebuilt in 20 seconds. This is because Oracle reads the existing index in order to gather the index node information for the new index. After the index has been read, Oracle replaces the old index tree in the same spot in the tablespace as the old index. For even faster execution time, the **UNRECOVERABLE** clause can be used with the **REBUILD** command.

Listing 8.11   The output from rebuilding indexes.

```
ALTER INDEX DON.DON_EK REBUILD TABLESPACE INDX_1;

index rebuilt

ALTER INDEX DON.DON_FK_ACT REBUILD TABLESPACE INDX_1;

index rebuilt

. . .
```

Oracle Bitmapped Indexes

Prior to release 7.3, Oracle never recommended that DBAs create an index on any field that was not "selective" and had less than 50 unique values. Imagine, for example, how a traditional B-tree index would appear if a column such as **region** were indexed. With only four distinct values in the index, the SQL optimizer would rarely determine that an index scan would speed up a query; consequently, the index would never be accessed. Of course, the only alternative would be to invoke a costly full-table scan of the table. Today, we are able to use bitmapped indexes for low cardinality indexes. *Cardinality* is defined as the number of distinct key values expressed as a percentage of the number of rows in the table. Hence, a million-row index with four distinct values has a low cardinality while a 100-row table with 80 distinct values has a high cardinality.

It is interesting to note that bitmapped indexes have been used in commercial databases since Model 204 was introduced in the late 1960s. However, their usefulness had been ignored until the data warehouse explosion of 1994, making it evident that a new approach to indexing was needed to resolve complex queries against very large tables.

Bitmapped indexes are a new feature of Oracle 7.3 that allow for very fast boolean operations against low cardinality indexes. Complex **AND** and **OR** logic is performed entirely within the index—the base table never needs to be accessed. Without a bitmapped index, some decision support queries would be impossible to service without a full-table scan.

Bitmaps are especially important for data warehouses and decision support systems where ad hoc, unanticipated queries make it impractical for the Oracle DBA to index all possible combinations of columns. To illustrate, assume that a manager wants to know the average income for all college-educated customers who drive red or blue cars in Wyoming or Nevada. Furthermore, assume there are 1 million rows in the customer table. The following query would be very hard to service using traditional indexing:

```
SELECT avg(yearly_income)
FROM
    CUSTOMER
WHERE
    education IN ('B','M','D')
AND
    car_color IN ('RED','BLUE')
AND
    state_residence IN ('WY','NV')
ORDER BY
    avg(yearly_income);
```

In a bitmapped index, it is not necessary to read all 1 million rows in the **CUSTOMER** table. Instead, the query manager would build rowid lists for all **1** values for **education**, **car_color**, and **state_residence**, and then match up the rowids for instances appearing in all three columns. When the query is ready to access the rows, it already has a list of rowids for all rows that meet the selection criteria.

To understand bitmapped indexes, imagine a very wide, fat table with only a few rows. In a bitmapped index, each unique value has one row, such that our **region** index contains only four rows. Across the bitmap, each row in the base table is represented by a column, with a **1** in the bitmap array if the value is true and a **0** if the value is false. Because of the high amount of repeating ones and zeros, bitmapped indexes can be compressed very effectively and expanded at runtime. In fact, the lower the cardinality, the better the compression. For example, we can expect a higher compression of a **gender** index with 2 distinct values than with a **state** index with 50 distinct values. Uncompressed, the **state** index would be 48 times larger than the **gender** bitmap, because 1 row in the bitmap array is required for each unique value.

Oracle bitmapped indexes can consume far less space than a traditional B-tree Oracle index. In fact, the size of a bitmapped index can be computed easily, as follows:

```
bitmap size = (cardinality_of_column * rows_in_table)/8
```

To illustrate, suppose that a **region** index has four distinct values in 1,000,000 rows. The entire index would only consume 4,000,000 bits uncompressed—and with Oracle's compression, this index would be far smaller than 500,000 bytes (8 bits per byte). In fact, with compression this index could probably be read entirely into the Oracle buffer with a few I/Os.

As you can see in the diagram shown in Figure 8.11, Oracle bitmapped indexes can dramatically reduce I/O for certain types of operations. For example, assume we are interested in knowing the number of corporations in the Western region. Because this information is contained entirely within the bitmapped indexes, we have no need to access the table. In other words, the query can be resolved entirely within the index.

How can we identify candidates for bitmapped indexes? The savvy data warehouse analyst starts by analyzing the existing database. There are two methods to use, based on whether your system is using the cost-based optimizer or the rule-based optimizer. If you are using the cost-based optimizer, then the **DBA_INDEXES** view will contain the cardinality information that you need to determine which index should be changed to bitmapped indexes. Listing 8.12 can be run for cost-based optimizer systems.

Listing 8.12   Locate bitmapped candidates for cost-based optimizer.

```
REM idx_bad2.sql -- Copyright (c) 1996 by Donald K. Burleson
SET PAGESIZE 60;
SET LINESIZE 100;

COLUMN c1 HEADING 'Index'    FORMAT a25;
COLUMN c2 HEADING 'Status'   FORMAT a10;
COLUMN c3 HEADING 'Level'    FORMAT 999;
```

```
COLUMN c4 HEADING 'dist. Keys' FORMAT 99,999,999;

SPOOL ind_bad2.lst;

PROMPT Change to bitmapped index if distinct_keys < 50

SELECT
  owner||'.'||index_name      c1,
  status                      c2,
  blevel                      c3,
  distinct_keys               c4
FROM DBA_INDEXES
WHERE
distinct_keys < 50 AND leaf_blocks > 500
ORDER BY distinct_keys desc;

SPOOL OFF;
```

Listing 8.13 shows the output from the script shown in Listing 8.12.

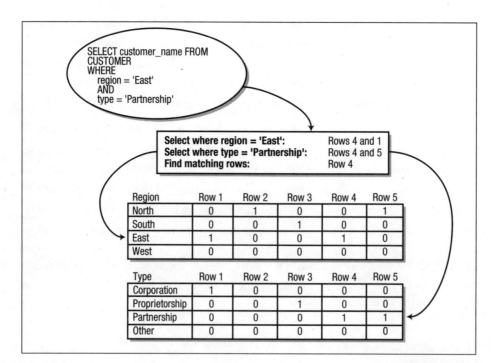

Figure 8.11

Oracle bitmapped indexes.

Listing 8.13 Bitmapped candidate report for cost-based optimizer.

```
sql> @idx_bad2

Index                       Status     Level  dist. Keys
------------------------    ---------- ----   ----------
DON.DON_FK_ACT              VALID        2          47
DON.CSB_EK_MONTH_YEAR       VALID        2          37
DON.DON_EK_ROLE_TY_DEST     VALID        2          10
DON.DON_FK_SRC              VALID        2          10
DON.SHL_FK_SRC              VALID        2           9
DON.DON_FK_PLT              VALID        2           4
DON.INF_EK_ABBR_CD_LOADED   VALID        2           4
DON.DON_FK_SPT              VALID        2           4
DON.INV_FK_INT              VALID        2           3
DON.INV_FK_SRC              VALID        2           1
DON.DON_FK_RAT              VALID        2           1

11 rows selected.
```

Other systems, which use Oracle's rule-based optimizer, must examine each index to determine the cardinality. Listing 8.14 can be run to check B-tree indexes, and it provides a list of candidates in ascending order of cardinality.

Listing 8.14 bitmap.sql identifies low cardinality indexes for bitmapped indexes.

```
REM  Written by Don Burleson

PROMPT Be patient. This can take awhile . . .

SET PAUSE OFF;
SET ECHO OFF;
SET TERMOUT OFF;
SET LINESIZE 300;
SET PAGESIZE 999;
SET NEWPAGE 0;
SET FEEDBACK OFF;
SET HEADING OFF;
SET VERIFY OFF;

REM  First create the syntax to determine the cardinality . . .


SPOOL idx1.sql;
```

```
SELECT 'set termout off;' FROM DUAL;
SELECT 'spool idx2.lst;' FROM DUAL;
SELECT 'column card format 9,999,999;' FROM DUAL;

SELECT 'select distinct count(distinct '
     ||A.column_name
     ||') card, '
     ||''' is the cardinality of '
     ||'Index '
     ||A.index_name
     ||' on column '
     ||A.column_name
     ||' of table '
     ||A.table_owner
     ||'.'
     ||A.table_name
     ||''' from '
     ||index_owner||'.'||a.table_name
     ||';'
FROM DBA_IND_COLUMNS A, DBA_INDEXES B
  WHERE
  A.index_name = B.index_name
AND
  tablespace_name NOT IN ('SYS','SYSTEM')
;

SELECT 'spool off;' FROM DUAL;
SPOOL OFF;

SET TERMOUT ON;


@idx1

!sort idx2.lst
```

Listing 8.15 shows the results of bitmap.sql and displays the indexes according to the number of distinct keys.

Listing 8.15   The results of bitmap.sql.

```
   3  is the cardinality of Index GEO_LOC_PK on column GEO_LOC_TY_CD
      of table DON.GEM_LCC
   4  is the cardinality of Index REGION_IDX on column REHION of
      table DON.CUSTOMER
```

```
    7  is the cardinality of Index GM_LCK on column GEO_LC_TCD of
       table DON.GEM_LCC
    8  is the cardinality of Index USR_IDX on column USR_CD of
       table DON.CUSTOMER
   50  is the cardinality of Index STATE_IDX on column STATE_ABBR of
       table DON.CUSTOMER
 3117  is the cardinality of Index ZIP_IDX on column ZIP_CD of
       table DON.GEM_LCC
71,513 is the cardinality of Index GEO_LOC_PK on column GEO_LOC_CD of
       table DON.GEM_LCC
83,459 is the cardinality of Index GEO_KEY_PK on column GEO_LOC_TY_CD
       of table DON.GEM_LCC
```

Of course, columns such as **gender** and **region** should be made into bitmaps—but what about **state** with 50 values, or **area_code** with a few hundred values? Intuition tells us that the benefits from bitmapped indexes are a function of the cardinality and the number of rows in the table, but no hard-and-fast rule exists for identifying what type of index is always best. A heuristic approach is called for, and it is relatively easy for a DBA to create a B-tree index, run a timed query, re-create the index with the **BITMAP** option, and re-execute the timed query.

Regardless, bitmapped indexes are critical to the performance of decision support systems, especially those that are queried in an ad hoc fashion against hundreds of column values. See Chapter 11, *Tuning The Oracle Warehouse Architecture*, for a discussion of the applications of bitmapped indexes.

Referential Integrity And Warehouse Performance

Before relational database-supported referential integrity, it was the responsibility of the programmer to guarantee the maintenance of data relationships and business rules. While this was fine for applications, risk came into play when ad hoc updated SQL commands were issued using Oracle SQL*Plus. With these ad hoc update tools, the programmatic SQL could be bypassed easily, skipping the business rules and creating logical corruption.

Relational database system such as Oracle allow for the control of business rules with constraints. Constraints, or referential integrity (RI) rules, are used to enforce one-to-many and many-to-many relationships within relational tables. For example, RI ensures that a row in the **CUSTOMER** table could not be deleted if orders for that customer exist in the **ORDER** table (see Figure 8.12).

Referential integrity has earned a bad reputation in Oracle because of the overhead created when enforcing business rules. In almost every case, it will be faster and more efficient to write your own rules for enforcing RI instead of having Oracle do it for you. Provided that your application does not allow ad hoc query, it is relatively easy to attach a trigger with a PL/SQL routine to enforce RI on your behalf. In fact, this is one of the best uses of a trigger because the DML **DELETE** event will not take place if the RI rules are invalid. For example, consider the following foreign-key constraint that protects a customer from being deleted if they have outstanding orders:

```
CREATE TABLE CUSTOMER (
    cust_id                 number
    CONSTRAINT cust_ukey UNIQUE (cust_id),
    cust_name               varchar(30),
    cust_address            varchar(30);

CREATE TABLE ORDER (
    order_id                number,
    order_date              date,
    cust_id                 number
    CONSTRAINT cust_fk REFERENCES CUSTOMER (cust_id) ON DELETE RESTRICT,
);
```

To ensure that SQL*Plus has no ad hoc updates, a constraint can be configured to disallow update operations. This is accomplished with the **PRODUCT_USER_PROFILE** table. Issuing the following row into this table will disable any ad hoc updates with SQL*Plus:

```
INSERT INTO PRODUCT_USER_PROFILE (product, user_id, attribute)
VALUES (
        'SQL*Plus',
        '%'
        'UPDATE');
```

Are you now free to write you own procedural RI without fear of accidental corruption? The answer is no because you can't guarantee that your end users always use your application to access the database. Remember, end users can use Oracle's SQL*Plus to access Oracle, thereby bypassing your business rules. A user on a PC (with SQL*Net installed) can access Oracle using ODBC without ever entering

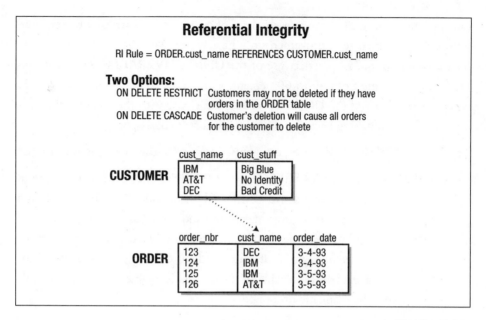

Referential Integrity

RI Rule = ORDER.cust_name REFERENCES CUSTOMER.cust_name

Two Options:

ON DELETE RESTRICT Customers may not be deleted if they have
orders in the ORDER table

ON DELETE CASCADE Customer's deletion will cause all orders
for the customer to delete

CUSTOMER

cust_name	cust_stuff
IBM	Big Blue
AT&T	No Identity
DEC	Bad Credit

ORDER

order_nbr	cust_name	order_date
123	DEC	3-4-93
124	IBM	3-4-93
125	IBM	3-5-93
126	AT&T	3-5-93

Figure 8.12

An overview of referential integrity.

SQL*Plus. So beware, and be sure that all ad hoc holes have been plugged before attempting to write your own RI rules.

Another problem with RI occurs when two tablespaces contain tables that have foreign key rules in the other tablespace. The DBA must commonly drop and rebuild tablespaces as a part of routine database compression. For example, when trying to drop a tablespace (say TS1) that has RI into another tablespace, the **DROP TABLESPACE CASCADE** will fail because foreign key references are contained in table B in tablespace TS2. Conversely, the DBA can't drop tablespace TS2 because it has references in tablespace TS1. This turns DBA maintenance into a nightmare because all constraints must be identified and disabled from TS2 in order to drop tablespace TS1.

Using Oracle's UNRECOVERABLE Option

At specific times, Oracle allows its internal transaction logging mechanism to be turned off. With Oracle, the software maintains a read-consistent image of the data for long-running queries, while at the same time providing rollback capability for each update transaction. Of course, this level of recoverability carries a price tag, and significant performance improvements can be achieved with the prudent use of the *unrecoverable* option. In practice, use of the **UNRECOVERABLE** clause will improve response time from 40 to 60 percent. Care needs to be taken, of course, to synchronize the use of the **UNRECOVERABLE** clause with the traditional procedures used when making backups of the archived redo logs.

The **UNRECOVERABLE** option can be used for any of the following operations:

- **CREATE TABLE . . . AS SELECT . . . UNRECOVERABLE**—This type of operation is generally performed when a table is *cloned*, or replicated, from a master table, usually with a subset of columns and rows. For example, you would use this command to create a subset of a customer table, containing only those customers in a specific region. Of course, a failure during the creation of the table would leave a half-built table in the destination tablespace, and the table would need to be manually dropped.

- **CREATE INDEX . . . UNRECOVERABLE**—This is the most common use of the **UNRECOVERABLE** clause, and certainly the use that makes the most sense from an Oracle perspective. Regardless of any transaction failures, an index can always be re-created by dropping and redefining the index, so having an incomplete or corrupt index would never be a problem.

- **ALTER TABLE . . . ADD CONSTRAINT . . . UNRECOVERABLE**—When a referential integrity constraint is added to a table, the Oracle software sometimes creates an index to enforce the constraint. Primary key, foreign key, and unique constraints may cause Oracle to create an index, which is built in unrecoverable mode.

- **SQL*Loader**—SQL*Loader is generally used when initially populating Oracle tables from external flat files. For very large numbers of inserts, it is best to leave the default. In the unlikely event of an abnormal termination, the incomplete tables must be dropped and SQL*Loader run again.

Oracle Tablespace Management

Unlike the CODASYL databases of the 1980s, today's Oracle databases allow for tables to grow according to specified rules and procedures. In the Oracle model, one or more tables may reside in a tablespace. As you may recall from earlier chapters, a *tablespace* is a predefined container for the tables that map to fixed files of a finite size. Tables assigned to a tablespace may grow according to the specified growth rules, but the size of the tablespace supersedes the expansion rules. In other words, a table may have more extents available according to the table definition, but there may not be room in the tablespace to allocate those extents.

Several Oracle parameters influence the growth of tables within a tablespace:

- **db_block_size**—Size of each physical database block.

- **INITIAL**—Initial size of each extent.

- **NEXT**—Subsequent size of new extents.

- **MINEXTENTS**—Minimum number of initial extents (used for striping).

- **MAXEXTENTS**—Maximum allowable number of extents. (Note: Oracle 7.3 supports **MAXEXTENTS UNLIMITED**.)

- **PCTINCREASE**—Percentage by which each subsequent extent grows (normally set to 1).

- **PCTFREE**—Percentage of space to be kept on each data block for future expansion.

Parameters of special note to Oracle warehouse developers are **PCTFREE** and **db_block_size**. Let's take a closer look at these two parameters.

Reserving Tablespace Using PCTFREE

The **PCTFREE** parameter is used to reserve space on each data block for the future expansion of row values (via the SQL **UPDATE** command). Table columns may be defined as allowing **NULL** values that do not consume any space within the row, or with **varchar** datatypes. A **varchar** datatype specifies the maximum allowable length for the column instance, but the acceptable range of values may be anywhere from 4 bytes (the size of the length holder) to the size of the field plus 4 bytes. Hence, a **varchar(2000)** may range in size from 4 bytes through 2004 bytes.

If an application initially stores rows with empty values and later fills in the values, the **PCTFREE** parameter can dramatically reduce I/O contention. If a block of storage is filled by the addition of a row, subsequent updates to that row to fill in column values will cause the row to fragment—usually fragmenting into the next available contiguous block.

Sizing Oracle Data Blocks With db_block_size

It is ironic that an Oracle developer must choose a blocksize when the data warehouse is initially created—a time when knowledge of system performance is extremely limited. While it is possible to use the Oracle import/export utility to change block sizes, too little attention is given to the proper sizing of database blocks. The physical block size is set with the **db_block_size** parameter in the init.ora file. While the default is to have 4 K block sizes, many Oracle developers choose at least 8 K block sizes for large, distributed data warehouses. Some DBAs believe that 16 K is the best block size, even for OLTP systems that seldom perform full-table scans. Depending on the host platform and operating system, Oracle block sizes may be set anywhere from 2 K to 32 K. The Oracle OS manual provides acceptable ranges for most operating systems, but the generally accepted wisdom is to create your database blocks as large as your operating system will allow. Remember, minimizing disk I/O is one of the most important factors in data warehouse tuning.

Disk I/O is the single most expensive and time-consuming operation within an Oracle database. As such, the more data that can be read in a single I/O, the faster the performance of the Oracle database. This principle is especially true for databases that have many reports that read the entire contents of a table. For systems that read random single rows from the database, block size is not as important—especially with database clusters. An Oracle *cluster* is a mechanism whereby an owner row will reside on the same database block as its subordinate rows in other tables. For example, if we cluster **order** rows on the same block as their **CUSTOMER** owners, Oracle will only need to perform a single I/O to retrieve the **CUSTOMER** and all of the **order** rows. Of course, in a distributed database where joins take place across different Oracle instances, clustering can not be used, and additional I/O will be required to read the rows individually.

Bear in mind that increasing the block size of an Oracle database will also affect the number of blocks that can be cached in the buffer pool. For example, if we set the

db_block_buffers init.ora parameter to 8 MB, Oracle will be able to cache 1,000 4-K blocks, but only 500 8-K blocks.

Oracle Tablespace Considerations

Choosing how to place tables and indexes into tablespaces has a great impact on the performance of your data warehouse. Warehouse designers have many choices, so it is a good idea to explore all available options. In general, you should consider the following characteristics when creating tablespaces in a data warehouse:

- *Group tables with similar characteristics in a tablespace.* For example, all tables that are read-only can be grouped into a single, read-only tablespace. Tables with random I/O patterns can also be grouped together; all small tables should be grouped together, and so on.

- *Create at least two tablespaces for use by the TEMP tablespaces.* This approach has the advantage of allowing a designer to dedicate numerous **TEMP** tablespaces to specific classes of users. As we know, the **TEMP** tablespace is used for large sorting operations, and assigning appropriately sized **TEMP** tablespaces to users depending upon their sorting requirements can enhance performance. Remember, in a distributed SQL query, rows are fetched from the remote database and sorted on the Oracle server that initiated the request. The use of multiple **TEMP** tablespaces has the added advantage of allowing a developer to switch **TEMP** tablespaces in case of disk failure.

- *Use many small, manageable tablespaces.* This approach makes it easier to take a single tablespace offline for maintenance without affecting the entire system. Oracle highly recommends that no tablespace should ever become greater than 10 GB, and placing all tables into a single tablespace reduces recoverability in case of media failure. However, this approach does not advocate creating a single tablespace for each table in a system. For example, Oracle recommends that the system tablespace contains only systems tables and that a separate tablespace is created for the exclusive use of the rollback segments.

- *Place the rollback segments in a separate tablespace.* This isolates the activity of the rollback segments (which tend to have a high I/O rate) from the data files belonging to the application.

- *If you have Oracle8, partition large table and indexes into separate tablespaces.* For a discussion of this method, see Chapter 14, *Oracle8 For The Warehouse.*

Tablespace Fragmentation

As rows are added to tables, the table expands into unused space within the tablespace. Conversely, when rows are deleted, a table may coalesce extents, releasing unused space back into the tablespace. As this happens, it is possible for there to be discontiguous chunks, or fragments, of unused space within the tablespace. Whenever the value for a table as specified by **STORAGE (INITIAL xx)** is exceeded, Oracle creates a new extent for the table. If the **PCTINCREASE** is set to zero, a new extent of the size specified in **STORAGE (NEXT xx)** will be added to the table. If **PCTINCREASE** is non-zero, the extent size will be equal to the value of the most recent extent size multiplied by **PCTINCREASE**.

Beware Of PCTINCREASE=0

PCTINCREASE for a tablespace should never be set to zero in Oracle 7.x because this disables the automatic coalesce facility for Oracle tablespaces. In general, all tablespaces except the system tablespaces (SYSTEM, RBS) should have PCTINCREASE set to 1. The PCTINCREASE parameter for tablespaces is generally only used when a table is allocated without a STORAGE clause— although Oracle also uses it for coalescing.

This allocation of new extents will be physically contiguous to the table's initial location, as long as the next physical data blocks are empty. Unfortunately, since many tables populate a tablespace, a table may not have contiguous data blocks for its next extent, which means it must fragment the extents onto another spot in the data file, as shown here:

```
CREATE TABLESPACE SALES
   DATAFILE '/Data/ORACLE/sales/sales.dbf'
   SIZE 500M REUSE
   DEFAULT STORAGE (INITIAL 500K  NEXT 50K  PCTINCREASE 1);
```

Here, you can see that the **SALES** tablespace has been allocated to a physical file called Data/ORACLE/sales/sales.dbf, created at a size of 500 MB. Assuming the tables within this tablespace use default storage, each table will be initially allocated at 500 K and will extend in chunks of 50 K.

But what happens if the tablespace gets full? Processing will cease against the tablespace, and the Oracle DBA will have to intervene and add another data file to the tablespace with the **ALTER TABLESPACE** command, as follows:

```
ALTER TABLESPACE SALES
ADD DATAFILE '/Data/ORACLE/sales/sales1.dbf'
SIZE 200M REUSE;
```

Obviously, the DBA should carefully monitor tablespace usage so tablespaces never fill, but Oracle version 7.2 and above offer an alternative that is especially useful for data warehouses. The **AUTOEXTEND** command can be used to allow a data file to grow automatically on an "as needed" basis. Following are the different permutations of this command:

```
ALTER DATABASE DATAFILE '/Data/ORACLE/sales/sales.dbf' AUTOEXTEND ON;

ALTER DATABASE DATAFILE '/Data/ORACLE/sales/sales.dbf' AUTOEXTEND
    MAXSIZE UNLIMITED;

ALTER DATABASE DATAFILE '/Data/ORACLE/sales/sales.dbf' AUTOEXTEND
    MAXSIZE (500M);

ALTER DATABASE DATAFILE '/Data/ORACLE/sales/sales.dbf' RESIZE (600M);
```

When tables fragment, additional I/O will be required to access the table data because the disk must access blocks on two noncontiguous spots on the data file. The script in Listing 8.16 will detect all tablespaces whose tables have taken more than 10 extents. These tablespaces will become candidates for a reorganization.

Listing 8.16 An SQL*Plus script to display tablespace extents.

```
REM tblsp_fr.sql - shows all tablespaces with more than 10 extents
SET PAGES 9999;
COLUMN c1 HEADING "Tablespace Name"
COLUMN c2 HEADING "Number of Extents"
TTITLE " Tablespaces with more than 10 extents"

SELECT tablespace_name c1,
       MAX(extent_id)  c2
FROM DBA_EXTENTS
WHERE
extent_id > 9
GROUP BY tablespace_name
;
```

Listing 8.17 displays the output of the script shown in Listing 8.16.

Listing 8.17   Report displaying tablespace extents.

```
SQL> @tblsp_fr

Fri Mar 15                                                        page    1
                          Tablespaces with more than 10 extents

Tablespace Name                    Number of Extents
------------------------------     -----------------
INDX                                              113
SALES                                              57
SYSTEM                                             56
```

Contrary to popular opinion, tables with noncontiguous extents do not cause performance problems. It is only the row fragmentation that sometimes accompanies discontiguous extents that negatively affects performance. In some studies, a table with discontiguous extents (and no row fragmentation) actually performed faster than a table in a single extent. However, it is often useful to display the amount of free space within a tablespace and the location of the free space pieces within the tablespace. Listings 8.18 and 8.19 show two useful scripts to display free space within a tablespace. The free_space.sql script (shown in Listing 8.18) needs to be run only once to create the view used by the tsfree.sql script (shown in Listing 8.19) to generate a detailed tablespace report. Listing 8.20 displays the resultant tablespace report.

Listing 8.18   free_space.sql creates the view used by tsfree.sql.

```
REM free_space.sql
REM run this script first, to create the free_space view;
DROP VIEW SYS.FREE_SPACE;

CREATE VIEW SYS.FREE_SPACE AS
SELECT tablespace_name tablespace,
       file_id,
       count(*) pieces,
       sum (bytes) free_bytes,
       sum (blocks) free_blocks,
       max (bytes) largest_bytes,
       max (blocks) largest_blks
FROM   SYS.DBA_FREE_SPACE
GROUP  BY tablespace_name, file_id;
```

Listing 8.19   tsfree.sql.

```
REM tsfree.sql - Shows all free space within tablespaces.
PROMPT be sure that you have run free_space.sql prior to this script

CLEAR BREAKS;
CLEAR COMPUTES;
SET VERIFY OFF;
SET PAGESIZE 66;
SET LINESIZE 79;
SET NEWPAGE 0;

COLUMN temp_col new_value spool_file noprint;


COLUMN today new_value datevar noprint;
COLUMN tablespace_name          FORMAT A15     HEADING 'Tablespace';
COLUMN pieces                   FORMAT 9,999   HEADING 'Tablespace|Pieces';
COLUMN file_mbytes              FORMAT 99,999  HEADING 'Tablespace|Mbytes';
COLUMN free_mbytes              FORMAT 99,999  HEADING 'Free|Mbytes';
COLUMN contiguous_free_mbytes FORMAT 99,999 HEADING
'Contiguous|Free|Mbytes';
COLUMN pct_free                 FORMAT 999     HEADING 'Percent|FREE';
COLUMN pct_contiguous_free      FORMAT 999     HEADING
'Percent|FREE|Contiguous';

TTITLE LEFT datevar RIGHT sql.pno -
       CENTER ' Instance Data File Storage' SKIP 1 -
       CENTER ' in ORACLE Megabytes (1048576 bytes)' -
       SKIP skip;

BREAK ON REPORT
COMPUTE SUM OF FILE_MBYTES ON REPORT

SELECT to_char(sysdate,'mm/dd/yy') today,
       tablespace_name,
       pieces,
       (D.bytes/1048576) file_mbytes,
       (F.free_bytes/1048576) free_mbytes,
       ((F.free_blocks / D.blocks) * 100) pct_free,
       (F.largest_bytes/1048576) contiguous_free_mbytes,
       ((F.largest_blks / D.blocks) * 100) pct_contiguous_free
FROM SYS.DBA_DATA_FILES D, SYS.FREE_SPACE F
WHERE D.status = 'AVAILABLE' AND
```

```
      D.file_id = F.file_id AND
      D.tablespace_name = F.tablespace_name
ORDER BY tablespace_name;
```

Listing 8.20 Detailed tablespace report.

Tablespace	Tablespace Pieces	Tablespace Mbytes	Free Mbytes	Percent FREE	Contiguous Free Mbytes	Percent Free Contiguous
MASTER1_DETAILS	1	18	2	10	2	10
MASTER1_DETAILS	1	20	20	100	20	100
MASTER2_DETAILS	1	2	1	65	1	65
MASTER3_DETAILS	1	5	5	95	5	95
MASTER4_DETAILS	2	3	1	36	1	35
RBS_ONE	11	490	380	78	280	57
RBS_TWO	11	490	379	77	279	57
SYSTEM	17	60	45	76	45	75
TEMP	1	650	650	100	650	100
TOOLS	2	15	9	61	8	55
USERS	41	100	31	31	4	4

While this report is useful for finding the largest chunk of free space in a tablespace, it is not a substitute for some of the graphical tablespace display tools, such as Oracle's Performance Pack Tablespace Manager or the Eventus AdHawk Spacer tool. These tools display a picture of each tablespace, showing exactly where the chunks of free space reside.

Tablespace Reorganization

Because Oracle databases are dynamic, they will always fragment over time and may require periodic cleanup. In general, reorganization ensures that all tables and indexes do not have row fragmentation and that they reside in a single extent, with all free space in a tablespace in a single, contiguous chunk. Reorganizing a tablespace can be accomplished in several ways, as we'll discuss in this section. Fortunately, rather than bringing down the entire Oracle database to perform a full export/import, there are some other options.

First, let's take a look at how a tablespace can become fragmented. At initial load time, all Oracle tables within a tablespace are contiguous—that is, only one chunk of free space resides at the end of the tablespace. As tables extend and new extents are added to the tablespace, the free space becomes smaller but it still remains contiguous.

Basically, a table can fragment in two ways:

- *A table extends (without row chaining)*—Contrary to popular belief, this is not a problem and performance will not suffer.

- *Rows fragment within the tablespace (due to SQL UPDATEs)*—This causes a serious performance problem, and the offending tables must be exported, dropped, and reimported.

Tablespace fragmentation occurs when some "pockets" of free space exist within the tablespace. So, how do these pockets of free space appear? If tables are dropped and re-created, or if individual tables are exported and imported, space that was once reserved for a table's extent will now be vacant.

To see the fragmentation within a tablespace, you can run the script shown in Listing 8.21.

Listing 8.21   tsfrag.sql shows a tablespace map.

```
REM written by Don Burleson

SET LINESIZE 132;
SET PAGES 999;

REM set feedback off;
REM set verify off;
REM set heading off;
REM set termout off;

BREAK ON file_id SKIP PAGE;
BREAK ON free SKIP 1;
COMPUTE sum OF KB ON free;

SPOOL tsfrag;

COLUMN owner            FORMAT a10;
COLUMN segment_name     FORMAT a10;
COLUMN tablespace_name  FORMAT a14;
COLUMN file_id          FORMAT 99 heading ID;
COLUMN end              FORMAT 999999;
COLUMN KB               FORMAT 9999999;
COLUMN begin            FORMAT 999999;
COLUMN blocks           FORMAT 999999;
```

```
SELECT
   tablespace_name,
   file_id,
   owner,
   segment_name,
   block_id begin,
   blocks,
   block_id+blocks-1 end,
   bytes/1024 KB,
   '' free
FROM SYS.DBA_EXTENTS
WHERE tablespace_name NOT IN ('RBS','SYSTEM','TEMP','TOOLS','USER')
UNION
SELECT
   tablespace_name,
   file_id,
   '' owner,
   '' segment_name,
   block_id begin,
   blocks,
   block_id+blocks+1 end,
   bytes/1023 KB,
   'F' free
FROM SYS.DBA_FREE_SPACE
WHERE tablespace_name NOT IN ('RBS','SYSTEM','TEMP','TOOLS','USER')
ORDER BY 1, 2, 5
;

/

SPOOL OFF;

!cat tsfrag.lst
```

Listing 8.22 displays the results of the tsfrag.sql script.

Listing 8.22 Results of the tsfrag.sql script.

TS_NAME	ID	OWNER	SEGMENT_NA	BEGIN	BLOCKS	END	KB	F
DONALD3_DETAILS	15	DON	ZIP_UPS	2	5	6	20	
DONALD3_DETAILS	15	DON	ACCC_TY	7	2	8	8	
DONALD3_DETAILS	15	DON	BUS_UNIT	9	35	43	140	
DONALD3_DETAILS				44	2	45	8	F

DONALD3_DETAILS	15	DON	PLANT	46	3	48	12	
DONALD3_DETAILS				49	10	58	40	F
DONALD3_DETAILS	15	DON	DON_TABLES	59	4	62	16	
DONALD3_DETAILS	15	DON	ZONE	63	2	64	8	
							--------	*
							252	s
DONALD3_DETAILS	15			65	1216	1282	4869	F
							--------	*
							4869	s

In the tablespace fragmentation report, you can see two discontiguous chunks of free space, as indicated by the **F** column on the far right-hand side of the report. Here, you can see that blocks 44 and 45 are free, as are blocks 49 through 58. As I mentioned earlier, there are other tools that provide this information in a graphical format, such as Oracle's Performance Pack's Tablespace Manager and the Eventus AdHawk Spacer product.

Oracle version 7.3 can automatically detect and coalesce tablespaces—provided that every affected tablespace contains a default storage clause setting **PCTINCREASE** to 1. The coalesce mechanism for tablespace coalescing is the **SMON** process, which periodically wakes up to coalesce free space. Between **SMON** coalesces, any transaction that requires an extent larger than any available free extent will trigger a coalesce on the tablespace to move all free space into a single chunk—hopefully making room for the required extent.

Also in Oracle 7.3 is a new dictionary view, **DBA_FREE_SPACE_COALESCED**, which provides details about the number of extents, bytes, and blocks that have been coalesced in each tablespace.

The following query will display coalesce information:

```
SELECT
    tablespace_name,
    bytes_coalesced,
    extents_coalesced,
    percent_extents_coalesced,
    blocks_coalesced,
    percent_blocks_coalesced
FROM
```

```
    SYS.DBA_FREE_SPACE_COALESCED
ORDER BY
    tablespace_name;
```

To change all tablespaces' **PCTINCREASE** from zero to one (so that tables will automatically coalesce), run the script presented in Listing 8.23.

Listing 8.23   coalesce.sql changes all tablespaces with **PCTINCREASE** not equal to one.

```
REM written by Don Burleson

SET LINESIZE 132;
SET PAGESIZE 999;
SET FEEDBACK OFF;
SET VERIFY OFF;
SET HEADING OFF;
SET TERMOUT OFF;

SPOOL COALESCE;

SELECT
    'alter tablespace '||
    tablespace_name||
    ' storage ( pctincrease 1 );'
FROM DBA_TABLESPACES
WHERE
 tablespace_name NOT IN ('RBS','SYSTEM','TEMP','TOOLS','USER')
AND
 pct_increase = 0;

SPOOL OFF;

SET FEEDBACK ON;
SET VERIFY ON;
SET HEADING ON;
SET TERMOUT ON;

@coalesce.lst
```

Manual Tablespace Coalescing

If you detect that a single tablespace has fragmented, you can quickly coalesce it with the following steps:

1. Alter session by retrieving the tablespace number from **SYS.TS$**:

```
SELECT * FROM SYS.TS$;
```

2. In SQL*DBA, issue the command

```
ALTER SESSION SET EVENTS (immediate trace name coalesce level
&tsnum);
```

where **tsnum** is the tablespace number from Step 1.

3. To manually coalesce from SQL*Plus, enter:

```
ALTER TABLESPACE <xxxx> COALESCE;
```

Using Oracle's Read-Only Tablespaces

In a busy environment where many different applications require access to a tablespace, it is sometimes desirable to use the read-only tablespace feature of Oracle 7.3. With read-only tablespaces, separate instances can be mapped to the same tablespaces, each accessing the tablespace in read-only mode. Of course, sharing a tablespace across Oracle instances increases the risk that I/O against the shared tablespaces may become excessive. As we can see in Figure 8.13, a read-only tablespace does not have the same overhead as an updatable tablespace.

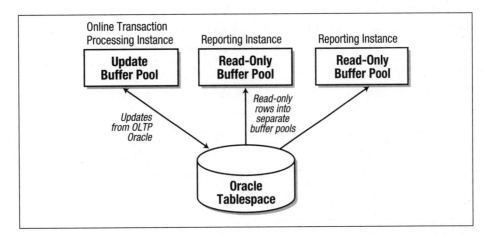

Figure 8.13
Oracle read-only tablespaces.

This approach has several advantages:

- *Buffer pool isolation*—The foremost advantage is the isolation of the buffer pools for each instance accessing the tablespace. If user A on instance A flushes his buffer by doing a full-table scan, user B on instance B will still have the blocks needed in memory.

- *Easy sharing of table data*—Read-only tablespaces offer an alternative to table replication and the update problems associated with replicated tables. Because a read-only tablespace may only be defined as updatable by one instance, updates are controlled at the system level.

When we examine the backup and recovery of an Oracle data warehouse, we generally find that the Oracle warehouse runs in two modes: load processing mode and query processing mode. Most Oracle data warehouses are refreshed periodically, and you can see different configurations for Oracle during load processing when compared to the configuration used during query processing. During query time, the database is generally optimized for queries, and it is not uncommon to see Oracle's recovery mechanisms disabled. Oracle provides several sophisticated mechanisms for read consistency and roll-forward.

Read consistency is defined as the ability of Oracle to "fix" a query such that a 30-minute query will retrieve data as it existed when the query started, even if information is being changed while the query is running. Oracle implements read consistency by referring to the online redo logs whenever a requested data item has been changed during a query, and the "old" value for the data is read from the online redo log. Of course, using the online redo logs adds to the overhead.

Another source of update overhead occurs as Oracle archives the online redo logs. Redo logs store the before and after images of all rows that have been added, modified, or deleted. In addition, the redo log contains log checkpoints such as begin-job, end-job, commit, and abort checkpoints for every transaction that runs under Oracle. As redo logs fill, Oracle directs the online log to be archived to a disk file. Periodically, these archived redo logs are written to tape media in case the Oracle database administrator needs to use them for a roll-forward.

These features are essential for maintaining the integrity of an updated Oracle database, but they are not necessary when your Oracle data warehouse is running in read-only mode. As such, many Oracle DBAs configure their data warehouses to use

Oracle's read-only tablespaces. Read-only tablespaces prohibit update operations against a tablespace. The main purpose of read-only tablespaces is to eliminate the need to perform backup and recovery operations against a static tablespace. Therefore, the primary purpose of read-only tablespaces in a data warehouse is to segregate those parts of the warehouse that are "historic" and will never be altered from the more recent warehouse information, which may be updated.

> **Note**: A read-only tablespace may only be online in the database that created the tablespace. The concept of Oracle read-only tablespaces has not yet been extended to allow multiple instances to access a read-only tablespace (except, of course, with Oracle parallel server).

Read-Only Tablespaces In The Real World

For a production Oracle data warehouse, it is very important to develop a method for determining when the data becomes permanent. For example, a large data warehouse may store historical data for the past decade, but the last 18 months' worth of data are subject to updates as the data status changes within the OLTP database. Figure 8.14 shows a data warehouse with fact tables that have been horizontally partitioned. In other words, even though the fact tables contain rows going back three years in time, the tables are separated to govern smaller periods of time.

Here, you can see that the main fact table has been logically partitioned into 3 horizontal partitions, and only the most recent section of the table (**FACT_97**) is subject to update. The other partitions for the fact table are static and will never change. For details on using horizontal table partitioning with Oracle tables, see Chapter 4, *Oracle Data Warehouse Design*. For details on automatic table and index partitioning with Oracle8, see Chapter 14, *Oracle8 For The Warehouse*.

Note that each chunk of the fact table in Figure 8.14 is segregated into its own tablespace, such that there are three independent tablespaces for each table. Also note that this is a rolling strategy. As **FACT_96** ages into the static category, the Oracle DBA will reorganize this table chunk and tightly pack it into a static tablespace. This is achieved by calculating the precise amount of storage for the table, and using Oracle **export/import** utility to offload the data and pack it into the new chunk. The index for each chunk also resides in its own tablespace, and this is packed into its new, static tablespace.

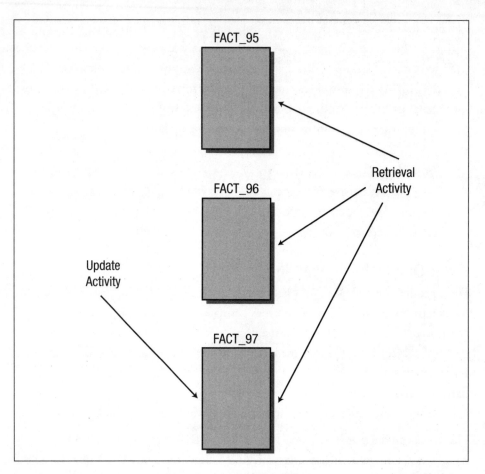

Figure 8.14
Horizontal partitioning of an Oracle warehouse.

But how do you "pack" Oracle data for use as a read-only tablespace? Essentially, there are two places where space is wasted within an Oracle table: the percentage free on each data block, and leftover space at the end of the table's extent. On each data block, Oracle will reserve an amount for row expansion, and this value is controlled by the **PCTFREE** table parameter, as discussed earlier in this chapter. The **PCTFREE** parameter is useful when you are loading incomplete rows that have columns defined with **varchar** data definitions. After initial loading, Oracle reserves space at the end of each data block for row expansion. For example, if a table is defined with 8-K blocks and **PCTFREE** = 25, 2,000 bytes are reserved at the end of each and every data block for row expansion. Later, if the DBA issues an SQL **UPDATE** command to add column values for a null value, the row size will expand into the free space. The second area of free space in a tablespace is the space left over at the end of the table (see Figure 8.15). Here, the DBA might see that the **CUSTOMER**, **ORDER**, and **ITEM** tables consume only 75 percent of their allocated extent, allowing for the table to extend as new rows are added. In short, tables grow wider as column values are added (in each data block), and tables grow longer as rows are added (to the end of the tablespace).

If you know that a table chunk is static, you can export the table into a flat file, and redefine the table and tablespace characteristics to maximize the amount of occupied space. At the table level, set **PCTFREE** equal to zero, not reserving any space within

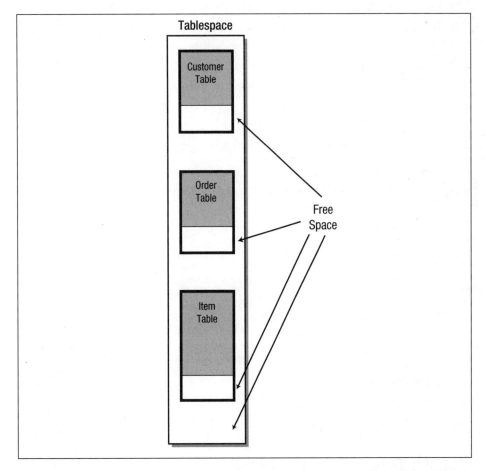

Figure 8.15
Free space distribution within a tablespace.

the data blocks for growth. At the tablespace level, redefine the tablespace to consume only as much space as the table requires. (The total amount of space for a table can be estimated fairly accurately by estimating the average row length and multiplying by the number of rows.)

After you have packed the row data and the indexes within their respective tablespace, you can now alter the tablespaces to make them read-only. Once the tablespace has been altered to become read-only, a single backup can be used for all future recovery. Unlike ordinary tablespaces, online backups never need to issue the **ALTER TABLESPACE FACT_96 BEGIN BACKUP** commands. During the startup of an Oracle instance, Oracle verifies that a tablespace is in read-only mode and recognizes that it does not need any media recovery. In short, a recovery of an Oracle data warehouse will only consist of applying the redo logs against tablespaces that were in update mode. This greatly simplifies database recovery for a very large Oracle warehouse. This technique also allows a tablespace to avoid the time-consuming overhead of writing to the online redo logs because roll-forward operations are performed by rerunning the nightly update routines. In addition, read-only tablespaces will never write to the database file headers, which saves system I/O.

With Oracle version 7.1 and above, any Oracle tablespace may be made read-only by issuing the **ALTER TABLESPACE** command, as follows:

```
SVRMGRL > shutdown;

SVRMGRL > startup restrict;

SVRMGRL > ALTER TABLESPACE WAREHOUSE_ONE READ ONLY;

SVRMGRL > ALTER DATABASE OPEN;
```

> **Note**: In order to change the status of a tablespace, the Oracle database must be quiesced. That is, there must be no active transactions running against the tablespace at the time the **ALTER TABLESPACE** command is issued. In the previous example, Oracle was shut down, and the database was in restricted mode.

Oracle And CD-ROM Media

It is not uncommon in an Oracle data warehouse for a tablespace to be transferred onto a CD-ROM when a tablespace will no longer be updated. Read-only media such as a CD-ROM disk is far cheaper and more compact than disk storage, and it is not substantially slower. While every data warehouse uses a different technique, the following shell script demonstrates how a read-write tablespace may be archived onto a CD-ROM and made into a read-only tablespace:

```
ORACLE_HOME=my.oracle.home
export ORACLE_HOME

ORACLE_SID=my_sid_name
export ORACLE_SID

PATH=$PATH:$ORACLE_HOME/bin
export PATH

svrmgrl << ALL_DONE
shutdown immediate;
EXIT;
ALL_DONE

cp read_write_tablespace_file CD_ROM_tablespace_file;

svrmgrl << ALL_DONE
startup mount;

ALTER TABLESPACE FACT_97 RENAME DATAFILE
        read_write_tablespace_file TO CD_ROM_tablespace_file;

startup restrict;

ALTER TABLESPACE WAREHOUSE_ONE READ ONLY;

ALTER DATABASE OPEN;
EXIT;
ALL_DONE

rm -f read_write_tablespace_file
```

After a tablespace has been packed and copied to cheaper media, a DBA can perform some system tuning tricks to boost performance. Oracle recommends that the data warehouse DBA use the table cache option (discussed earlier in this chapter) and issue a full-table scan against all small, frequently accessed tables in the read-only tablespace to ensure that they have been loaded into the Oracle buffer pool. For small tables defined with the cache option, issuing the following **SELECT count(*)**

against the table at database startup time will cache the table in the most frequently used portion of Oracle's data buffer:

```
SVRMGRL>  SELECT count(*) FROM SALES_FACT_TABLE;
```

Now, let's invalidate our entire discussion on read-only tablespaces by noting that in a few years, it will not be necessary to use these techniques because system performance will be so fast that this type of tuning will not significantly influence performance. To illustrate, let's take a look at how unbelievable speed is achieved using Oracle data warehouses on 64-bit processors.

Oracle's 64-Bit Option—A Look Into The Future

For very large data warehouses where sub-second response time is critical, few database engines can beat the performance of Oracle with the 64-bit option. Designed for use with Digital Equipment Corporation's Alpha series (DEC-Alpha), Oracle's 64-bit architecture performs more than 1,000 times faster than standard Oracle7 software. It is interesting to note that the DEC-Alpha family of 64-bit processors has been around since 1991, and the database vendors are only now beginning to realize their potential for data warehousing. Because most major hardware vendors have caught on and are creating 64-bit systems, let's take a look into the future by examining the existing state of Oracle's 64-bit option for data warehousing.

SQL Complexity And Response Time

As you probably know, when Oracle performs n-way joins of a very large fact table against dimension tables, Oracle denigrates in performance as the number of joined tables increases (see Figure 8.16). However, Oracle claims that using Oracle's STAR query hints with 64-bit databases actually improves response times as the complexity of SQL queries increases. In an Oracle study, a DEC-Alpha with Oracle's 64-bit option showed response times improving as the number of joined tables increased.

An Oracle STAR query maps the selection criteria conditions from a query and creates a cross-product of the dimension tables. This cross-product is then compared to the fact table by using a multikey index in the fact table.

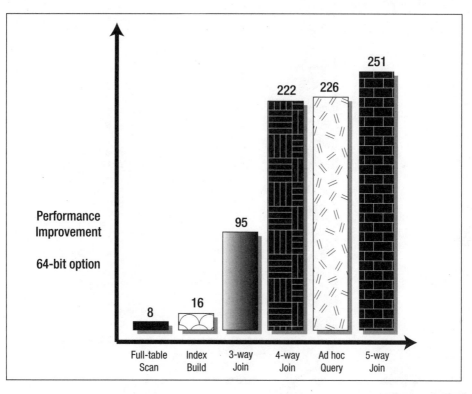

Figure 8.16
An Oracle benchmark.

Using a large SGA configuration with Oracle 64 on a DEC-Alpha, Oracle corporation demonstrated that a query that took more than one hour on a Unix Oracle database ran in less than three seconds on a 64-bit processor with a STAR schema and 6 gigabytes of data buffer (see Figure 8.17).

What About BOB?

The Oracle 64-bit option has two enhanced features: Big Oracle Blocks (BOB) and Large SGA (LSGA). BOB is probably one of the most important features of Oracle on 64-bit machines. Because block sizes can reach 32 K, an entire track of data can be read with a single I/O, and system performance can be improved dramatically. This is especially important in data warehouses that scan large ranges of tables. When used with the init.ora parameter, **db_multiblock_read_count**, physical I/O for table scan operations will be greatly reduced. BOB is also very useful if you are storing

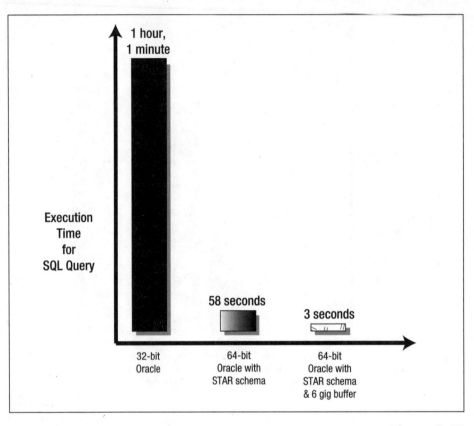

Figure 8.17
Query speed comparison—32-bit versus 64-bit processors.

nontabular data in your Oracle database, as is the case with Oracle's spatial data option. In these cases, binary large objects (BLOBs), such as images, can be accessed with a single physical disk I/O.

LSGA is extremely important in the future of Oracle data warehouse systems. As the cost of RAM memory falls, you will see huge Oracle SGAs, some of which will be able to cache an entire database. In some 64-bit Oracle warehouses, large tables are read into an Oracle data buffer using the table cache option. For example, assume we have a 10 gigabyte data warehouse with 32-K blocks and **db_block_buffers** parameter set to 10,000, for a total buffer size of 320 megabytes. Here, we have an SGA large enough to hold the entire database, which can be read at startup where it will remain for the entire processing day without any disk I/O (assuming, of course, that we are in query mode). Because accessing RAM takes 50 nanoseconds, compared to the 50 milliseconds required to access disk I/O, you can see that I/O will proceed one million times faster in a system that does not perform disk I/O.

Sixty-four bit architectures also remove many of the traditional barriers of Unix systems. File sizes can now exceed 2 gigabytes, SGA regions can reach up to 14 gigabytes, and database block sizes can now be made 32 K, the same as Oracle's mainframe cousins.

Summary

Now that we have explored the internals of Oracle tables, indexes, and tablespaces in relation to data warehouses, let's take a look at how distributed data warehouses are designed using Oracle SQL*Net. Then, we'll proceed to explore Oracle utilities and the tuning of Oracle SQL.

Distributed Oracle Data Warehouses

CHAPTER

9

HIGH PERFORMANCE

Distributed Oracle Data Warehouses

Managing an Oracle data warehouse becomes very challenging when we move into the distributed database environment. The challenge arises because so many components within the database software contribute to the overall performance. The number of concurrent users, the availability of space within the buffer and lock pools, and the balancing of access across processors all can affect database performance.

When a data warehouse accesses several remote databases in a single warehouse query, another dimension of complexity is added to the data warehouse. Not only must the database administrator (DBA) look at each individual database, but the DBA also must consider transactions that span several servers. While accessing several servers in a distributed warehouse query may seem trivial, performance problems can be introduced by PC hardware, LAN and network bottlenecks, router overloads, and many other sources. Let's take a look at distributed data warehouses and examine how they differ from traditional data warehouse environments.

A Definition Of Distributed Databases

There is an ongoing debate over the standard definition of distributed database systems, and to muddy the waters further, vendors have implemented distributed database technology in different manners. To many database vendors, a distributed database is a geographically distributed system composed entirely of one brand of database products. On the other hand, front-end applications vendors define a distributed database as a system distributed architecturally, using a blend of database products and access methods. Finally, to hardware vendors, a distributed database is a system composed of different databases running on the same hardware platforms.

So, the question remains—What is a distributed database? The most widely accepted, general definition of distributed databases was developed by Chris J. Date, the popular author and coinventor of the relational database model. In his definition, Chris Date defined the following 12 characteristics of a distributed database:

- Local autonomy
- No reliance on a central site
- Continuous operation
- Location independence
- Fragmentation independence
- Replication independence
- Distributed query processing
- Distributed transaction management (update processing)
- Hardware independence
- Operating system independence
- Network independence
- Database independence

A distributed database contains all 12 of these characteristics. Let's take a look at each one.

Local Autonomy

Local autonomy means that data in the distributed network is owned and managed by local hosts. For example, a site in California could have a remote database that participates in a national distributed system. While functioning as a part of the nationally distributed network, the California database continues to process local operations, independent from the overall distributed system.

No Reliance On A Central Site

Ideally, all sites are equally remote, in the sense that no one site has governing authority over another node in the distributed network. Each site retains its own data dictionary and security, and each site functions as an independent database management system.

Continuous Operation

While each site maintains a unique identity and controls its own database management system, the site also functions as part of a unified federation. Functioning as a part of a larger system enables remote systems to access information from the site in a seamless fashion. Continuous operation refers to the ability of each node to be available to the overall system 24 hours per day, 7 days per week. To accomplish this goal, remote sites may use Oracle's hot backups to back up the database while it remains available for update by other nodes in the distributed system.

Location Independence

End users do not necessarily know, or care, about the physical location of each component in a distributed database. In a distributed database, information can be retrieved without specifically referencing physical locations, making the database appear to end users as a unified whole.

Fragmentation Independence

Fragmentation independence refers to the ability of end users to store logically related information at different physical locations. There are two types of fragmentation independence: vertical partitioning and horizontal partitioning. *Horizontal partitioning* allows for different rows of the same table to be stored at different remote sites. This is commonly used by organizations that maintain several branch offices, each with an identical set of table structures. *Vertical partitioning* refers to the ability of a distributed system to fragment information such that the data columns from the same logical tables are maintained across a network.

Replication Independence

Replication is the ability of a database to create copies of a master database at remote sites. These copies are called *snapshots* within Oracle, and a snapshot may contain an entire database or any component of a database. For example, in an Oracle data warehouse, a fact table may be replicated by geographic region, and copies of subsets of the fact tables could reside at different locations for the northern region, southern region, and so on. Remember, disk space is cheap, and data warehouse replication at different geographic locations can dramatically improve response times for end users. In addition, subsets of a fact table may be specified, such that only specific rows and columns appear in a replicated table, and the replicated items are refreshed on a periodic basis.

Distributed Query Processing

Within Oracle, distributed query processing is much more than the ability to execute a query against more than one database. In Oracle, a distributed query splits the execution, sharing resources from each Oracle instance. In Oracle warehouses, a distributed query might query data items from widely distributed databases in a single query. For example, consider the following:

```
SELECT CUSTOMER.name, CUSTOMER.address, ORDER.order_number,
    ORDER.order_date
    FROM CUSTOMER@tokyo, ORDER@paris
        WHERE
        CUSTOMER.customer_number = ORDER.customer_number;
```

Let's assume that the query is initiated from an Oracle database in New York. The retrieval of the rows from Tokyo and Paris will take place using the resources on their respective Oracle instances, while the New York host will perform the merge join of the results from the customer and order queries.

Distributed Transaction Management (Update Processing)

Distributed transaction management refers to Oracle's ability to manage an **UPDATE**, **INSERT**, or **DELETE** operation on multiple databases using a single query. Oracle uses a common mechanism called a *two-phase commit* to implement this process. The two-phase commit ensures that remote databases have successfully completed their sub-updates before the entire transaction is committed to the database. A failure at one of the remote databases will cause the entire transaction to fail. To avoid transaction failures, some new techniques now allow partial **COMMIT**s, which store the unavailable updates and applies them as soon as the unavailable database is online.

For example, consider a distributed database with a **CUSTOMER** table residing in New York and an **ORDER** table residing in Paris. The control mechanisms for the database ensure that the business rules for related tables are maintained even though component data resides on different processors. When a user attempts to add a row to the **ORDER** table in Paris, the Oracle manager can be made to check the referential integrity to ensure that the customer exists in the **CUSTOMER** table in New York.

Hardware Independence

Hardware independence refers to the ability to query and update information regardless of the hardware platform on which the data resides. For example, a single query initiated on a PC might retrieve information from an IMS on a mainframe, a Lotus database on a PC, and an Oracle database on a midrange host.

Operating System Independence

In a truly distributed database, a query should not be dependent on any operating system. For example, a distributed database should have no problem allowing PC-based queries to be entered from either MS-DOS or OS/2 systems, and users should be able to access databases residing on MVS/ESA, Unix, or any other operating system.

Network Independence

Network protocols should not be an issue for distributed databases, and Oracle has included a multiple community feature as part of SQL*Net to address different protocols. Oracle allows LU6.2 nodes to coexist with TCP/IP protocols, and automatic conversion routines allow synchronous channels (such as those on IBM mainframes) to communicate in the asynchronous world of Unix.

Database Independence

Database independence refers to the ability to retrieve and update information from many different database architectures. Oracle implements this feature via its gateway products that allow communication with legacy databases.

Types Of Database Distribution

As mentioned earlier, *distributed database* means something different to different database designers. Furthermore, there are several flavors of distributed databases.

Each type of database has unique characteristics and unique solutions. By taking a careful look at each type of distributed database, we can shed some light on the major issues of distributed databases. Oracle supports all of the following types of distributed databases. There are actually very few types of data distribution that cannot be implemented with Oracle.

Geographical Distribution (Horizontal Distribution)

Geographical distribution refers to several databases that run under the control of different processors, as shown in Figure 9.1. In terms of database distribution, it is irrelevant whether the databases are separated by several inches or several thousand miles. In fact, it is possible to have a distributed database architecture within a single machine, as in the case of an SMP system with a quadratic processor. Numerous Unix processors have several CPUs contained within the box, and separate database systems can be run on each half of the CPU. Each database enjoys the benefit of an isolated processor, but distributed database communication tools such as Oracle's SQL*Net are required to make the processors communicate with each other.

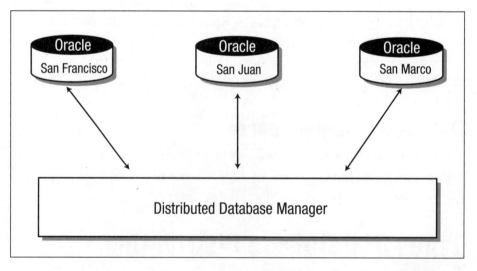

Figure 9.1
Geographically distributed databases.

Platform Distribution (Vertical Distribution)

Platform distribution refers to the existence of databases that reside on a diversity of hardware platforms (see Figure 9.2). An example would be a FoxPro system on a PC-LAN using DB2 to communicate with a mainframe. Platform distribution is often used with client/server software applications so shared databases can be distributed to PCs connected to wide area networks.

Architectural Distribution

Architectural distribution, shown in Figure 9.3, refers to distributed databases that involve different database architectures, many of which are not relational. Examples of architectural distribution include an object-oriented database that communicates with a relational database or a CODASYL database that communicates with a hierarchical database.

Contrary to popular opinion, architectural distribution can be the simplest form of database distribution to implement. By using the language preprocessors that come with a database, it is simple to embed commands for each of the databases in an architecture into a single program. When the program is compiled, each preprocessor is invoked, and the database calls are replaced by native calls. Using this method,

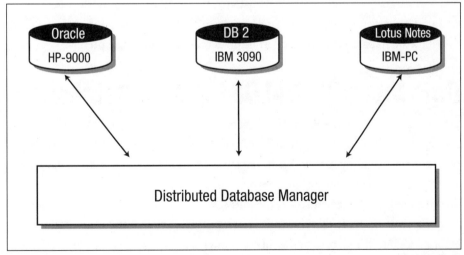

Figure 9.2
Platform database distribution.

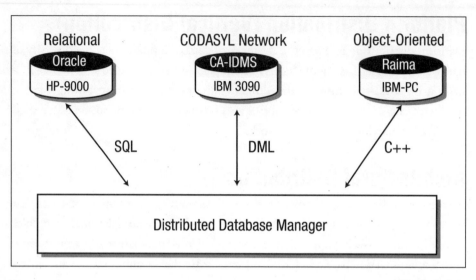

Figure 9.3
Architectural database distribution.

a programmer can write a batch program that simultaneously communicates with a relational database and a non-relational database. For example, a JCL job stream on MVS could easily make Oracle MVS communicate with an IMS database. This approach is commonly used in the "master-slave" distributed database model where a master database is updated and a daily batch COBOL program reads this database and updates several query-only databases in a different architecture. Master-slave distributed databases are discussed in more detail later in this chapter.

Data Integrity And Distributed Databases

Data integrity refers to the ability of a distributed Oracle warehouse to manage concurrent updates to data in many physical locations while ensuring that all of the data is physically and logically correct. While data integrity is managed very effectively within a single database with row locking, deadlock detection, and roll-back features, distributed data integrity is far more complex. Recovery in a distributed database environment involves ensuring that the entire transaction has completed successfully before issuing a **COMMIT** to each of the subcomponents in the overall transaction. This can often be a cumbersome chore, and the issue of the two-phase commit is addressed in detail later in this text. One popular alternative to the two-phase commit is replicating information and relying on asynchronous replication techniques to enforce the data integrity. Asynchronous replication refers to Oracle snapshots and requires a master-slave type of configuration, whereby a master database relays updates to the slave database on a periodic basis (using Oracle snapshots to create master-slave replication is discussed in more detail later in this chapter). The snapshot approach makes sense when an overall system does not require instant integrity.

Data Partitioning

When a single Oracle database is split into separate entities, we sometimes see a schema where tables are split into smaller tables. These tables may reside within the same schema as the other pieces of the tables, or they may reside on other Oracle databases.

Because the smaller table pieces are no longer a part of the base schema, distributed SQL can be issued across a horizontal partition that treats each table as if it were a single entity. This technique uses Oracle's SQL*Net distributed communications facility, and anytime you see a table name ending with **@location**, you can assume that you are dealing with a distributed Oracle transaction. Horizontal partitioning refers to the ability of the system to store similar information at many sites while the information continues to maintain its sameness with other information in the network. In an Oracle warehouse, this might mean, for example, that some rows from a fact table may reside in Paris while other rows from the fact table reside in London. From the viewpoint of the application, the fact table appears as a unified table. Oracle provides many tools to assist in this process, using remote update capabilities, stored procedures, and database triggers. Vertical partitioning refers to splitting columns from a table into different locations. For example, an employee table might be vertically partitioned to move the salary column into a secured database where the data is protected from nosey coemployees.

The following SQL demonstrates how the SQL **UNION** operator is used to reassemble partitioned tables. Here we see two employee tables being queried as if they were a single table:

```
SELECT *
FROM    EMPLOYEE@tucson
UNION
SELECT *
```

```
FROM    EMPLOYEE@albuquerque
ORDER BY eMP_ID;
```

In vertical partitioning, tables can also be reassembled into a single entity by using SQL to re-add the desired columns. In the following example, we can query the employee salary, which is kept as a separate partition in Dallas:

```
SELECT EMPLOYEE.emp_id, emp_name, phone, salary
FROM EMPLOYEE@denver, EMPLOYEE@phoenix, SALARY@dallas
ORDER BY emp_id;
```

Figure 9.4 shows an example of horizontal and vertical partitioning.

Note that table partitioning is not always used with distributed databases. You may choose to partition a very large fact table according to month to make the indexes easier to manage, while leaving the horizontal partitions within the same schema. However, there are some benefits to distributing tables, and these benefits will be

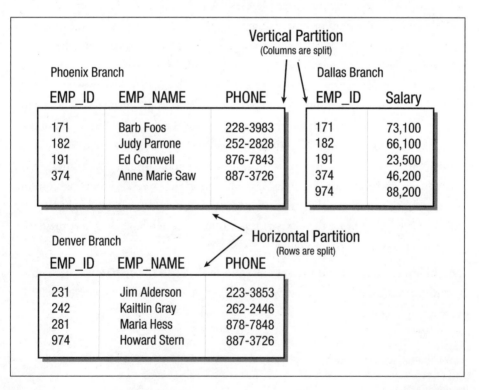

Figure 9.4
The two types of data partitioning.

addressed in detail later in this chapter. While vertical and horizontal partitioning are helpful for Oracle data warehouses, both methods suffer from some drawbacks. Because each database continues to maintain two identities—one for the local location and another for the overall federation—response times can vary widely depending on the local demands on the tables. There is also the problem of data dependence. Unlike a replicated distributed database, a failure at any one of the remote nodes makes a part of the overall system unavailable.

Location Transparency

Location transparency refers to the ability of a distributed database to function as a unified whole and appear to end users as if they are accessing a single database. The end users of a distributed warehouse most likely do not care where data resides or what access method the database invokes to service their queries. Location transparency is rather complex, and it becomes even more complex when we are dealing with distributed transactions among different relational databases. While many third-party vendors have achieved this type of transparency, it is not without cost. Even a distributed system composed entirely of relational databases still has to deal with variances in each database's "100% ANSI compliant" SQL. As we see in Figure 9.5, the tools must translate the dialect of each database vendor's SQL.

One of the most pressing problems with distributed databases is managing the various dialects of SQL. Every major database vendor adds features and extensions to the standard SQL, ostensibly to improve their implementation of SQL. Consequently, any queries that use special features may fail in a distributed multivendor architecture.

SQL dialect problems are even more aggravating when the distributed database is composed of databases from non-relational architectures. Sophisticated techniques must be used to interrogate a distributed query to identify which data components reside in which architectures. Then, sub-queries must be decomposed into appropriate access languages (see Figure 9.6).

Implementing Location Transparency With Oracle

To clarify location transparency further, let's consider the following example. Assume we have a parts inventory system with separate databases in London, Paris, Washington, and Albuquerque. The manager wishes to know the number of clocks

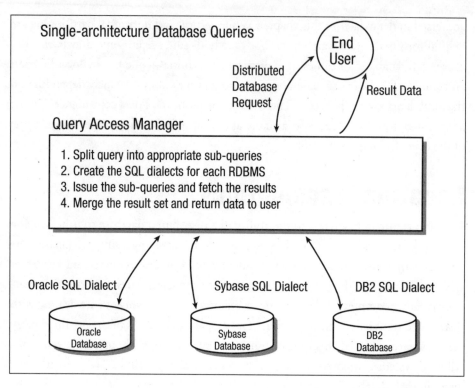

Single-architecture Database Queries

Distributed Database Request

End User

Result Data

Query Access Manager

1. Split query into appropriate sub-queries
2. Create the SQL dialects for each RDBMS
3. Issue the sub-queries and fetch the results
4. Merge the result set and return data to user

Oracle SQL Dialect

Sybase SQL Dialect

DB2 SQL Dialect

Oracle Database

Sybase Database

DB2 Database

Figure 9.5

Relational architectural distribution.

on hand in all of the locations and issues the following SQL command to the distributed database manager:

```
SELECT count(*) FROM PART WHERE partname = 'clock';
```

This example is called a *global transaction*, and the end user does not know or care what databases are interrogated to satisfy the request. In this example, it is the responsibility of the database to query all of the distributed **INVENTORY** tables, collect the counts from each table, and merge the responses into a single result set. Using Oracle SQL*Net, location transparency is achieved by creating database links to the remote database and then assigning a global synonym to the remote tables.

Database links are created with a link name that corresponds to a Transparent Network Substrate (TNS) name, which is declared in the **USING** clause of the database link statement. In the following example, the link name is *london*, which

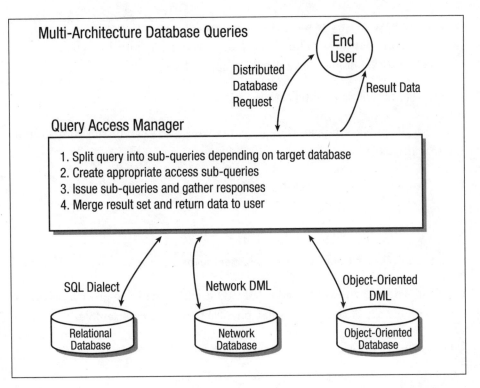

Figure 9.6

Multiple database architecture database queries.

corresponds to a TNS name of *london_host*. The **london_host** string is then looked up in the tnsnames.ora file, and the host name, database name, and protocol are gathered.

```
SQL>   CREATE PUBLIC DATABASE LINK london
       CONNECT TO london_user IDENTIFIED BY secret_password
           USING london_host;
```

Now that we have defined the database link, we can now include any tables from the London sites by qualifying the remote site name directly in the SQL query.

```
SELECT    CUSTOMER.customer_name,
          ORDER.order_date
   FROM   CUSTOMER@london,
          ORDER
   WHERE
   CUSTOMER.cust_number = ORDER.customer_number;
```

Because we have to specify **CUSTOMER@london**, we have not yet achieved real location transparency. The DBA may assign a public synonym for **CUSTOMER@london** to make the query appear local.

```
CREATE PUBLIC SYNONYM CUSTOMER FOR CUSTOMER@london;
```

Now that the public synonym is in place, the same query can be run with location transparency, as follows:

```
SELECT    CUSTOMER.customer_name,
          ORDER.order_date
   FROM   CUSTOMER,
          ORDER
   WHERE
   CUSTOMER.cust_number = ORDER.customer_number;
```

Oracle stored procedures can also be defined for remote tables so procedures can be called without referencing other tables' physical locations. For example:

```
CREATE PROCEDURE add_customer ( cust_name char(8) ) AS
BEGIN
   INSERT INTO CUSTOMER VALUES (cust_name);
END;
```

This procedure could be called with the statement **add_customer("Tytler, Sarah")**.

Oracle Domains And Location Transparency

Many Oracle warehouse designers recognize the need to track the locations of remote databases while, at the same time, provide location transparency to end users and programmers. Oracle domains are especially important in situations of horizontal partitioning, where tables with identical names are kept at numerous locations. Domains establish a logical hierarchy of physical locations for an enterprise. The sample database depicted in Figure 9.7 shows how a domain hierarchy can be established for remote databases.

Each database in a distributed federation can have a synonym assigned for all unique tables within the distributed network. In situations where duplicate table structures exist at many locations, abbreviated domains can be created. For example, assume that both Japan and Ohio have a **CUSTOMER** table, identical in structure but containing different rows. We could assign Oracle synonyms as follows:

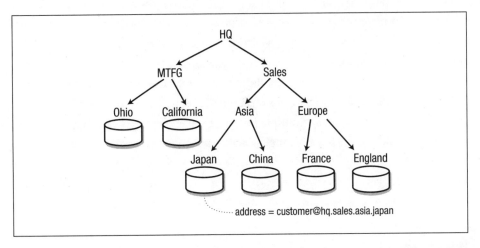

Figure 9.7
An Oracle TNS domain name hierarchy.

```
CREATE SYNONYM georgia_customer FOR
      CUSTOMER@georgia;

CREATE SYNONYM arizona_customer FOR
      CUSTOMER@arizona;
```

Table Replication Techniques

One of the easiest ways to improve warehouse availability is with data replication. In order to bypass many of the problems inherent with network communications, data is copied and stored in multiple Oracle databases. Mainly, warehouses replicate information to improve reliability and maximize query response times. As you may know, in a client/server environment, it is often difficult to get all of the data to all of the users who require the information. It is also difficult to balance processing requirements between light data users (e.g., online transaction processing systems) and heavy data users (e.g., data warehouse systems for marketing). Data replication is often a desirable choice when processing requirements demand that online systems get fast response times while intensive I/O analysis is performed concurrently against the same information.

Another benefit of table replication is that if there is a failure with one of the component databases, the replicated database information remains available. This type of data replication is commonly called *data distribution*. Data distribution is not always the same as a distributed database. With data distribution, information can be redundantly copied to another database, whereas in "true" distributed databases the information is not replicated even though the data may reside in many databases. As mentioned earlier, some installations create master-slave replication, where a master database is used for updating multiple query, or slave, databases each day. The master-slave method usually has a "change" database that keeps track of all changes made to the master database. When the time comes to propagate the changes to the slave databases, a background task is triggered to copy the data, and the changed entries are then removed from the change database.

Master-Slave Oracle Replication

Using Oracle snapshots to create master-slave replication has become a very popular method for distributing warehouse data. In order to create a master-slave configuration with Oracle, the following three steps are required:

1. Define and populate the slave database, using copies of the table descriptions from the master catalog tables. This is done with the **CREATE SNAPSHOT** command.

2. Create the propagation routines on the host database, and establish host gateways into the slave databases. This is done with the **REFRESH** clause of the **CREATE SNAPSHOT** statement.

3. Define snapshot log tables to hold updates that will be propagated from the original table to the replicated table.

The foremost concern when creating snapshots is the time interval in which the replicated tables will be refreshed. Data warehouse developers use database replication because they cannot afford the overhead of instant database updates (the two-phase commit issue). When using replication, developers must determine the length of the time lag between master database updates and slave table updates. Some data warehouse developers choose to allow updates to occur at predefined time intervals (say, each day), ensuring that updates occur when the time interval is reached. Another approach is to base slave table updates on the level of activity in the slave databases. A predefined threshold can be defined to start the slave updates when all of the slave databases fall below the activity threshold. This method allows slave tables to be updated when they are not busy, but, on the downside, end users can never be sure about the currency of their slave database. One interesting approach to this problem is to have each slave database automatically poll the master when it is not busy to see if there are any updates awaiting propagation.

When using Oracle snapshots, developers also have to face the issue of what to do when a slave database becomes unavailable. Should the update proceed to update only the available slave databases, or should the update wait until all slave databases are online and available for updating? If the developer chooses the simpler of the two methods—waiting for all slave databases to be available—then the developer takes the risk that a major failure of one slave database will affect the currency of the other slave databases. The developer will also have to account for the possibility that a transaction may abort due to some shortage of database resources (i.e., shortage in storage area, shortage of available tablespace, and so forth) and the previously made changes to the slave databases will have to be rolled back.

On the other hand, if developers choose to propagate changes regardless of availability, the change propagation subsystem must be able to track the changes to each slave database. The most common approach for slave tracking is to have the propagator task reference a change table that keeps a list of all changes and a set of flags to indicate which slave databases have been updated. Only after all of the slave databases are successfully updated will a row be deleted from the change database.

Another popular approach for warehouse replication is to avoid the use of Oracle snapshots and simply copy the tables using the Oracle **export/import** utility. Updates are achieved by rerunning nightly warehouse population jobs once for each replicated table.

Replication And Referential Integrity

If a distributed Oracle database uses table replication such that the business rules span physical databases, then we need to address the maintenance of referential integrity (RI). A problem with RI sometimes occurs when periodic updates to replicated tables violate some business rules. For example, consider the simple business rule that no customers may be deleted if they still have outstanding orders in the order table. While this rule can be maintained easily in the master database, what happens when the dependent tables are replicated? (See Figure 9.8.) If a local task on a slave database deletes a row for a customer named *Smith,* it may do so without the knowledge that orders exist on the master database for customer Smith.

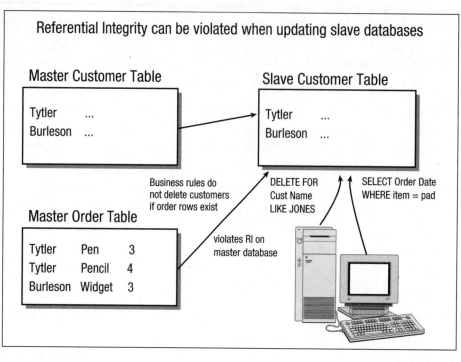

Figure 9.8
Replication and referential integrity.

There are two methods that an Oracle developer can use to solve the problem of maintaining referential integrity while using table replication. The first method is to run a query against the master order table to see if rows exist for a particular customer. The second solution is to feed the slave task back to the master database so Oracle can detect the RI violations.

Realtime Table Updates

An alternative to refreshing our replicated tables once each day is to synchronize the master database with the slave database and have all updates instantly propagated to all replicated tables. The choice between refreshing and synchronization depends on the volatility of the data and the currency needs of the user community. For example, a static, nonchanging database can easily be refreshed daily, provided that the end users understand that their data is only current to within 24 hours. For highly dynamic databases with constantly changing information, a synchronization scheme can be developed, but it is important to remember that there can be tremendous overhead when updating a replicated database. The overhead is especially noticeable when system indexes are updated. Indexes share a common root node, so performance can degenerate if updates are being applied while an index tree reconfigures itself to accommodate new data. Speaking from experience, it is often faster to refresh a small database hourly than to incur the performance problems that accompany realtime updating.

Some warehouses choose to completely refresh their replicated tables. This is done by either dropping and re-copying the replicated table or using the **REFRESH COMPLETE** clause of the **CREATE SNAPSHOT** statement. For example:

```
CREATE SNAPSHOT UNFILLED_orders
       REFRESH COMPLETE
       START WITH to_date ('DD-MON-YY' HH23:MI:55)
       NEXT sysdate + 7
AS
SELECT customer_name, customer_address, order_date
FROM CUSTOMER@paris, ORDER@london
WHERE
    CUSTOMER.cust_number = ORDER.customer_number
AND
  order_complete_flag = "N";
```

Here, you can see that a snapshot will be taken on Monday at 11:55 PM, and, thereafter, every seven days. The end users will be told about the refreshing period, and the database software will automatically perform the extract. The DBA could also perform the extract manually by issuing the following command:

```
EXECUTE UNFILLED_ORDERS.refresh_all;
```

Now, let's take a detailed look at how Oracle snapshots are used to replicate tables.

Table Replication With Oracle Snapshots

Oracle snapshots are used to create read-only copies of tables in other Oracle databases. This is a highly effective way to avoid expensive cross-database joins of tables. As you probably know, an SQL join with a table at a remote server is far slower than a join with a local table because SQL*Net overhead increases as it retrieves and transfers data across a network.

> *Note:* *For more information about table replication utilities see Chapter 10, Oracle Data Warehouse Utilities.*

It is interesting to note that the general attitude about data replication has shifted dramatically in the past 10 years. In the 1980s, replication was frowned upon. Database designers believed that there was no substitute for the third normal form database. Today, the practical realities of distributed processing have made replication a cheap and viable alternative to expensive cross-database joins.

Table replication is so stable and has been so successful within Oracle version 7 that Oracle is now introducing the concept of updatable snapshots with Oracle version 7.3. However, replication is not to be used without justification, and the following guidelines exist for using replicated tables to the best advantage:

- *Replicated tables should be read-only.* Obviously, a table snapshot cannot be updated because the master copy of the table is on another server.

- *Replicated tables should be relatively small.* Ideally, a replicated table is small enough that the table can be dropped and re-created each night, or the **REFRESH COMPLETE** option can be used. Of course, large tables can be replicated with the **REFRESH FAST** option, but this involves a complicated mechanism for holding table changes and propagating them to the replicated table.

- *Replicated tables should be used frequently.* It does not make sense to replicate a table if it is only referenced a few times per day, and the cost of the replication would outweigh the cost of the cross-database join.

Despite any claims by Oracle to the contrary, snapshots are not to be used indiscriminately. Only tables that meet the above criteria should be placed in snapshots. In practice, snapshots are not maintenance-free, and many points of failure are possible—especially if the snapshot is created with the **REFRESH FAST** option. Problems can occur while writing to the **SNAPSHOT_LOG** table, and SQL*Net errors can cause update failures to transfer to the replicated tables.

How Oracle Snapshots Work

A snapshot is created on a destination system with the **CREATE SNAPSHOT** command, and the remote table is immediately defined and populated from the master table.

After creation, a snapshot may be refreshed periodically. There are two types of refreshing: complete and fast. A *complete refresh* can be done in several ways, but most savvy Oracle developers drop and re-create snapshots using a Unix **cron** job to achieve full refreshes, especially if the table is small and easily re-created. Optionally, a *fast refresh* can be used, which refreshes tables with only the changes made to the master table. This requires additional work on the slave database to create an Oracle refresh process (in the init.ora) and the definition of a snapshot log on the master database (see Figure 9.9).

Several steps need to be completed before your Oracle data warehouse is ready to use snapshots. First you need to run CATSNAP.SQL, which can be found in your $ORACLE_HOME/rdbms/admin directory. This script will populate the Oracle dictionary with the necessary system tables to manage the snapshots. You'll also need to run DBMSSNAP.SQL, which can also be found in the $ORACLE_HOME/rdbms/admin directory. This script creates the stored procedures that can be used to manipulate the snapshots. In addition, the following parameters must be added to the init.ora file before your Oracle data warehouse can use snapshots:

- **SNAPSHOT_REFRESH_INTERVAL=60**—This sets the interval (in minutes) for the refresh process to wake up.

- **SNAPSHOT_REFRESH_PROCESSES=1**—This is the number of refresh processes on the instance (the minimum is 1 refresh per instance).

- **SNAPSHOT_REFRESH_KEEP_CONNECTIONS=FALSE**—This specifies whether the database should keep remote connections after refreshing the tables. Always use **FALSE**.

For snapshots small enough to be totally repopulated, the following steps are necessary. Note that it is possible to do a **REFRESH COMPLETE** or a **REFRESH FORCE** rather than a **cron** job, but using a **cron** is a simple way to guarantee that the replicated table will be fully repopulated. (A **cron** job is a method of scheduling tasks inside Unix.) Oracle also allows the **REFRESH FAST** option as an alternative to fully repopulating the replicated table. With **REFRESH FAST**, Oracle keeps copies of all of the table changes and moves them to the replicated table at intervals that are specified when the snapshot is created. To avoid the **REFRESH FAST** option with a Unix **cron**, the following two steps are required:

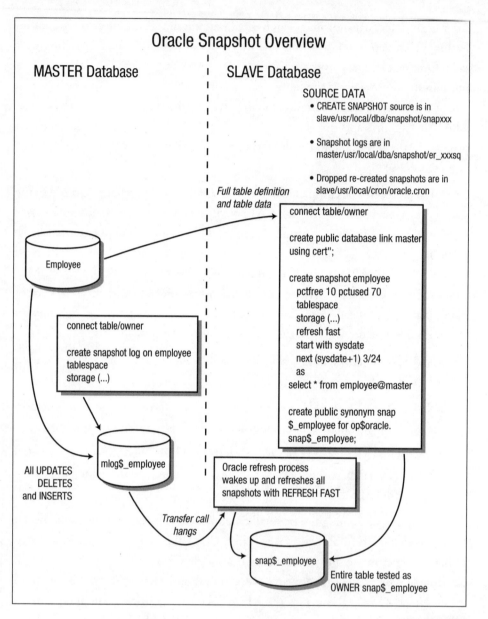

Figure 9.9
A high-level overview of Oracle snapshots.

1. Create the snapshot with the **REFRESH COMPLETE** option.

2. Alter oracle.cron to drop and re-create the snapshot.

For snapshots on large tables, you may want to use the **REFRESH FAST** option. For **REFRESH FAST**, the following three steps are required:

1. *On the destination system*—Create the snapshot with the **REFRESH FAST** option signed on as user **SYS**. (Be sure to define a database link with **CONNECT TO XXX IDENTIFIED BY ZZZ** and ensure that user **XXX** has **SELECT** privileges against the master table.

2. *On the master system* —Create a snapshot log on each master table.

3. Bounce the **DESTINATION SYSTEM** to begin the refreshes based on the interval specified in the **CREATE SNAPSHOT** statement.

Listing 9.1 shows a sample snapshot.

Listing 9.1   An example of a snapshot that reads a table from an instance called *london*.

```
CONNECT sys/xxxx;
DROP PUBLIC DATABASE LINK london;
CREATE PUBLIC DATABASE LINK london
CONNECT TO db_link IDENTIFIED BY db_pass USING 'london';
----------------------------
DROP SNAPSHOT MY_REPLICATED_TABLE;
----------------------------
CREATE SNAPSHOT MY_REPLICATED_TABLE
        PCTFREE 10 PCTUSED 40
        TABLESPACE TS2
        STORAGE (INITIAL 60K NEXT 10K PCTINCREASE 1)
        REFRESH FAST
                START WITH sysdate
                NEXT (sysdate+1) + 3/24
        AS SELECT * FROM ORACLE.MY_MASTER_TABLE@london;

GRANT ALL ON MY_REPLICATED_TABLE  TO PUBLIC;
--********************************************************
--    Add the appropriate synonyms for the snapshots...
--********************************************************
CONNECT /;
CREATE PUBLIC SYNONYM snap$_MY_REPLICATED_TABLE
FOR ops$oracle.snap$_MY_REPLICATED_TABLE;
```

Here, you can see that **MY_REPLICATED_TABLE** is refreshed each morning at 3:00 AM, and the read-only name **SNAP$_ MY_REPLICATED_TABLE** has been replaced with the synonym **MY_REPLICATED_TABLE**. Following is an example of the snapshot log syntax that needs to be run on the master database:

```
CREATE SNAPSHOT LOG ON CUSTOMER_TABLE
TABLESPACE TS2
STORAGE (INITIAL 20K NEXT 20K);
```

The **dbms_snapshot.refresh_all** procedure can be run at any time on the destination data warehouse to refresh the snapshot tables. To force a refresh of an individual table, execute the following:

```
EXECUTE dbms_snapshot.refresh('office','f');
```

> **Note:** Any refresh errors are written to the alert.log file.

The snapshot log is a table that resides in the same database as the master table, which can be seen in the **DBA_TABLES** view as a table with the name **MLOG$_tablename**. In our example, the snapshot log would be called **MLOG$_CUSTOMER**.

Real-World Tips And Techniques For Oracle Snapshots

Even with Oracle's distributed features, it is still far faster to process a table on a local host than it is to process a remote table across SQL*Net's distributed communication lines. As such, table replication is a very desirable technique for improving processing speeds.

Several factors influence the decision about replicating tables. The foremost considerations are the size of replicated tables and the volatility of the tables. Large, highly active tables with many updates, deletes, and inserts require a lot of system resources to replicate and keep the tables synchronized with the master table. Smaller, less active tables are ideal candidates for replication, because the creation and maintenance of the tables will not consume a high amount of system resources.

Oracle's snapshot facility is relatively mature, and it generally works as noted in the Oracle documentation. However, the flexibility of the snapshot tool gives developers many choices in how snapshots can be created and refreshed. Developers can refresh a replicated table in full, re-create a snapshot at will, choose periodic refreshes of a snapshot, and use database triggers to propagate changes from a master table to a snapshot table. While the choice of techniques depends on individual applications, some general rules apply.

If a replicated table is small and relatively static, it is usually easier to drop and re-create a snapshot than to use Oracle's **REFRESH COMPLETE** option. A crontab file can be set up to invoke a drop and re-create at a predetermined time each day, completely refreshing the entire table.

Another popular alternative to the snapshot is using Oracle's distributed SQL to create a replicated table directly on the slave database. In the following example, the New York database creates a local table called **EMP_NY**, which contains New York employee information from the master employee table at corporate headquarters:

```
CREATE TABLE EMP_NY
AS
    SELECT
            emp_nbr,
            emp_name,
            emp_phone,
            emp_hire_date
    FROM EMP@hq WHERE department = 'NY';
```

Very large replicated tables consume too much time when dropping and re-creating the snapshot or using the **REFRESH COMPLETE** option. For static tables, a snapshot log would not contain very many changes—you could direct Oracle to propagate the changes to the replicated table at frequent intervals. Let's take a look at some different refresh intervals that can be specified for a snapshot.

In the first example, Oracle is instructed to take the snapshot log and apply it to the replicated table every seven days:

```
CREATE SNAPSHOT CUST_SNAP1
REFRESH FAST
    START WITH sysdate
    NEXT sysdate+7
AS SELECT cust_nbr, cust_name FROM CUSTOMER@hq WHERE department = 'NY';
```

The next example shows a table that is refreshed each Tuesday at 6:00 AM:

```
CREATE SNAPSHOT CUST_SNAP1
REFRESH FAST
```

```
        START WITH sysdate
        NEXT next_day(trunc(sysdate),'TUESDAY')+6/24
AS SELECT cust_nbr, cust_name FROM CUSTOMER@hq WHERE department = 'NY';
```

For very static tables, designers can specify refreshes to run quarterly. The following example refreshes a table completely on the first Tuesday of each quarter:

```
CREATE SNAPSHOT CUST_SNAP1
REFRESH COMPLETE
        START WITH sysdate
        NEXT next_day (ADD_MONTHS(trunc(sysdate,'Q'),3),'TUESDAY')
AS SELECT cust_nbr, cust_name FROM CUSTOMER@hq WHERE department = 'NY';
```

For dynamic tables that require refreshing daily, designers can specify that a table is refreshed at 11:00 AM each day:

```
CREATE SNAPSHOT CUST_SNAP1
REFRESH FAST
        START WITH sysdate
        NEXT sysdate+11/24
AS SELECT cust_nbr, cust_name FROM CUSTOMER@hq WHERE department = 'NY';
```

In addition to using a time range specified in the **CREATE SNAPSHOT** syntax, you can also use Oracle stored procedures to achieve the same results. If you run the dbmssnap.sql script, you can refresh a snapshot by issuing the following command:

```
EXECUTE dbms_snapshot.refresh('customer','c');  /* complete refresh */
EXECUTE dbms_snapshot.refresh('customer','f');  /* forced   refresh */
EXECUTE dbms_snapshot.refresh('customer','?');  /* fast     refresh */
```

Using Triggers To Update Snapshots

But what about replicated tables that require faster propagation? Oracle version 7.3 offers updatable snapshots, but users of previous releases of Oracle can use database triggers to simulate the realtime propagation of changes from a master table to replicated tables. In the following example, an update trigger is placed on a customer table, and relevant changes will be propagated to the New York branch:

```
CREATE TRIGGER ADD_CUSTOMER
        AFTER INSERT ON CUSTOMER
AS
```

```
IF :dept = 'NY' THEN
(INSERT INTO CUSTOMER@NY
    VALUES(:parm1, parm2,:parm3);
);
```

But, what can we do about rows that are deleted from the customer table? Using the same technique, a delete trigger can be placed on the customer table to remove rows from the replicated tables as follows:

```
CREATE TRIGGER DELETE_CUSTOMER
    AFTER DELETE ON CUSTOMER
AS
IF :dept = 'NY' THEN
(DELETE FROM CUSTOMER@NY
    WHERE
    cust_nbr = :customer_parm
);
```

Using Snapshots To Propagate Subsets Of Master Tables

As you have seen, snapshot replication is very handy for taking a master and copying it to a remote location. But, what if we only want to replicate a portion of the tables? Fortunately, Oracle provides a method for excluding certain rows and columns from replicated tables. For example, let's assume we are replicating a central employee table for use by our New York branch. However, we only want to replicate employee records for those who work at the New York branch, and we want to exclude confidential columns, such as the employee's salary. The snapshot would appear as follows:

```
CREATE SNAPSHOT EMP_NY
REFRESH FAST
    START WITH sysdate
    NEXT next_day(trunc(sysdate),'TUESDAY')+6/24
AS
    SELECT
            emp_nbr,
            emp_name,
            emp_phone,
            emp_hire_date
    FROM EMP@hq WHERE department = 'NY';
```

Warehouse Table Partitioning And Distributed Oracle

In data warehouses that allow cross-database access, a very common method of distribution uses horizontal partitioning. For example, customer service organizations commonly allow their remote sites to maintain customer information while maintaining a location-transparent access mode to every customer, regardless of their physical location. Horizontal partitioning is achieved by taking a subset of each remote site's customer table and populating a master look-up table that is accessible from any node in the distributed data warehouse, as shown in Figure 9.10.

In a Unix-based distributed data warehouse, the **cron** utility can be used to schedule a periodic refresh of a master table. An SQL script automatically extracts **customer_name** from the remote site and repopulates the master customer table, leaving the customer details at the remote site. The Oracle SQL might look like this:

```
/*  Delete remote rows in the master table... */

DELETE FROM CUSTOMER@master
WHERE
location = :OUR_SITE;

/*  Repopulate the master table...  */

SELECT customer_name, ':our_site'
FROM CUSTOMER@:OUR_SITE
AS
INSERT INTO CUSTOMER@master
VALUES CUSTOMER_NAME, site_name;
```

Once populated, the master look-up can be accessed by any node and used to redirect the database query to the appropriate remote database for customer detail, as shown in Figure 9.11.

Because of the dynamic substitution in the SQL, a common application can be made to access any customer in a federation, regardless of location, without making any changes to the application code.

Dynamic transparency is especially useful for situations where remote locations have "ownership" of data, but a corporate entity requires access to the data at a central location.

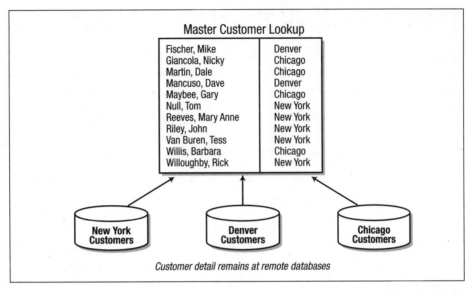

Figure 9.10

Horizontal data partitioning.

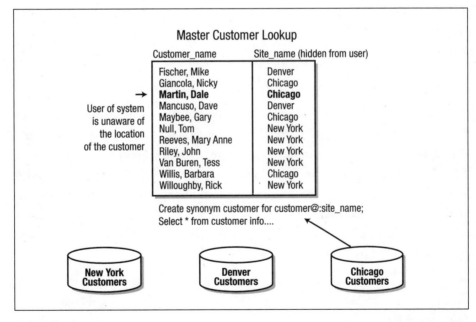

Figure 9.11

Dynamic location transparency.

The Internals Of Oracle's SQL*Net

In its most basic form, SQL*Net is a software tool that allows a network of Oracle clients and servers to communicate transparently on top of any underlying network topology or protocol using SQL. Although SQL*Net is a very robust and sophisticated tool, you must appreciate the inherent complexity that goes along with the flexibility of SQL*Net. This section provides a no-nonsense overview of the SQL*Net architecture. All of the examples are based on Unix.

Due to its sophisticated architecture, it is not trivial to install SQL*Net on a client or server. For Unix systems, the following files are necessary to operate SQL*Net 2.0:

- *etc/tnsnames.ora*—Used for outgoing database requests, this file contains all of the database names (sids) running on the processor, as well as the domain name, protocol, host, and port information. When a new database is added to a box, you must update this file (changes to tnsnames.ora become effective instantly). Note that the SQL*Net version 1.0 file equivalent is etc/oratab.

- *etc/listener.ora*—This file contains a list of local databases for use by incoming connections. When you add a new destination database to a Unix host, you must also add it to this file.

- *etc/hosts*—This file lists all of your network addresses.

- *etc/services*—This file lists all of the SQL*Net services.

In version 2.0, Oracle has added several important enhancements to SQL*Net. Aside from the badly needed bug fixes, SQL*Net now allows multiple community access. A *community* is a group of computers that shares a common protocol (such as TCP/IP to LU6.2). In addition, the Oracle database engine now defines a multithreaded server (MTS) for servicing incoming data requests. In the MTS, all communications to the database are handled through a single dispatcher. In SQL*Net version 1.0, a separate process is spawned for each connection. These connections are easily viewed by using the Unix **ps** command.

When upgrading from SQL*Net 1.0 to SQL*Net 2.0, you should be aware of subtle differences between how the two versions handle communications (see Figure 9.12). SQL*Net version 1.0 uses an **orasrv** component on the destination database to listen for incoming requests, while SQL*Net 2.0 uses a process called **tnslsnr** (TNS listener). In addition, SQL*Net 1.0 cannot use the multithreaded server.

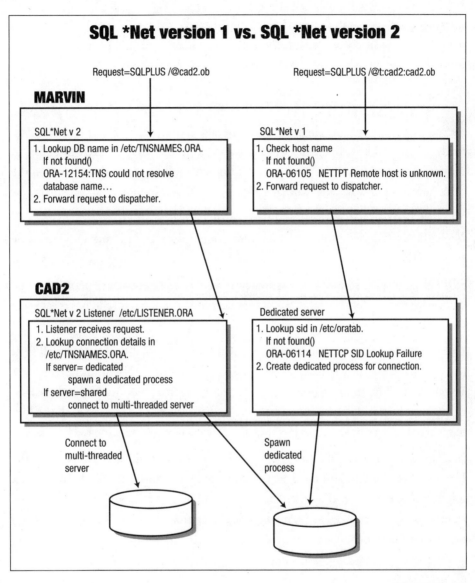

Figure 9.12
The two versions of SQL*Net.

When a connection is made to SQL*Net, it passes the request to its underlying layer—the transparent network substrate (TNS)—where the request is transmitted to the appropriate server. At the server, SQL*Net receives the request from TNS and passes the SQL to the database. *Transparent network substrate* is a fancy phrase meaning a single, common interface to all protocols that allows you to connect to databases in physically separate networks. At the lowest level, TNS communicates to other databases with message-level send and receive commands.

On the client side, the User Programmatic Interface (UPI) converts SQL to associated **PARSE**, **EXECUTE**, and **FETCH** statements. The UPI parses the SQL, opens the SQL cursor, binds the client application, describes the contents of returned data fields, executes the SQL, fetches the rows, and closes the cursor. Oracle attempts to minimize messages to the server by combining UPI calls whenever possible. On the server side, the Oracle Programmatic Interface (OPI) responds to all possible messages from the UPI and returns requests.

No UPI exists for server-to-server communication. Instead, a Network Programmatic Interface (NPI) resides at the initiating server, and the responding server uses its OPI.

SQL*Net supports network transparency such that the network structure may be changed without affecting the SQL*Net application. Location transparency is achieved with database links and synonyms.

Let's trace a sample data request through SQL*Net. Essentially, SQL*Net will look for the link name in the database link table (**DBA_DB_LINKS**) and extract the service name. The service name is then located in the tnsnames.ora file, and the host name is extracted. Once again, we have a two-stage process beginning with the link name referencing the service name, then the service name referencing the host name.

In Unix environments, the host name is found in a host file (etc/hosts), and the Internet Protocol (IP) address is gathered. In the following example, **london_unix** might translate into an IP address of 143.32.142.3. The following four steps illustrate how SQL*Net takes a remote request and translates it into the IP address of a destination database:

1. *Issue a remote request.* Check the database link called **LONDON**.

   ```
   SELECT * FROM CUSTOMER@london
   ```

2. *Database link.* Get the service name (**london_unix_d**) using the **link_name** (**LONDON**).

   ```
   CREATE PUBLIC DATABASE LINK london
   CONNECT TO london_unix_d;
   ```

3. *tnsnames.ora*. Get the sid name (**london_sid**) using service name (**london_unix_d**).

```
london_unix_d = (description=(address=(protocol=tcp) (host=seagull)
(port=1521) (connect_data=(sid=london_sid) (server=dedicated))))
```

4. *etc/hosts*. Get the IP address (143.32.142.3) using the sid name (**london_sid**).

```
143.32.142.3     london_sid          london_unix.corporate.com
```

As you can see, this translation occurs in a multistage process. The tnsnames.ora file specifies the name of the host containing the destination database. For Unix environments, the host name is then looked up in the etc/hosts file to get the IP address of the destination box.

The service name is looked up in tnsnames.ora. If the service exists, the IP address is found in the etc/hosts file and a communications request is sent to the destination IP address. Note that both of the entries in this file connect to London, but **london_unix_d** directs SQL*Net to spawn a dedicated process, while **london_unix** uses the multithreaded server component because a shared server is specified.

Now that you have the tnsnames.ora and etc/hosts files in place, you can include any tables from the London sites by qualifying the remote site name in the SQL query. For example:

```
SELECT CUSTOMER.customer_name, ORDER.order_date
   FROM CUSTOMER@london, ORDER
   WHERE CUSTOMER.cust_number = ORDER.customer_number;
```

This query joins two tables at different locations, and the database link called *london* determines how the Oracle connection will be established on the destination system. Regardless of how the connection is made to the destination, however, the user ID must have **SELECT** privileges against the customer table, or this query will fail.

Establishing SQL* Net Sessions

On systems running SQL*Net version 2.0, the session script can be used to query the number of dedicated and shared servers on the system. For example, Listing 9.2 shows an SQL*Plus script to view all sessions.

Listing 9.2   session.sql displays all connected sessions.

```
SET ECHO OFF;
SET TERMOUT ON;
SET LINESIZE 80;
SET PAGESIZE 60;
SET NEWPAGE 0;
TTITLE "dbname Database|UNIX/Oracle Sessions";
SPOOL /tmp/session
SET HEADING OFF;
SELECT 'Sessions on database '||substr(name,1,8) from v$database;
SET HEADING ON;
SELECT
        substr(B.serial#,1,5) ser#,
        substr(B.machine,1,6) box,
        substr(B.username,1,10) username,
        substr(B.osuser,1,8) os_user,
        substr(B.program,1,30) program
FROM V$SESSION B, V$PROCESS A
WHERE
B.paddr = A.addr
AND TYPE='USER'
ORDER BY spid;
TTITLE OFF;
SET HEADING OFF;
SELECT 'To kill, enter SQLPLUS>  ALTER SYSTEM KILL SESSION',
''''||'SID, SER#'||''''||';' FROM DUAL;
SPOOL OFF;


[oracle]ram2: sqlx session

Wed Sep 14

                                                 Page    1
                                            ram2db Database
                                          Sessions for SQL*Net


SERVER      Oracle user  O/S    User   Machine Program
------      -----------  ----   -----  ----------------



DEDICATED   SYS          oracle ram2   sqldba@ram2 (Pipe Two-Task)

DEDICATED   OPS$REDDY    risdon ram2   runform30@ram2 (Pipe Two-Task)
```

```
DEDICATED   GLINT        jones    ram2   sqlplus@ram2 (Pipe Two-Task)

DEDICATED   OPS$ORACLE   oracle   clt2   sqlplus@clt2 (TNS interface)

DEDICATED   OPS$JOKE     joke     ram2   ?  @ram2 (TCP Two-Task)

DEDICATED   OPS$WWRIGHT  wwright  ram2   runmenu50@ram2 (Pipe Two-Task)

DEDICATED   OPS$ORACLE   oracle   ensc   sqlplus@ensc (TCP Two-Task)

DEDICATED   SECTION144   OraUser         C:\PB3\PBSYS030.DLL

DEDICATED   OPS$ORACLE   oracle   ram2   sqlplus@ram2 (Pipe Two-Task)

DEDICATED   OPS$JSTARR   jstarr   ram2   sqlforms30@ram2 (Pipe Two-Task)

DEDICATED   OPS$WWRIGHT  wwright  ram2   RUN_USEX@ram2 (Pipe Two-Task)


12 rows selected.
```

Here, we see each of the following four types of SQL*Net connections:

- *Pipe Two-Task*—Used for internal tasks (**SQLPLUS /**).

- *TNS Interface*—Used when connection is made with a v2 service name (**SQLPLUS /@ram2**).

- *TCP Two-Task*—Used when connection is made with a v1 *connect string* (**SQLPLUS /@t:ram2:ram2db**).

- *PC Connection Task*—Denoted by the PC DLL name (c:\pb3\pbsys030.dll = initiated via PowerBuilder DLL).

Application Connection With SQL*Net

Now that we have seen how SQL*Net connections are made to Oracle, let's take a look at how an application specifies a remote database. Connections to remote databases can be made by specifying either *service names* or *connect strings*. Connect strings use the full connection. In the following example, the **t:** means a TCP/IP connection, **host:** is the name of the remote processor, and **database:** is the name of the databases on that processor:

- Connect with a service name.

```
EMP@my_db
```

- Connect with a server connect string.

```
sqlplus /@t:host:database
```

- Connect strings are stored in the **DBA_DBLINKS** table, and they are created with the **CREATE DATABASE LINK** command.

```
CREATE PUBLIC DATABASE LINK ny_emp FOR NY_EMP@t:myhost:mydatabase
```

SQL*Net For Oracle Distributed Data Warehouses

SQL*Net can establish database communications in three ways: remote connection, remote request, or distributed request. A *remote connection* is the easiest way to make a database connection. The sending database simply makes a request by specifying a table name suffixed by @. SQL*Net takes it from there, seamlessly accessing the remote database and returning the data to the initiating system. Communication is established by making a distributed request to a remote database. Within Oracle, @ specifies the remote database name, but the functionality of the @ operator depends upon where it is used. Here's an example:

```
sqlplus scott/tiger@london

SELECT count(*) FROM EMPLOYEE;

COUNT(*)
--------
     162
```

In this request, **scott** is using the Oracle SQL*Plus command line interface to connect to the London database, and **@london** is the service name, as defined in the tnsnames.ora file. SQL*Net recognizes this as a remote connection and determines the appropriate linkage to establish communications with London. Internally, Oracle will check the tnsnames.ora file to ensure that **london** is a valid destination.

Now, observe another way of connecting to London from the same database. This is called a *remote request:*

```
sqlplus scott/tiger
SELECT count(*) FROM EMPLOYEE@london;

COUNT(*)
--------
     162
```

Unlike a remote connection made directly from SQL*Plus, this remote request has **scott** connecting to the local copy of SQL*Plus to specify the remote table (in this case, **EMPLOYEE@london**). In order for a remote request to work, a database link must define **london**. As mentioned earlier, a database link is a connection pathway to a remote database that specifies the service name of the remote database. Without the database link, the following request would fail:

```
sqlplus scott/tiger
SELECT count(*) FROM EMPLOYEE@london;
```

This request will give you an error message that reads: *ORA-02019: connection description for remote database not found.* This message is received because of the way Oracle defines the @ operator. When entering an Oracle service such as SQL*Plus, the @ operator will go directly to the tnsnames.ora file to manage the request, while the @ operator from within an Oracle program specifies the use of a database link.

To make the code functional, you must define a database link that specifies the service name used to establish the connection. Note that the database link name and the service name are the same in this example, but the database link and the connect descriptor are not related in any way:

```
CREATE DATABASE LINK london USING 'london';
SELECT count(*) FROM EMPLOYEE@london;

COUNT(*)
-------
     162
```

Let's take a closer look at the database link. In this simple example, no mention is made of the user ID used to establish the connection on the remote database.

Because **scott** is the user connecting to SQL*Plus, Scott will be the user ID when the remote connection is established to the London database. Therefore, **scott** must have **SELECT** privileges against the employee table in London in order for the query to work properly. **scott's** privileges on the initiating Oracle have no bearing on the success of the query.

> **Note**: If you are using the Oracle Names facility, you must be sure that your database service names are the same as the **global_databases_names** and the **DOMAIN** init.ora parameter.

In cases where **SELECT** security is not an issue, you can enhance the database link syntax to include a remote connect description, as follows:

```
CREATE DATABASE LINK london USING 'london'
CONNECT TO scott1 IDENTIFIED BY tiger1;
```

This way, all users who specify the **london** database link will connect as **scott1** and will have whatever privileges **scott1** has on the London system.

Once you establish a communications pathway to the remote database, it is often desirable to implement location transparency. In relational databases such as Oracle, you can obtain location transparency by creating database links to the remote database and then assigning a global synonym to the remote tables. The database link specifies a link name and an SQL*Net service name. You can create database links with a location suffix that is associated with a host name (in this example, **london**).

You can use database links to allow applications to point to other databases without altering the application code. For data warehousing applications, you can replicate a table on another machine and establish links to enable the application to point transparently to the new box containing the replicated table.

To see the links for a database, query the Oracle dictionary, as follows:

```
SELECT DISTINCT db_link FROM dba_db_links;
```

Keep in mind that SQL*Net bypasses all operating system connections when it connects to a database. All externally identified user accounts (that is, accounts without an Oracle password) will not be allowed in SQL*Net transactions unless the init.ora parameter is changed. The identified externally clause (**OPS$**) in Oracle version 6 allows the operating system to manage passwords, but because SQL*Net bypasses the operating system, impostor accounts can be created from other platforms. The result is that security can be bypassed. Consequently, Oracle now recommends forbidding externally identified accounts when using distributed connections, and the **OPS$** feature is seldom used in Oracle7 or Oracle8.

It is interesting to note that Oracle will allow you to create accounts with an **OPS$** prefix. Therefore, the operating system can manage its passwords, while you also have passwords within Oracle. For example, assume the following user definition:

```
CREATE USER ops$scott IDENTIFIED BY tiger;
```

Assuming that **scott** has logged onto the operating system, **scott** could enter SQL*Plus either with or without a password, as follows:

```
sqlplus /
sqlplus scott/tiger
```

Understanding The SQL*Net Listener

To see what the Oracle listener is doing, Oracle provides a series of listener commands, including:

- *lsnrctl reload*—Refreshes the listener.

- *lsnrctl start*—Starts the listener.

- *lsnrctl stop*—Stops the listener.

- *lsnrctl status*—Shows the status of the listener.

Following is the output of a **lsnrctl** status command:

```
[oracle]ram2: lsnrctl stat

LSNRCTL for HPUX:Version 2.0.15.0.0 - Production on 16-SEP-94 15:38:00

Copyright (a)  Oracle Corporation 1993.  All rights reserved.

Connecting to (ADDRESS=(PROTOCOL=TCP)(HOST=ram2)(PORT=1521))
STATUS of the LISTENER
------------
Alias                     LISTENER
Version                   TNSLSNR for HPUX:Version 2.0.15.0.0-Production
```

```
Start Date              29-AUG-94 13:50:16
Uptime                  18 days 1 hr. 47 min. 45 sec
Trace Level             off
Security                OFF
Listener Parameter File /etc/listener.ora
Listener Log File       /usr/oracle/network/log/listener.log
Services Summary...
  dev7db                has 1 service handlers
  ram2db                has 1 service handlers
The command completed successfully


lsnrctl services      - lists all servers and dispatchers

[oracle]seagull: lsnrctl services

LSNRCTL for HPUX:Version 2.0.15.0.0-Production on 16-SEP-94 15:36:47

Copyright (a)  Oracle Corporation 1993. All rights reserved.

Connecting to (ADDRESS=(PROTOCOL=TCP)(HOST=dogpatch)(PORT=1521))
Services Summary...
  tdb000                has 4 service handlers
    DISPATCHER established:1 refused:0 current:2 max:55 state:ready
      D001 (machine: dogpatch, pid: 4146)
      (ADDRESS=(PROTOCOL=tcp)(DEV=5)(HOST=999.123.224.38)(PORT=1323))
    DISPATCHER established:1 refused:0 current:2 max:55 state:ready
      D000 (machine: dogpatch, pid: 4145)
      (ADDRESS=(PROTOCOL=tcp)(DEV=5)(HOST=999.123.224.38)(PORT=1321))
    DISPATCHER established:0 refused:0 current:1 max:55 state:ready
      D002 (machine: dogpatch, pid: 4147)
      (ADDRESS=(PROTOCOL=tcp)(DEV=5)(HOST=999.123.224.38)(PORT=1325))
    DEDICATED SERVER established:0 refused:0
The command completed successfully
```

As a service request is intercepted by an Oracle server, the listener may direct the request via a dedicated server, an MTS, or an existing process (pre-spawned shadow). The key is whether the connection contacts the listener via a service name or bypasses the listener with the **TWO_TASK** connect string. If the listener is contacted as part of the connection and the MTS parms are defined to init.ora, the client will use the MTS.

There are five basic listener commands: **RELOAD, START, STOP, STATUS,** and **SERVICES.** Based on the request, the listener decides whether to dispatch a connection to a dedicated-server process (which it spawns) or use the MTS. The programmer has several options when deciding how Oracle will manage the process. Dedicated requests can be specified by a version 1.0 connect string or by using a service name that specifies **server=dedicated** in the tnsnames.ora file.

> **Note**: *Local connections will use the listener if multithreaded servers are defined. Even internal invocations to Oracle (for example, **sqlplus/**) will add a connection to an MTS.*

Managing SQL* Net Connections

Listing 9.3 describes some of the utilities you can use to manage SQL*Net sessions effectively. You should be aware that some of the examples in this section are operation system-dependent and may not apply to your environment.

Listing 9.3   Commit point strength.

```
commit.sql -  Reports the commit point strength for the database.

SET FEEDBACK OFF
COLUMN NAME   FORMAT a30 HEADING 'Name'
COLUMN TYPE   FORMAT a7  HEADING 'Type'
COLUMN VALUE  FORMAT a60 HEADING 'Value'

PROMPT Commit Point-strength Report Output:
PROMPT
PROMPT
SELECT name,
       decode(type,1,'boolean',
                   2,'string',
                   3,'integer',
                   4,'file') type,
       replace(replace(value,'@','%{sid}'),'?','%{home}') value
FROM   V$PARAMETER
WHERE  name = 'commit_point_strength';
```

Managing A Multithreaded Server (MTS)

One of the problems faced by developers using SQL*Net version 1.0 was that each incoming transaction was spawned by the listener as a separate operating system task. With SQL*Net version 2.0, Oracle now has a method for allowing the listener connection to dispatch numerous sub-processes. With the MTS, all communications to a database are handled through a single dispatcher instead of separate Unix process IDs (PIDs) on each database. This translates into faster performance for most online tasks. Even local transactions will be directed through the MTS, and you will no longer see a PID for your local task when you issue **ps -ef|grep oracle**.

However, be aware that the MTS is not a panacea, especially at times when you want to invoke a dedicated process for your program. For Pro*C programs and I/O-intensive SQL*Forms applications—or any processes that have little idle time—you may derive better performance using a dedicated process.

In general, the MTS offers benefits such as reduced memory use, fewer processes per user, and automatic load balancing. However, it is often very confusing to tell whether the MTS is turned on—much less working properly.

Remember the following rules of thumb when initially starting the MTS:

- The MTS is governed by the init.ora parameters. If no MTS parms are present in init.ora, the MTS is disabled.

- The MTS is used when the MTS parms are in the init.ora and requests are made by service name (such as **@myplace**). In other words, you must retrieve the **ROWID** of all version 1.0 connect strings (such as **t:unix1:myplace**).

- Each user of the MTS requires 1 K of storage, so plan to increase your **SHARED_POOL_SIZE**.

- The **V$QUEUE** and **V$DISPATCHER** system tables indicate when the number of MTS dispatchers is too low. Even though the number of dispatchers is specified in the init.ora file, you can change it online in SQL*DBA with the **ALTER SYSTEM** command, as follows:

```
SQLDBA> ALTER SYSTEM SET MTS_DISPATCHERS = 'TCPIP,4';
```

- If you encounter problems with the MTS, you can quickly regress to dedicated servers by issuing an **ALTER SYSTEM** command. The following command turns off the MTS by setting the number of MTS servers to zero:

```
SQLDBA> ALTER SYSTEM SET MTS_SERVERS=0;
```

- In order to use **OPS$**, you must set two init.ora values to **TRUE** (they default to **FALSE**).

```
remote_os_authent = TRUE
remote_os_roles = TRUE
```

- When both SQL*Net 1.0 and 2.0 are installed, the user may connect to the server either via a dedicated server or the MTS. However, you cannot stop and restart the listener when connecting via the MTS. You must connect to SQL*DBA with a dedicated server.

- In some cases, the instance must be bounced if the listener is stopped, or the listener will restart in dedicated mode. Whenever an instance is to be bounced, stop the listener, shut down the instance, restart the listener, and start up the instance. The listener reads the MTS parameters only if it is running before the startup of the instance. Therefore, bouncing the listener will disable the MTS.

Managing The Listener Process

As mentioned earlier, the listener is a software program that runs on each remote node that listens for incoming database requests. When a request is detected, the listener may direct the request to any of the following:

- A dedicated server

- A multithreaded server

- An existing process or pre-spawned shadow

Note that the configuration of an Oracle listener is a direct result of the parameters specified in the startup deck for the Oracle database. This parameter file, called init.ora, contains the following parameters to define the multithreaded server and listener.

```
# -----------
# Multithreaded Server
# -----------

MTS_DISPATCHERS = "tcp,3"

MTS_LISTENER_ADDRESS = "(ADDRESS=(PROTOCOL=tcp) (HOST=dogpatch)
                                 (PORT=1521))"

MTS_MAX_DISPATCHERS = 5

MTS_MAX_SERVERS = 20
```

```
# -------------
# Distributed systems options
# -------------

DISTRIBUTED_LOCK_TIMEOUT = 60

DISTRIBUTED_RECOVERY_CONNECTION_HOLD_TIME = 200

DISTRIBUTED_TRANSACTIONS = 6
```

Managing Two-Phase Commits (2PCs) With SQL*Net

When a distributed update (or delete) has finished processing, SQL*Net will coordinate **COMMIT** processing, which means that the entire transaction will roll back if any portion of the transaction fails. The first phase of this process is a prepare phase to each node, followed by the **COMMIT**, and then terminated by a forget phase.

If a distributed update is in the process of issuing the 2PC and a network connection breaks, Oracle will place an entry in the **DBA_2PC_PENDING** table. The recovery background process (RECO) will then roll back or commit the good node to match the state of the disconnected node to ensure consistency. You can activate RECO via the **ALTER SYSTEM ENABLE DISTRIBUTED RECOVERY** command.

The **DBA_2PC_PENDING** table contains an **advice** column that directs the database to either commit or roll back the pending item. You can use the **ALTER SESSION ADVICE** syntax to direct the 2PC mechanism. For example, to force the completion of an **INSERT**, you could enter the following:

```
ALTER SESSION ADVISE COMMIT;
INSERT INTO PAYROLL@london . . . ;
```

When a 2PC transaction fails, you can query the **DBA_2PC_PENDING** table to check the **state** column. You can enter SQL*DBA and use the Recover In-Doubt Transaction dialog box to force either a roll back or a commit of the pending transaction. If you do this, the row will disappear from **DBA_P2C_PENDING** after the transaction has been resolved. If you force the transaction the wrong way (for example, roll back when other nodes committed), RECO will detect the problem, set the **MIXED** column to yes, and the row will remain in the **DBA_2PC_PENDING** table.

Internally, Oracle examines the init.ora parameters to determine the rank that the commit processing will take. The **COMMIT_POINT_STRENGTH** init.ora parameter determines which of the distributed databases is to be the commit point site. In a distributed update, the database with the largest value of **COMMIT_POINT_STRENGTH** will be the commit point site. The commit point site is the database that must successfully complete before the transaction is updated at the other databases. Conversely, if a transaction fails at the commit point site, the entire transaction will be rolled back at all of the other databases. In general, the commit point site should be the database that contains the most critical data. Listing 9.4 shows a script that will identify a two-phase commit transaction that has failed to complete.

Listing 9.4   pending.sql reports on any pending distributed transactions.

```
SET PAGESIZE 999;
SET FEEDBACK OFF;
SET WRAP ON;
COLUMN local_tran_id  FORMAT a22 HEADING 'Local Txn Id'
COLUMN global_tran_id FORMAT a50 HEADING 'Global Txn Id'
COLUMN state          FORMAT a16 HEADING 'State'
COLUMN mixed          FORMAT a5  HEADING 'Mixed'
COLUMN advice         FORMAT a5  HEADING 'Advice'

SELECT local_tran_id,global_tran_id,state,mixed,advice
FROM   DBA_2PC_PENDING
ORDER  BY local_tran_id;
```

Miscellaneous Management Tips For SQL*Net

Just as the etc/oratab file for SQL*Net version 1.0 is interpreted, the tnsnames.ora file is also interpreted. This means that you can change it at any time without fear of bouncing anything. However, changes to listener.ora require the listener to be reloaded with **lsnrctl reload***.*

When a database is accessed remotely via a database link, SQL*Net uses the temporary tablespace on the destination database, regardless of the processor invoking the task or the original database location. That way, SQL*Net will use the temporary tablespace on the destination database—not the initiating database. In other words, applications on one processor that access another processor with a database link will use the temporary tablespaces on the terminal processor—not the processor that contains the link.

- Always remember to change your *$ORACLE_HOME/bin/oraenv* file to unset **ORACLE_SID** and set **TWO_TASK=sid**.

- The following three logs appear in SQL*Net:

  - listener log—usr/oracle/network/log/listener.log

  - sqlnet log—usr/oracle/network/log/sqlnet.log

  - trace log—Destination set with the **TRACE_DIRECTORY_LISTENER** parameter of the etc/listener.ora file

  - Three levels of tracing are found in SQL*Net:

  - lsnrctl trace admin

  - lsnrctl trace user

  - lsnrctl trace off

- It is possible to run two listeners simultaneously, one for version 1.0 and another listener for version 2.0. If a version 1.0 connect string is sent, a version 1.0 listener (**tcpctl**) will be used. Conversely, if a TNS connect description is sent, the version 2.0 listener (**lsnrctl**) will be used. A connect description is the name of a database (such as **@mydata**), which maps to the tnsnames.ora on the sending side and listener.ora on the receiving side.

- It is essential to note that the functions of the **ORACLE_SID** and **TWO_TASK** variables have changed between SQL*Net versions 1.0 and 2.0. To use the MTS while you are local to the database, you should unset the **ORACLE_SID** variable and set the **TWO_TASK** to the SID name (**EXPORT TWO_TASK=mydb**). If the **ORACLE_SID** is active, you will still be able to connect—although you will not be able to take advantage of the MTS. You must change all login scripts and *$ORACLE_HOME/bin/oraenv* files to reflect this new functionality.

- We now have three ways to establish distributed database communications with MTS. We can choose from a shared service name (**sqlplus /@ram2db**) or a dedicated service name (**sqlplus /@d_ram2db**—prefixing the SID with **d_** will direct the listener to spawn a dedicated process for your program). And, we can also use a (**TWO_TASK**) server connect string (**sqlplus /@t:host:sid**). This latter approach will bypass the MTS and use a dedicated process.

As systems continue to evolve into complex distributed networks, inter-database communications will become even more complex, requiring even more sophisticated tools. While object-orientation promises to make inter-database communications simple, the DBA in the trenches will continue to struggle with implementing everyday distributed database communications.

Summary

Now that you understand how distributed databases function with table replication techniques, let's take a look in Chapter 10 at some of the specific types of utilities that can be used for the Oracle warehouse.

Oracle Data Warehouse Utilities

CHAPTER

10

HIGH PERFORMANCE

Oracle Data Warehouse Utilities

This chapter provides an overview of the Oracle utilities that can assist the Oracle Data Warehouse manager. The basic utilities are Oracle export/import utilities, the SQL*Loader utility, and the Oracle procedural gateway utilities. By virtue of the great size of Oracle data warehouses, extra discussion has been added about selectively repairing chained rows, determining extended tables, partitioning Oracle table rebuilding, and other methods for avoiding a wholesale reorganization of the Oracle data warehouse.

The older conventional wisdom stated that Oracle databases should be periodically reorganized to clean up extended tables and indexes. Extended tables and indexes impede performance and may reach maximum extents, causing database outages. In addition, Oracle indexes may become out of balance, and table rows may become chained, causing excessive I/O. Let's start by taking a tour of Oracle import/export utilities.

Oracle's Import/Export Utilities

In a traditional Oracle environment, the Oracle DBA would periodically use the Oracle export utility to archive the entire database to disk, drop the database, and completely rebuild the database using Oracle's import utility to read the export file. This had the net effect of putting the Oracle tables and indexes into a single extent and rebuilding the index trees. Now the conventional wisdom dictates that table and index extension is not bad, per se, and some Oracle experts have conducted tests that show extended tables sometimes outperform tables residing in a single extent. Therefore, table and index extension is not a sufficient reason for performing a database reorganization. Oracle data warehouse DBAs can appreciate this because databases are often far too large to be reorganized using the Oracle export/import utilities.

Before exploring export and import techniques, let's take a look at some SQL utilities that will help you determine when your database needs reorganization.

Note: For scripts to detect and correct out-of-balance indexes, see Chapter 8, Oracle Features For The Data Warehouse.

Table Row Fragmentation Utilities

Row fragmentation is one of the most problematic events that can happen to an Oracle system. Fragmentation commonly occurs when an SQL **UPDATE** operation lacks sufficient room to expand a row on its data block. When this happens, the row must extend onto the next available data block, causing an extra I/O when the row is accessed.

In Figure 10.1, the next five blocks are filled with rows. When an SQL **UPDATE** adds 1,500 bytes to row 1, the database chains to the next block. Finding no space, it then chains to the next block, and then the next block, before finding 1,500 bytes of free space on block four. The fragment is stored in block four, and a chain is established from the block header of block one to point to the next block header, and so on, until the fragment is located. Most databases have some type of "free list" at each block header to determine the total available space on each block.

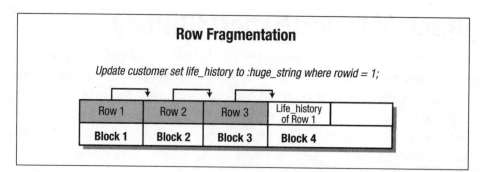

Row Fragmentation

Update customer set life_history to :huge_string where rowid = 1;

Row 1	Row 2	Row 3	Life_history of Row 1	
Block 1	**Block 2**	**Block 3**	**Block 4**	

Figure 10.1

An example of Oracle row chaining.

In order to retrieve the entire row, any subsequent retrieval of row one will require the database to perform four physical block I/Os. I/O time is usually the largest component of overall response time, so this type of row fragmentation can greatly reduce performance.

Several preventative measures can be taken to avoid this situation. If the row will eventually contain all of its column values, and the values are of fixed length, the table could be defined with the parameter **NOT NULL**. This reserves space in the row when it is initially stored. If the row contains variable length columns, then the **PCTFREE** parameter is increased to reserve space on each block for row expansion. By the way, this issue is not confined to Oracle. Most databases offer a utility that can be run periodically to check for row fragmentation. If row fragments are found, the data must be exported to a flat file, the table redefined with different storage parameters, and the table repopulated from the flat file.

Listing 10.1 contains a script, called *chain.sql.* This script detects the number of chained rows for all Oracle tables. Chain.sql consists of a series of queries that acquires a list of the Oracle tables and writes the **ANALYZE TABLE** syntax to an intermediate file. The intermediate file is then used to count the total number of chained rows found in the tables. A chained row occurs when an SQL **UPDATE** operation has increased the size of a row, causing it to fragment onto another data block.

Check Your optimizer_mode

*Running the script in Listing 10.1 creates table statistics that may force the use of the cost-based SQL optimizer. This can be prevented by ensuring that the init.ora file parameter **optimizer_mode** is set to RULE instead of CHOOSE.*

Listing 10.1   chain.sql shows all chained rows in the database tables.

```
set echo off;
set heading off;
set feedback off;
set verify off;

drop table chained_rows;
@/opt/oracle/product/7.1.6/rdbms/admin/utlchain.sql

--define owner = &tableowner
```

```
spool /opt/oracle/admin/adhoc/chainrun.sql;

SELECT 'analyze table ' || owner || '.' ||table_name ||
       ' list chained rows;'
FROM dba_tables
WHERE owner NOT IN ('SYS','SYSTEM');

spool off;

--!more chainrun.sql
@chainrun.sql

SELECT 'There are ' || count(*) || ' chained rows in this database.'
FROM chained_rows;

SELECT DISTINCT owner_name, table_name, count(*)
FROM chained_rows
GROUP BY owner_name, table_name;


prompt
prompt You may now query the chained_rows table.
prompt This table contains one row for each chained row.
prompt
prompt suggested query:   select table_name, head_rowid, timestamp
prompt                          from chained_rows
prompt
prompt Refer to Oracle Administrators guide page 22-8 for directions
prompt regarding cleaning-up chained rows.

@chain

ANALYZE TABLE ORACLE.PUMPDATA list chained rows;
ANALYZE TABLE ORACLE.SALESORG list chained rows;
ANALYZE TABLE ORACLE.EMP list chained rows;
ANALYZE TABLE ORACLE.LOB list chained rows;
ANALYZE TABLE ORACLE.PRODUCT list chained rows;
ANALYZE TABLE ORACLE.PAC1 list chained rows;
ANALYZE TABLE ORACLE.PAC12 list chained rows;
ANALYZE TABLE ORACLE.PAC23 list chained rows;
ANALYZE TABLE ORACLE.MGC list chained rows;
ANALYZE TABLE ORACLE.FILM_CODE list chained rows;
ANALYZE TABLE ORACLE.CUST_CAT list chained rows;
```

```
ANALYZE TABLE ORACLE.SALES_SUM list chained rows;
ANALYZE TABLE ORACLE.DEPT list chained rows;
ANALYZE TABLE ORACLE.BONUS list chained rows;
ANALYZE TABLE ORACLE.SALGRADE list chained rows;
ANALYZE TABLE ORACLE.DUMMY list chained rows;

SQL>
SQL> spool off;
SQL>
SQL> @chainrun.sql
SQL> select 'analyze table ' || owner || '.' ||table_name || ' list
     chained rows;'
SQL>   2  from dba_tables
SQL>   3  where owner not in ('SYS','SYSTEM');
SQL>

SQL> analyze table ORACLE.LOB list chained rows;
SQL> analyze table ORACLE.PRODUCT list chained rows;
SQL> analyze table ORACLE.PAC1 list chained rows;
SQL> analyze table ORACLE.PAC12 list chained rows;
SQL> analyze table ORACLE.PAC23 list chained rows;
SQL> analyze table ORACLE.MGC list chained rows;
SQL> analyze table ORACLE.FILM_CODE list chained rows;
SQL> analyze table ORACLE.CUST_CAT list chained rows;
SQL> analyze table ORACLE.SALES_SUM list chained rows;
SQL> analyze table ORACLE.DEPT list chained rows;
SQL> analyze table ORACLE.BONUS list chained rows;
SQL> analyze table ORACLE.SALGRADE list chained rows;
SQL> analyze table ORACLE.DUMMY list chained rows;
```

Listing 10.2 shows the results from the script shown in Listing 10.1.

Listing 10.2   The results from the chain.sql script.

```
There are 16784 chained rows in this database.

SQL>
SQL> select distinct owner_name, table_name, count(*)
  2  from chained_rows
  3  group by owner_name, table_name;

ORACLE                  SALESMAN                    16784
ORACLE                  SALES                         432
ORACLE                  CUST                       126744
```

So, now that we have identified the tables with chained rows, what can we do? Remember, row fragmentation is caused by a failure to reserve enough room on the database block for row expansion. The remedy involves the following steps:

1. Export the chained row table.

2. Drop the table.

3. Re-create the table definition with a higher **PCTFREE** value.

4. Import the rows from the export file using the **ignore=y** parameter.

As you can see, in addition to reconsolidating the chained rows, we must ensure that the new table reserves enough free space to accommodate updates to column values without fragmenting the row in the future. If an export/import is not feasible, the **PCTFREE** can be altered for the existing table, ensuring that new rows on new data blocks will have extra free space. This is done by changing the value of the **PCTFREE** clause of the Oracle **CREATE TABLE** statement. For example:

```
sql > Alter table fact_97  storage (pctfree 30);
Table Altered.
```

> *Note*: For a detailed description of the Oracle table parameters, see Chapter 8, Oracle Features For The Data Warehouse.

Now, let's examine a simple technique for determining which tables are approaching the maximum extent value.

Table Fragmentation Utilities

Again, it needs to be emphasized that table fragmentation does not cause performance problems. Rather, it is the row chaining that often accompanies table fragmentation that seriously impedes performance. In fact, some Oracle DBAs have reported that extended tables (without row chaining) sometimes outperform tables that reside in a single extent.

Listing 10.3 shows a simple script that can be run to see the number of times a table has extended.

Listing 10.3 tblexts.sql lists all tables with more than 10 extents.

```
set pause off;
set echo off;
set linesize 150;
set pagesize 60;

column c1  heading "Tablespace";
column c2  heading "Owner";
column c3  heading "Table";
column c4  heading "Size (KB)";
column c5  heading "Alloc. Ext";
column c6  heading "Max Ext";
column c7  heading "Init Ext (KB)";
column c8  heading "Next Ext (KB)";
column c9  heading "Pct Inc";
column c10 heading "Pct Free";
column c11 heading "Pct Used";
break on c1 skip 2 on c2 skip 2

ttitle "Fragmented Tables";

SELECT  substr(seg.tablespace_name,1,10) c1,
        substr(tab.owner,1,10)           c2,
        substr(tab.table_name,1,30)      c3,
        seg.bytes/1024                   c4,
        seg.extents                      c5,
        tab.max_extents                  c6,
        tab.initial_extent/1024          c7,
        tab.next_extent/1024             c8,
        tab.pct_increase                 c9,
        tab.pct_free                     c10,
        tab.pct_used                     c11
FROM    sys.dba_segments seg,
        sys.dba_tables   tab
WHERE   seg.tablespace_name = tab.tablespace_name
  AND   seg.owner = tab.owner
  AND   seg.segment_name = tab.table_name
  AND   seg.extents > 10
ORDER BY 1,2,3;
```

Listing 10.4 shows the results of the script shown in Listing 10.3.

Listing 10.4   The results from the tblexts.sql script.

```
SQL> @tblexts

Thu Mar 14

                                                    page    1
                                              Fragmented Tables


Tablespace Owner  Table     Size  Alloc  Max   Init  Next Pct Pct  Pct
                            (KB)  Ext    Ext   Ext   Ext  Inc Free Used
                                         (KB)  (KB)

---------- -----  ------    ----- -----  ---   ----  ---- --- ---- ---
ORACLE     CUST   UST_CAT   5800  58     249   100   100   0  20   40
SYSTEM     SYS    AUD$      1724  11     249   12    840  50  10   40
                  CHAINED_ROWS 684 57    249   12    12    0  10   40
                  SOURCE$   1724  11     249   12    840  50  10   40
```

Warehouse Backups Using Oracle's Export/Import Utilities

When we examine the backup and recovery of an Oracle data warehouse, we generally find that the Oracle warehouse runs in two modes: read-only mode during the processing day, and update mode at night when the tables are being refreshed with new data. Most Oracle data warehouses are refreshed periodically. In addition, there can be different configurations during Oracle load processing versus query processing. During query processing, the database is generally optimized for queries, and it is not uncommon to see Oracle's recovery mechanisms disabled. Oracle provides several sophisticated mechanisms for read consistency and roll forward.

Read consistency is defined as Oracle's ability to "fix" a query, such that a 30-minute query will retrieve data as it exists when the query starts, even if the information changes while the query is running. Oracle implements read consistency by referring to the online redo logs whenever a requested data item has been changed during a query, and the "old" value for the data is read from the online redo log. Of course, using the online redo logs adds to the overhead for Oracle.

Another source of update overhead occurs when Oracle archives the online redo logs. Redo logs store the before and after images of all rows that have been added, modified, or deleted. In addition, the redo log contains log checkpoints such as begin-job, end-job, commit, and abort checkpoints for every transaction that runs under Oracle. As redo logs fill, Oracle directs the online log to be archived to a disk file. Periodically, these archived redo logs are written to tape media in case the Oracle database administrator needs to use them for a roll forward. (Oracle allows a database to be recovered in the case of disk failure even if some time has passed since the last backup. Oracle keeps track of all changes to the database with online redo logs, and writes these logs to flat files where they can be applied to the database, thereby re-creating the transactions that happened since the last backup. This process is called a *roll forward*.)

These features are essential for maintaining the integrity of an updated Oracle database, but they are not necessary when your Oracle data warehouse is running in read-only mode. As such, many Oracle DBAs configure their data warehouses to use Oracle's read-only tablespaces. Read-only tablespaces allow a tablespace to avoid the time-consuming operations of writing to the online redo logs. In addition, many Oracle data warehouses are run in **NOARCHIVELOG** mode, and roll-forward operations are performed by rerunning the nightly update routines. For more information about read-only tablespaces, see Chapter *8, Oracle Features For The Data Warehouse.*

Oracle Export/Import Data Warehouse Issues

Many vendor tools can aid in database reorganization, but generally, Oracle administrators write a script that exports all tables within a tablespace, re-creates the tablespace, and then imports and compresses the tables and indexes into a single extent. However, be forewarned that referential integrity (RI) may make it difficult to drop a tablespace. *Referential integrity* occurs when one tablespace contains a table that has a foreign-key constraint from a table in another tablespace.

Most often, the administrator will reorganize the entire database, performing the following steps:

1. Export the full database.

2. Generate the create database script.

3. Generate a list of data files to remove.

4. Remove the data files.

5. Create the database.

6. Import the full database.

7. Bounce the database and, optionally, turn on archive logging.

When Oracle's export utility is executed, the parameters may specify a set of tables or an entire database to be exported. The exports are governed by the values in a parameter file, as shown in Listing 10.5. In the following example, we see the entire database is exported without the index.

Listing 10.5 A sample of an Oracle export parameter file.

```
USERID=SYSTEM/warehouse
CONSTRAINTS=Y
BUFFER=102400
GRANTS=Y
INDEXES=N
ROWS=Y
COMPRESS=N
FULL=Y
LOG=full_tranp1.log
```

We can also specify a range of tables in an export, as shown in Listing 10.6. This feature is especially useful for Oracle data warehouses due to the large size of the database and the constraints surrounding online file sizes in Unix.

Listing 10.6 An export parameter file with selected tables.

```
SYSTEM/warehouse
VOLSIZE=0
LOG=shpmt.log
GRANTS=Y
ROWS=Y
CONSTRAINTS=Y
INDEXES=Y
COMPRESS=N
tables=RPT.LOB_SHPMT_ALLOC,
       RPT.LOB_SHPMT,
       RPT.SHPMT
```

Issues Of Scale With Export/Import

Oracle database reorganization is problematic as the database grows in size. Any time an export file grows larger than 2 GB, the file can no longer be stored on disk because of the 2 GB file size limit imposed by the Unix operating system. For export files larger than 2 GB, one of several alternatives must be chosen:

- Direct the export to a tape device. A tape device can hold a very large export file, but tape can be an unreliable medium.

- Run the Oracle export through a compressed pipe. This tactic increases the runtime slightly, but it greatly reduces the size of the compressed file. This is useful for a 3 GB file than can be compressed into 1.5 GB to make it fit onto disk. Unfortunately, compression does not guarantee that the compressed file will be less than 2 GB, so this method will not work for compressed files that are larger then 2 GB.

- Partition the export into small chunks by specifying table names. The drawback of partitioning is that it is time consuming for database administrators.

Let's take a quick look at each export option.

Exporting To Tape

The option of writing an export to a tape device is undesirable for several reasons. First, tape media is far more unreliable than disk, and there is always the possibility that a medium failure could prevent a successful import. Another consideration is speed. Oracle import operations run faster when importing from a disk than when importing from a tape. Consequently, DBAs should take a closer look at the disk file options.

Compressing Oracle Exports

Following is a sample compressed export job using Unix **crontab** to submit the compressed export:

```
crontab entry: 00 05 * * 0 /apps/oracle/admin/mysid/exp/exp_full 2>&1
```

This C shell script will compress small Oracle data warehouses (those where the export file will fit into 2 GB) and can be run on a scheduled basis.

Listing 10.7 shows a complete C shell script for running an Oracle export through a named pipe. Note that the script is fully parameterized, which means it can be re-used on many systems simply by changing the variable declarations in the beginning of the script.

Listing 10.7 A sample compressed Oracle export.

```csh
#! /bin/csh
# Copyright (c) 1994 by Don Burleson
set path = ( . $path /var/opt/bin )
setenv ORAENV_ASK  NO


#*********************************************************
# user-defined variables are here . . .
#*********************************************************
setenv ORACLE_SID mysid
setenv EXPORT_HOME /apps/oracle/admin/mysid/exp
setenv EXPORT_DATA /disk7/ORACLE/MYSID/exp
setenv EXP_FILE $EXPORT_DATA/full_weekly_$ORACLE_SID.dmp
setenv EXP_LOG $EXPORT_HOME/full_$ORACLE_SID.log
setenv PARMFILE exp_full.parms
setenv DBA_MAILBOX your.email.address
#*********************************************************

source /var/opt/bin/coraenv
cd $EXPORT_DATA

set RM = /bin/rm
set MAIL = mail

set clobber
unset noclobber
unalias rm

if ("'whoami'" != "oracle") then
   echo 'You must be the ORACLE user to run this.'
   echo 'Please change your UNIX ID and try again.'
   exit
endif

#
#    STEP1.  Remove the old export file and pipe.
#

 if (-e    $EXP_FILE) then
   $RM -f $EXP_FILE
 endif

echo 'Starting export at ' 'date' > $EXP_LOG

# STEP2 is optional, and is intended to ensure that the database
# will not be updated while the export is running.
```

```
#
#      STEP2.   startup restrict
#
#sqldba <<! >> $EXP_LOG
#   connect internal;
#   shutdown abort;
#   startup restrict;
#   exit;
#!
#
#      3.  Full export of the db files in this instance.
#

# Create the named pipe
        mknod $EXP_FILE p
# Others in your group may need to use it, too.
        chmod g+w $EXP_FILE

# Set up the compress to pipe in the background. It will wait for
# the export. Take what's in the pipe and use as input to the
# compress command. Output it to the compressed file name of choice.
# Note the '&'.

 (compress < $EXP_FILE > $EXP_FILE.Z &) > $EXP_LOG

# Perform the export to the named pipe. Compress is waiting for it.
# Don't put this in the background because we want to wait for it
# to finish and test to see if it ran ok.

cd $EXPORT_HOME
exp FILE=$EXP_FILE parfile=$PARMFILE >>& $EXP_LOG

# Did it give any errors?
set EXP_RC = $status

if ($EXP_RC == 0) then
   echo 'Ending export at ' 'date' >> $EXP_LOG
   $MAIL -s 'MPTVI Full export ran OK' $DBA_MAILBOX
else
   echo 'Export FAILED at ' 'date' >> $EXP_LOG
   echo 'Export FAILED at ' 'date'
   $MAIL -s 'MPTVI Full export FAILED' $DBA_MAILBOX
endif

echo 'Ending job at ' 'date' >> $EXP_LOG

exit
```

Following is the parameter file for the export shown in Listing 10.7:

```
USERID=SYSTEM/secret_password
CONSTRAINTS=Y
BUFFER=102400
GRANTS=Y
INDEXES=N
ROWS=Y
COMPRESS=N
FULL=Y
LOG=full_mysid1.log
```

Let's briefly explore the functions in Listing 10.7. As you can see, the first step of the script is to ensure that the Unix user ID is set to **ORACLE**. This is done to ensure that the export has the proper Oracle privileges to execute the export. The next step is to remove any previous copy of the export file, and create the named pipe for the export. Finally, the compress command is issued using the Oracle export script as input.

Partitioning Oracle Exports

Partitioning Oracle exports has the advantage of allowing faster recovery of data warehouse tables. It can take hours to recover a single table from a compressed 2 GB export file, whereby a smaller table can be recovered very quickly if it was segregated into its own export file. You can use the output listing from a previous Oracle export to determine the amount of disk file storage an individual table consumes (see Listing 10.8).

Listing 10.8   A listing from an Oracle export.

```
Connected to: Oracle7 Server Release 7.1.6.2.0 - Production Release
With the distributed, replication and parallel query options
PL/SQL Release 2.1.6.2.0 - Production

About to export specified tables ...
Current user changed to RPT
. exporting table              FACT       226654 rows exported
. exporting table              DON_SHPMT 2931690 rows exported
. exporting table              OLD_SHPMT 2388343 rows exported
Export terminated successfully without warnings.
```

Here, we see that the FACT table consists of 226,000 rows. If we know that the row size is 100 bytes, then we can estimate that the FACT table consumes 226 MB and can easily fit into a Unix file system. This table can now be exported. The table can be dropped, and the rows can be re-added from the export file using Oracle's import utility with the **ingore=n** parameter.

Loading Export Files Using The SQL*Loader Utility

While the import and export utilities are very useful for moving data between Oracle databases, we need a method for loading non-Oracle data into an Oracle database. The loader utility can be very useful for populating Oracle tables with information extracted from legacy systems in other database architectures such as IMS and CA-IDMS. When faced with loading an Oracle warehouse from flat files extracted from other data sources, the database designer has a choice: write a customized load program using Oracle's Pro*C or use the Oracle SQL*Loader utility. Because customized load programs are so varied, this section focuses on using SQL*Loader.

SQL*Loader can be used to validate, massage, and load flat-file data directly into Oracle tables. For data warehouse loads, it is interesting to note that SQL*Loader is also upwardly compatible with the DB2 load utility and DB2 control files can be used within SQL*Loader. SQL*Loader has the following built-in features:

- Enables splitting one load file into many tables.

- Enables consolidating many load files into one table.

- Allows SQL functions to massage data prior to load.

- Allows the creation of primary keys from load file field values.

- Provides fast load capability by using "direct" loading.

For data warehouses, it is not uncommon to see files extracted from legacy databases that contain numerous pieces of a single logical entity (see Figure 10.2). For example, some customer data may be extracted from a DB2 database, while other customer data is extracted from an IMS database. SQL*Loader allows different load files to be consolidated and loaded into a single Oracle table.

In other cases, we may have a denormalized load file that contains data fields that need to be loaded into many different Oracle tables (see Figure 10.3). In these cases, SQL*Loader can read a record from the load file and use the fields to populate many Oracle tables.

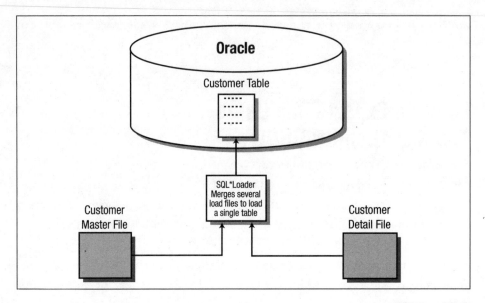

Figure 10.2
Consolidation of flat files for a table load.

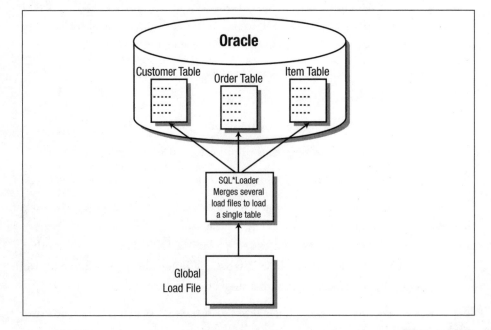

Figure 10.3
Splitting a single load file into many Oracle tables.

As SQL*Loader executes, it reads a record, validates the input, and continues reading data until an internal array is filled with row data. When the internal array is filled, Oracle proceeds to insert row information into the target tables.

SQL*Loader produces two types of error files: the *bad* file and the *discard* file (see Figure 10.4). It is important to understand how these files are generated and what anomalies cause records to be dumped into these files.

- *Bad files* contains SQL*Loader and Oracle rejects:

    - *SQL*Loader Rejects*—When the data in a load file does not match the definition in a control file, an SQL*Loader reject occurs. SQL*Loader rejects include instances when the specified length of an input record is exceeded or a field delimiter is missing.

    - *Oracle Rejects*—After records have been validated by SQL*Loader for insertion into Oracle, the possibility remains that the records may be rejected by Oracle. A record may be rejected because it contains a duplicate column value for a unique index, a **NOT NULL** column doesn't contain a value, or a numeric column is passed character values.

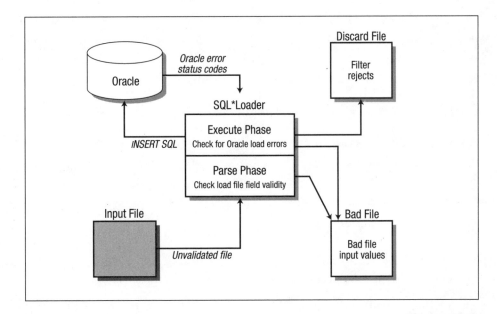

Figure 10.4
SQL*Loader writes to two types of error files.

- *Discard files* contain records that were not loaded into an Oracle table because of filtering statements in the control file. For example:

```
sqlldr user/pass control=xxxx.ctl log=xxxx.log
```

Conventional Path Loading

In conventional path loading, SQL*Loader reads input records into an internal array and then issues **INSERT** statements to Oracle from the array. All **INSERT** triggers and referential integrity remain active, and each row must pass all foreign key checks before it is accepted into the database.

Conventional loads use SQL **INSERT** commands to load data from a bind array buffer, and consequently, conventional loads pass SQL statements to Oracle for execution—one at a time. In short, using the conventional path is slow, but it performs a valuable scrubbing function on data. If any of the data to be loaded is even slightly suspect, the conventional path should be used.

Direct Path Loading

Using the direct path option with SQL*Loader is a double-edged sword. On the one hand, the data will load much faster and more efficiently. On the other hand, the delay of foreign key referential integrity checking can cause cleanup problems after the load has completed. The following code example shows a sample SQL*Loader command to load data from a file called my_control_file:

```
sqlldr control=my_control_file, direct=true
```

Whenever data loading occurs, the checking of foreign key constraints can slow down processing. For example, let's assume we are loading an **ORDER** table (see Figure 10.5). Here, we see that the **ORDER** table has referential integrity coming into the table as well as referential integrity going out of the table. As a new row is inserted, the following RI checks must take place:

- Validation that the **salesperson** row corresponds to **salesperson_name**.

- Verification that a valid **customer** row corresponds to the **customer_nbr**.

The RI checks results in additional I/O operations for each row inserted into the **ORDER** table. Unlike conventional path loading, direct path loading disables all constraints except the **NOT NULL, UNIQUE,** and primary key constraints.

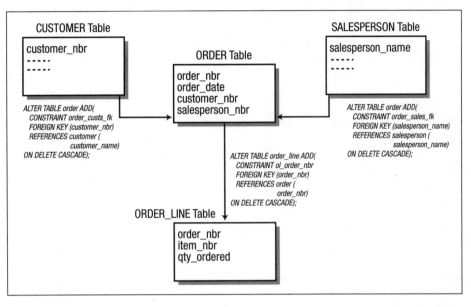

Figure 10.5
Referential integrity checking at table load time.

Therefore, all foreign key constraints within the target table that reference other tables are disabled prior to the data load. Also, all **INSERT** triggers are disabled when using a direct load. If you want the foreign key constraints re-enabled immediately after the load, you may use the **REENABLE** clause.

Foreign Key Constraints

*If your load places invalid rows into your target table, the foreign key constraints may fail to re-enable. For example, an **order** row that has a wrong **customer_nbr** will load, but the foreign key constraint will not re-enable because there is not a corresponding **customer_nbr** in the customer table. You must then manually correct the table rows and then re-enable constraints. Also, note that all **INSERT** triggers are disabled when using direct loads. After loading, the **INSERT** trigger could be copied as the **UPDATE** trigger and run for each of the newly loaded rows.*

Again, the direct load option is not recommended unless you have a very high degree of confidence in the quality of the data entering your warehouse. The foreign key constraints serve a very useful purpose for ensuring data warehouse validity.

Using The SQL*Loader Control File

Oracle uses a file called a *control file* to direct the process of reading, checking, and filtering incoming Oracle data. Let's examine the following control file:

```
LOAD DATA
INFILE      'emp.dat'
BADFILE     'badfile.out'
DISCARDFILE 'discard.out'
APPEND
INTO TABLE EMPLOYEE
(
person_num       POSITION (1:6)     CHAR,
department_num   POSITION (26:28)   INTEGER EXTERNAL,
first_name       POSITION (52:71)   CHAR "initcap(:first_name)",
middle_initial   POSITION (72)      CHAR "upper(:middle_initial)",
last_name        POSITION (73:97)   CHAR "initcap(:last_name)",
created_by       CONSTANT 'Don Burleson',
date_created     sysdate
)
```

Following the **INTO TABLE EMPLOYEE** statement, the first data field from columns one through six are defined as character fields inserted into the **person_num** column of the **EMPLOYEE** table. Note that the specification of **CHAR** allows numeric values to be inserted into the column. The second data field comes from columns 26 through 28 of the input file, and the values will be inserted into the **department_num** column only if these columns contain an **INTEGER** value. The next two fields demonstrate the use of Oracle's built-in functions to massage the incoming data. The **first_name** resides in columns 52 through 71 of the input file as uppercase letters. The Oracle **initcap** function is used to convert a string, such that *JONES* is converted to *Jones* upon loading. The **upper** function is used by the **middle_initial** column to ensure that this is always an uppercase value. The **created_by** column of the **EMPLOYEE** table is set to the literal string of **Don Burleson**, and the **date_created** column is set to the current date with Oracle's **sysdate** function.

Improving Loading Speed

Now that we understand how data can be cleansed, validated, and loaded using SQL*Loader, let's take a look at some tricks that can be used to improve loading speeds. There are many features of SQL*Loader specially designed for the data warehouse, and these features can be extremely useful for shortening the time required to load new information into your warehouse.

Oracle provides many parallelization techniques, and SQL*Loader is no exception. In fact, there are many techniques that can be used to improve loading speed. Following is a list of some useful loading tips and SQL*Loader features:

- *Parallel data loading*—SQL*Loader allows for multiple concurrent sessions to simultaneously load the same table. To use this feature, set **PARALLEL=TRUE** in your control file. This feature creates temporary segments to hold the rows from the parallel load and then merges the rows into the target table after the parallel loads have been completed.

- *Pre-allocate space*—Pre-allocating space can save time because table extending consumes system resources and can slow down processing. For example, a table could be exported, dropped, and redefined with a very large **INITIAL** extent, such that the space for future loads already exists within the table.

- *Pre-sort the load file*—An input file can easily be sorted using the Unix **sort** command, and pre-sorting can help load performance while ensuring that the table is clustered with an index. This reduces the need for temporary segments to sort the loaded data and also speeds up loading time. With indexes on tables, SQL*Loader bypasses internal sorting and moves directly into the merge phase of index creation— quickly inserting key values into the index at load time. To invoke this option, you need to tell SQL*Loader which index should be sorted in the same order as the load file. This is done by indicating the index name in the **SORTED INDEXES** parameter. For more information on index clustering, see Chapter 8, *Oracle Features For The Data Warehouse*. If you are using the direct load option, you can also specify the **SORTED INDEXES** option. For example, stating **SORTED INDEXES last_name_ix** tells SQL*Loader that the input file has been pre-sorted in the same sequence as the **last_name_ix** index. This will greatly reduce the load time for the file.

- *Use the **UNRECOVERABLE** clause*—This option turns off media recovery for the loaded table. While this means an aborted load cannot roll back to its original state, it will dramatically improve load speed because the roll back segment writes are not needed during the **INSERT**s. Of course, this option is only for very stable loads that have functioned flawlessly for a great period of time. If a load process fails, the table would need to be completely restored from a backup.

- *Drop and re-create the indexes*—In situations where the load is for a large percentage of the total table, dropping the indexes and re-creating them later will save resources in the temporary tablespace. Again, this option should only be used for very large loads or loads that strain the temporary segment space.

Now that we have covered how SQL*Loader can be used to populate our Oracle warehouse, let's take a look at other methods for linking legacy databases with the Oracle data warehouse.

Linking Oracle Warehouses With Other Databases

Now is the time to take a look at methods for linking databases from various vendors. In general, the Oracle warehouse needs to have links into other databases for loading purposes and perhaps for asynchronous data replication. In general, we have the following three approaches to achieving these links:

- *Manual consolidation*—Data is extracted from a variety of databases and loaded into a common repository—an approach commonly used with data warehouses. Red Brick systems are an example of manual consolidation.

- *Remote connection*—Many databases are monitored via a common console. In this scenario, status information is shipped from a variety of databases to a common console that is used to alert the operations staff to extraordinary conditions. Patrol, by BMC Software, is an example of this type of linking.

- *Online applications*—An online application (usually running on a PC) accesses data from a variety of databases, presenting the data to the user as if the data was coming from a single source. EDA-SQL and UniFace are examples of this type of linking.

You will find two schools of thought concerning applications that span multiple vendor databases. One group maintains that a single vendor should be able to provide a global, omniscient database capable of supporting all types of data requirements—from online transaction processing to decision support. Many vendors foster this belief by marketing their database products as suitable for every type of application. The vendors point out the nightmares that result when a multidatabase application attempts to make diverse databases communicate with each other in a seamless fashion. The opposing philosophy believes the only way to successfully implement database technology is to use numerous databases, leveraging the strengths of each engine. As recently as five years ago, database vendors touted their products as a corporate panacea, appropriate for all types of data and application systems.

The whole multidatabase trend is a reaction to corporate acquisitions and weak systems development strategies. Companies have had little or no strategic direction for databases, although it is doubtful that any company ever decided to go heterogeneous, either. Having heterogeneous databases means duplicating licenses and talent, and few companies have a large enough talent pool to support multiple databases.

External influences have also impacted the database configuration of shops. Corporate acquisitions, mergers, and "right-sizing" efforts have had the side effect of leaving a plethora of database engines within newly reformed organizations. Regardless of the wisdom of having multiple types of databases, most IS departments must link more than one database, and cross-database connectivity has become commonplace. Sentry Market Research estimates that the average corporation has approximately nine different databases. End users are demanding applications that integrate legacy data from mainframes with data in open systems, while MIS designers are faced with the incredible challenge of making these diverse systems function as a unified whole.

While linking non-relational databases such as IMS and CA-IDMS into Oracle databases is considered challenging, it is a common misconception that relational databases are basically the same and, therefore, easy to link together. Even linking databases that share the same architecture is difficult, especially with different vendor implementations of relational databases. The idea that relational databases are "plug-and-play" is pure fantasy. For example, the popular PowerBuilder application development tool was primarily designed for use with a Sybase relational database. To accommodate PowerBuilder, Oracle had to add an init.ora parameter to cache cursors for PowerBuilder because PowerBuilder doesn't give the user control over specific cursors (which results in many SQL re-parses). Locking between Oracle and Sybase is also totally different. If you use Oracle and want to build a high performance OLTP application, you should first lock all records (which doesn't exist in Sybase); set a transaction boundary to roll back everything except the locks, in case of a transaction error; then perform array operations such as array **INSERT**s, **DELETE**s, **UPDATE**s, and **SELECT**s (all of which are not supported by Sybase). Even the SQL syntax differs, and the procedural extensions between the two applications' SQL are never equal.

So, how do large IS shops deal with these problems? Should companies invest in training their employees for many different relational databases? The cost of this comprehensive training is difficult to justify.

To further illustrate the stumbling blocks, consider the cost of converting an application from one relational database to another. First, do you even have the talent to make it happen when the interfaces are diverse? Even more confounding is the lack of clarity about the "truths" of the differences. Rarely is a relational database (RDBMS) chosen over another on the basis of which RDBMS is best for the type of application.

The challenge of linking multivendor databases is not one of syntax—we can solve that problem through standard query languages, data dictionaries, and the like. The real challenge is one of semantics: *How do we extract meaning from data contained in many different locations?* I believe this challenge can only be met by building executable business models that pull related information out of multiple databases as a side effect of their ongoing operations.

Even the major DBMS vendors are recognizing that extensions into other products are necessary for their survival. The crux of the situation is becoming evident—most shops are not capable of moving their data into a single database.

While there are dozens of third-party vendors who offer utilities that will link Oracle with other databases, let's begin by examining the characteristics of Oracle's procedural gateway utility.

Oracle Gateway Utilities

In response to the realities of linking multivendor databases, just about every database vendor has created a tool that claims to allow seamless communication between its engine and other vendors' products. For example, Oracle's philosophy emphasizes the need for a smooth transition path for non-Oracle databases by offering a three-phase program. Oracle recognizes that customers can't be expected to shift into Oracle overnight, so this gateway strategy allows for a smooth transition into an Oracle environment.

Gateway Utilities—Phase One

In phase one, Oracle applications provide gateways into non-Oracle databases, allowing Oracle applications to make calls (using Oracle SQL) to non-Oracle databases. The converter then translates the Oracle SQL into the native SQL for the foreign database. Now, the developer can use the robust extensions found in Oracle SQL with a non-Oracle database, while the Oracle open gateway relies on "SQL compensation" to perform Oracle SQL functions against the non-Oracle database. This technology allows an Oracle application to join, for example, a DB2 table with a Sybase table—all within the gateway product. Oracle believes in connectivity into all databases—not just relational databases. For this reason, Oracle is packaged with Information Builders Incorporated, using its EDA-SQL product to help insulate the front-end application from the foreign data source. This takes the form of an access manager that handles the communications to and from the Oracle database, allowing Oracle to access non-relational databases. (See Figure 10.6.)

While this approach seems noble, Oracle has experienced some problems with a few of its SQL extensions that do not have equivalents in other relational databases. For example, Oracle's **DECODE** function cannot be implemented in Informix, because the **DECODE** verb has no direct equivalent in Informix SQL. (See Figure 10.7.)

Gateway Utilities—Phase Two

Phase two of Oracle's strategy allows a foreign application to access Oracle. For example, a CICS COBOL customer may require access to Oracle data. In phase two of

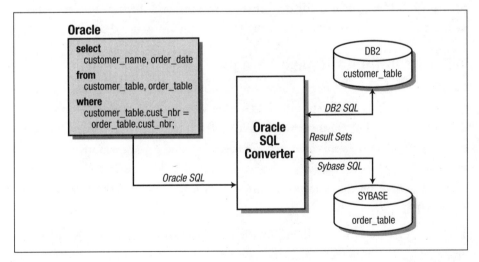

Figure 10.6
Oracle transparent gateway—phase one.

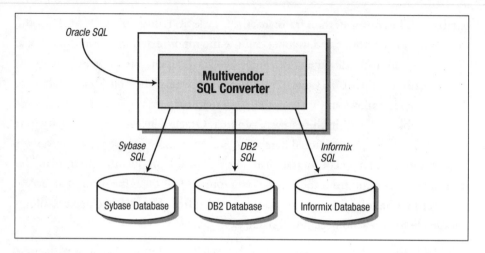

Figure 10.7
Oracle's open gateway.

the Oracle gateway, the non-Oracle application on the mainframe can access Oracle as if it resided on a local host. However, some middleware vendors do not feel that the gateway approach is the best long-term solution for database connectivity. Unlike the gateway products that have a single interface, some products have separately tuned drivers for each target database. This movement away from general interfaces such as ODBC is primarily for performance reasons, and it is not uncommon for each product to have its own custom interface for each supported database.

Gateway Utilities—Phase Three

Phase three of Oracle's strategy is heterogeneous replication. At this point, we have a solution that allows us to replicate data from a variety of sources and import table data into Oracle. The third phase of the Oracle gateway provides a mechanism to constantly update the replicated non-Oracle data. The gateway approach is commonly used with data warehouse applications, but it also allows updates to non-Oracle data to be quickly transported into a replicated Oracle database, as shown in Figure 10.8.

The replication can work in the other direction as well—taking Oracle tables and propagating them into the foreign database where they behave as native tables within the foreign database, as shown in Figure 10.9.

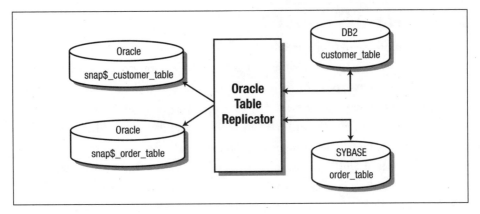

Figure 10.8
Foreign tables imported into Oracle.

The ability to replicate in both directions gives the database designer enormous flexibility in choosing the best approach for data replication, based on the needs of the client/server application. However, we need to be aware that replication interfaces are complicated and often require manual intervention, especially when data is being transferred from one hardware architecture to another. For example, populating EBCDIC data from DB2 tables into the ASCII world of Oracle involves translating characters unknown to ASCII, such as the cent sign.

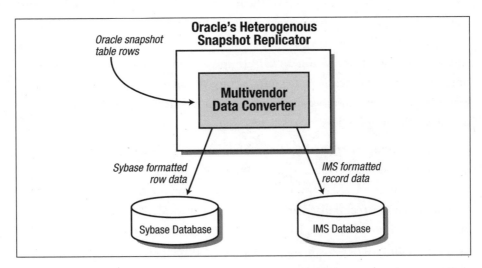

Figure 10.9
Oracle tables exported into foreign databases.

Middleware Solutions

Many new middleware packages allow applications to be developed independently of databases, providing drivers for more than 25 database products. Some products, such as UniFace, accomplish this with *data choreography*, where the developer specifies the data with query by example. The developer does not have to write SQL, and UniFace takes care of all I/O and relationship management. A middleware product capable of enforcing business rules across database architectures is also needed. One important aspect of UniFace is the ability to enforce referential integrity across platforms. For example, a customer database may exist at corporate headquarters using Oracle, but the orders are taken in the field using a C/ISAM database. The tool will maintain the business rules between these tables, even though the tables are in different databases at different locations.

Some large IS shops have had great success using middleware gateway technology to link multiplatform databases. For example, consider a company that supports IMS, DB2, and Oracle. After looking at various solutions to make these databases communicate, they may choose two different gateway products. One gateway might be Oracle's transparent gateway for communication from Oracle applications to DB2 and IMS, and the other gateway could be IBM's DDCS and Data Joiner to handle communications from DB2 into Oracle databases. Many companies use Oracle's transparent gateway because it allows them to treat calls to DB2 as if DB2 was just another Oracle database. The gateway product takes care of the translation into DB2 SQL. The company will then have the capability to join two DB2 tables, each on a separate processor, from within an Oracle application. While these gateway solutions are definitely functional, the long-term goal for most companies is to avoid gateways altogether and move into a three-tiered architecture with a protocol layer such as CORBA or DCE.

It is interesting to note that the demand for mainframe resources does not always decline after a company embraces a commitment to open systems. Having a single database may have offered definite advantages in the mainframe days, but most large IS shops are now decentralized and distributed worldwide. To complicate matters, many of the remote locations have the authority to choose their own database—usually selecting whatever is in vogue at the time or perhaps the cheapest database available. This approach can lead to a realtime support load problem. Interestingly, even after a large company completes its push into open systems, the migration away from the mainframes may still take years. Some legacy systems on mainframes required hundreds of thousands of hours to create, and they cannot be removed overnight. Consequently, many managers are surprised to see that the largest system costs may still be incurred by the mainframe. Although new development is moving to open systems, companies continue to see mainframe expenditure requirements grow at a rate of 15 to 20 percent per year.

As we move further away from proprietary operating systems to open systems, it seems evident that the days of single-vendor environments are numbered. We are already witnessing the shift toward a plug-and-play RDBMS environment.

Clearly, the differences between proprietary databases will be less problematic as robust interfaces are developed. Very few theoretical reasons can support remaining bound to the technology of a single database vendor. Within the next few years, we will be entering an era of cross-platform joins. Vendors who do not provide the capability to do so will be seen as hampering the flow of information, thereby decreasing productivity. This doesn't mean that vendors will abandon their notable differences in favor of a standardized database environment. In fact, vendor-specific differences are likely to intensify with the addition of new functionality because each RDBMS will need to emphasize its strengths to establish superiority over the competition.

Some vendors have recognized a market opportunity for a tool that can easily access multivendor databases, both for retrieval and update purposes. One such product is called *Passport*, an object-oriented tool that makes the development of three-tiered multivendor applications unbelievably easy. Passport started out as a front-end tool when Oracle and Ingres dominated the market. As more database applications started to hit the shelves, customers began to want to mix-and-match databases. Passport provided the solution—and continues to provide the solution today. For example, if a customer wants one database's tool set and another database's SQL, the customer can use a tool such as Passport to switch databases on an as-needed basis.

Some of the new middleware products have the capability of leveraging on their object-oriented architecture to easily access multiple databases. For example, some middleware treats each database as an object with its own attributes and behaviors, making it trivial to swap out one database for another. These middleware products use an inherent distributed database model to manage two-phase commits across numerous midrange and PC databases. That way, a single update screen can display data from many different databases. At update time, the tool uses synchronous communications to ensure that all databases are updated.

Summary

Now that we understand how the Oracle import/export and gateway utilities can assist the Oracle data warehouse manager, let's dive deep into the waters of Oracle and examine how the Oracle memory region (the instance) can be optimized for a data warehouse application. Later, we will take a look at the Oracle8 features for the data warehouse and see how data mining will evolve in Oracle.

Tuning The Oracle Warehouse Architecture

CHAPTER
11

Tuning The Oracle Warehouse Architecture

A holistic approach to the tuning of the overall Oracle architecture is paramount to the development of effective client/server systems. Regardless of how slick and well-tuned the client performs, poor response time at the server level will cause the entire development effort to fail. Whether your server is private to your application or shared among many client applications, the optimal use of Oracle resources can ensure that the system performs at an acceptable level. Topics in this chapter include the Oracle architecture, Oracle's internal structures, tuning Oracle memory, and Oracle interoperability features.

The Oracle Architecture

Oracle is the world's leading relational database, continuing to dominate the marketplace for mid-range computer platforms. Since Oracle's inception in 1971, it has evolved to the point where Oracle7 bears little resemblance to the original offering. While Oracle has many extensions, the base product consists of the following components:

- *The Oracle SGA*—This is the region in RAM memory that is created when Oracle is started.

- *SQL*Plus*—This is the online interface to the Oracle database. Like SPUFI on DB2 and IDD for CA-IDMS, SQL*Plus is used to allow ad hoc queries and updates to be issued against the database.

- *SQL*DBA*—This is the interface to Oracle for the database administrator. It allows the DBA to create databases, tablespaces, tables, clusters, indexes, and other Oracle constructs.

- *Server Manager and Enterprise Manager*—This is the visual reporting component to Oracle. Server Manager provides a graphical interface to online reports that give fast, visual access to the database. Enterprise Manager can be run with Windows using Oracle SQL*Net for communications to the database, or it can be run on an individual server using Motif.

- *SQL*Net*—This is the communications protocol that allows remote database servers to communicate with each other. SQL*Net is described extensively in Chapter 9.

- *PL/SQL*—This is Oracle's proprietary implementation of the ANSI SQL standard. PL/SQL can be used within Oracle application tools called SQL*Forms or embedded into remote tools, such as C programs or PC GUIs. A fully functional programming language by itself, PL/SQL adds extensions to the SQL to allow sophisticated processing.

- *SQL*Menu*—This is the menu builder for Oracle that allows individual SQL*Forms screens to be linked together.

The following list represents related Oracle products that may also be of interest, including some utilities:

- *Oracle Express*—Formerly called *Express* by IRI Corporation, Oracle Express is a multidimensional database for supporting data warehouses and online analytical processing (OLAP). This product has yet to be integrated with the standard Oracle engine, and communications with the relational database are usually accomplished by extracting data from Oracle7 and loading it into Oracle Express.

- *Oracle*ConText*—A text database, Oracle*ConText is used primarily for creating hypertext documents.

- *Import/Export*—A utility that allows the developer to dump the contents of tables into a flat file and allows the flat file to be restored to the database.

- *SQL*Loader*—A utility that allows delimited flat files to be loaded into Oracle tables. For example, an extract from a DB2 database could be created with commas delimiting each table column. SQL*Loader would be used to import this flat file into an Oracle table.

- *Designer 2000*—A utility that is part of the Oracle family of CASE tools. Designer 2000 allows the developer to maintain logical table definitions and create a physical model from the logical structure.

Oracle's Internal Structures

When Oracle is started, a region of memory is configured according to initial parameters defined in two files: the init.ora and the config.ora. These files tell the database software how to configure the system global area (SGA), which is the term used to describe a running Oracle. In addition to the SGA, each application that accesses Oracle receives a program global area, or PGA.

SGA And PGA

Because the SGA resides within an operating system, it is dependent on the operating environment (see Figure 11.1). In Unix, Oracle must share space with many other memory regions, competing for the limited memory and processing resources, as shown in Figure 11.2. These other memory regions may include the program global area (PGA) for external Oracle programs and perhaps memory regions for other teleprocessing and database instances.

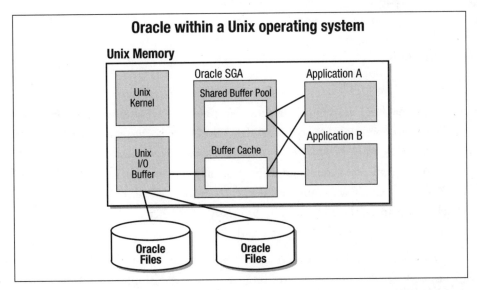

Figure 11.1

A sample Oracle instance in Unix.

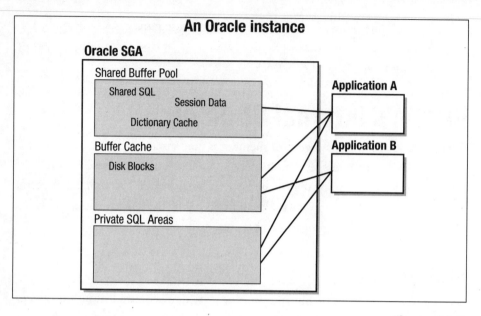

An Oracle instance

Oracle SGA

Shared Buffer Pool

Shared SQL

Session Data

Dictionary Cache

Buffer Cache

Disk Blocks

Private SQL Areas

Application A

Application B

Figure 11.2
The relationships between Oracle and applications.

The SGA consists of several main components, each of which is configured at database startup time:

- Buffer cache
- Log buffer
- Shared pool
- Private SQL areas

At the internal level, each Oracle instance has predefined interfaces to the hardware to allow it to communicate with the physical devices. Being a database software product, Oracle must be able to communicate with disk devices and CD-ROMs, and it must be able to retrieve and store information from these devices. When the DBA defines a tablespace, a physical data file is associated with the tablespace, and Oracle will manage the addressability to this file. In other words, Oracle manages the mapping of the logical tablespaces to the physical data files.

The configuration of the SGA is critical to designing high performance client/server applications. The sizes allocated to the program pool and the buffer pools have a direct impact on the speed at which Oracle retrieves information. Remember, most business applications are I/O bound—the single greatest delay being the time required to access data from disk. As such, tuning for I/O becomes a critical consideration.

The single most important component for tuning an Oracle database is the size of the database buffer. The database buffer is where Oracle holds blocks that have already been retrieved by a prior database request. Whenever a new request for data is made, Oracle will first check this buffer. If the block is already in memory, Oracle can deliver the block to the user 10,000 times faster than if Oracle had to perform an I/O to go to the external disk for information. Access time on disks now reaches an impressive speed—between 10 and 25 milliseconds. However, data that already resides in the RAM area of Oracle SGA can be retrieved in microseconds. The parameter controlling the size of the buffer is called **db_block_buffers**, and it is one of the parameters in the init.ora file. For more information on **db_block_size**, see Chapter 8, *Oracle Features For The Data Warehouse*.

The other important region of the SGA is the shared pool, which keeps a number of sub-areas. One of the confounding problems with Oracle is that all of these areas are sized by only one parameter: **SHARED_POOL_SIZE**. It is impossible to dedicate separate regions of memory for the components within the shared pool.

The shared pool is the SGA's second largest memory component, second only to the Oracle data buffer. The shared pool holds memory for the following purposes:

- *Library Cache*—An area that holds the plan information for SQL that is currently being executed. This area also holds stored procedure and trigger code.

- *Dictionary Cache*—Keeps environmental information, including referential integrity, table definitions, indexing information, and other metadata, that is stored within Oracle's internal tables.

- *Session Information*—Session information is only kept for systems that are using SQL*Net version 2 with Oracle's multithreaded server. See Chapter 9 for details on using the multithreaded server.

In addition to the SGA, each application that accesses Oracle receives a program global area. The PGA contains private SQL areas that are used by individual programs and keep application-specific database information. The PGA keeps the current values of cursors and other program-dependent information.

Now that we have a high-level overview of the internal memory structures of Oracle, let's take a look at the internal views that Oracle uses to provide internal information.

The Oracle V$ Views

The V$ tables are internal structures built into memory when an Oracle instance is started. Although they appear to be tables, they are really internal memory structures implemented in the C language. Therefore, the V$ tables only exist during the execution of the instance and are destroyed at shutdown time. The V$ tables are used by Oracle to capture information about the overall status of the database, and the information from the V$ tables can provide tremendous insight into the internal operations. While dozens of V$ tables exist, only a handful can be used for Oracle performance and tuning.

The V$ tables have limited use for measuring time-dependent information because they accumulate information from the moment an Oracle instance is started until the present time. As such, measures such as the buffer hit ratio are normalized, presenting only the average for the entire time that the instance has been running.

Interoperability Facilities

It is very important for a distributed database to have the ability to address information regardless of the hardware platform or the architecture of the database, especially in volatile environments where hardware and network configurations may change frequently. Two types of interoperability come into play with distributed databases: hardware and database.

Hardware interoperability refers to the ability of the distributed system to address resources at many locations on an as-needed basis. At the hardware level, it is possible for a single sub-query of a distributed query to run on numerous processors, and load balancing tools are available for assigning multiple processors to a single database.

Database interoperability refers to the ability of a database to function autonomously to allow the distributed database to access many different types of databases within the domain of a unified environment. Tools such as UniFace and PowerBuilder attempt to serve this market, providing mechanisms for subtasking database queries and merging result sets automatically.

Creating Batch-Oriented Oracle Instances

In some cases, widely differing applications may access the same tables. An excellent example of this scenario would be a banking application that processes fast online transactions during the day and is updated with long-running background tasks in the evening.

A fundamental difference exists between the database resources required for transaction processing and those for batch processing. Online transactions are usually small and require few resources from the database lock manager. Batch processes are generally lock intensive, sweeping a table in a linear fashion.

Oracle's buffer pool offers a finite amount of RAM storage within the region. This storage may be allocated to lock pools or buffer pools, but it is impossible to reallocate these resources as the applications change unless the system is brought down and then restarted with a new configuration (a process called *bouncing*). For online transaction systems with hundreds of concurrent users, the demands on the database buffer pool are much more intensive than with system-wide updates. Conversely, batch updates make very little use of large buffers, but they require a lot of room in the lock pools to hold row locks between commit checkpoints.

One simple solution to these application-specific requirements is to create two database configurations, each with a different configuration of buffers and lock pools. At the end of the online transaction day, the online system may be brought down and a batch version of the database may be started with a different memory configuration.

Oracle Stored Procedures

As objects such as stored procedures and triggers become more popular, more application code will move away from external programs and into the database engine. Oracle has been encouraging this approach in anticipation of the object-oriented features of Oracle version 8. However, Oracle DBAs must be conscious of the increasing memory demands of stored procedures, and they must carefully plan for the days when all of the database access code resides within the database.

Today, most Oracle databases have only a small amount of code in stored procedures—but this is rapidly changing. Many compelling benefits can be derived by placing all Oracle SQL inside stored procedures. These include:

- *Encapsulation*—The code resides in the database instead of in external programs. With the proper use of Oracle packages, stored procedures can be logically grouped together into a cohesive framework of SQL statements.

- *Flexibility*—By keeping all database access inside Oracle packages, the applications contain no SQL, becoming little more than a set of calls to the stored procedures. As such, the application is insulated from the database and will easily be able to migrate to another platform or database product.

- *Better performance*—Stored procedures are loaded once into the SGA and remain there unless they become paged out. Subsequent executions of the stored procedure are far faster than external code.

- *Coupling of data with behavior*—Relational tables can be coupled with the behaviors that are associated with them by using naming conventions. For example, if all behaviors associated with the employee table are prefixed with the table name (as in **EMPLOYEE.hire** and **EMPLOYEE.give_raise**), then the data dictionary can be queried to list all behaviors associated with a table (for instance, **SELECT * FROM DBA_OBJECTS WHERE OWNER = 'EMPLOYEE'**), and code can be readily identified and reused.

One of the foremost reasons why stored procedures and triggers function faster than traditional code is related to Oracle System Global Area (SGA). After a procedure has been loaded into the SGA, it will remain in the library cache until it is paged out of memory. Items are paged out of memory based on a least-recently-used algorithm. Once loaded into the RAM memory of the shared pool, the procedure will execute very quickly. The trick is to prevent pool-thrashing during the period when many procedures are competing for a limited amount of library cache within the shared pool memory.

When tuning Oracle, two init.ora parameters emerge as more important than all of the other parameters combined. These are the **db_block_buffers** and the **shared_pool_size** parameters. These two parameters define the size of the in-memory region that Oracle consumes on startup and determines the amount of storage available to cache data blocks, SQL, and stored procedures.

Oracle also provides a construct called a *package*. Essentially, a package is a collection of functions and stored procedures, and can be organized in a variety of ways. For example, functions and stored procedures for employees can be logically grouped together in an employee package like this:

```
CREATE PACKAGE EMPLOYEE AS

    FUNCTION compute_raise_amount (percentage NUMBER);
    PROCEDURE hire_employee();
```

```
    PROCEDURE fire_employee();
    PROCEDURE list_employee_details();

END employee;
```

Here, all employee "behaviors" are encapsulated into a single package that will be added into Oracle's data dictionary. If the DBA forces programmers to use stored procedures, the SQL moves out of the external programs and into the database, reducing the application programs into nothing more than a series of calls to Oracle stored procedures.

As systems evolve and the majority of process code resides in stored procedures, Oracle's shared pool becomes very important. The shared pool consists of the following sub-pools:

- Dictionary cache
- Library cache
- Shared SQL areas
- Private SQL areas (these exist during cursor open/cursor close)
    - persistent area
    - runtime area

As we have mentioned, the shared pool utilizes a least-recently-used algorithm to determine which objects are paged out of the shared pool. As this paging occurs, fragments or discontiguous chunks of memory are created within the shared pool.

This means that a large procedure that initially fits into memory may not fit into contiguous memory when it's reloaded after paging out. Consider a problem that occurs when the body of a package has been paged out of the instance's SGA because of other more recent or frequent activity. Fragmentation occurs, and the server cannot find enough contiguous memory to reload the package body, resulting in an ORA-4031 error.

When To Use Oracle Stored Procedures

Certain rules apply in deciding when to use a trigger and when to use a stored procedure. The choice revolves around the nature of the desired SQL, and whether it is specific to a DML event or is global in nature. In general, the validation of input data is ideally suited to an **INSERT** trigger, especially when it involves accessing another Oracle table. If you are writing your own referential integrity, **DELETE** triggers are appropriate. Triggers are generally associated with SQL that is closely tied to a single DML event, such as the insertion, deletion, or updating of a row. In practice, **SELECT** triggers are only used in situations where hand-rolled auditing is used to keep a log of those who are viewing secure rows.

Stored procedures are generally used when an SQL query creates an aggregate object, which accesses rows from many tables to create a single result set. The creation of an invoice, an order form, or a student's schedule are examples of these types of queries.

One of the problems with utilizing Oracle stored procedures and triggers is keeping track of the SQL once it has been entered into the database. Unlike the object database products, Oracle does not yet provide a mechanism for directly associating a stored procedure with the tables that it touches.

Oracle version 8 promises to make this less of a problem, but in the meantime, client/server programmers must be able to identify and reuse queries that have already been written and tested. To achieve reusability, you can use naming conventions to ensure that all SQL is logically associated with the tables against which it operates. For example, the SQL to insert a row into the customer table could be given a meaningful name, say **customer_insert**(). This way, the data dictionary can be interrogated to identify all existing SQL that touched a table. The use of naming conventions is tricky when a single SQL statement joins many tables, but prudent use of naming conventions can help ensure that the SQL can be easily located.

Pinning Oracle Packages In The SGA

To prevent paging, packages can be marked as non-swappable, which tells the database that after their initial load, they must always remain in memory. This is called *pinning* or *memory fencing*. Oracle provides a procedure called **dbms_shared_pool.keep** to pin a package. Packages can also be unpinned with **dbms_shared_pool.keep**.

> **Note:** *Only packages can be pinned. Oracle stored procedures cannot be pinned unless they are placed into a package.*

The choice of whether to pin a package in memory is a function of the size of the object and the frequency of its use. A very large, frequently called package might benefit from pinning, but any performance differences may go unnoticed because the frequent calls to the procedures have kept the package loaded into memory. Therefore, because the object never pages out, the pinning has no effect. Also, the way procedures are grouped into packages may have some influence. Some Oracle DBAs identify high-impact procedures and group them into a single package, which is pinned in the library cache.

In an ideal world, the **shared_pool** parameter of the init.ora should be large enough to accept every package, stored procedure, and trigger that may be used by the applications. However, reality dictates that the shared pool cannot grow indefinitely, and wise choices must be made in terms of which packages are pinned.

Because of their frequent usage, Oracle recommends that the **standard**, **dbms_standard**, **dbms_utility**, **dbms_describe** and **dbms_output** packages always be pinned in the shared pool. The following snippet demonstrates how a stored procedure called SYS.STANDARD can be pinned:

```
CONNECT INTERNAL;

@/usr/oracle/rdbms/admin/dbmspool.sql

EXECUTE dbms_shared_pool.keep('sys.standard');
```

A standard procedure can be written to pin all of the recommended Oracle packages into the shared pool. Here is the script:

```
EXECUTE dbms_shared_pool.keep('DBMS_ALERT');
EXECUTE dbms_shared_pool.keep('DBMS_DDL');
EXECUTE dbms_shared_pool.keep('DBMS_DESCRIBE');
EXECUTE dbms_shared_pool.keep('DBMS_LOCK');
EXECUTE dbms_shared_pool.keep('DBMS_OUTPUT');
EXECUTE dbms_shared_pool.keep('DBMS_PIPE');
EXECUTE dbms_shared_pool.keep('DBMS_SESSION');
EXECUTE dbms_shared_pool.keep('DBMS_SHARED_POOL');
EXECUTE dbms_shared_pool.keep('DBMS_STANDARD');
EXECUTE dbms_shared_pool.keep('DBMS_UTILITY');
EXECUTE dbms_shared_pool.keep('STANDARD');
```

Automatic Re-Pinning Of Packages

Unix users may want to add code to the /etc/rc file to ensure that the packages are re-pinned after each database startup. This guarantees that all packages are re-pinned with each bounce of the box. A script might look like this:

```
[root]: more pin
ORACLE_SID=mydata
export ORACLE_SID
su oracle -c "/usr/oracle/bin/svrmgrl /<<!
connect internal;
select * from db;
   @/usr/local/dba/sql/pin.sql
exit;
!"
```

The database administrator also needs to remember to run pin.sql whenever the database must be restarted. This is done by reissuing the pin command from inside SQL*DBA immediately after the database has been restarted.

How To Measure Pinned Packages

Listing 11.1 shows a script called MEMORY.SQL, which is used to display pinned packages in the SGA.

Listing 11.1   Display pinned SGA packages.

```
memory.sql - Display used SGA memory for triggers, packages, & procedures

SET PAGESIZE 60;

COLUMN EXECUTIONS FORMAT 999,999,999;
COLUMN Mem_used    FORMAT 999,999,999;

SELECT substr(owner,1,10)  Owner,
       substr(type,1,12)   Type,
       substr(name,1,20)   Name,
       executions,
       sharable_mem        Mem_used,
       substr(kept||' ',1,4)    "Kept?"
 FROM V$DB_OBJECT_CACHE
 WHERE TYPE IN ('TRIGGER','PROCEDURE','PACKAGE BODY','PACKAGE')
 ORDER BY EXECUTIONS DESC;
```

Listing 11.2 shows the output of MEMORY.SQL.

Listing 11.2   Output of MEMORY.SQL.

```
SQL> @memory
```

OWNER	TYPE	NAME	EXECUTIONS	MEM_USED	KEPT
SYS	PACKAGE	STANDARD	867,600	151,963	YES
SYS	PACKAGE BODY	STANDARD	867,275	30,739	YES
SYS	PACKAGE	DBMS_ALERT	502,126	3,637	NO
SYS	PACKAGE BODY	DBMS_ALERT	433,607	20,389	NO
SYS	PACKAGE	DBMS_LOCK	432,137	3,140	YES
SYS	PACKAGE BODY	DBMS_LOCK	432,137	10,780	YES
SYS	PACKAGE	DBMS_PIPE	397,466	3,412	NO
SYS	PACKAGE BODY	DBMS_PIPE	397,466	5,292	NO
HRIS	PACKAGE	S125_PACKAGE	285,700	3,776	NO
SYS	PACKAGE	DBMS_UTILITY	284,694	3,311	NO
SYS	PACKAGE BODY	DBMS_UTILITY	284,694	6,159	NO
HRIS	PACKAGE	HRS_COMMON_PACKAGE	258,657	3,382	NO
HRIS	PACKAGE BODY	S125_PACKAGE	248,857	30,928	NO
HRIS	PACKAGE BODY	HRS_COMMON_PACKAGE	242,155	8,638	NO
HRIS	PACKAGE	GTS_SNAPSHOT_UTILITY	168,978	11,056	NO
HRIS	PACKAGE BODY	GTS_SNAPSHOT_UTILITY	89,623	3,232	NO
SYS	PACKAGE	DBMS_STANDARD	18,953	14,696	NO
SYS	PACKAGE BODY	DBMS_STANDARD	18,872	3,432	NO
KIS	PROCEDURE	RKA_INSERT	7,067	4,949	NO
HRIS	PACKAGE	HRS_PACKAGE	5,175	3,831	NO
HRIS	PACKAGE BODY	HRS_PACKAGE	5,157	36,455	NO
SYS	PACKAGE	DBMS_DESCRIBE	718	12,800	NO
HRIS	PROCEDURE	CHECK_APP_ALERT	683	3,763	NO
SYS	PACKAGE BODY	DBMS_DESCRIBE	350	9,880	NO
SYS	PACKAGE	DBMS_SESSION	234	3,351	NO
SYS	PACKAGE BODY	DBMS_SESSION	165	4,543	NO
GIANT	PROCEDURE	CREATE_SESSION_RECOR	62	7,147	NO
HRIS	PROCEDURE	INIT_APP_ALERT	6	10,802	NO

Here is an easy way to tell the number of times a non-pinned stored procedure was swapped out of memory and required a reload. To effectively measure memory, two methods are recommended. The first method is to regularly run the **ESTAT/BSTAT** utility (usually located in ~/rdbms/admin/utlbstat.sql and utlestat.sql) for measuring SGA consumption over a range of time. The second method is to write a **SNAPDUMP** utility to interrogate the SGA and note any exceptional information relating to the library cache. This would include the following measurements:

- Data dictionary hit ratio
- Library cache miss ratio
- Individual hit ratios for all namespaces

Also, be aware that the relevant parameter, **SHARED_POOL_SIZE**, is used for other objects besides stored procedures. This means that one parameter fits all, and Oracle offers no method for isolating the amount of storage allocated to any subset of the shared pool.

Now, let's take a look at a sample report used for gathering information relating to **SHARED_POOL_SIZE**. Some DBAs run utlbstat.sql, wait one hour, and run utlestat.sql to produce a report similar to the report in Listing 11.3, which shows system-wide statistics over an elapsed time interval.

Listing 11.3   The generated report showing system-wide statistics.

```
============================
DATA DICT HIT RATIO
----------------------------
(should be higher than 90 else increase shared_pool_size in init.ora)


  Data Dict. Gets    Data Dict. cache misses   DATA DICT CACHE HIT RATIO
------------------   -----------------------   -------------------------
    41,750,549               407,609                      99


=============================
LIBRARY CACHE MISS RATIO
-----------------------------
(If > 1 then increase the shared_pool_size in init.ora)


  executions  Cache misses while executing  LIBRARY CACHE MISS RATIO
  ----------  ----------------------------  ------------------------
  22,909,643             171,127                     .0075


=============================
Library Cache Section
-----------------------------
hit ratio should be > 70, and pin ratio > 70 ...
```

NAMESPACE	Hit ratio	pin hit ratio	reloads
SQL AREA	84	94	125,885
TABLE/PROCEDURE	98	99	43,559
BODY	98	84	486
TRIGGER	98	97	1,145
INDEX	0	0	
CLUSTER	31	33	
OBJECT	100	100	
PIPE	99	99	52

As you can see, the data dictionary hit ratio is above 95 percent and the library cache miss ratio is very low. However, you can see over 125,000 reloads in the SQL area namespace, in which case the DBA may want to increase the **SHARED_POOL_SIZE**. When running this type of report, always remember that statistics are gathered from startup, and the numbers may be skewed. For example, for a system that has been running for six months, the data dictionary hit ratio will be a running average over six months. Consequently, data from the **V$** structures is meaningless if you want to measure today's statistics.

Let's take a look at the SQL*Plus script (Listing 11.4) that generated Listing 11.3.

Listing 11.4 The script that generated Listing 11.3.

```
PROMPT
PROMPT
PROMPT             ===========================
PROMPT             DATA DICT HIT RATIO
PROMPT             ===========================
PROMPT (should be higher than 90 else increase shared_pool_size
PROMPT in init.ora)

COLUMN "Data Dict. Gets"           FORMAT 999,999,999
COLUMN "Data Dict. cache misses"   FORMAT 999,999,999
SELECT sum(gets) "Data Dict. Gets",
       sum(getmisses) "Data Dict. cache misses",
       trunc((1-(sum(getmisses)/sum(gets)))*100)
       "DATA DICT CACHE HIT RATIO"
FROM V$ROWCACHE;

PROMPT
PROMPT
PROMPT             ===========================
PROMPT             LIBRARY CACHE MISS RATIO
```

```
PROMPT          ============================
PROMPT (If > 1 then increase the shared_pool_size in init.ora)
PROMPT
COLUMN "LIBRARY CACHE MISS RATIO" FORMAT 99.9999
COLUMN "executions"               FORMAT 999,999,999
COLUMN "Cache misses while executing"   FORMAT 999,999,999
SELECT sum(pins) "executions", sum(reloads) "Cache misses while executing",
     (((sum(reloads)/sum(pins)))) "LIBRARY CACHE MISS RATIO"
FROM V$LIBRARYCACHE;

PROMPT
PROMPT          ============================
PROMPT          LIBRARY CACHE SECTION
PROMPT          ============================
PROMPT hit ratio should be > 70, and pin ratio > 70 ...
PROMPT

COLUMN "reloads" FORMAT 999,999,999
SELECT namespace, trunc(gethitratio * 100) "Hit ratio",
       trunc(pinhitratio * 100) "pin hit ratio", reloads "reloads"
FROM V$LIBRARYCACHE;
```

Just as the wisdom of the 1980s dictated that data should be centralized, the 1990s have begun an era where SQL is also centralized and managed. With the centralization of SQL, many previously impossible tasks have become trivial. For example:

- SQL can easily be identified and reused.

- SQL can be extracted by a DBA, allowing the DBA to run **EXPLAIN PLAN** utilities to determine the proper placement of table indexes.

- SQL can be searched, allowing for fast identification of "where used" information. For example, when a column changes definition, all SQL that references that column can be quickly identified.

As memory becomes less expensive, it will eventually become desirable to have all of an application's SQL and code loaded into the Oracle library cache where the code will be quickly available for execution by any external application, regardless of the its platform or host language. The most compelling reasons for putting all SQL within packages are portability and code management. If all application, become "SQL-less," with calls to stored procedures, then entire applications can be ported to other platforms without touching a single line of the application code.

As the cost of memory drops, 500 MB Oracle regions will not be uncommon. Until that time, however, the DBA must carefully consider the ramifications of pinning a package in the SGA.

Oracle Triggers

Many database systems now support the use of *triggers* that can be fired at specific events. The insertion, modification, or deletion of a record may fire a trigger, or business events, such as **place_order**, may initiate a trigger action. Oracle Corporation claims that the design of their triggers closely follow the ANSI/ISO SQL3 draft standard (ANSI X3H6), but Oracle triggers are more robust in functionality than the ANSI standard. Triggers are defined at the schema level of the system, and they will fire whenever an SQL **SELECT**, **UPDATE**, **DELETE**, or **INSERT** command is issued. Remember, a trigger is always associated with a single DML event.

Deciding When To Use A Trigger

The choice of when to use a trigger and when to use a stored procedure can have a profound impact on the performance of a system. In general, triggers are used when additional processing is required as a row is inserted into a table. For example, assume that whenever a **CUSTOMER** row is added, the system is required to look for the customer in the **BAD_CREDIT** table. If the customer appears in the **BAD_CREDIT** table, then its **shipping_status** column is set to 'COD'. In this case, a trigger on **INSERT OF CUSTOMER** can fire the PL/SQL procedure to do the necessary lookup and set the **shipping_status** field to its appropriate value.

Oracle triggers have the ability to call procedures, and a trigger may include SQL statements, thus providing the ability to nest SQL statements. Oracle triggers are stored as procedures that may be parameterized and used to simulate object-oriented behavior. For example, assume that we want to perform a behavior called **CHECK_TOTAL_INVENTORY** whenever an item is added to an order (see Figure 11.3).

The trigger definition would be as follows:

```
CREATE TRIGGER CHECK_TOTAL_INVENTORY
          AFTER  SELECT OF ITEM
FOR EACH ROW
```

```
   SELECT count(*) INTO :count
    FROM QUANTITY WHERE item_# = :myitem:

IF :count < ITEM.TOTAL then
    ......
END IF;
```

Triggers could also be combined to handle multiple events, such as the reordering of an **ITEM** when the quantity-on-hand falls below a predefined level. For example:

```
CREATE TRIGGER REORDER BEFORE UPDATE ON ITEM
   FOR EACH ROW WHEN (new.reorderable = 'Y')
       BEGIN
               IF new.qty_on_hand + old.qty_on_order < new.minimum_qty
               THEN
               INSERT INTO REORDER VALUES (item_nbr, reorder_qty);
               new.qty_on_order := old.qty_on_order + reorder_qty;
               END IF;
       END
```

Oracle Hash Tables

Oracle7 now supports the concepts of hash clusters. A hash cluster is a construct that works with Oracle clusters and uses the **HASHKEYS** command to allow fast access to the primary key for the cluster. Oracle relies on a *hashing algorithm*, which takes a symbolic key and converts it into a row ID (**ROWID**), as shown in Figure 11.4. The hashing function ensures that the cluster key is retrieved in a single I/O, which is faster than reading multiple blocks from an index tree. Because a hashing algorithm

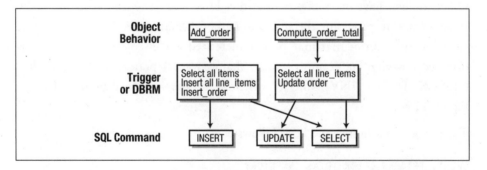

Figure 11.3
The relationship among objects, triggers, and SQL.

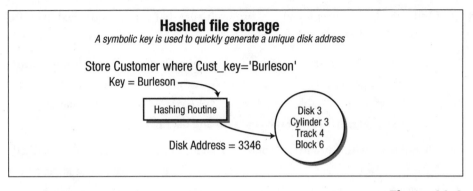

Figure 11.4
A sample hashing routine.

always produces the same key each time it reads an input value, duplicate keys have to be avoided. In Oracle, these "collisions" result when the value of **HASHKEYS** is less than the maximum number of cluster key values. For example, if a hash cluster uses the **cust_nbr** field as the key, and you know that there will be 50,000 unique **cust_nbr** values, then you must be sure that the value of **HASHKEYS** is set to at least 50,000. Also, you should always round up your value for **HASHKEYS** to the next highest prime number. Here is an example of a hash cluster:

```
CREATE CLUSTER my_cluster (customer_nbr     VARCHAR(10))
   TABLESPACE user1
        STORAGE (initial 50K next 50K pctincrease 1)
        SIZE 2K
        HASH IS customer_nbr hashkeys 50000;
```

Now, a table is defined within the cluster, as follows:

```
CREATE TABLE CUSTOMER (
        customer_nbr  NUMBER PRIMARY KEY )
CLUSTER my_cluster (customer_nbr);
```

The **SIZE** parameter is usually set to the average row size for the table. Oracle recommends the following:

- Use hash clusters to store tables that are commonly accessed by **WHERE** clauses that specify equalities.

- Only use hash clusters when you can afford to keep plenty of free space on each database block for updates. This value is set by the **PCTFREE** statement in the **CREATE TABLE** parameter.

- Only use a hash cluster if you are absolutely sure that you will not need to create a new, larger cluster at a later time.

- Do not use a hash cluster if your table is commonly accessed by full-table scans, especially if a great deal of extra space for future growth has been allocated to the hash cluster. In a full-table scan, Oracle will read all blocks of the hash cluster, regardless of whether or not they contain any data rows.

- Do not use a hash cluster if any of the hash cluster keys are frequently modified. Changing the value of a hash key causes the hashing algorithm to generate a new location, and the database will migrate the cluster to a new database block if the key value is changed. This is a very time-consuming operation.

Keep in mind that the total size of the index columns must fit inside a single Oracle block. If the index contains too many long values, additional I/O will be required and **UPDATE**s and **INSERT**s will cause serious performance problems. Note the sample hashing routine shown in Figure 11.4.

As discussed earlier in this chapter, the database designer may choose to make the buffer blocks large to minimize I/O if the application clusters records on a database page.

Oracle Clusters

Clustering is a very important concept for improving client/server performance. When traversing a database, reducing I/O always improves throughput. The concept of clusters is very similar to the use of the VIA set in the CODASYL Network database model where member records are stored physically near their parent records. For Oracle, clusters can be used to define common one-to-many access paths, and the member rows can be stored on the same database block as their owner row. For example, assume that you have a one-to-many relationship between customers and orders. If your application commonly accesses the data from customer to order, you can cluster the order rows on the same database block as the customer row. In this way, you'll receive the list of all orders for a customer in a single I/O (see Figure 11.5). Of course, you will need to size the database blocks with **db_block_size** so that an entire order will fit onto a single database block.

One important issue needs to be addressed, however. While a cluster will tremendously improve performance in one direction, queries in the other direction will suffer. For example, consider the many-to-many relationship among customers and

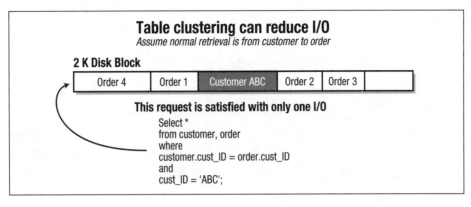

Figure 11.5
A sample Oracle cluster.

orders. Let's say there is a junction table, **ORDER_LINE**, at the intersection of this many-to-many relationship and you need to decide which owner, **ORDER** or **ITEM**, will be the anchor for your cluster. If you commonly traverse from order to item (for example, when displaying an order form), it would make sense to cluster the **ORDER_LINE** records on the same database block as their **ORDER** owner. If, on the other hand, you commonly traversed from **ITEM** to **ORDER** (for example, when requesting the details for all orders containing widgets), you would cluster the **ORDER_LINE** rows near their **ITEM** owner. If you cluster on the **ORDER** owner, database queries that display order forms will be very fast, while queries in the other direction will have to do additional I/O.

Now let's take a look at how Oracle's memory structures can be tuned to provide optimal throughput for database transactions.

Tuning Oracle Memory

The way Oracle memory is managed can have a huge impact on performance, and each SGA can be tuned according to the needs of the application. However, one must remember that the SGA faces dynamic forces, and one transaction can cause problems for other transactions that are accessing Oracle. Hundreds of transactions may be serviced concurrently, each requesting different data. Tuning the memory for an activity at one point in time may not be suitable at another time. Because of the dynamic nature of the Oracle database, only general tuning is possible.

Fortunately, this general approach works out well because of Oracle's high level of sophistication. Now let's take a look at the issues involved with determining the sizes of the memory regions for an Oracle warehouse.

Sizing The System Global Area (SGA)

The init.ora file and the config.ora file not only determine the overall size of the SGA, but they also determine which Oracle constructs get a specified amount of memory. Init.ora parameters rank in the dozens. To see all of the init.ora parameters, enter SQL*DBA and issue this command:

```
SQLDBA> SHOW PARAMETERS
```

The results are shown in Listing 11.5.

Listing 11.5   The results of the **SHOW PARAMETERS** command.

NAME	TYPE	VALUE
async_read	boolean	TRUE
async_write	boolean	TRUE
audit_file_dest	string	/opt/oracle/admin/my_sid/ audit
audit_trail	string	TRUE
background_core_dump	string	full
background_dump_dest	string	/opt/oracle/admin/my_sid/ bdump
blank_trimming	boolean	FALSE
cache_size_threshold	integer	40
ccf_io_size	integer	134217728
checkpoint_process	boolean	FALSE
cleanup_rollback_entries	integer	20
close_cached_open_cursors	boolean	FALSE
commit_point_strength	integer	1
compatible	string	
compatible_no_recovery	string	
control_files	string	/Data/d09/ORACLE/mysid/ control1.dbf, /Data/d10/ORACLE/my_sid/ control2.dbf, /Data/d01/ORACLE/mysid/ control3.dbf
core_dump_dest	string	/opt/oracle/admin/mysid/ cdump

```
cursor_space_for_time                   boolean   FALSE
db_block_buffers                        integer   400
db_block_checkpoint_batch               integer   8
db_block_lru_extended_statistics        integer   0
db_block_lru_statistics                 boolean   FALSE
db_block_size                           integer   4096
db_domain                               string    WORLD
db_file_multiblock_read_count           integer   16
db_file_simultaneous_writes             integer   4
db_files                                integer   30
db_name                                 string    my_sid
db_writers                              integer   1
dblink_encrypt_login                    boolean   FALSE
discrete_transactions_enabled           boolean   FALSE
distributed_lock_timeout                integer   60
distributed_recovery_connection_hol     integer   200
distributed_transactions                integer   19
dml_locks                               integer   100
enqueue_resources                       integer   177
event                                   string
fixed_date                              string
gc_db_locks                             integer   400
gc_files_to_locks                       string
gc_lck_procs                            integer   1
gc_rollback_locks                       integer   20
gc_rollback_segments                    integer   20
gc_save_rollback_locks                  integer   20
gc_segments                             integer   10
gc_tablespaces                          integer   5
global_names                            boolean   FALSE
ifile                                   file      /opt/oracle/admin/my_sid/
                                                  configmptp.ora

instance_number                         integer   0
job_queue_interval                      integer   60
job_queue_keep_connections              boolean   FALSE
job_queue_processes                     integer   0
license_max_sessions                    integer   0
license_max_users                       integer   0
license_sessions_warning                integer   0
log_archive_buffer_size                 integer   64
log_archive_buffers                     integer   4
log_archive_dest                        string    /opt/oracle/admin/my_sid/
                                                  arch/my_sid
log_archive_format                      string    %t_%s.dbf
log_archive_start                       boolean   TRUE
log_buffer                              integer   32768
log_checkpoint_interval                 integer   10000
```

```
log_checkpoint_timeout                integer  0
log_checkpoints_to_alert              boolean  FALSE
log_files                             integer  255
log_simultaneous_copies               integer  2
log_small_entry_max_size              integer  800
max_commit_propagation_delay          integer  90000
max_dump_file_size                    integer  500
max_enabled_roles                     integer  20
max_rollback_segments                 integer  30
max_transaction_branches              integer  8
mts_dispatchers                       string
mts_listener_address                  string   (address=(protocol=
                                               ipc)(key=%s))

mts_max_dispatchers                   integer  0
mts_max_servers                       integer  0
mts_servers                           integer  0
mts_service                           string   my_sid
nls_currency                          string
nls_date_format                       string
nls_date_language                     string
nls_iso_currency                      string
nls_language                          string   AMERICAN
nls_numeric_characters                string
nls_sort                              string
nls_territory                         string   AMERICA
open_cursors                          integer  100
open_links                            integer  4
optimizer_comp_weight                 integer  0
optimizer_mode                        string   CHOOSE
os_authent_prefix                     string
os_roles                              boolean  FALSE
parallel_default_max_instances        integer  0
parallel_default_max_scans            integer  0
parallel_default_scansize             integer  100
parallel_max_servers                  integer  5
parallel_min_servers                  integer  0
parallel_server_idle_time             integer  5
post_wait_device                      string   /devices/pseudo/pw@0:pw
pre_page_sga                          boolean  FALSE
processes                             integer  60
recovery_parallelism                  integer  0
reduce_alarm                          boolean  FALSE
remote_login_passwordfile             string   NONE
remote_os_authent                     boolean  FALSE
remote_os_roles                       boolean  FALSE
resource_limit                        boolean  FALSE
```

```
rollback_segments                       string    rolb1, rolb2, rolb3, rolb4
row_cache_cursors                       integer   10
row_locking                             string    default
sequence_cache_entries                  integer   10
sequence_cache_hash_buckets             integer   7
serializable                            boolean   FALSE
session_cached_cursors                  integer   0
sessions                                integer   71
shadow_core_dump                        string    full
shared_pool_reserved_min_alloc          integer   5000
shared_pool_reserved_size               integer   0
shared_pool_size                        integer   6000000
single_process                          boolean   FALSE
snapshot_refresh_interval               integer   60
snapshot_refresh_keep_connections       boolean   FALSE
snapshot_refresh_processes              integer   0
sort_area_retained_size                 integer   65536
sort_area_size                          integer   65536
sort_mts_buffer_for_fetch_size          integer   0
sort_read_fac                           integer   5
sort_spacemap_size                      integer   512
spin_count                              integer   2000
sql92_security                          boolean   FALSE
sql_trace                               boolean   FALSE
temporary_table_locks                   integer   71
thread                                  integer   0
timed_statistics                        boolean   FALSE
transactions                            integer   78
transactions_per_rollback_segment       integer   34
use_ism                                 boolean   TRUE
use_post_wait_driver                    boolean   FALSE
use_readv                               boolean   FALSE
user_dump_dest                          string    /opt/oracle/admin/mysid/
                                                  user_dump
```

> *Note: The SQL*DBA **SHOW PARAMETERS** command does not display some of the specialized Oracle parameters that begin with an underscore, such as **_offline_rollback_segments** and **_db_block_write_batch**.*

To see the size of the SGA, you can issue the **SHOW SGA** command from SQL*DBA, as follows:

```
SQLDBA> SHOW SGA
```

This command would return results similar to the following:

```
Total System Global Area        8252756 bytes
Fixed Size                      48260 bytes
Variable Size                   6533328 bytes
Database Buffers                1638400 bytes
Redo Buffers                    32768 bytes
```

Oracle has only four parameters that affect the size of the parts of the SGA: **db_block_buffers, db_block_size, log_buffer,** and **shared_pool_size.**

- **db_block_buffers**—This parameter determines the number of database block buffers in the Oracle SGA and represents the single most important parameter to Oracle memory.

- **db_block_size**—The size of the database blocks can make a huge improvement in performance. While the default value is 2,000 bytes, databases that have large tables with full-table scans will see a tremendous improvement in performance by increasing **db_block_size** to a larger value.

- **log_buffer**—This parameter determines the amount of memory to allocate to Oracle's redo log buffers. The higher the amount of update activity, the more space needs to be allocated to the **log_buffer.**

- **shared_pool_size**—This parameter defines the pool that is shared by all users in the system, including SQL areas and data dictionary caching.

Now that we have a general understanding of the basic memory components, let's explore how the size of the database blocks will affect the performance of an Oracle data warehouse.

Using The db_block_size With db_file_multiblock_read_count

The **db_block_size** parameters can have a dramatic impact on data warehouse performance. Minimizing I/O is essential to performance, so the less physical I/O incurred by Oracle, the faster the database will run.

In general, **db_block_size** should never be set to less than 8 K, regardless of the type of application. Even online transaction processing (OLTP) systems will benefit from using 8 K blocks, while data warehouses that perform many full-table scans may benefit from even larger block sizes. Depending on the operating system, Oracle can support up to 32 K block sizes.

Also, note the relationship between **db_block_size** and the **multiblock_read_count** parameter. At the physical level in Unix, Oracle always reads in a minimum of 64 K blocks. Therefore, the values of **multiblock_read_count** and **db_block_size** should be set such that their product is 64 K. For example:

- *8 K blocks*   db_block_size=8192
  db_file_multiblock_read_count=8

- *16 K blocks*   db_block_size=16384
  db_file_multiblock_read_count=4

Note that the block size for Oracle is not immutable. Eventually, all Oracle databases should be compressed (export/import) to reduce fragmentation, and it becomes trivial at this time to alter the value of **db_block_size**.

Remember that increasing the size of **db_block_size** will increase the size of the Oracle SGA. The values of **db_block_size** are multiplied by the value of **db_block_buffers** to determine the total amount of memory to allocate for Oracle's I/O buffers.

In addition to the memory structures, significant performance improvements can be achieved by tuning the way that Oracle manages sorting operations.

Tuning Oracle Sorting

A small but very important component of SQL syntax, sorting is a frequently over-looked aspect of Oracle tuning. In general, the Oracle database will automatically perform sorting operations on row data as requested by a **CREATE INDEX** or an SQL **ORDER BY** or **GROUP BY** statement. In Oracle, sorting occurs under the following circumstances:

- Using the **ORDER BY** clause in SQL

- Using the **GROUP BY** clause in SQL

- Creating an index

- Invoking a **MERGE SORT** using the SQL optimizer because inadequate indexes exist for a table join

At the time a session is established with Oracle, a private sort area is allocated in memory for sorting by the session. Unfortunately, the amount of memory must be the same for all sessions—it is not possible to add additional sort area for tasks that are sort intensive. Therefore, the designer must strike a balance between allocating enough sort area to avoid disk sorts for the large sorting tasks, keeping in mind that the extra sort area will be allocated and not used by tasks that do not require intensive sorting.

The size of the private sort area is determined by the **SORT_AREA_SIZE** init.ora parameter. The size for each individual sort is specified by the **SORT_AREA_RETAINED_SIZE** init.ora parameter. Whenever a sort cannot be completed within the assigned space, a disk sort is invoked using the temporary tablespace for the Oracle instance. As a general rule, only index creation and **ORDER BY** clauses using functions should be allowed to use a disk sort.

Disk sorts are expensive for several reasons. First, they consume resources in the temporary tablespaces. Oracle must also allocate buffer pool blocks to hold the blocks in the temporary tablespace. In-memory sorts are always preferable to disk sorts, and disk sorts will surely slow down an individual task, as well as impact other concurrent tasks on the Oracle instance. Also, excessive disk sorting will cause a high value for free buffer waits, paging other tasks' data blocks out of the buffer. To see the amount of disk and in-memory sorts, issue the following query against the **V$SYSSTAT** table:

```
sorts.sql - Displays in-memory and disk sorts
SPOOL /tmp/sorts
COLUMN value FORMAT 999,999,999
SELECT NAME, VALUE FROM V$SYSSTAT
    WHERE NAME LIKE 'sort%';
SPOOL OFF;
```

Here is the output:

```
SQL> @sorts

NAME                                               VALUE
--------                                           ---------
sorts (memory)                                     7,019
sorts (disk)                                       49
sorts (rows)                                       3,288,608
```

You can see that there were 49 sorts to disk. Out of a total of 3.2 million sorts, this is well below 1 percent and is probably acceptable for the system.

> **Note:** *For tips on avoiding disk sorts, see Chapter 12, Tuning Oracle SQL, where we'll take a look at specific techniques for assuring in-memory sorts.*

With Oracle version 7.2, several new parameters were added to the init.ora file to allocate a new in-memory sort area. The **sort_write_buffer_size** parameter defines the size of this new buffer, and the **sort_write_buffers** defines the number of buffer blocks. You must also set the parameter **sort_direct_writes_true** to use this feature. Writing sorts to this buffer bypasses the need for the sort to contend for free blocks in the buffer cache, thereby improving sorting performance by up to 50 percent. Of course, this is done at the expense of additional memory with the SGA. This move towards segmenting the buffer into individual components can dramatically improve response time in Oracle.

The Oracle Program Global Area (PGA)

As mentioned earlier in the chapter, the SGA is not the only memory area available to programs. PGA is a private memory area allocated to external tasks. The PGA is used for keeping application-specific information, such as the values of cursors, and it allocates memory for internal sorting of result sets from SQL queries. The following two init.ora parameters influence the size of the PGA:

- **open_links**—Defines the maximum number for concurrent remote sessions that a process may initiate. Oracle's default is four, meaning that a single SQL statement may reference up to four remote databases within a query.

- **sort_area_size**—Defines the maximum amount of PGA memory that can be used for disk sorts. For very large sorts, Oracle will sort the data in its temporary tablespace, and the **sort_area_size** memory is used to manage the sorting process.

In order to effectively tune Oracle databases, we must be conscious of the other internal memory structures that are used to cache the SQL and stored procedures inside database memory.

Tuning The shared_pool_size

The shared pool component of the Oracle SGA is primarily used to store shared SQL cursors, stored procedures, and the cache for data from the data dictionary cache. The library and dictionary cache are the two components of the shared pool. The shared SQL areas and the PL/SQL areas are called the *library cache*; the other main component of the shared pool is the *dictionary cache*.

Tuning The Oracle Library Cache

The library cache miss ratio tells the DBA whether or not to add space to the shared pool, and it represents the ratio of the sum of library cache reloads to the sum of pins (pinning is discussed in more detail later in this chapter). In general, if this ratio is more than one, you may want to consider increasing the **shared_pool_size**. Library cache misses occur during the compilation of SQL statements. The compilation of an SQL statement consists of two phases: the parse phase and the execute phase. When the time comes to parse an SQL statement, Oracle first checks to see if the parsed representation of the statement already exists in the library cache. If not, Oracle will allocate a shared SQL area within the library cache and then parse the SQL statement. At execution time, Oracle checks to see if a parsed representation of the SQL statement already exists in the library cache. If not, Oracle will reparse and execute the statement.

Within the library cache, the hit ratios can be determined for all dictionary objects that are loaded. These include stored procedures, triggers, indexes, package bodies, and clusters. If any of the hit ratios fall below 75 percent, you are well advised to add to the **shared_pool_size**.

The table **V$LIBRARYCACHE** is the V$ table that keeps information about library cache activity. The table has three relevant columns. The first is the **namespace**, which states whether the measurement is for the SQL area, a table or procedure, a package body, or a trigger. The second value in this table is **pins**, which counts the number of times an item in the library cache is executed. The **reloads** column counts the number of times a parsed representation did not exist in the library cache, forcing Oracle to allocate the private SQL areas in order to parse and execute the statement.

Listing 11.6 shows an example of a SQL*Plus query for the interrogation of the **V$ LIBRARYCACHE** to retrieve the necessary performance information.

Listing 11.6 An SQL*Plus query interrogating the V$LIBRARYCACHE table.

```
library.sql - lists the library cache
PROMPT
PROMPT          ==============================
PROMPT             LIBRARY CACHE MISS RATIO
PROMPT          ==============================
PROMPT (If > 1 then increase the shared_pool_size in init.ora)
PROMPT
COLUMN "LIBRARY CACHE MISS RATIO" FORMAT 99.9999
COLUMN "executions"     FORMAT 999,999,999
COLUMN "Cache misses while executing"    FORMAT 999,999,999
SELECT sum(pins) "executions", sum(reloads)
    "Cache misses while executing",
    (((sum(reloads)/sum(pins)))) "LIBRARY CACHE MISS RATIO"
FROM v$librarycache;


PROMPT
PROMPT          ==============================
PROMPT             LIBRARY CACHE SECTION
PROMPT          ==============================
PROMPT hit ratio should be > 70, and pin ratio > 70 ...
PROMPT

COLUMN "reloads" FORMAT 999,999,999
SELECT namespace, trunc(gethitratio * 100) "Hit ratio",
        trunc(pinhitratio * 100) "pin hit ratio", RELOADS "reloads"
FROM V$LIBRARYCACHE;
```

Listing 11.7 shows the output from the query in Listing 11.6.

Listing 11.7 The output of the query in Listing 11.6.

```
SQL> @temp


==============================
LIBRARY CACHE MISS RATIO
==============================
(If > 1 then increase the shared_pool_size in init.ora)

  executions Cache misses while executing LIBRARY CACHE MISS RATIO
---------- ---------------------------- -----------------------
     251,272                        2,409                    .0096
```

```
==============================
Library Cache Section
==============================
hit ratio should be > 70, and pin ratio > 70 ...


namespace              Hit ratio    pin hit ratio     reloads
-----------            ----------   --------------    --------
SQL AREA                  90             94            1,083
TABLE/PROCEDURE           93             94            1,316
BODY                      96             95            9
TRIGGER                   89             86            1
INDEX                     0              31            0
CLUSTER                   44             33            0
OBJECT                    100            100           0
PIPE                      100            100           0

8 rows selected.
```

One of the most important steps a developer can take to reduce the usage of the library cache is to ensure that all SQL is written within stored procedures. For example, Oracle library cache will examine the following SQL statements and conclude that they are not identical:

```
SELECT * FROM Customer;

SELECT * FROM CUSTOMER;
```

While capitalizing a single letter, adding an extra space between verbs, or using a different variable name may seem trivial, the Oracle software is not sufficiently intelligent to recognize that the statements are identical. Consequently, Oracle will reparse and execute the second SQL statement, even though it is functionally identical to the first SQL statement.

Another problem occurs when values are hard-coded into SQL statements. For example, Oracle considers the following statements to be different:

```
SELECT count(*) FROM CUSTOMER WHERE STATUS = 'NEW';

SELECT count(*) FROM CUSTOMER WHERE STATUS = 'PREFERRED';
```

This problem is easily alleviated by using an identical bind variable, such as:

```
SELECT count(*) FROM CUSTOMER WHERE STATUS = :var1;
```

The best way to prevent reloads from happening is to encapsulate all SQL into stored procedures and bundle the stored procedures into packages. This removes all SQL from application programs and moves them into Oracle's data dictionary. This method also has the nice side effect of making all database calls as functions. This creates a layer of independence between the application and the database. Again, by efficiently reusing identical SQL, the number of reloads will be kept to a minimum, and the library cache will function at optimal speed.

The **cursor_space_for_time** parameter can be used to speed executions within the library cache. Setting **cursor_space_for_time** to **false** tells Oracle that a shared SQL area may be deallocated from the library cache to make room for a new SQL statement. Setting **cursor_space_for_time** to **true** means that all shared SQL areas are pinned in the cache until all application cursors are closed. When set to **true**, Oracle will not bother to check the library cache on subsequent execution calls because it has already pinned the SQL in the cache. This technique can improve the performance for some queries, but **cursor_space_for_time** should not be set to **true** if there are cache misses on execution calls. Cache misses indicate that the **shared_pool_size** is already too small, and forcing the pinning of shared SQL areas will only aggravate the problem.

Another way to improve performance on the library cache is to use the init.ora **session_cached_cursors** parameter. As we know, Oracle checks the library cache for parsed SQL statements, but **session_cached_cursors** can be used to cache the cursors for a query. This is especially useful for tasks that repeatedly issue parse calls for the same SQL statement—for instance, where an SQL statement is repeatedly executed with a different variable value. An example would be an SQL request that performs the same query 50 times, once for each state:

```
SELECT sum(sale_amount)
FROM SALES
WHERE
state_code = :var1;
```

Once the library cache has been tuned, we can take a look at the other cache area within Oracle memory, the Oracle dictionary cache.

Tuning The Oracle Dictionary Cache

The data dictionary cache is used to hold rows from the internal Oracle metadata tables, including SQL that is stored in packages. Based on my experience, I highly recommend storing all SQL in packages, so let's take a look at how packages interact with the dictionary cache.

When a package is invoked, Oracle will first check the dictionary cache to see if the package is already in memory. Of course, a package will not be in memory the first time it is requested, and Oracle will register a *dictionary cache miss*. Consequently, it is virtually impossible to have an instance with no dictionary cache misses because each item must be loaded once.

The **V$ROWCACHE** table is used to measure dictionary cache activity. Three columns are of interest: **parameter**, **gets**, and **misses**. The first column, **parameter**, describes the type of dictionary object that has been requested. The second parameter, **gets**, provides the total number of requests for objects of that type. The last column, **misses**, counts the number of times Oracle had to perform a disk I/O to retrieve a row from its dictionary tables. The data dictionary cache hit ratio is used to measure the ratio of dictionary hits to misses.

> **Note:** The **V$** tables are only good for measuring the average hit ratio for the life of an instance. For a snapshot of the Oracle hit ratios, use Oracle **ESTAT/BSTAT** utilities located in $ORACLE_HOME/rdbms/admin. These utilities are named utlbstat.sql and utlestat.sql.

The data dictionary cache hit ratio can be measured using the script shown in Listing 11.8.

Listing 11.8   The script that measures the cache hit ratio.

```
dict.sql - Displays the dictionary cache hit ratio
PROMPT
PROMPT
PROMPT          =============================
```

```
PROMPT          DATA DICT HIT RATIO
PROMPT          ============================
PROMPT (should be higher than 90 else increase shared_pool_size
PROMPT in init.ora)

COLUMN "Data Dict. Gets"            FORMAT 999,999,999
COLUMN "Data Dict. cache misses"    FORMAT 999,999,999
SELECT sum(gets) "Data Dict. Gets",
       sum(getmisses) "Data Dict. cache misses",
       trunc((1-(sum(getmisses)/sum(gets)))*100)
          "DATA DICT CACHE HIT RATIO"
FROM V$ROWCACHE;


SQL> @t2


============================
DATA DICT HIT RATIO
============================

(should be higher than 90 else increase shared_pool_size in init.ora)


Fri Feb 23                                              page    1
                        dbname Database
                    Data Dictionary Hit Ratios

Data Dict. Gets Data Dict. cache misses DATA DICT CACHE HIT RATIO
---------  ---------------  ---------------------------------------
409,288        11,639                    97

1 row selected.
```

Listing 11.9 measures the contention for each dictionary object type.

Listing 11.9   The script that measures the contention.

```
ddcache.sql - Lists all data dictionary contention
REM SQLX SCRIPT
SET PAUSE OFF;
SET ECHO OFF;
SET TERMOUT OFF;
SET LINESIZE 78;
SET PAGESIZE 60;
SET NEWPAGE 0;
```

```
TTITLE "dbname Database|Data Dictionary Hit Ratios";
SPOOL /tmp/ddcache
SELECT     substr(PARAMETER,1,20) PARAMETER,
           gets,getmisses,count,usage,
           ROUND((1 - getmisses / decode(gets,0,1,gets))*100,1) hitrate
FROM       V$ROWCACHE
ORDER BY 6,1;
SPOOL OFF;
```

Here is the output of the script shown in Listing 11.5:

```
SQL> @t1

Fri Feb 23                                              page    1
                         dbname Database
                    Data Dictionary Hit Ratios
```

PARAMETER	GETS	GETMISSES	COUNT	USAGE	HITRATE
dc_object_ids	136	136	12	0	0
dc_free_extents	1978	1013	67	48	48.8
dc_used_extents	1930	970	63	5	49.7
dc_database_links	4	2	3	2	50
dc_sequence_grants	101	18	121	18	82.2
dc_synonyms	527	33	34	33	93.7
dc_objects	18999	947	389	387	95
dc_columns	163520	6576	2261	2247	96
dc_segments	8548	314	127	117	96.3
dc_constraint_defs	7842	250	218	210	96.8
dc_table_grants	26718	792	772	763	97
dc_sequences	4179	75	11	7	98.2
dc_users	1067	14	20	14	98.7
dc_tables	49497	261	272	271	99.5
dc_tablespace_quotas	957	4	5	4	99.6
dc_indexes	59548	172	329	328	99.7
dc_tablespaces	1162	3	7	3	99.7
dc_tablespaces	1201	4	27	4	99.7
dc_user_grants	9900	14	24	14	99.9
dc_usernames	18452	18	20	18	99.9
dc_users	14418	17	18	17	99.9
dc_column_grants	0	0	1	0	100
dc_constraint_defs	0	0	1	0	100
dc_constraints	0	0	1	0	100
dc_files	0	0	1	0	100
dc_histogram_defs	0	0	1	0	100

```
dc_profiles              0       0       1       0      100
dc_rollback_segments  18560      6      17       7      100
```

28 rows selected.

Multithreaded Server Tuning

Remember, if you are using SQL*Net version 2 with the multithreaded server, Oracle will allocate storage in the library cache to hold session information. As new connections are established through the MTS, Oracle will allocate memory, and the amount of memory can be measured with the **V$SESSSTAT** table. Listing 11.10 shows a sample query using **V$SESSSTAT**.

Listing 11.10   A sample query using **V$SESSSTAT**.

```
SELECT (sum(value) || ' bytes' "Total memory for all sessions"
   FROM V$SESSSTAT, V$STATNAME
WHERE
NAME = 'session memory'
AND
V$SESSSTAT.statistics# = V$STATNAME.statistic#;


SELECT (sum(value) || ' bytes' "Total maximum memory for all sessions"
   FROM V$SESSSTAT, V$STATNAME
WHERE
NAME = 'max session memory'
AND
V$SESSSTAT.statistics# = V$STATNAME.statistic#;
```

The output might look like this:

```
Total memory for all sessions
-----------------------------
203460 bytes

Total maximum memory for all sessions
-------------------------------------
712473 bytes
```

Based on an instance in time, this report shows that 204 K is allocated to sessions, while the maximum memory for all sessions is 712 K. When deciding whether or not to increase the **shared_pool_size** parameter, the total memory for all sessions is the best guideline because it is unlikely that all sessions will reach maximum memory allocation at the same moment in time.

Now let's take a look at tuning the single most important parameter in the system, **db_block_buffers**.

Tuning The db_block_buffers Parameter

When a request is made to Oracle to retrieve data, Oracle will first check the internal memory structures to see if the data is already in the buffer. In this fashion, Oracle avoids unnecessary I/O. It would be ideal if we could create one buffer for each database page, ensuring that Oracle would only read each block once. However, the costs of memory in the real world make this prohibited.

At best, we can only allocate a small number of real-memory buffers, and Oracle will manage this memory for us. Oracle utilizes a least-recently-used algorithm to determine which database pages are to be flushed from memory. Another related memory issue emerges that deals with the size of the database blocks. In most Unix environments, database blocks are sized to only 2 K. Unlike the mainframe ancestors that allowed blocks of up to 16,000 bytes, large blocks are not possible because of the way Unix handles its page I/O. Remember, I/O is the single most important slowdown in a client/server system, and the more relevant the data that can be grabbed in a single I/O, the better the performance. The cost of reading a 2 K block is not significantly higher than the cost of reading an 8 K block. However, the 8 K block read will be of no benefit if we only want a small row in a single table. On the other hand, if the tables are commonly read from front to back, or if you make appropriate use of Oracle clusters, you can reap dramatic performance improvements by switching to large block sizes. Oracle clusters are described in detail later in this chapter.

For batch-oriented reporting databases, very large block sizes are always recommended. However, many databases are used for online transaction processing during the day, while the batch reports are run in the evenings. Nevertheless, as a general rule, 8 K block sizes will benefit most systems.

Fortunately, Oracle allows for large block sizes, and the **db_block_size** parameter is used to control the physical block size of the data files. Unlike other relational databases, Oracle allocates the data files on your behalf when the **CREATE TABLESPACE** command is issued. One of the worst things that can happen to a buffer cache is the running of a full-table scan on a large table.

Predicting The Benefit Of Adding Additional Block Buffers

As database blocks are retrieved from disk into the database, they are stored in RAM memory, in an area called a *buffer*. The record remains in the buffer until it is overwritten by another database request. At read time, the database first checks to see if the data already resides in the buffer before incurring the overhead of a disk I/O, as shown in Figure 11.6.

The size of the buffer is determined by the database administrator—and for some databases, separate buffers may be created for different tables. The method for maximizing the use of buffers is to perform a check on the buffer hit ratio. The *buffer hit ratio* is the ratio of logical requests to physical disk reads. A logical read is a request from a program for a record, while a physical read is real I/O against a database. A one-to-one ratio correspondence does not always exist between logical and physical reads because some records may have been fetched by a previous task and still reside in the

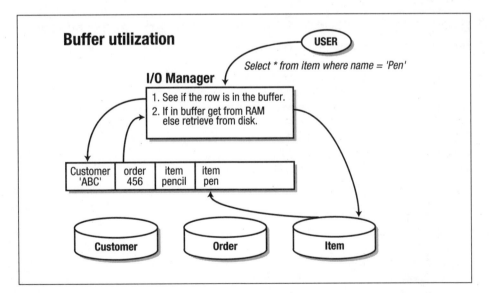

Figure 11.6
Oracle's data buffer operation.

buffer. In other words, the buffer hit ratio is the probability of finding the desired record in the memory buffer. The following calculation determines the hit ratio:

```
Hit Ratio = Logical Reads - Physical Reads / Logical Reads
```

Listings 11.11 and 11.12 show two scripts for calculating the buffer hit ratio.

Listing 11.11   Method 1: Script for calculating the buffer hit ratio.

```
buffer1.sql - displays the buffer hit ratio
PROMPT **********************************************************
PROMPT  HIT RATIO SECTION
PROMPT **********************************************************
PROMPT
PROMPT           ============================
PROMPT           BUFFER HIT RATIO
PROMPT           ============================
PROMPT (should be > 70, else increase db_block_buffers in init.ora)

SELECT trunc((1-(sum(decode(name,'physical reads',value,0))/
               (sum(decode(name,'db block gets',value,0))+
               (sum(decode(name,'consistent gets',value,0)))))
            )* 100) "Buffer Hit Ratio"
FROM V$SYSSTAT;
```

Listing 11.12   Method 2: Script for calculating the buffer hit ratio.

```
buffer2.sql - displays the buffer hit ratio

PROMPT **********************************************************
PROMPT  HIT RATIO SECTION
PROMPT **********************************************************
PROMPT
PROMPT           ============================
PROMPT           BUFFER HIT RATIO
PROMPT           ============================
PROMPT (should be > 70, else increase db_block_buffers in init.ora)

COLUMN "logical_reads" FORMAT 99,999,999,999
COLUMN "phys_reads"    FORMAT 999,999,999
COLUMN "phy_writes"    FORMAT 999,999,999
SELECT A.value + B.value  "logical_reads",
       C.value            "phys_reads",
       D.value            "phy_writes",
       ROUND(100 * ((A.value+B.value)-C.value) / (A.value+B.value))
```

```
     "BUFFER HIT RATIO"
FROM V$SYSSTAT a, V$SYSSTAT b, V$SYSSTAT c, V$SYSSTAT d
WHERE
   A.statistic# = 37
AND
   B.statistic# = 38
AND
   C.statistic# = 39
AND
   D.statistic# = 40;
```

Listing 11.13 shows the output from the Method 2 script (presented in Listing 11.12).

Listing 11.13   Output from the Method 2 script.

```
SQL> @t3
***********************************************************
Hit Ratio Section
***********************************************************


==============================
BUFFER HIT RATIO
==============================

(should be > 70, else increase db_block_buffers in init.ora)

Fri Feb 23                                              page    1
                        dbname Database
                   Data Dictionary Hit Ratios

 logical_reads    phys_reads   phy_writes BUFFER HIT RATIO
 --------------   ----------   ---------- ----------------
     18,987,002      656,805       87,281               97

1 row selected.
```

Be aware that the buffer hit ratio (as gathered from the V$ tables) measures the overall buffer hit ratio of the system since the Oracle instance was started. Because the V$ tables keep their information forever, the current buffer hit ratio may be far worse than the 97 percent shown in the preceding listing. To get a measure of the buffer hit ratio over a specific time period, use Oracle's **BSTAT/ESTAT** utility in $ORACLE_HOME/rdbms/admin.

While some of the mainframe databases allow for individual buffers for each record type, mid-range databases such as Oracle provide only one database-wide buffer for the database I/O. In general, the buffer hit ratio is a function of the application and of the size of the buffer pool. For example, an application with a very large customer table is not likely to benefit from an increase in buffers because the I/O is widely distributed across the tables. However, smaller applications will often see an improvement as the buffer size is increased because this also increases the probability that frequently requested data will remain in the buffer. For example, the high-level nodes of an index are generally used by all applications, and response time can be improved if these blocks can be kept in the buffers at all times.

Databases that allow segmented buffer pools (such as the CA-IDMS) can be configured such that small indexes will be kept in the buffer at all times. This is accomplished by allocating an index to a separate area and assigning the area to a separate buffer in the Device Media Control Language (DMCL).

If the buffer hit ratio is less then 70 percent (i.e., two-thirds of data requests require a physical disk I/O), you may want to increase the number of blocks in the buffer. In Oracle, a single buffer pool exists and is controlled by a parameter called **db_block_buffers** in the init.ora process.

To estimate statistics, the following init.ora parameters must be set, and the database must be bounced:

```
db_block_lru_statistics = true
db_block_lru_extended_statistics = #buffers
```

> **Note:** Where **#buffers** is the number of buffers to add, be aware that the SGA will increase in size by this amount, such that a value of 10,000 would increase an SGA by 40 MB (assuming a 4 K block size). Make sure that your host has enough memory before trying this. Also, note that performance will be degraded while these statistics are running, and it is a good idea to choose a noncritical time for this test.

Oracle uses two system tables called **SYS.X$KCBRBH** (to track buffer hits) and **SYS.X$KCBCBH** (to track buffer misses). Note that these are temporary tables and must be interrogated before stopping Oracle. An SQL query can be formulated against this table to create a chart showing the size of the buffer pool and the expected buffer hits, as follows:

```
REM morebuff.sql - Predicts benefit from added blocks to the buffer

SET LINESIZE 100;
SET PAGES 999;

COLUMN "Additional Cache Hits" FORMAT 999,999,999;
COLUMN "Interval"    FORMAT a20;

SELECT  250*trunc(indx/250)+1
               ||' to '||250*(trunc(indx/250)+1) "Interval",
               sum(count) "Additional Cache Hits"
FROM SYS.X$KCBRBH
GROUP BY trunc(indx/250);
```

This SQL creates the following result, which shows the range of additional buffer blocks that may be added to the cache and the expected increase in cache hits:

```
SQL> @morebuff

Interval                Additional Cache Hits
-------------           -----------------------
1 to 250                                   60
251 to 500                                 46
501 to 750                                 52
751 to 1000                               162
1001 to 1250                              191
1251 to 1500                              232
1501 to 1750                              120
1751 to 2000                               95
2001 to 2250                               51
2251 to 2500                               37
2501 to 2750                               42
```

You can see that the number of cache hits peaks at 232 with the addition of 1,500 buffer blocks. You can then see a decreasing marginal benefit from adding more buffers. This is very typical of online transaction processing databases that have common information frequently referenced by all end users.

The following sample is from a database that primarily performs reports that invoke full-table scans:

```
SQL> @morebuff

Interval                Additional Cache Hits
```

```
- - - - - - - - - - - -     - - - - - - - - - - - - - - - - - - - - -
1 to 250                    60
251 to 500                  46
501 to 750                  52
751 to 1000                 62
1001 to 1250                51
1251 to 1500                24
1501 to 1750                28
1751 to 2000                35
2001 to 2250                31
2251 to 2500                37
2501 to 2750                42
```

Here, you can see no peak and no marginal trends with the addition of buffers. This is very typical of databases that read large tables from front to back. Doing a full-table scan on a table that is larger than the buffer will cause the first table blocks to eventually page out as the last table rows are read. Consequently, we will see no specific "optimal" setting for the **db_block_buffers** parameter.

As a general rule, all available memory on the host should be tuned, and Oracle should be given **db_block_buffers** up to a point of diminishing returns. There is a point where the addition of buffer blocks will not significantly improve the buffer hit ratio, and these tools give the Oracle DBA the ability to find the optimal amount of buffers.

In other words, as long as marginal gains can be achieved from adding buffers and you have the memory to spare, you should increase the value of **db_block_buffers**. Increases in buffer blocks increase the amount of required RAM memory for the database, and it is not always possible to "hog" all of the memory on a processor for the database management system. Therefore, the DBA should carefully review the amount of available memory and determine an optimal amount of buffer blocks.

> **Note:** If you over-allocate SGA memory on a Unix system, such as Oracle user's sign-on, the Unix kernel will begin to swap out chunks of active memory in order to accommodate the new users and cause a huge performance problem.

Today, many databases reside alone on a host. When this is the case, you can predict the amount of "spare" memory and run your Oracle SGA up to that amount. For example, assume that your host machine has 350 MB of available memory. The Unix kernel consumes 50 MB, leaving 300 MB available for your Oracle database. You know that each online user will need to allocate a PGA when accessing the application, and the largest share of the PGA is determined by the value of the **sort_area_size** init.ora parameter. Therefore, assuming that you have a **sort_area_size** of 20 MB and 10 online users, you can assume that about 200 MB of real memory must be reserved for end-user sessions, leaving 100 MB for the Oracle SGA.

In many cases, you will see conditions where memory may be subtracted from the SGA without causing any serious performance hits. Oracle provides the **X$KCBCBH** table for this purpose, and you can query this table to track the number of buffer misses that would occur if the SGA was decreased in size. For example:

```
REM lessbuff.sql - Predicts losses from subtracting
REM                 db_block_buffer values

SET LINESIZE 100;
SET PAGES 999;

COLUMN "Additional Cache Misses" FORMAT 999,999,999;
COLUMN "Interval"    FORMAT a20;

SELECT 250*trunc(indx/250)+1
       ||' To '||250*(trunc(indx/250)+1) "Interval",
       sum(count) "Additional Cache Misses"
FROM X$KCBCBH
WHERE indx > 0
GROUP BY trunc(indx/250);
```

Following is an example of how the output might appear:

```
SQL>@lessbuff

Interval                Additional Cache Misses
------------            ------------------------
1 To 250                              3,895,959
251 To 500                               35,317
501 To 750                               19,254
751 To 1000                              12,159
```

1001 To 1250	9,853
1251 To 1500	8,624
1501 To 1750	7,035
1751 To 2000	6,857
2001 To 2250	6,308
2251 To 2500	5,625
2501 To 2750	5,516
2751 To 3000	5,343
3001 To 3250	5,230
3251 To 3500	5,394
3501 To 3750	4,965

You can clearly see that this database has some shared information, with nearly 4 million cache hits in the first 250 buffer blocks. From 250 on up, you can see a slowly decreasing downward trend, indicating that this application is doing some full-table scans or is not referencing a lot of common information.

For more sophisticated databases, you can control not only the number of buffer blocks—but you can also control the block size for each buffer. For example, on an IBM mainframe, the DBA might want to make the buffer blocks very large so that I/O contention can be minimized. An I/O for 32,000 bytes is not a great deal more expensive than an I/O for 12,000 bytes, so the database designer may choose to make the buffer blocks large to minimize I/O if the application clusters records on a database page. If a customer record is only 100 bytes, the DBA will not gain by retrieving 32,000 bytes to get the targeted 100 bytes needed. However, if the DBA clusters the orders physically near the customer (i.e., on the same database page), and if I/O usually proceeds from customer to order, the DBA won't need further I/O to retrieve orders for the customer. The orders will already reside in the initial read of 32,000 bytes, as shown in Figure 11.7. Oracle clusters are described in detail later in this chapter.

Now, let's take a look at tuning the memory cache within Oracle.

Memory Cache Tuning

When I/O contention causes a performance problem, there are alternatives to disk striping (disk striping is discussed in more detail later in this chapter). For very small and high-impact data tables, it is possible to make these tables reside in RAM memory. The access time against RAM is 10,000 times faster than disk I/O, and this solution can often make a huge performance difference. Two approaches to caching are possible. The first is a hardware solution that uses extra RAM memory to hold the data

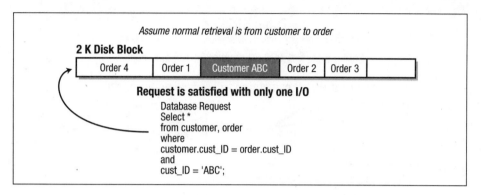

Figure 11.7
Using table clusters to reduce I/O.

table (table caching). The other alternative uses software mechanisms to reserve buffer memory for the exclusive use of the data table. While not all databases support this feature, some allow the memory buffer to be "fenced" or partitioned for the exclusive use of specific tables.

I/O-Based Tuning

In a distributed database environment, it is important to understand that the overall distributed system is only going to perform as well as the weakest link. Therefore, most distributed database tuning treats each remote node as an independent database, individually tuning each one and thereby improving overall distributed system requests.

Input/Output is the single most important factor in database tuning. Business systems, by their very nature, are relatively light on processing and heavy on their demands from the disks that comprise the database. Several tricks are available to reduce I/O time from disk, including cache memory, buffer expansion, file placement, and file striping.

Disk Striping

Striping involves taking a very large or very busy data table and distributing it across many disks. When a performance problem occurs on a regular basis, it is most often the result of disks waiting on I/O. By distributing the file across many physical devices, the overall system response time will improve. Disk striping is generally done for tables that are larger than the size of a disk device, but striping can be equally effective for small, heavily accessed tables (see Figure 11.8).

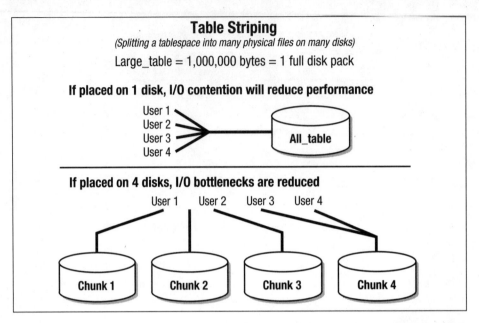

Figure 11.8
Striping a table across many disks.

Note that the data file appears to the database management system as a single logical file, which avoids any I/O problems from within the database when doing table striping. As rows are requested from the table, the SQL I/O module will request physical data blocks from the disk—one at a time—unaware that the logically continuous table actually contains many physical data files.

In an Oracle database, disk striping is done in a similar fashion. Consider the following Oracle syntax:

```
CREATE TABLESPACE TS1
    DATA FILE "/usr/disk1/bigfile1.dbf"  SIZE=30M
    DATA FILE "/usr/disk2/bigfile2.dbf"  SIZE=30M


CREATE TABLE BIG_TABLE (
    big_field1    char(8)
    big_field2    varchar(2000))
TABLESPACE TS1
STORAGE (INITIAL 25M   NEXT 25M   MINEXTENTS 2   PCTINCREASE 1);
```

Here, you can see that a tablespace is created with two data files—bigfile1 and bigfile2—each with a size of 30 MB. When you are ready to create a table within the tablespace, you would size the extents of the table such that the database is forced to allocate the table's initial extents into each data file. As the table is created in the empty tablespace, the **MINEXTENT** parameter tells the database to allocate two extents, and the **INITIAL** parameter tells the database that each extent is to be 25 MB each. The database then goes to bigfile1 on disk1 and allocates an extent of 25 MB. It then tries to allocate another extent of 25 MB on bigfile1, but only 5 MB of free space are available. The database must move to bigfile2 to allocate the final extent of 25 MB, as shown in Figure 11.9.

After the table has been initially created, the value for the **NEXT** extent should be changed to a smaller value than the **INITIAL** extent, as follows:

```
ALTER TABLE BIG_TABLE
STORAGE ( NEXT 1M);
```

Some database administrators recommend striping all tables across each and every physical disk. If a system has 10 tables and the CPU is configured for two disks, then each of the 10 tables would be striped into each disk device.

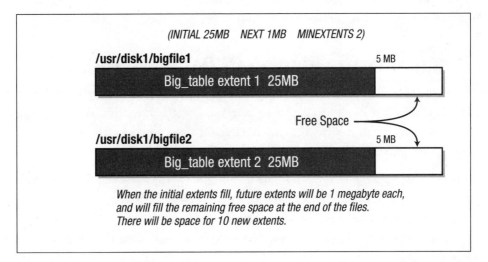

Figure 11.9
Allocating an Oracle table with striped extents.

It is unfortunate that the relational databases require the DBA to "trick" the database allocation software into striping the files rather than allowing direct control over the file placement process. This lack of control can be a real problem when tables are compressed.

Several methods will ensure that the tables are striped across the disks. Many databases with a sophisticated data dictionary allow queries that reveal the striping of the files. Oracle relies on the following script:

```
striping.sql - displays striped file names
SELECT DISTINCT file_name,
FROM   dba_data_files a, dba_extents b
WHERE
    A.file_id = B.file_id
AND
    segment_name = :striped_table_name;

(WHERE :striped_table_name = 'BIG_TABLE')
```

Other databases offer utilities that report on the physical file utilization for a specific table or database record type.

Now that we have reviewed the basics of memory cache tuning, let's take a look at some DBA tricks that can be used to improve performance.

Simulating The Pinning Of Database Rows

Unfortunately, Oracle does not yet support the pinning of database blocks within its buffer cache. If it were possible to keep specific data blocks from swapping-out, commonly used blocks such as common reference tables and the high-level nodes of indexes could be kept in memory.

Fortunately, tricks can be used to simulate this type of buffer pinning. Introduced in Oracle 7.2, read-only tablespaces allow for the creation of separate instances that concurrently access the same tablespace. For example, assume that your application has a common set of look-up tables, commonly referenced by every user. This table could be placed inside a separate instance, sized only for the look-up tables. Because the instance has its private buffer pool, you can ensure that the reference tables will always reside in memory. This type of architecture is also beneficial for systems that must do full-table scans because it alleviates the buffer flushing that occurs when an online transactions system is slowed by a single task requiring a full-table scan on a large table.

But what if the table is read both by the online transaction processing and by the full-table scan request? With read-only tablespaces and Oracle parallel server, a tablespace can be in update-mode for the online transactions processing instance while a separate instance handles read-only full-table scans (see Figure 11.10). The Oracle DBA should make every possible effort to identify and isolate read-only tables into a read-only tablespace because performance is dramatically faster in read-only processing mode.

> **Note:** For details on implementing read-only tablespaces, refer to Chapter 8, Oracle Features For The Data Warehouse.

The ability to identify and correct performance problems has plagued distributed systems from their genesis. Even within the context of a single transaction, distributed query optimization can be a formidable challenge. On a single database, query tuning takes place by running an SQL **EXPLAIN** and performing the appropriate tuning. However, when a query is "split" into distributed databases, the overall query tuning becomes much more complex. Many distributed database managers take a distributed query and partition it into sub-queries which are then independently optimized and run (sometimes simultaneously) on the distributed databases. The

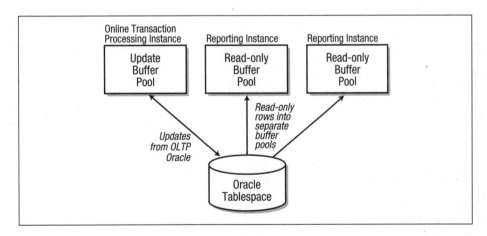

Figure 11.10
Oracle's read-only tablespaces.

query is considered complete when the last sub-query has completed successfully and the results are returned to the user. This approach is sometimes called *the weakest link architecture*. If a distributed query partitions into four sub-queries, for example, the longest running of the four sub-queries, determines the overall performance for the entire query, regardless of how fast the other three sub-queries execute.

Clearly, when tuning a distributed query, you must take into consideration the load on the network, the physical location of the database, and the availability of multiple CPUs. Today, tools are available to perform "load balancing," whereby a processor may borrow CPU cycles in order to balance the query and achieve maximum throughput.

Summary

By now, you should have a good understanding of the Oracle memory utilities for data warehouse applications. However, system-level tuning can often be futile if the individual SQL statements are not optimized for the Oracle database. The next chapter investigates the tuning of Oracle SQL and shows how individual queries can be tuned. After that, we'll look into Oracle locking and see how to remove bottlenecks on update operations.

Tuning Oracle SQL

CHAPTER

12

HIGH PERFORMANCE

Tuning Oracle SQL

While several books have been devoted to the efficient use of Oracle SQL, only a few general rules and guidelines are actually effective in guaranteeing the best performance from Oracle data warehouses. In addition to basic SQL syntax tuning, this chapter focuses on the types of SQL queries that are most commonly used in data warehouse queries, including the new data warehouse query techniques. This chapter also focuses on the basic techniques for quickly achieving the maximum SQL performance in a data warehouse with the least amount of effort.

Tuning Oracle SQL Syntax

Because SQL is a declarative language, we can write the same query in many different ways. And although each query will return identical results, the execution time can vary dramatically. To illustrate this concept, let's consider a small employee table with only 100 rows and an index on **sex** and **hiredate**. Assume that we're using Oracle's rule-based optimizer, and we issue the following query to retrieve all female employees who have been hired within the last 90 days:

```
SELECT emp_name
FROM EMPLOYEE
WHERE
sex = 'F'
AND
hiredate BETWEEN sysdate-90 AND sysdate;
```

Because the table has only 100 rows, the most efficient way to service this request would be to use a full-table scan. However, Oracle will walk the index that exists, performing dozens of extra I/Os as it reads the index tree to access the rows in the table. While this is a simplistic example, it serves to illustrate the concept that the execution time of SQL is heavily dependent on the way a query is stated as well as the internal index structures within Oracle.

The first step is to look at the relative costs for each type of SQL access. Oracle has published the cost list shown in Table 12.1 that describes the relative cost of each type of row access.

As you can see, the fastest way to retrieve a row is by knowing its row ID. A row ID (called a *ROWID* in Oracle) is the number of the database block followed by the "displacement" or position of the row on the block. For example, the **ROWID** 1221:3 refers to a row on block number 1221, and the row is the third on the page. Many savvy programmers capture the **ROWID** for a row if they plan to retrieve it. In Oracle, **ROWID** is a valid column statement, such that you can select the **ROWID** along with your data in a single statement, as follows:

```
SELECT ROWID FROM EMPLOYEE INTO :myvar;
```

Table 12.1 Costs for SQL access.

Cost	Type Of Operation
1	Single row by row ID (**ROWID**)
2	Single row by cluster join
3	Single row by hash cluster key with unique or primary key
4	Single row by unique or primary key
5	Cluster join
6	Hash cluster key
7	Indexed cluster key
8	Use of a multi-column index
9	Use of a single-column index
10	Bounded range search on indexed columns
11	Unbounded range search on un-indexed columns
12	Sort-merge join
13	**MAX** or **MIN** search of an indexed column
14	Use of **ORDER BY** on an indexed column
15	Full-table scan

On the other end of the cost spectrum is the full-table scan. As you may know, a full-table scan is acceptable for small tables, but it can wreak havoc in Oracle when a full-table scan is invoked against a large data warehouse table. Therefore, more than any other SQL tuning technique, avoiding full-table scans is a primary consideration. In short, full-table scans can *always* be avoided by using indexes and index hints. However, another issue must be considered. While a full-table scan may be the fastest for an individual query with many complex **WHERE** conditions, the full-table scan is done at the expense of other SQL on the system. The question then becomes: Do we tune an individual query for performance, or do we tune the database as a whole?

General Tips For Efficient Oracle SQL

Fortunately, some simple rules are available for writing efficient SQL in Oracle. These rules may seem simplistic, but following them in a diligent manner will relieve more than half of the SQL tuning problems of your data warehouse:

- Never do a calculation on an indexed column (e.g., **WHERE salary*5 > :myvalue**).

- Whenever possible, use the **UNION** statement instead of **OR**.

- Avoid the use of **NOT IN** or **HAVING** in the **WHERE** clause. Instead, use the **NOT EXISTS** clause.

- Always specify numeric values in numeric form, and character values in character form (e.g., **WHERE emp_number = 565, WHERE emp_name = "Jones"**).

- Avoid specifying **null** on an indexed column.

- Avoid the **LIKE** parameter if = will suffice. Using any Oracle functions will invalidate the index, causing a full-table scan.

- Never mix datatypes in Oracle queries, as it will invalidate the index. If the column is numeric, remember not to use quotes (e.g., **salary = 50000**). For **char** index columns, always use quotes. (e.g., **name = "BURLESON"**).

- Remember that Oracle's rule-based optimizer looks at the order of a table name in the **FROM** clause to determine the driving table. Always make sure that the last table specified in the **FROM** clause is the table that will return the smallest number of rows. In other words, specify multiple tables with the largest result set table specified first in the **WHERE** clause.

- Avoid using sub-queries when a **JOIN** will do the job.

- Use the Oracle **DECODE** function to minimize the number of times a table has to be selected.

- To turn off an index that you do not want to use (only with cost-based), concatenate a **null** string to the index column name (e.g., **name||""**) or add zero to a numeric column name (e.g., **salary+0**).

- If your query will return more than 20 percent of the rows in the table, use a full-table scan rather than an index scan.

- Always use table aliases when referencing columns.

One of the historic problems with SQL involves queries. Simple queries can be written in many different ways, each variant of the query producing the same result but with widely different access methods and query speeds. For example, a simple query such as "What students received an A last semester?" can be written in three ways, as shown in Listings 12.1, 12.2, and 12.3, and each query will return an identical result.

Listing 12.1 A standard join.

```
SELECT *
FROM STUDENT, REGISTRATION
WHERE
    STUDENT.student_id = REGISTRATION.student_id
AND
    REGISTRATION.grade = "A";
```

Listing 12.2 A nested query.

```
SELECT *
FROM STUDENT
WHERE
    student_id =
    (SELECT student_id
        FROM REGISTRATION
        WHERE
        grade = "A"
    );
```

Listing 12.3 A correlated sub-query.

```
SELECT *
FROM STUDENT
WHERE
    0 <
    (SELECT count(*)
        FROM REGISTRATION
        WHERE
        grade = "A"
        AND
        student_id = STUDENT.student_id
    );
```

Each of these queries will return identical results, though the standard join will have the fastest response and the correlated sub-query will be the slowest.

The following discussion will review the basic components of an SQL query, showing how to optimize a query for remote execution. It is important to note that several steps are required to understand how SQL is used in a distributed database. Distributed SQL queries function in the same way as queries within a single database, with the exception that cross-database joins and updates may utilize indexes that reside on different databases. Regardless, a basic understanding of the behavior of SQL can lead to dramatic performance improvements.

Tuning SQL With Indexes

As a general rule, indexes will always increase the performance of a database query. For Oracle, indexes are recommended for two reasons: to speed the retrieval of a small set of rows from a table and to "presort" result sets so that the SQL **ORDER BY** clause does not cause an internal sort. However, the presence of a column within an index is not a guarantee that the SQL optimizer will use the index. In order to use an index, the SQL optimizer must recognize that the column has a valid value for index use. This is called a *sargeable predicate*, and it is used to determine the index access. Listing 12.4 shows some valid predicates, and Listing 12.5 shows invalid predicates.

Listing 12.4 Valid predicates.

```
SELECT * FROM EMPLOYEE WHERE emp_no = 123;

SELECT * FROM EMPLOYEE WHERE dept_no = 10;
```

Listing 12.5 Invalid predicates.

```
SELECT * FROM EMPLOYEE WHERE emp_no = "123";

SELECT * FROM EMPLOYEE WHERE salary * 2 < 50000;

SELECT * FROM EMPLOYEE WHERE dept_no != 10;
```

As you can see from these examples, whenever a transformation to a field value takes place, the Oracle database will not be able to use the index for that column.

The Oracle software has been enhanced to recognize when a full-table scan is taking place on a large table. When Oracle detects this condition, it will invoke a type of "sequential pre-fetch" to look ahead, reading the next data block while the previous data block is being fetched by the application. The use of this feature requires that the **db_file_multiblock_read_count** be set in the init.ora file. At the physical level in Unix, Oracle always reads-in a minimum of 64 K blocks. Therefore, the values of **db_file_multiblock_read_count** and **db_block_size** should be set such that their product is 64 K. An example is shown in Table 12.2.

As a general rule, any SQL query that retrieves more than 15 percent of the table rows in a table will probably run faster if the optimizer chooses a full-table scan than if it chooses to use an index. For example, assume that a student table has 1,000 rows, representing 900 undergraduate students and 100 graduate students. A non-unique index has been built on the **student_level** field that indicates **undergrad** or **grad**. The same query will benefit from different access methods depending on the value of the literal in the **WHERE** clause. The following query will retrieve 90 percent of the rows in the table, and will run faster with a full-table scan than it will if the SQL optimizer chooses to use an index:

```
SELECT * FROM STUDENT WHERE student_level = 'UNDERGRAD';
```

Table 12.2 Establishing the settings.

Blocksize	db_block_size	db_file_multiblock_read_count setting
8 K blocks	db_block_size=8192	db_file_multiblock_read_count=8
16 K blocks	db_block_size=16384	db_file_multiblock_read_count=4

This next query will only access 10 percent of the table rows and will run faster by using the index on the **student_level** field:

```
SELECT * FROM STUDENT WHERE student_level = 'GRAD';
```

Unfortunately, the Oracle database cannot predict in advance the number of rows that will be returned from a query. Many SQL optimizers will invoke an index access even though it may not always be the fastest access method.

To remedy this problem, some dialects of SQL allow users to control index access. This is a gross violation of the declarative nature of theoretical SQL—the user does not control access paths. But in practice, these extensions can improve performance. Oracle, for example, allows the concatenation of a null string to the field name in the **WHERE** clause to suppress index access. The previous query could be rewritten in Oracle SQL to bypass the **student_level** index, as follows:

```
SELECT * FROM STUDENT WHERE student_level||'' = 'UNDERGRAD';
```

The concatenation (||) of a **NULL** string to the field tells the Oracle SQL optimizer to bypass index processing for this field and instead invoke a faster-running full-table scan.

This is a very important point. While SQL optimizers are becoming more intelligent about their databases, they still cannot understand the structure of the data and will not always choose the best access path.

Concatenated Indexes

A concatenated index (sometimes called a *composite index*) is a single index that is created with multiple columns. This type of index can greatly speed up a query where all of the index columns are specified in the query's SQL **WHERE** clause and the composite index keys are in the proper order. For example, assume the following index on the **STUDENT** table:

```
CREATE INDEX idx1
ON STUDENT
(student_level, major, last_name) ascending;
```

The following concatenated index could be used to speed up queries that reference both **student_level** and **major** in the **WHERE** clause:

```
SELECT student_last_name FROM STUDENT
WHERE
    student_level = 'UNDERGRAD'
AND
    major = 'computer science';
```

However, some queries using **major** or **student_level** will not be able to use this concatenated index. In this example, only the major field is referenced in the query:

```
SELECT * FROM STUDENT
WHERE
    major = 'computer science';
```

In the next example, even though **student_level** is the high-order index key, the index will not be used because the **major** column is not referenced. Because **major** is the second column in the index, Oracle will conclude that the index cannot be used.

```
SELECT last_name FROM STUDENT
WHERE
    student_level = 'PLEBE'
ORDER BY last_name;
```

Because **student_level** is the first item in the index, the leading portion of the index can be read and the SQL optimizer will invoke an index scan. Why have we chosen to add the **last_name** to the index, even though it is not referenced in the **WHERE** clause? Because Oracle will be able to service the request by reading only the index, and the rows of the **STUDENT** table will never be accessed. Also, the **ORDER BY** clause asks to sort by **last_name**, so Oracle will not need to perform a sort on this data.

The **NOT** (!) operator will cause an index to be bypassed, and the query "Show all undergrads who are not computer science majors" will cause a full-table scan, for instance:

```
SELECT * FROM STUDENT
WHERE
    student_level = 'UNDERGRAD'
AND
    major != 'COMPUTER SCIENCE';
```

Here, the **NOT** condition isn't a sargeable predicate and will cause a full-table scan. In short, concatenated indexes are excellent ways of improving performance of Oracle data warehouses, but they do require some forethought about the types of queries that will be executed against the database.

Using Oracle's Explain Plan Utility

Oracle's **explain plan** utility is used to see the hidden access method that your SQL is using to deliver the data. To see the output of an explain plan, you must first create a plan table. Oracle provides a script in $ORACLE_HOME/rdbms/admin called utlxplan.sql. To prepare for an explain plan, execute utlxplan.sql and create a public synonym for the **PLAN_TABLE**, as follows:

```
sqlplus > @utlxplan
table created.

sqlplus > CREATE PUBLIC SYNONYM PLAN_TABLE FOR SYS.PLAN_TABLE;
synonym created.
```

Oracle takes the SQL statement as input, runs the SQL optimizer, and outputs the access path information into a **PLAN_TABLE**, which can then be interrogated to see the access methods. Listing 12.6 runs a query against the student database that shows the sum of all items' sales for a specific month, grouped by sales territory.

Listing 12.6   An item query.

```
EXPLAIN PLAN SET statement_id = 'test1' FOR
SET statement_id = 'RUN1'
INTO PLAN_TABLE
FOR
SELECT   'T'||ITEM_NET.terr_code, 'P'||DETITEM.pac1 || DETITEM.pac2 ||
DETITEM.pac3, 'P1',
sum(ITEM_NET.ytd_d_ly_tm),
 sum(ITEM_NET.ytd_d_ty_tm),
 sum(ITEM_NET.jan_d_ly),
 sum(ITEM_NET.jan_d_ty),
FROM item_net, detitem
WHERE
    ITEM_NET.mgc = DETITEM.mktgpm
AND
    DETITEM.pac1 IN ('N33','192','195','201','BAI',
    'P51','Q27','180','181','183','184','186','188',
    '198','204','207','209','211')
GROUP BY 'T'||ITEM_NET.terr_code, 'P'||DETITEM.pac1
            ||DETITEM.pac2 || DETITEM.pac3;
```

This syntax is piped into the SQL optimizer, which will analyze the query and store the plan information in a row in the plan table identified by **RUN1**. Please note that the query will not execute; it will only create the internal access information in the plan table. The plan table contains the following fields:

- **operation**—The type of access being performed. Usually table access, table merge, sort, or index operation.

- **options**—Modifiers to the operation, specifying a full table, a range table, or a join.

- **object_name**—The name of the table being used by the query component.

- **process_id**—The identifier for the query component.

- **parent_id**—The parent of the query component. Note that several query components may have the same parent.

Now that the **PLAN_TABLE** has been created and populated, you may interrogate it to see your output by running the following query:

```
REM plan.sql - displays contents of the explain plan table
SET PAGES 9999;
SELECT  lpad(' ',2*(level-1))||operation operation,
        options,
        object_name,
        position
FROM PLAN_TABLE
START WITH ID=0
AND
statement_id = 'RUN1'
CONNECT BY PRIOR ID = parent_id
AND
statement_id = 'RUN1';
```

Listing 12.7 shows the output from the plan table, displaying the sequence of operations.

Listing 12.7   The plan table's output.

```
SQL> @list_explain_plan

OPERATION
-----------------------------------
OPTIONS                         OBJECT_NAME            POSITION
-----------------------------   ------------           ----------
SELECT STATEMENT
```

```
        SORT
    GROUP BY                                                    1

        CONCATENATION
                                                                1

            NESTED LOOPS
                                                                1
            TABLE ACCESS FULL      ITEM_NET                     1

            TABLE ACCESS BY ROWID  DETITEM                      2

                INDEX RANGE SCAN   DETITEM_INDEX                1

        NESTED LOOPS
```

From this output, you can see the dreaded **TABLE ACCESS FULL** on the **ITEM_NET** table. To diagnose the reason, we need to return to the SQL and look for any **ITEM_NET** columns in the **WHERE** clause. There, we see that the **ITEM_NET** column called **mgc** is being used as a join column in the query, indicating that an index is necessary on **ITEM_NET.MGC** to alleviate the full-table scan.

While the plan table is useful for determining the access path to the data, it does not tell the entire story. The configuration of the data is also a consideration. While the SQL optimizer is aware of the number of rows in each table and the presence of indexes on fields, the SQL optimizer is not aware of data distribution factors, such as the number of expected rows that will be returned from each query component.

For those Oracle professionals who are using Oracle's Enterprise Manager Performance Pack, the explain plan can be easily gathered online inside the Top Sessions tool (see Figure 12.1). The only requirement for gathering an explain plan with this tool is that the connected user must have defined a plan table, and the SQL must be marked as active on the main Top Sessions screen.

The other tool used with the plan table is an SQL **trace** facility. Most database management systems provide a trace facility that shows the resources consumed within each query component. The trace table will show the number of I/Os required to perform an SQL query, as well as the processor time for each query component.

Some other relational databases, such as DB2, allow the DBA to specify the physical sequence for storing the rows on a data block. Generally, this sequence will correspond to the column value that is most commonly used when the table is read

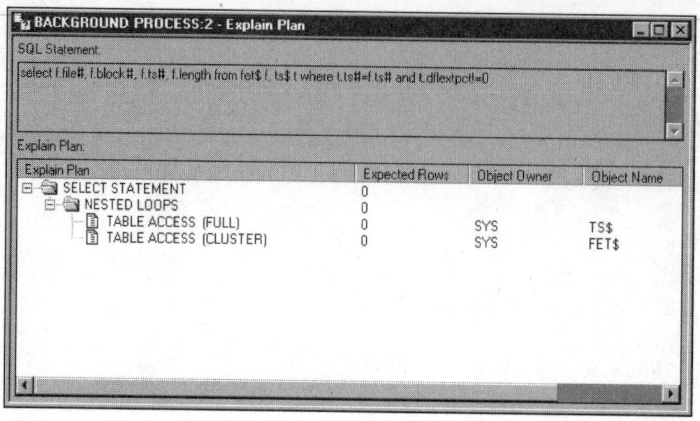

Figure 12.1
An SQL Explain Plan from OEM Performance Pack Top Sessions.

sequentially by an application. If a customer table is frequently accessed in customer ID order, then the rows should be physically stored in customer ID sequence. Even though Oracle does not have a provision for the physical ordering of rows onto data blocks, Oracle performance can be greatly improved in many cases. There are some tricks that can be performed to change the physical sequence of rows and cluster the physical rows in the table with the keys in an index. For more information on these techniques, see the section titled "How To Create A Clustered Index" in Chapter 8, *Oracle Features For The Data Warehouse*.

As you may know, interpreting the output from the explain plan is not always straight-forward or easy. The explain plan output will display many database access methods, and the developer must understand how each of them works. The major access techniques that might appear in an explain plan include:

- **AND-EQUAL**—Indicates that tables are being joined and that Oracle will be able to use the values from the indexes to join the rows.

- **CONCATENATION**—Indicates an SQL **UNION** operation.

- **COUNTING**—Indicates the use of an SQL **count** function.

- **FILTER**—Indicates that the **WHERE** clause is removing unwanted rows from the result set.

- **FIRST ROW**—Indicates that a cursor has been declared for the query.

- **FOR UPDATE**—Indicates that returned rows were write locked (usually by using **SELECT . . . FOR UPDATE OF . . .**).

- **INDEX (UNIQUE)**—Indicates that an index was scanned for a value specified in the **WHERE** clause.

- **INDEX (RANGE SCAN)**—Indicates that a numeric index was scanned for a range of values (usually with the **BETWEEN, LESS_THAN,** or **GREATER_THAN** specified).

- **INTERSECTION**—Indicates a solution set from two joined tables.

- **MERGE JOIN**—Indicates that two result sets were used to resolve the query.

- **NESTED LOOPS**—Indicates that the last operation will be performed *n* times, once for each preceding operation.

- **PROJECTION**—Indicates that only certain columns from a selected row are to be returned.

- **SORT**—Indicates a sort, either into memory or the **TEMP** tablespace.

- **TABLE ACCESS (ROWID)**—Indicates a row access by **ROWID** that is very fast.

- **TABLE ACCESS (FULL)**—Indicates a full-table scan and is usually cause for concern unless the table is very small.

- **UNION**—Indicates that the **DISTINCT** SQL clause was probably used.

- **VIEW**—Indicates that an SQL view was involved in the query.

Database statistics packages can be made to capture this information, but they tend to be very resource intensive. Turning on SQL trace statistics for a very short period of time during processing is a good practice to follow in order to gather a representative sample of the SQL access.

Using Temporary Tables To Improve Performance

The prudent use of temporary tables can dramatically improve Oracle performance. Any time an SQL query contains a sub-query, you can replace the sub-query with two SQL statements: one to select data into a temporary table and a second to join the temporary table with the outer table. This simple technique can more than triple the speed of many queries. Consider the following example: We want to identify all users who exist within Oracle, but have not been granted a role. We could formulate the following query:

```
SELECT username FROM DBA_USERS
WHERE
username NOT IN
(SELECT grantee FROM DBA_ROLE_PRIVS);
```

This query runs in 18 seconds. Now, let's rewrite the same query to utilize temporary tables, as follows:

```
CREATE TABLE TEMP1 AS
   SELECT DISTINCT username FROM DBA_USERS;

CREATE TABLE TEMP2 AS
   SELECT DISTINCT grantee FROM DBA_ROLE_PRIVS;

SELECT username FROM TEMP1
WHERE username NOT IN
(SELECT grantee FROM TEMP2);
```

This query runs in less than three seconds. Clearly, this technique is very useful in a situation when the end users have either correlated sub-queries or noncorrelated sub-queries. Of course, there is always a cost for these techniques, and this is no exception. The end users will need to be granted **CREATE TABLE** privileges, and there will be additional maintenance as the temporary tables must be dropped after the query has been completed. Most savvy programmers simply reuse the same temporary table name for all of their queries, dropping the table immediately before issuing the **CREATE TABLE AS SELECT** statement.

Now, let's take a look at the optimizers for Oracle SQL. Essentially, there are two optimizers for Oracle: the rule-based optimizer and the cost-based optimizer. The rule-based optimizer has been a part of the Oracle engine for many years, and it generally does a very good job in choosing access paths for data. The cost-based optimizer was introduced as the next evolution of the optimizer, whereby statistics from the tables are used to determine the best path to the data.

Tuning The Rule-Based Optimizer

In Oracle's rule-based optimizer, the ordering of the table names in the **FROM** clause determines the driving table. The driving table is important because it is retrieved first, and the rows from the second table are then merged into the result set from the first table. Therefore, it is essential that the second table returns the least amount of rows based on the **WHERE** clause. *This is not always the table with the least amount of rows* (i.e., the smallest cardinality).

For example, consider two **EMP_TABLE**s—one in London and another in New York—shown in Table 12.3.

In this example, the following total select from the **EMP_TABLE** should specify the New York table first because London has the least amount of returned rows:

```
SELECT *
FROM EMP@new_york, EMP@london;
```

The following SQL specifies a **WHERE** condition to include only Department 100, so the order of table names should be reversed:

```
SELECT *
FROM EMP@london, EMP@new_york
WHERE
    dept = 100;
```

Because it is not always known what table will return the least amount of rows, procedural code could be used to interrogate the tables and specify the tables in their proper order. This type of SQL generation can be very useful for ensuring optimal database performance, as shown in Listing 12.8.

Listing 12.8 Automatic generation of optimal rule-based SQL.

```
SELECT count(*) INTO :my_london_dept
    FROM EMP@london
```

Table 12.3 New York and London **EMP_TABLE**s.

	Rows	Dpt 100	Dpt 200
New York	1000	100	900
London	200	150	50

```
        WHERE dept = :my_dept;

SELECT count(*) INTO :my_ny_dept
    FROM EMP@new_york
    WHERE dept = :my_dept;

IF my_london_dept >= my_ny_dept
{
    TABLE_1 = EMP@london
    TABLE_2 = EMP@new_york
ELSE
    TABLE_1 = EMP@new_york
    TABLE_2 = EMP@london
}

/* Now we construct the SQL*/

SELECT *
FROM :TABLE_1, :TABLE_2
WHERE
    dept = :my_dept;
```

As you know, Oracle version 7 offers two methods of tuning SQL. If you are running version 7.2 or above, you can use the cost-based optimizer. Releases of Oracle version 7.1 and below require the rule-based optimizer. The rule-based method was the only method available in version 6. With the rule-based optimizer, the indexing of tables and order of clauses within the SQL statement controls the access path in rule-based optimization. The cost-based optimizer automatically determines the most efficient execution path, and the programmer is given *hints* that can be added to the query to alter the access path. The cost-based optimizer or the rule-based optimizer is set in the init.ora file by setting the **optimizer_mode** to **RULE, CHOOSE, FIRST_ROWS**, or **ALL_ROWS**. Be careful when using the **CHOOSE** option. When you give Oracle the ability to choose the optimizer mode, Oracle will favor the cost-based approach if *any* of the tables in the query have statistics. (Statistics are created with the **ANALYZE TABLE** command.) For example, if a three-table join is specified in **CHOOSE** mode and statistics exist for one of the three tables, Oracle will decide to use the cost-based optimizer and will issue an **ANALYZE TABLE ESTIMATE STATISTICS** at runtime. This will dramatically slow down the query.

The optimizer option (rule versus cost) can be controlled at the database level or at the program level. Prior to version 7.0.16, the cost-based analyzer had significant problems, and Oracle recommended the use of the rule-based optimizer.

Here are some tips for effective use of Oracle's rule-based optimizer:

- Try changing the order of the tables listed in the **FROM** clause. Page 19-15 in *Oracle RDBMS Database Administrator's Guide* states that "Joins should be driven from tables returning fewer rows rather than tables returning more rows." In other words, the table that returns the fewest rows should be listed *last*. This *usually* means that the table with the most rows is listed *first*. If the tables in the statement have indexes, the driving table is determined by the indexes. One Oracle developer recently slashed processing in half by changing the order of the tables in the **FROM** clause! Another developer had a process shift from running for 12 hours to running in 30 minutes by changing the **FROM** clause.

- Try changing the order of the statements in the **WHERE** clause. Here's the idea: Assume than an SQL query contains an **IF** statement with several boolean expressions separated by **AND**s. Oracle parses the SQL from the bottom of the SQL statement, in reverse order. Therefore, the most restrictive boolean expression should be on the bottom. For example, consider the following query:

```
SELECT last_name
FROM STUDENT
WHERE
eye_color = 'BLUE'
AND
national_origin = 'SWEDEN';
```

Here, we assume that the number of students from Sweden will be smaller than the number of students with blue eyes. To further confound matters, if an SQL statement contains a compound **IF** separated by **OR**s, the rule-based optimizer parses from the top of the **WHERE** clause. Therefore, the most restrictive clause should be the first boolean item in the **IF** statement.

- Analyze the existence/nonexistence of indexes. Understand your data. Again, unlike the cost-based optimizer, the rule-based optimizer only recognizes the existence of indexes and does not know about the selectivity or the distribution of the index column. Consequently, use care when creating indexes, especially when using rule-based optimization. Consider *all* programs that use a field in a **WHERE** clause of a **SELECT**. A field should only be indexed when a very small subset (less than 5 to 10 percent) of the data will be returned.

- Determine whether the target table is fragmented. For example, a table could be fragmented if it constantly has a large number of rows inserted and deleted. This is especially true in **PCTFREE** because the table has been set to a low number. Regular compression of the table with Oracle export/import utility will restore the table row and remove the fragmentation.

- Always run questionable SQL through **explain plan** to examine the access path.

- Understand which "query paths" are the fastest. For example, accessing a table by **ROWID** is the fastest access method available where a full-table scan is 17 out of 18 for the ranking of query paths. (Reference Table 12.1 for the complete list of relative costs.)

- Avoid joins that use database links into Oracle version 6 tables.

- Make effective use of arrays, as array processing significantly reduces database I/O. Consider the following example: A table has 1,000 rows to be selected. The records are manipulated and then updated in the database. Without using array processing, the database receives 1,000 reads and 1,000 updates. With array processing (assuming an array size of 100), the database receives 10 reads (1,000/ 100) and 10 updates. According to Oracle, increasing the array size to more than 100 has little benefit.

Beware of an Oracle rule-based "feature" whereby a join of numerous large tables will always result in a full-table scan on one of the tables, even if all of the tables have indexes and the join could be achieved with an index scan. Of course, full-table scans are costly, and SQL hints can be used to force the query to use the indexes. You can use hints with the rule-based optimizer.

Listing 12.9 is a script that can be run to view SQL that has been loaded into the SGA shared pool.

Listing 12.9   qltext.sql shows all SQL in the SGA shared pool.

```
REM Written by Don Burleson

SET PAGESIZE 9999;
SET LINESIZE 79;
```

```
SET NEWPAGE 0;
SET VERIFY OFF;
BREAK ON address SKIP 2;

COLUMN address FORMAT 9;
SELECT
        address,
        sql_text
FROM
        V$SQLTEXT
ORDER BY
address, piece;
```

Listing 12.10 shows the output from sqltext.sql.

Listing 12.10   The output for sqltext.sql.

```
D09AFC4C    select decode(object_type, 'TABLE', 2,  'VIEW', 2, 'PACKAGE',
            3,'PACKAGE BODY', 3, 'PROCEDURE', 4, 'FUNCTION', 5,  0) from
            all_objects where object_name = upper('V_$SQLTEXT')   and
            object_type in ('TABLE', 'VIEW', 'PACKAGE', 'PACKAGE BODY',
            'PROCEDURE', 'FUNCTION') and owner = upper('SYS')


D09B653C    select owner, table_name, table_owner, db_link from
            all_synonyms where synonym_name = upper('V_$SQLTEXT') and
            owner = upper('SYS')


D09BC5AC    select owner, table_name, table_owner, db_link from
            all_synonyms where synonym_name = upper('v$sqltext') and
            (owner = 'PUBLIC' or owner = USER)


D09C2D58    select decode(object_type, 'TABLE', 2,  'VIEW', 2,
            'PACKAGE', 3, 'PACKAGE BODY', 3, 'PROCEDURE', 4,
            'FUNCTION', 5,  0) from user_objects where object_name
            = upper('v$sqltext')   and   object_type in ('TABLE', 'VIEW',
            'PACKAGE', 'PACKAGE BODY',  'PROCEDURE', 'FUNCTION')

D09CFF4C    UPDATE SHPMT SET
            AMT_SUM_ILI=:b1,PMT_WGHT_SUM_ILI=:b2,
            CUST_PMT_W
            GHT_SUM_ILI=:b3 WHERE SHPMT_ID = :b4
            AND SHPMT_SYS_SRC_CD = :b5
```

Of course, this script could be extended to feed the SQL statements into Oracle's **explain plan** utility, where long-table full-table scans could be detected and indexes created for these queries.

> **Note:** *Oracle's **bstat/estat** utility also provides information on the number of full-table scans incurred by the database as a whole. Please see Chapter 11, Tuning The Oracle Warehouse Architecture, for more information.*

Tuning The Cost-Based Optimizer

The rule-based optimizer was supposed to become obsolete with the introduction of Oracle8, but its replacement—the cost-based optimizer—is available today. Unlike the rule-based optimizer, which uses heuristics to determine the access path, the cost-based optimizer uses data statistics to determine the most efficient way to service a request.

> **Note:** *The cost-based optimizer requires far more management than the rule-based optimizer. Table and index statistics must be collected on a regular basis, and care must be taken to ensure that the end-user community is making use of hints within their data warehouse queries.*

The basic difference between the optimizers is the way Oracle handles the access path to the data. In the rulebased optimizer, access decisions are made without any regard for the physical characteristics of the tables and indexes. In the cost-based optimizer, table and index statistics are gathered using the **ANALYZE** command and stored in the **ALL_TABLES** and **ALL_INDEXES** views. At runtime, Oracle will access these statistics to make a more intelligent decision about which access path is the most efficient.

In order to make the cost-based optimizer work efficiently, all of the tables and indexes must be reanalyzed after any large changes. For data warehouses, any time more than 25 percent of the rows change as a result of SQL **INSERT**, **UPDATE**, or **DELETE** operations, it is a good idea to reanalyze the table and indexes to obtain current statistics.

As a general rule, it is always a good idea to use the **ESTIMATE STATISTICS SAMPLE nn ROWS** clause of the **ANALYZE** command. Sampling an entire table or index seldom results in better quality statistics, and the runtimes for complete analysis can be very long. As a rule of thumb, statistics should be estimated at between 20 to 30 percent of the number of rows in the table.

Here is a summary of the most common hints that can be added to SQL:

- **ALL_ROWS**—This is the cost-based approach designed to provide the best overall throughput.

- **CLUSTER**—Requests a cluster scan of the table(s).

- **FIRST_ROWS**—This is the cost-based approach designed to provide the best response time.

- **FULL**—Requests the bypassing of indexes, doing a full-table scan.

- **INDEX**—Requests the use of the specified index. If no index is specified, Oracle will choose the best index.

- **ROWID**—Requests a **ROWID** scan of the specified table.

- **RULE**—Indicates that the rule-based optimizer has been invoked (recommended in some cases to avoid full-table scans).

- **ORDERED**—Requests that the tables should be joined in the order that they are specified. For example, if you know that a **STATE** table has only 50 rows, you may want to use this hint to make **STATE** the driving table.

- **USE_NL**—Requests a nested loop operation with the specified table as the driving table.

- **USE_MERGE**—Requests a sort merge operation.

Remember, the cost-based optimizer will only be as accurate as the statistics that are computed from the tables. Your DBA will need to create a periodic **cron** job to reestimate statistics for all tables that are volatile and change columns frequently. While a full **ANALYZE TABLE xxx ESTIMATE STATISTICS** will interrogate every row of the table, a faster method can be used by issuing **ANALYZE TABLE ESTIMATE STATISTICS SAMPLE nn ROWS**. By taking a sample of the rows within the table, the statistics generation will run much faster. Keep in mind that one of the things that the **ANALYZE** command reviews is the selectivity and distribution of values within an index. As such, care should be taken to sample at least 100 rows from each table.

Here is a test that created a set of three tables—**DEPT, DEPT1, DEPT2**—each with an index on **deptno** and **optimizer_goal** set as **RULE** in the init.ora. Listing 12.11 shows the results of the query.

Listing 12.11   The results of the query.

```
SELECT /*+ INDEX(DEPT DEPT_PRIMARY_KEY) INDEX(DEPT2 i_dept2)
INDEX(DEPT1 i_dept1)*/
DEPT.deptno, DEPT1.dname, DEPT2.loc
FROM DEPT, DEPT1, DEPT2
WHERE DEPT.deptno=DEPT1.deptno AND
DEPT1.deptno=DEPT2.deptno

Misses in library cache during parse: 1
Optimizer hint: RULE
Parsing user id: 48   (DON)


Rows     Execution Plan
------   -------------------------------------------------------
0        SELECT STATEMENT    OPTIMIZER HINT: RULE
4          MERGE JOIN
4            SORT (JOIN)
4              NESTED LOOPS
5                INDEX (RANGE SCAN) OF 'DEPT_PRIMARY_KEY' (UNIQUE)
4                TABLE ACCESS (BY ROWID) OF 'DEPT1'
8                  INDEX (RANGE SCAN) OF 'I_DEPT1' (NON-UNIQUE)
4            SORT (JOIN)
4              TABLE ACCESS (BY ROWID) OF 'DEPT2'
5                INDEX (RANGE SCAN) OF 'I_DEPT2' (NON-UNIQUE)
```

Listing 12.12 shows what we receive without any hints.

Listing 12.12 The query results for no hints.

```
SELECT DEPT.deptno, DEPT1.dname, dept2.loc
FROM DEPT, dept1, DEPT2
WHERE DEPT.deptno=DEPT1.deptno AND
DEPT1.deptno=DEPT2.deptno

Misses in library cache during parse: 1
Optimizer hint: RULE
Parsing user id: 48   (JACK)


Rows     Execution Plan
------   -------------------------------------------------------
0        SELECT STATEMENT    OPTIMIZER HINT: RULE
4          NESTED LOOPS
4            NESTED LOOPS
4              TABLE ACCESS (FULL) OF 'DEPT2'
4              TABLE ACCESS (BY ROWID) OF 'DEPT1'
```

```
8           INDEX (RANGE SCAN) OF 'I_DEPT1' (NON-UNIQUE)
4        INDEX (UNIQUE SCAN) OF 'DEPT_PRIMARY_KEY' (UNIQUE)
```

If we add a hint for the **DEPT2** index, the full-table scan would be on **DEPT1**, and so on.

Tuning PL/SQL

PL/SQL is the acronym for Procedure Language/Structured Query Language, the standard procedural language for online Oracle applications. PL/SQL is commonly used within Oracle's SQL*Forms application framework, but the popularity of PL/SQL for non–SQL*Forms applications has reemerged because of the benefits of using Oracle stored procedures, which must be written with PL/SQL. PL/SQL offers the standard language constricts, including looping, **IF** statement structures, assignment statements, and error handling. There are several problems with PL/SQL, each of which warrants special attention. Each will be addressed in the following text.

PL/SQL offers two types of SQL cursors, the *explicit* cursor and the *implicit* cursor. Explicit cursors are manually declared in PL/SQL as follows:

```
DECLARE
CURSOR C1 IS
SELECT last_name
FROM CUSTOMER
WHERE
cust_id = 1234;
```

However, it is possible to issue the SQL statement directly in PL/SQL without specifying the cursor name. When this happens, Oracle opens an implicit cursor to handle the request. Implicit cursors create a tremendous burden for Oracle, as the implicit cursor must always reissue a **FETCH** command to be sure that only a single row was returned by the query. This will double the amount of **FETCH** statements for the query. The moral is simple: Always declare all cursors in your PL/SQL.

PL/SQL allows certain types of correlated sub-queries to run much faster than a traditional Oracle SQL query. Consider a situation where a bank maintains a general ledger table and a transaction table. At the end of the banking day, the check transaction table is applied to the **GENERAL_LEDGER** table, making the requisite deductions from the **account_balance** column. Let's assume that the **GENERAL_LEDGER** table contains 100,000 rows and 5,000 daily checks need to be processed.

A traditional SQL query (shown in Listing 12.13) used to accomplish the updating of **account_balance** would involve a correlated sub-query.

Listing 12.13   Using a traditional SQL query.

```
UPDATE general_ledger
SET account_balance = account_balance -
   (SELECT check_amount FROM transaction
     WHERE
     transaction.account_number = GENERAL_LEDGER.account_number)
WHERE
EXISTS
(SELECT 'x' FROM TRANSACTION
 WHERE
 TRANSACTION.account_number = GENERAL_LEDGER.account_number);
```

As you may recall, a correlated sub-query involves executing the sub-query first and then applying the result to the entire outer query. In this case, the inner query will execute 5,000 times, and the outer query is executed once for each row returned from the inner query. This Cartesian product problem has always been a problem for correlated sub-queries.

Now, consider the identical query as written in PL/SQL, shown in Listing 12.14.

Listing 12.14   The PL/SQL query.

```
DECLARE
  CURSOR C1 IS
  SELECT account_number,
    check_amount
  FROM TRANSACTION;

    keep_account_number      number;
    keep_check_amount        number;

BEGIN

    OPEN C1;
    LOOP
            FETCH C1 INTO keep_account_number, keep_check_amount;
    EXIT WHEN C1%NOTFOUND;

    UPDATE GENERAL_LEDGER
    SET account_balance = account_balance - keep_check_amount
```

```
        WHERE account_number = keep_account_number;
    END LOOP;
END;
```

Here, you can see that each check amount is retrieved in a separate transaction and fetched into cursor **C1**. For each **check_amount**, the balance is applied to the **GENERAL_LEDGER** row, one at a time.

Now that we have covered the basics of SQL and PL/SQL, let's take a detailed look at how SQL is used within an Oracle data warehouse. While the basic syntax of the language remains unchanged, we must address the features that are specific to Oracle data warehousing.

New Oracle SQL Tuning Features

has added several new features to the implementation of cost-based of release 7.2, and the cost-based optimizer is now considered robust for most Oracle data warehouse applications. Some of the more im- enhancements include:

R query support—Oracle 7.3 allows for the use of virtual indexing to dra- ically speed up STAR queries for data warehouses.

sh join support—Oracle now allows for hash joins to improve execution speed by up to 300 percent.

- *Altering of improper outer joins*—The Oracle optimizer is now intelligent enough to detect an improper outer join operation and will internally correct the improperly specified query into a less expensive inner join.

- *Weighting of access options*—The cost-based optimizer is programmed to apply more logic to expensive queries and simple queries. The more complex and time-consuming the query, the more effort the cost-based optimizer will expend in searching for optimal access paths.

- *Improved detection of superfluous conditions*—In situations where the SQL specifies queries with several criteria that are **OR**ed together, Oracle may automatically simplify the query and remove syntax errors. For example,

```
SELECT * FROM CUSTOMER WHERE zip_code = 14450 OR zip_code > 12000;
```

will be changed to

```
SELECT * FROM CUSTOMER WHERE zip_code > 12000;
```

Oracle will also remove all literal predicates from queries. For example,

```
SELECT * FROM CUSTOMER WHERE 3=1 and zip_code = 14450;
```

will be changed to

```
SELECT * FROM CUSTOMER WHERE zip_code = 14450;
```

The two most exciting features for the Oracle data warehouse administrator are the STAR query support and the use of hash tables. Let's take a look at these.

STAR Queries With Oracle 7.3

One very exiting new feature of Oracle 7.3 is the introduction of optimized STAR queries. With this new optimization, data warehouse queries can run at blistering speeds, in some cases dozens of times faster than the original query. As we have already discussed in Chapter 4, *Oracle Data Warehouse Design*, the STAR schema design involves creating a main fact table that contains all of the primary keys in the related tables. This massive denormalization of the database structure means that just about any query against the STAR schema is going to involve the joining of many large tables—including a large fact table and many smaller reference tables.

The new STAR query feature with release 7.3 detects STAR query joins and invokes a special procedure to improve performance of the query. Prior to release 7.3 of Oracle, this feature only worked with up to five tables, but this restriction has been eliminated. Also, release 7.3 no longer requires the use of STAR query hints. However, hints are still allowed in the SQL syntax and are generally a good idea for documentation purposes. The STAR query requires a single concatenated index to reside in the fact table for all keys. To invoke the STAR query path, the following characteristics must be present:

- There must be at least three tables being joined, with one large fact table and several smaller dimension tables.

- There must be a concatenated index on the fact table with at least three columns, one for each of the table join keys.

- You must verify with an explain plan that the **NESTED LOOPS** operation is being used to perform the join.

Essentially, Oracle follows a simple procedure for processing STAR queries. Oracle will first service the queries against the smaller dimension tables, combining the result set into a Cartesian product table that is held in Oracle memory. This virtual table will contain all of the columns from all of the participating dimension tables. The primary key for this virtual table will be a composite of all of the keys for the dimension tables. If this key matches the composite index on the fact table, then the query will be able to process very quickly. Once the sum of the reference tables has been addressed, Oracle will perform a nested-loop join of the intermediate table against the fact table. This approach is far faster than the traditional method of joining the smallest reference table against the fact table and then joining each of the other reference tables against the intermediate table. The speed is a result of reducing the physical I/O. The indexes are read to gather the virtual table in memory, and the fact table will not be accessed until the virtual index has everything it requires to go directly to the requested rows via the composite index on the fact table (see Figure 12.2).

> **Note**: The STAR query can be very tricky to implement, and careful consideration should be given to the proper placement of indexes. Each dimension table must have an index on the join key, and the large fact table must have a composite index consisting of all of the join keys from all of the dimension tables. In addition, the sequencing of the keys in the fact table composite index must be in the correct order, or Oracle will not be able to use the index to service the query.

Using Oracle's Bitmap Indexes

For data warehouse applications that must elicit as much performance as possible, some special situations can arise where Oracle bitmapped indexes may be useful. As we know, the sheer volume of rows in very large tables can make even a trivial query run for a long time. Oracle has introduced bitmapped indexes with release 7.3 in an attempt to improve index lookup performance for queries, especially decision support type queries that may have many conditions in the **WHERE** clause.

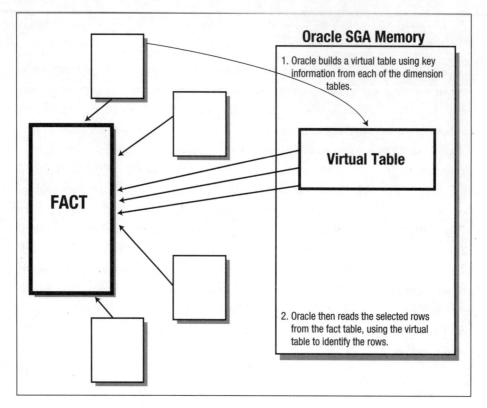

Figure 12.2
Oracle STAR query processing.

The bitmap approach to indexing is very different from the traditional B-tree style of indexes. In a traditional index, the index keys are sorted and carried in several tree nodes. In a bitmapped index, an array is created. This array has all possible index values as one axis, while the other axis contains all rows in the base table. For example, consider a bitmapped index on the **region** field of the **SALES** table, where the regions are **North**, **South**, **East**, and **West**. If the **SALES** table contains 1 million rows, the bitmapped index would create an array of 4×1 million bits to store the possible key values.

Within this array, the index data is binary. If a value is **TRUE**, it is assigned a binary 1—a **FALSE** reading is set to binary 0 (see Figure 12.3).

Here, you can see how this query runs faster than a traditional query. The Oracle optimizer will notice that the items in the **WHERE** clause have bitmapped indexes,

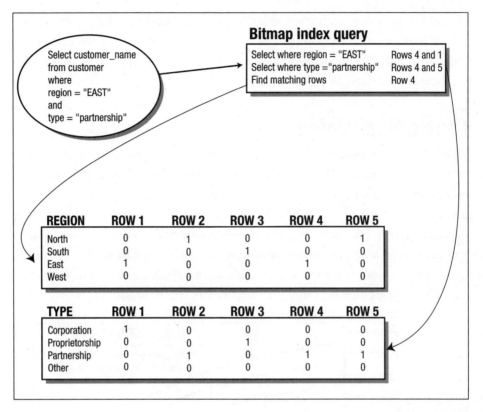

Figure 12.3
An Oracle bitmapped index.

scan for non-zero values in the proper array column, and quickly return the **ROWID** of the columns. A fast merge of the result set will then quickly identify the rows that meet the query criteria.

While it may appear that the index is very large, Oracle has developed a compression method whereby the binary zeros are omitted from the bitmap. This makes it very compact.

While this may look reasonable at first glance, some drawbacks to bitmapped indexing have to be considered. The first and most obvious is that bitmapped indexes work best for columns that only have a small amount of possible values. For columns that have many values, such as **state_name** or **city_name**, the index overhead would probably exceed any performance gains that might accrue from using bitmapped indexes.

However, for columns, such as **sex**, **color**, and **size**, that have a small number of finite values, bitmapped indexes will greatly improve query retrieval speeds. Bitmapped indexes are especially useful for decision support systems where many conditions are combined into a single **WHERE** clause.

Oracle Hash Joins

Oracle release 7.3 also provides another method for speeding up decision support and warehouse queries. This method is called the *hash join*. A hash join is a technique where Oracle bypasses the traditional sort-merge join technique and replaces it with a new access algorithm that automatically identifies the fact table and the dimension tables. This technique splits the small dimension tables into small chunks and then reads these chunks into memory where an internal hash table is created. Once the hash table is created, Oracle performs a full-table scan on the larger fact table and retrieves the rows using the hash key (see Figure 12.4).

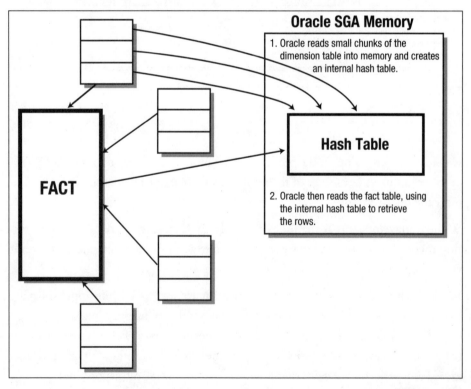

Oracle SGA Memory

1. Oracle reads small chunks of the dimension table into memory and creates an internal hash table.

Hash Table

2. Oracle then reads the fact table, using the internal hash table to retrieve the rows.

FACT

Figure 12.4
Using Oracle's hash table facility.

Partition pairs from the smaller dimension tables that do not fit into memory are placed in the **TEMP** tablespace. This technique alleviates the need for in-memory sorting and does not require that indexes exist on the target tables.

The following init.ora parameters must be set to use hash joins:

- **optimizer_mode=COST**
- **hash_join_enabled=TRUE**
- **hash_multiblock_io_count=TRUE**
- **hash_area_size=SIZE**

To execute a hash join, the hash-join hint must be used. Consider the following example:

```
SELECT /* USE_HASH*/
FROM CUSTOMER, ORDER
WHERE
CUSTOMER.cust_no = ORDER.cust_no
AND
credit_rating = 'GOOD';
```

Summary

While this review of SQL is far from exhaustive, it should hopefully provide a starting point in understanding the processes involved in optimizing data warehouse SQL queries. Now, let's move on to take a look at some of the recent performance and tuning offerings from Oracle 7.3, namely the Oracle Enterprise Manager and how it is used to monitor the Oracle data warehouse.

Monitoring The Oracle Data Warehouse

CHAPTER

13

HIGH PERFORMANCE

Monitoring The Oracle Data Warehouse

The latest release of Oracle 7.3 represents a significant improvement over the older, line-based methods of database monitoring. Whereas the SQL*DBA product was popular with the early Oracle version 7 release, Oracle improved on the tool with the introduction of the Oracle Server Manager. Then, with the general availability of Windows NT, Oracle introduced a powerful new product for the monitoring and maintenance of Oracle data warehouses. This product has been dubbed the *Oracle Enterprise Manager*, or OEM. OEM currently runs on Windows NT clients and can also be accessed using a Web browser.

Extending on the base functionality of Oracle Enterprise Manager, Oracle also offers an additional cost performance monitor called *Oracle Performance Pack* (OPP). The OPP product includes some very useful performance, tuning, and monitoring tools. This chapter discusses both the Oracle Enterprise Manager suite and the Oracle Performance Pack.

Oracle Enterprise Manager

Oracle Enterprise Manager (OEM) was first introduced with Oracle version 7.3. This suite of tools was not purely motivated by Oracle's desire to make life easier on the Oracle administrator. Rather, OEM was developed to meet a need for the rapidly growing market for Oracle databases that reside on NT-based hardware platforms. The introduction of Windows NT as a hardware platform made both SQL*DBA and Oracle Server Manager obsolete because both of those tools were designed to operate in a Unix environment.

With OEM, the Oracle administrator can utilize Oracle's SQL*Net to manage an Oracle database on any hardware platform and provide a consistent interface with the Oracle engine. Because Oracle databases on NT platforms no longer have a command-line interface with the database manager, many of the SQL commands that were used to alter tables, indexes, and tablespaces have become obsolete. The obsolete SQL commands have been replaced with a set of tools inside OEM.

Oracle Enterprise Manager—Standard Tools

OEM's tools allow Oracle database managers to maintain Oracle databases without having to manually type cumbersome and wordy SQL commands. Essentially, OEM consists of the following tools:

- *Oracle Schema Manager*—Allows the graphical display of schema objects, including tables, indexes, functions, and stored procedures. In addition, Schema Manager allows an administrator to alter many of the characteristics of schema objects.

- *Oracle Security Manager*—Provides a graphical interface where Oracle administrators can create users and grant schema privileges. The Security Manager is also used to maintain system privileges, object privileges, and role privileges.

- *Oracle Replication Manager*—Provides the ability to define and manage replicated tables in distributed Oracle environments. The Replication Manager allows for the definition of snapshots and snapshot logs for refreshing the replicated tables.

- *Oracle Data Manager*—Assists in the management of Oracle import and export utilities, including scheduling exports.

- *Oracle Storage Manager*—Displays the mapping of Oracle tablespaces to physical files. The Storage Manager is most commonly used to add physical files when a tablespace becomes full.

- *Oracle Backup Manager*—Schedules Oracle backups. By providing a scheduling facility, the Backup Manager allows the DBA to manage the backups of numerous Oracle instances.

- *Oracle Enterprise Manager Console*—Provides an interface used to schedule tasks and notify DBAs about Oracle events. Additional prewritten alerts are available with the purchase of OPP (discussed later in this chapter). These extra alerts allow the OEM Console to constantly monitor Oracle instances by using Oracle's intelligent agent. If a predefined threshold is exceeded, the OEM Console can be programmed to send email or activate a beeper.

- *Oracle SQL Worksheet*—Allows SQL to be executed to retrieve and update information in Oracle databases. This is the Enterprise Manager equivalent of the popular SQL*Plus interface.

- *Oracle Instance Manager*—Enables the administrator to display the initialization parameters from the init.ora file. The Instance Manager also allows the developer to start and stop Oracle instances.

Let's take a quick, high-level tour of these tools to see how they can assist Oracle DBAs.

Oracle Schema Manager

Oracle Schema Manager is one of the most commonly used Oracle utilities, and it is also one of the most helpful for the developers who want to see a graphical display of their database. The display begins with a selection list that shows all of the relevant schema objects in alphabetical order. Drilling down on any of these schema objects by double clicking will display a list of all of the schema owners for that object. In Figure 3.1, we have drilled into the table object and then drilled into the **EXPERT** table owner to see a list of table names that are owned by **EXPERT**.

The General, Storage, Constraints, and Status tabs in the Schema Manager allow a table to be altered according to the desires of the developer. The first screen, shown in Figure 13.1, shows all of the details for a table, including all of the columns and storage parameters. Many of these parameters can quickly be altered online, including the **NEXT**, **PCTINCREASE**, **PCTFREE**, and **PCTUSED** parameters.

In addition to changing the base table parameters, a developer can also look at the table constraints, as well as a table's status and whether any of its primary key constraints have been disabled.

While Oracle Schema Manager is the most commonly used of the standard OEM tools, there are other tools that are used fairly often. One often-used tool is the Oracle Security Manager, where Oracle users and roles are maintained.

Oracle Security Manager

Oracle Security Manager provides a quick method for displaying all of the privileges associated with an Oracle user. Figure 13.2 shows the main screen for Oracle

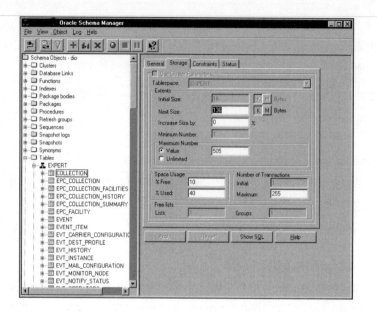

Figure 13.1

Changing the size of a table's **NEXT** extent in the Schema Manager.

Security Manager. Here, you can see that the system has three submenus: Users, Roles, and Profiles. Within User, you can drill down to get a list of Oracle users. Using the Oracle Security Manager, you can see the roles, system privileges, and object privileges that have been granted to users. Figure 13.2 shows the general information for a user, including the default profile, and the default and temporary tablespace names.

The Quotas tab shows all quotas for a user. These quotas describe the amount of system resources that are available to Oracle users. An example of quotas is the Unlimited Tablespace privilege.

A user's privileges can be viewed by clicking on the Privileges tab. Once there, an administrator can view a list of available privileges on the bottom of the screen and assign roles to users using the list. This screen also allows for revoking roles from users and allows roles to be granted with the ADMIN option.

Now that we have covered the administration of users and security, let's move on to take a look at the Oracle Replication Manager.

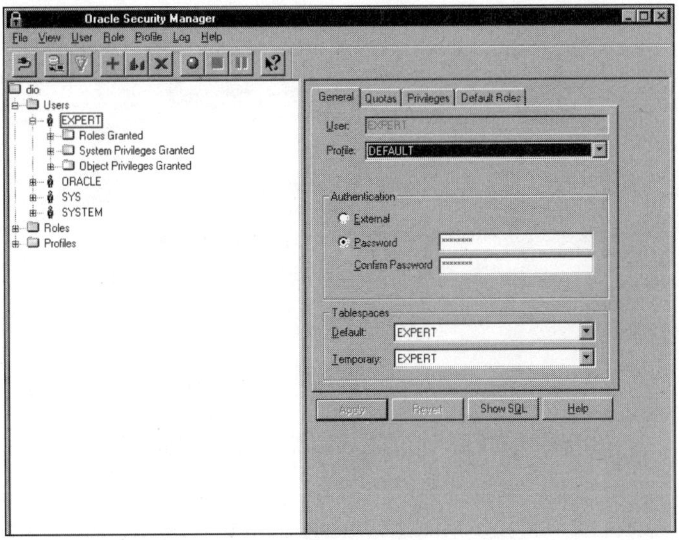

Figure 13.2
Displaying Oracle user information in the Security Manager.

Oracle Replication Manager

The Oracle Replication Manager was originally designed as an interface for an Oracle NT system where the standard Oracle snapshot syntax would not function. This section assumes that you are already familiar with the creation and maintenance of Oracle snapshots. For more information about Oracle snapshots, please refer to the book *High Performance Oracle Database Applications*, published by Coriolis Group Books. The main screen for Oracle Replication Manager (shown in Figure 13.3) contains options for Configuration, Scheduling, and Administration (deferred tasks and jobs).

From the main screen, the warehouse DBA can create a new snapshot group. The data collected for a snapshot group includes the name of the snapshot group and the link to the target database. The DBA can then easily define the tables in the snapshot group.

This tool also includes a definition screen for destination links in a snapshot. As you may know, a snapshot that is periodically refreshed must allow for a snapshot table on the target instance to hold the changes to the table.

A screen is also available to create the destination link. Here, the developer can specify transaction counts, execution seconds, delay in seconds, and batch size. These parameters are used to control the intervals for the refreshing of snapshots.

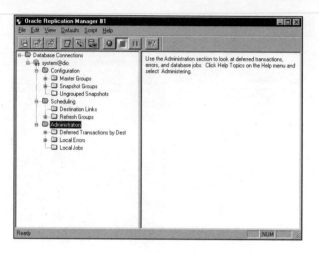

Figure 13.3
The main screen in the Oracle Replication Manager.

There is also a screen for defining snapshot refresh groups. A *refresh group* is a set of related tables that are always refreshed on the same schedule. On this screen, you can see three tabs: the General tab, where you specify the refresh group name; the Snapshot tab, where the snapshots that participate in the group are defined; and the Scheduling tab, where the refreshing jobs are scheduled.

Now that we have seen the functionality of the replication manager, let's take a look at how the Oracle Data Manager keeps track of Oracle data.

Oracle Data Manager

Oracle Data Manager is another tool that was designed exclusively for use by Oracle NT databases. Because Oracle Data Manager is not designed for Unix-based Oracle databases, many developers are surprised to see that the backup destinations are configured to point to local file systems on their NT client. Figure 13.4 shows the main screen for the Oracle Data Manager.

Here, we see that the basic functionality for the Data Manager tool is the management of export and import utilities and the interface to the SQL*Loader utility. For details on these utilities, refer to Chapter 10, *Oracle Data Warehouse Utilities*. In this first screen of the Data Manager, the developer may specify a local, PC file to hold the export file and then define a list of tables to be exported. This utility is useful for

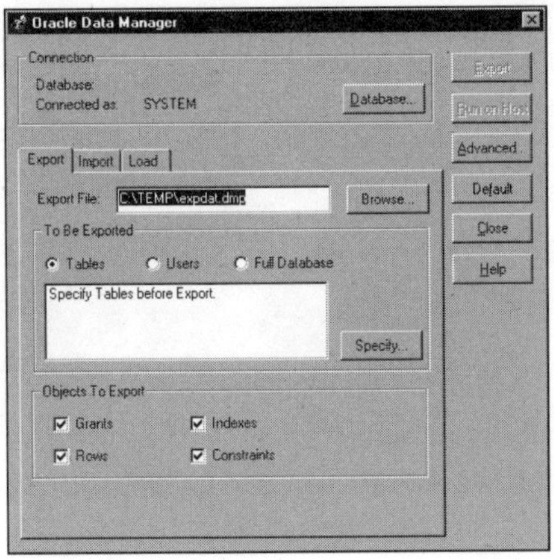

Figure 13.4

Setting up an export file in the Oracle Data Manager.

performing exports from Unix-based Oracle systems, where small tables can be exported from Unix and stored on cheaper PC-based disk media.

There is a set of tabs for the Oracle export definition. First, the developer specifies the name of the export file and an optional list of tables to be imported on by using the Import tab. In addition, this tab allows the developer to specify whether table grants and indexes will be imported. There is also a Load tab to interface to Oracle's SQL*Loader utility. This tab allows a developer to specify the name of a control file that will direct a load, the location of the data to be loaded, the bad file, the discard file, and all other parameters required by SQL*Loader.

Figure 13.5 shows the advanced setting for the load utility. These settings include the frequency that inserted rows will be committed and other parameters. For more details about setting these parameters, see Chapter 10, *Oracle Data Warehouse Utilities*.

In addition to Oracle Data Manager there is also an Oracle tool that manages the mapping of logical tablespaces to physical files. Let's take a look at the Oracle Storage Manager.

Oracle Storage Manager

The Oracle Storage Manager is used to manage data files and roll back segments. The highest level menu in the Storage Manager is shown in Figure 13.6. You can see that tablespaces are listed on the left side of the screen. This screen allows you to drill

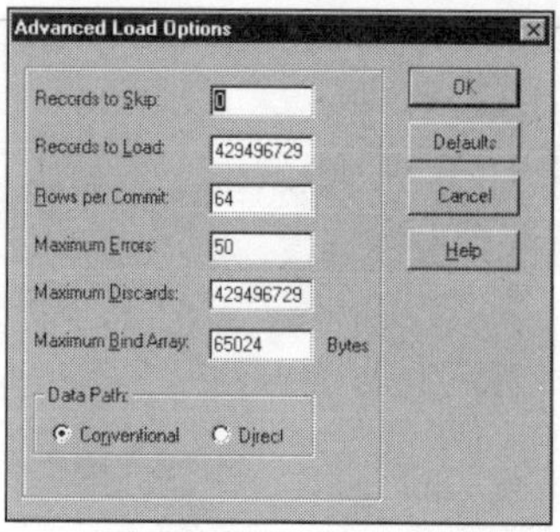

Figure 13.5

Setting the Advanced Load Options in the Oracle Data Manager.

down to see the data files or rollback segments associated with each tablespace. As you may know, a tablespace can have many data files and rollback segments. The information on the General tab on the right side of the screen shows the data files and the status of each data file.

Note that there is an Extents tab on the main Oracle Storage Manager screen. The Extents tab enables developers to alter the size of the **INITIAL**, **NEXT**, **PCTINCREASE**, and **MAXEXTS** default values for a tablespace. Remember, these are table parameters, and table parameters are only used in tablespace definitions

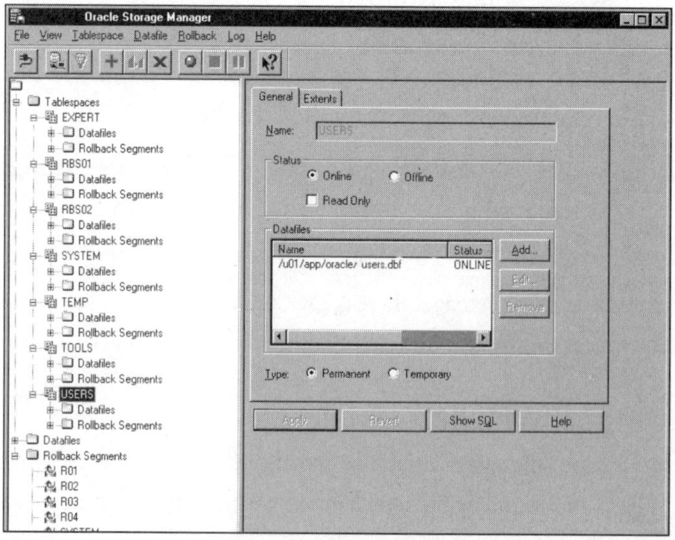

Figure 13.6

The Oracle Storage Manager main screen.

when a table is defined without storage parameters. If a tablespace is defined with storage parameters, the storage parameters are used for the table.

Now that we have covered the management of data and storage, let's take a look at how backups are managed within Oracle Enterprise Manager.

Oracle Backup Manager

The Oracle Backup Manager is another OEM tool created primarily for use by Oracle databases on NT servers. Just like the Storage Manager, the left side of the screen displays tablespaces, as shown in Figure 13.7. Note that the toolbar at the top of the screen includes a Backup Wizard button. The first button on the left allows a reconnection to another instance, and the next button to the left starts the Backup Wizard. This is the first time that Oracle has attempted to use a wizard for any database operations.

The first screen of the Wizard allows a developer to state whether the database is currently up or down, and whether the backup will be a hot backup (synchronized with the redo logs) or a cold backup (no update activity allowed). The users are then directed to a screen where they are allowed to choose which tablespaces should be backed up. Listing 13.1 is the output from the Wizard. It is interesting to note that

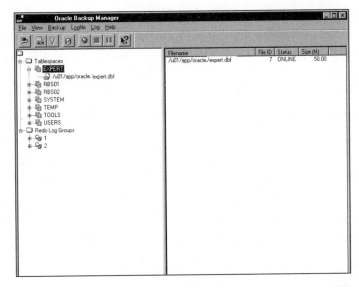

Figure 13.7

The main screen for the Oracle Backup Manager.

the script is written in the TCL language. As you may know, there are several portable scripting languages between Windows NT and Unix, including POSIX and Perl. At this point in the backup, the developer is free to execute the script or alter it according to specific backup needs.

Listing 13.1 The output from the Backup Wizard.

```
REM Wizard Backup Tcl Script Ver. 1.1
sam son
$SMP_USER/$SMP_PASSWORD@$SMP_SERVICE
"UP"
{\"ONLINE\"}
{{{EXPERT}}}
{{{1}}}
{{{/u01/app/oracle/sam son/expert.dbf}}}
{/tmp/backup}
CopyFilesToDirectory
```

While the Oracle Backup Manager may become more popular, there is still some debate about whether it will displace some of the third-party products that manage Oracle backup and recovery. Now let's take a look at the heart of Oracle's Enterprise Manager, the OEM console.

Oracle Enterprise Manager Console

The Oracle Enterprise Manager console is one of the most powerful components of OEM, and it is also one of the most confusing. Figure 13.8 shows the main display screen for the OEM Console, which is divided into four sections, each with its own functionality. One of the most important uses of the OEM Console is the interface with the Oracle intelligent agents on each of the remote servers. On each remote server, a program constantly runs in the background and interfaces the OEM Console with the scheduling of jobs and sending of alerts to the OEM Console. In Figure 13.8, you can see a listing of all of the available events within the OEM Console.

Many of the console alerts are only available with the purchase of the OEM Performance Pack (discussed later in this chapter). As you can see, these alerts can be made to constantly monitor numerous conditions and alert a DBA whenever any alert threshold has been exceeded.

The OEM console provides a complete environment for managing many aspects of Oracle, including database alert propagation, job scheduling, and distributed database

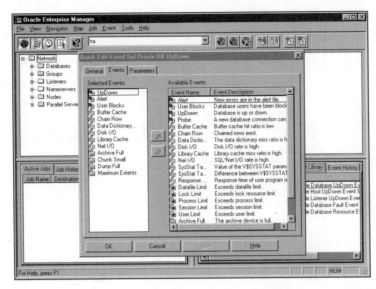

Figure 13.8
Event set management in the Oracle Enterprise Manager console.

management. Now, let's move on to take a look at the OEM replacement for the SQL*Plus facility, Oracle SQL Worksheet.

Oracle SQL Worksheet

The Oracle SQL Worksheet is essentially a GUI version of the Unix-based SQL*Plus product. In Figure 13.9, you can see the open script selection screen. Just as you can in Unix, you can browse the local Admin directory on the PC client and see the standard Oracle catalog SQL scripts. Figure 13.9 shows the scrolling output from executing an SQL script in the SQL Worksheet. This is a nice feature of OEM because the scrolled output can be saved and browsed easily.

The ability to easily browse and edit SQL statements using the GUI features is one of SQL Worksheet's biggest improvements over the Unix-based SQL*Plus. Now let's take a look at the OEM replacement for the Unix-based SQL*DBA utility, the OEM Instance Manager.

Oracle Instance Manager

The Oracle Instance Manager is a very simple tool. Its main function is to start and stop an Oracle instance. But you can also use this tool to display the init.ora parameters for an instance, as shown in Figure 13.10.

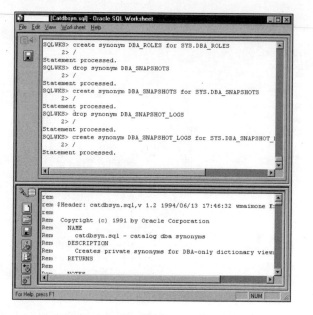

Figure 13.9
Executing catdbsyn.sql in the Oracle SQL Worksheet.

While the OEM tools function quite nicely on a Windows NT client, there has been a great interest in making the Oracle monitoring tools available from remote locations.

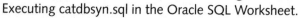

Figure 13.10
Viewing instance parameters in the Oracle Instance Manager.

The natural answer to this problem has been addressed by Oracle in their development of a Web-based front end for the Oracle Enterprise Manager. While this front end does not yet have all of the robust features of its NT cousin, it is a powerful alternative for database developers who do not possess Windows NT clients.

Oracle Enterprise Manager On The Web

One of the shortcomings of the OEM suite is the necessity of having an Oracle NT client to run the software. This was also a drawback of OEM's predecessor, Oracle Server Manager, which required an X-Windows interface and would only execute on Unix platforms. Oracle is beginning to address these issues by developing a Web-based edition of the OEM suite. The Web-based front end is still not fully functional, but Oracle is making rapid headway toward delivering OEM on a platform that can be accessed from any Web browser. There are options for the Database Manager, Security Manager, Data Manager, Session Manager, and Tablespace Manager.

The Database Manager has essentially the same functionality as the Instance Manager on NT platforms, with the notable exception of the new Self-Tune tab. The Self-Tune function claims to adjust the init.ora parameters according to the current requirements of the database.

The Web-based product also includes a new Security Manager, shown in Figure 13.11. In addition to the information available in the NT version of OEM, this new version also displays the date created for each Oracle user, including the internal user number. The Web version of Security Manager allows for exported tables to be listed by name, user, or full database.

Figure 13.12 displays the Tablespace Manager. Here, you can see the screen where the developer may enter tablespace information. Note the instructions that state that the tablespaces are self-expanding, indicating that this session is connected to an Oracle NT server.

A useful aspect of the Tablespace Manager is the Tablespace Status screen, where the amount of free space in the tablespace is reported. There are additional options for View, Expand, and Create. The Tablespace Manager also allows the adding of a data file in the Web-based version of OEM. In this screen, the developer can see a field for the entry of a new data file name and a space to specify the size of the new data file. Now that we understand the basic functionality of the Oracle Enterprise

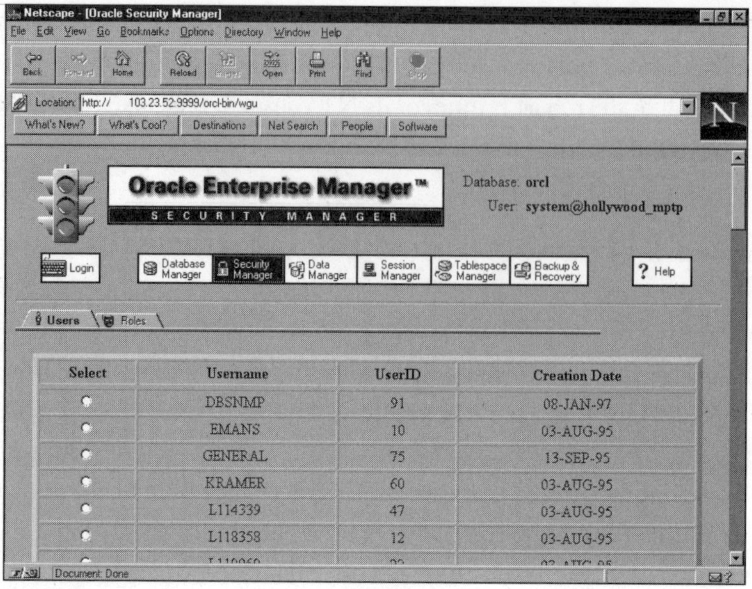

Figure 13.11
The OEM Security Manager as viewed in Netscape.

Manager, let's take a look at Oracle's exciting new product in the database performance and tuning market.

Oracle Performance Pack

As mentioned earlier, the Oracle Performance Pack (OPP) was introduced with Oracle 7.3. OPP and is one of the best new entries into the Oracle database monitoring market. While this tool set doesn't come free with Oracle and can be very expensive, it has functionality that can greatly aid in the performance and tuning of complex Oracle systems. In addition, OPP can be used to analyze databases running pre–7.3 versions of Oracle software. OPP consists of the following six tools:

- *Top Sessions*—Allows DBAs to quickly display the top Oracle sessions according to dozens of criteria. In addition, Top Sessions allows developers to drill into a task and display the explain plan for the SQL.

- *Oracle Expert*—Allows Oracle DBAs to apply the knowledge embedded in Oracle Expert to a specific database. This tool will inspect a schema definition, the SQL that currently resides in a shared pool, and the physical database itself.

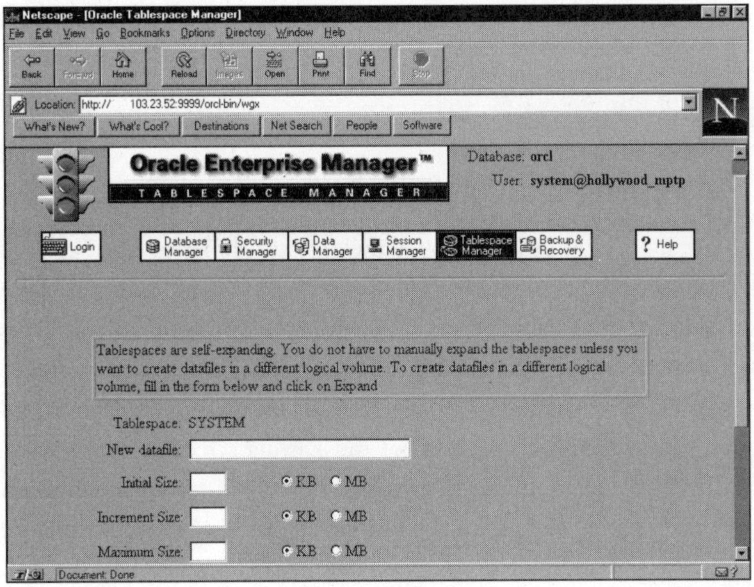

Figure 13.12
The OEM Tablespace Manager as viewed in Netscape.

Following these inspections, Oracle Expert will make recommendations, which can then be scheduled for implementation.

- *Oracle Performance Manager*—Provides a graphical display of many of the standard performance and tuning measures, such as the buffer cache hit ratio.

- *Oracle Tablespace Manager*—Allows for a graphical display of tables within their tablespaces. This can be an excellent tool for understanding table placement within a tablespace.

- *Oracle Lock Manager*—Allows developers to quickly see which tasks may be holding locks that block the execution of other tasks. This tool replicates the manual use of the **DBA_BLOCKERS** and **DBA_WAITERS** views except that it runs much faster that the script method. The Oracle Lock Manager appears in two places within OEM: as a standalone icon and as a sub-screen within Oracle's Performance Pack Top Sessions Monitor.

- *Oracle Trace*—Presents a GUI version of the standard Oracle trace utility, and allows developers to trace data as it is fetched from a specified SQL statement.

Oracle's Performance Pack is an exciting new tool for bringing detail to the complex task of tuning Oracle data warehouses. Let's take a high-level overview of the basic components of this tool.

Top Sessions

The Top Sessions monitor begins by allowing a developer to choose from a list of sorting criteria for the top sessions. This is an extremely useful tool because the top tasks can be sorted by just about every conceivable measurement criteria. These criteria include the number of cleanouts and rollbacks, the number of consistent gets, the amount of CPU used by a session, I/O performed by a session, calls to SQL*Net, and many other options. Figure 13.13 shows the starting screen to Top Sessions, where sorting criteria are chosen. In the real world, a developer may iterate through the sort criteria selection screen in order to sort the top Oracle tasks by several different criteria. This is done to help understand whether a task is CPU bound or I/O bound.

The Top Sessions screen then displays the top sessions (accompanied by useful top session information) according to the sort criteria. Note that the Oracle background processes are also listed on this screen. While statistics for all tasks may be gathered, details about an SQL explain plan may only be viewed for those tasks marked *ACTIVE*.

To view details about any task on this list, simply doubleclick on the task, and a screen similar to the one shown in Figure 13.14 will appear. This screen has four tabs: General, Statistics, Cursors, and Locks. Figure 13.14 shows the general information reported about an Oracle task.

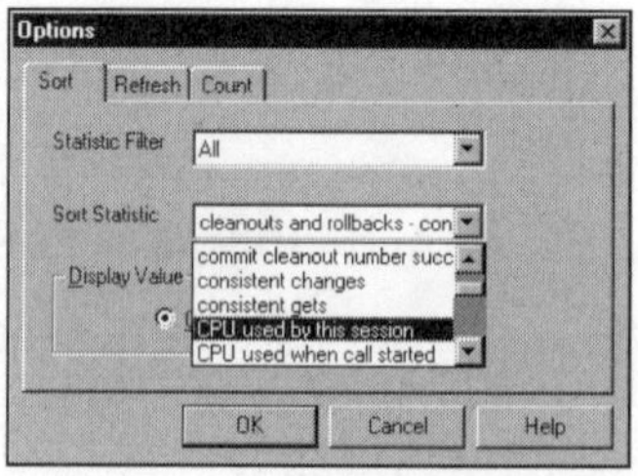

Figure 13.13
Selecting the Top Sessions sorting criteria.

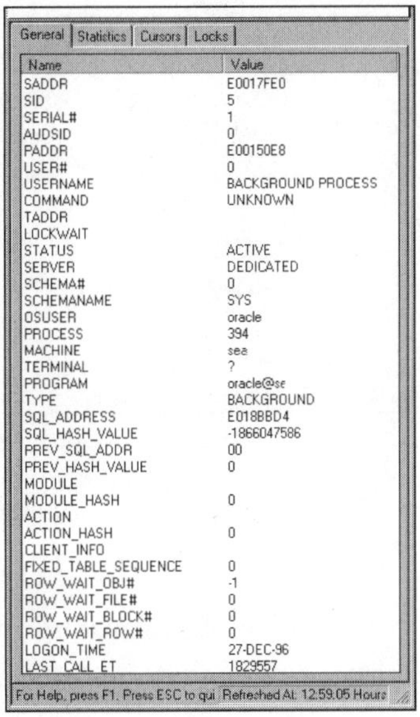

Figure 13.14
The general data for an individual Oracle task.

To display even more details about an Oracle task, the Statistics tab can be chosen. This screen provides some very useful information about a data warehouse query, including SQL*Net activity from client to server, CPU usage, and consistent gets.

The real value of the Session Details screen is gained by pressing the Cursors tab. For all SQL marked *ACTIVE* on the main screen, you can see the actual SQL as it exists in the library cache. Note that the Explain Plan button can be pressed to review the explain plan for the SQL.

In Figure 13.15, you can see the Explain Plan for SQL that is currently executing. This is one of the most powerful features of OPP because explain plan information can be captured and printed easily for further reference. In many cases, data warehouse queries can be shown to be performing full-table scans, even though the developers thought the queries were using indexes. This is especially important for systems where a lot of ad hoc queries are executed.

Now that you understand how individual tasks are investigated using OPP's Top Sessions tool, let's take a quick look at some of the system-wide tuning tools, starting with the Oracle Expert.

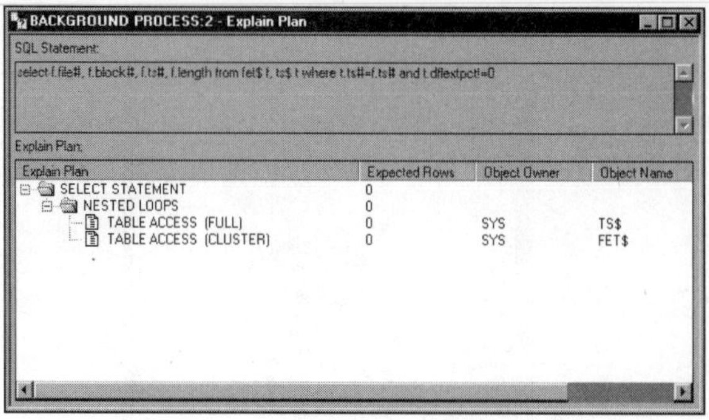

Figure 13.15
The Explain Plan for an SQL query.

Oracle Expert

The Oracle Expert aids DBAs in the performance and tuning of Oracle databases. Based on decision rules, Oracle Expert interrogates a database instance and schema definition, and recommends changes. In addition, Oracle Expert contains a facility for implementing any suggested changes. Oracle Expert makes tuning recommendations for three areas: instance tuning, application tuning, and structure tuning.

- *Instance Tuning*—Involves changes to the all of the parameters that affect the configuration of an Oracle instance, including the following:

  - *Initialization Parameters*—SGA parameters, such as **shared_pool_size** and **db_block_buffers**.

  - *I/O Parameters*—Parameters such as **checkpoint_processes** and **db_multiblock_read_count**.

  - *Parallel Query Parameters*—Parameters such as suggested settings for **parallel_min_servers** and **parallel_max_servers**.

  - *Sort Parameters*—Parameters such as suggestions for **sort_area_size**, **sort_area_retained_size**, and **sort_direct_writes**.

- *Application Tuning*—Involves tuning SQL statements, but only includes SQL statements that happen to reside in the SGA at the time Oracle Expert is running. Oracle Expert examines the applications, transactions, and SQL statements that are running at the moment. Application tuning categories include the following:

- *SQL Similarity Identification*—Oracle Expert identifies similar SQL statements that are treated as different SQL statements due to differences in capitalization and spacing. These duplicate SQL statements must be parsed as new SQL statements, causing unnecessary overhead for Oracle.

- *Index Placement*—Oracle Expert examines existing SQL and determines if any of the queries might benefit from new indexes. Oracle Expert may also make recommendations to remove indexes that are not used and may recommend changes to existing indexes, such as adding columns to existing indexes.

- *Structure Tuning*—Involves database structure tuning. Oracle Expert can create recommendations about the size and placement of database tables and indexes. The categories of structure tuning are as follows:

  - *Segment Size*—Oracle Expert makes recommendations for default storage parameters of a tablespace. These parameters provide default initial allocation and growth rate of segments created within a tablespace.

  - *Segment Placement*—Oracle Expert makes recommendations to isolate tables and indexes in separate tablespaces.

  - *User Analysis*—Oracle Expert makes recommendations on the proper assignment of default and temporary tablespaces.

It needs to be noted that Oracle Expert is still rather primitive and sometimes makes naive recommendations. For example, while Oracle recommends that **PCTINCREASE** be set to **1** for a tablespace in order for the tablespace coalesce feature to work, Oracle Expert will detect the non-zero value and recommend that **PCTINCREASE** be reset to **0**.

Also, the runtime for Oracle Expert can be frustrating, especially when Oracle Expert is asked to examine a database. Oracle Expert dutifully walks through indexes and tables, looking to make recommendations, but it does not report back to an end user about where the Expert is during the process. Even a relatively small database may take hours to examine, and the user often runs the risk that the SQL*Net connection may get dropped during these long-running examinations of the data.

Oracle Expert has tremendous potential to be a successful tool that automates the task of routine performance and tuning audits. Clearly, Oracle has made a commitment to this type of tool, and it will be exciting to see the Oracle Expert evolve into a robust and intelligent tool for tuning the database.

Now that we understand Oracle Expert, let's take a look at one of the most popular tools in the OPP tool set, Oracle's Performance Manager.

Oracle Performance Manager

The Oracle Performance Manager component of OPP is a very simple package that graphically displays salient system measures using pie charts and histograms. While this is not a new concept, Oracle has created numerous shortcuts to allow the quick, visual display of a database's performance.

While Oracle Performance Manager provides many different graphical capabilities, the most commonly used display is achieved by opening the Display menu and choosing the Overall option. This command provides a high-level graphical view of the system, as shown in Figure 13.16.

The Oracle Performance Manager tool is generally used to get a fast, high-level overview of the health of an instance. With just a few mouse clicks, the Oracle DBA can

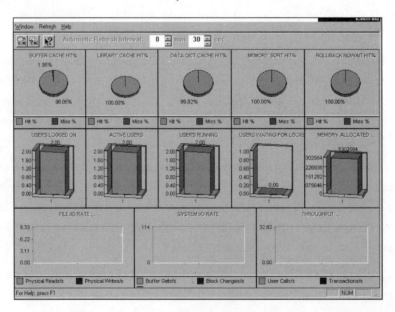

Figure 13.16
The overall statistics in the Performance Manager.

generate a report that displays all of the hit ratios, number of users logged on, number of active users, users waiting for locks, memory used, file I/O, system I/O, and system throughput.

The Oracle Performance Manager is an excellent tool for identifying the high-level characteristics of an Oracle warehouse. Now let's look at some of the other components of the Oracle arsenal.

Oracle Trace

The Oracle Trace tool allows the developer to directly view the data that is accessed while an SQL statement is executing. As a general rule the Oracle Trace facility is only used when a very critical SQL statement is giving strange results, and is seldom used by the Oracle data warehouse manager.

Now let's take a look at a tool that has proven very useful to the Oracle warehouse manager, the Oracle Tablespace Manager. This tool is indispensable for the identification of data warehouse file placement within the data warehouse.

Oracle Tablespace Manager

Another exciting addition to Oracle's performance pack is the Tablespace Manager tool. At last, the Oracle DBA has a tool that will display where tables reside within a tablespace. The Oracle Tablespace Manager can drill into schema owners and investigate any tablespace.

Figure 13.17 shows the details of a tablespace. On the left side, you can see the data files that comprise the tablespace. On the right side, you can see a list of segment names (tables or indexes) sorted by any number of selection criteria. In our example, the tablespaces are sorted in descending order by the number of extents. From this screen, the developer may highlight a segment and see details on the table. In Figure 13.17, you can see that the **XP_OBJECT** table has taken 18 extents and that the initial segment consumes 342 data blocks.

The real value of the Tablespace Manager lies in the ability to see where the segment extents reside within a tablespace. In Figure 13.17, the extents for the **XP_OBJECT** table are displayed in yellow, quickly providing information about the segment distribution within the tablespace.

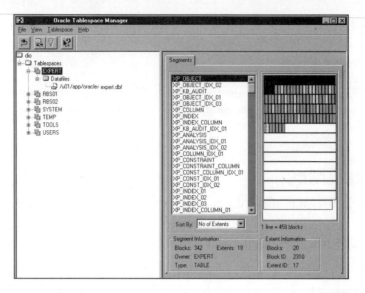

Figure 13.17
The tablespace detail display screen for the Oracle Tablespace Manager.

Overall, the Oracle Performance Pack is a direct competitor to numerous other third-party products that are used to monitor the Oracle database. In time, OPP will become increasingly popular by virtue of its tight integration with Oracle, and because of the commitment from Oracle to continue to enhance the tool set. Finally, let's take a look at the toolbar that is used to invoke the services of OEM and OPP.

The OEM And OPP Toolbar

When OEM and OPP is installed within Windows NT, the Oracle installer automatically ensures that the PC is configured as an SQL*Net client and adds the OEM components to the Program menu selection. However, Oracle also provides a toolbar, shown in Figure 13.18, that can be used to quickly access the OEM and OPP components.

This toolbar contains the entire set of tools from the OEM and OPP. To add or remove icons from the standard OEM toolbar, the icon on the bottom right can be clicked. One item that is often used is the SQL*Net Easy component of the Oracle installer. The icon displayed on the top left in Figure 13.18 invokes SQL*Net Easy. The purpose of SQL*Net Easy is to allow developers to quickly add new database names to the local TNSNAMES.ORA file on the PC client. The developer enters an

Figure 13.18
The Oracle Enterprise Manager toolbar.

instance name, a host name or IP address, and a Transparent Network Substrate (TNS) service name. This provides all of the information needed for an SQL*Net client to connect to the remote Oracle server.

All of the products within the OEM suite of tools require that the PC client sign-on to the remote Oracle host. Because OEM runs as an SQL*Net client, the developer is required to enter a valid Oracle user name, password, and TNS service name when connecting to the database.

Summary

This new generation of Oracle tools has proven that there will soon be changes in the ways that Oracle professionals monitor and tune their Oracle data warehouses. To understand some of the other changes that are in the works, let's move on to Chapter 14, where we'll take a look at some new Oracle features that will soon become available.

Oracle8 For The Warehouse

CHAPTER

14

HIGH PERFORMANCE

Oracle8 For The Warehouse

The new Oracle8 architecture is primarily focused on the introduction of objects into the relational model, but there are some significant new features that directly address data warehousing. The new features for data warehousing in Oracle8 fall into three categories:

- *Table And Index Partitioning*—Rather than manually splitting tables into horizontal partitions by date, Oracle8 provides a method for creating partitioned tables and indexes. This new feature allows a set of partitioned tables and indexes to function as a single entity, thereby allowing better manageability.

- *New Parallel Operations*—Oracle8 now allows for parallel DML and parallel index scans, and provides for parallelism within the new partitioned table and index structures.

- *Improved Join Optimization*—The join optimizer has been altered to allow faster joins when utilizing partitioned tables and indexes.

Table And Index Partitioning

The ability to partition tables and indexes will have a very positive impact on Oracle data warehouse managers. The partitioning of tables and indexes will allow the DBA to enhance the availability of a data warehouse by making structural maintenance simpler. In addition, Oracle data warehouses will perform faster because Oracle engines will recognize partitions and only query the partitions necessary to service a query.

Increased Availability

Because table and index partitions exist as separate physical entities within the Oracle database, they can be maintained independently without affecting the availability of other partitions (see Figure 14.1).

In an Oracle data warehouse, there are many times when partitioning can be extremely useful. As discussed in Chapter 8, *Oracle Features For The Data Warehouse,* an entire data warehouse is usually far too large for a complete, periodic reorganization. Of course, there are times when certain conditions require tables and indexes to be rebuilt. Partitioning enables you to successfully rebuild tables and indexes in most situations. Consider the following:

- *Disk Failures*—When a disk crashes in a partitioned data warehouse, the affected object partition can be taken offline, restored, and rolled forward without impacting the availability of the other partitions.

- *Backup Of Objects*—With object partitioning, portions of tables and indexes can be backed up without affecting the availability of other partitions.

- *Tables With Too Many Chained Rows*—Sometimes, a data warehouse table may be initially loaded with **null varchar** columns that are later updated to insert

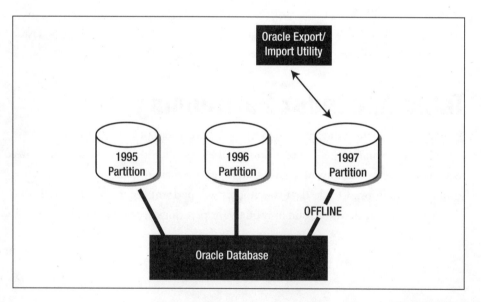

Figure 14.1
Partitions can be brought offline for maintenance.

expanded values. When this occurs, the rows can fragment into other data blocks, requiring additional I/O to access the row. To detect this condition, run the chain.sql script found on the CD-ROM.

- *Tables Approaching Maximum Extents*—In tables with a finite number of extents, the insertion of new rows will cause the table to extend. While table extending is not a problem, if the table approaches its maximum values for extents, new rows will not be allowed into the table until it has been exported and imported into a single extent.

- *Static Tables With **PCTFREE** Set Too High*—Because data warehouses are data sensitive, it is common to see a rolling effect where the most current partition of a table gets heavy updates. As this partition becomes older, it will no longer be updated, and space can be reclaimed by exporting the partition and re-creating it with smaller **PCTFREE** values, thereby packing the rows onto the data blocks and saving significant disk space. Sometimes, a data warehouse DBA may also want to migrate these partitions onto read-only tablespaces on a CD-ROM while the current partition remains in an updateable tablespace.

- *Indexes With Too Many Deleted Leaf Blocks*—Oracle data warehouse indexes can become unbalanced if there are too many deleted leaf blocks within the index. When this happens, the Oracle warehouse DBA should drop and re-create the index. For a script to detect this condition, see the id1.sql script on the CD-ROM.

- *Indexes With More Than Four Levels*—With heavy update activity, it is not uncommon to see a data warehouse index spawn to deeper levels in certain spots within the index. When this happens, the data warehouse DBA should drop and re-create the index, thereby balancing the levels. For a script to detect this condition, see the index.sql script on the CD-ROM.

- *Base-Table Indexes Not Clustered With The Base Table*—In Oracle, it is possible to have an index physically sequenced in the same order as the table. But, as rows are added onto the end of the table, the index will become less clustered. In these cases, the Oracle DBA should extract and sort the table, replace the table, and then rebuild the clustered index.

With table partitioning, some clustering of data with the index will take place automatically because new table rows will be directed to the partition that contains similar partition values. However, clustering within a partition may get out of synchronization when too many rows are added to the end of a partition.

When any of these conditions occurs, the DBA will be able to take the offending partition offline, rebuild the object, and reintroduce it into the data warehouse with minimal service interruption.

Increased Performance

The Oracle8 engine gains performance increases as a direct result of Oracle8's new architecture, which allows for the physical segregation of table and index partitions. The Oracle8 engine will take advantage of the new architecture in the following ways:

- *Query Optimization*—The Oracle8 optimizer can detect values within each partition and only access those partitions necessary to service a query. Because each partition can be defined with its own storage parameters, the Oracle8 SQL optimizer may choose a different optimization plan for each partition.

- *Load Balancing*—Table and index partitioning allows Oracle data warehouse DBAs to segregate portions of very large tables and indexes onto separate disk devices, thereby improving disk I/O throughput and ensuring maximum performance.

- *Parallel Query*—The partitioning of objects also greatly improves the performance of parallel query. When Oracle8 detects that a query is going to span several partitions, such as a full-table scan, Oracle can fire off parallel processes, each of which will independently retrieve data from each partition. This feature is especially important for indexes because parallel queries will no longer need to share a single index, and separate indexes can exist for each partition.

Now that we have reviewed the compelling reasons for using partitioning with Oracle tables and indexes, let's take a look at how partitioning is implemented within the Oracle8 architecture.

Table Partitioning With Oracle8

As we discussed in Chapter 4, *Oracle Data Warehouse Design,* table partitioning can greatly improve the manageability of very large data warehouse tables. Now, Oracle8 provides a method to automatically partition tables in a horizontal fashion during table-creation time (see Figure 14.2).

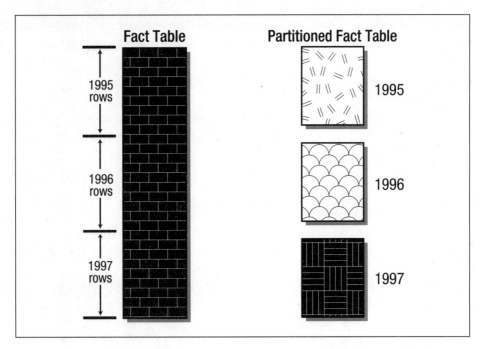

Figure 14.2
Horizontal partitioning of tables.

At first glance, table partitioning might seem to be a simple method of chunking tables, but Oracle has included the ability for each partition to have its own values set for **PCTFREE, PCTUSED, INITTRANS,** and **MAXTRANS.** Enabling partitions to have different table usage values can be especially useful in partitioned tables where only the most recent partition is updated. In this case, earlier partitions would have **PCTUSED** set to **100** and **PCTFREE** set to **0.** By allowing control over the partitions as if they were separate tables, a DBA can pack static data into Oracle blocks and save space. The current partition would have **PCTFREE** set to a higher number to allow for row expansion as the rows are updated.

Partitioning Syntax

The process of creating a partitioned table with Oracle8 is very straightforward. For example, if you have a table called **ALL_FACTS,** you would first need to choose a partition key for the operation. Generally, a partition key is a date value that specifies the range of rows participating in each partition. For some data warehouse applications, the partition key could be a non-date value, such as the case where an employee table is partitioned according to the value of each employee's department column. Listing 14.1 shows the SQL used to create a partitioned table definition in Oracle8.

Listing 14.1   A partitioned table definition in Oracle8.

```
CREATE TABLE ALL_FACTS
(
    order_date              date,
    order_year              number(2),
    order_quarter           char(2),
    order_month,            number(2),
    order_nbr               number(5),
    salesperson_name        varchar(20),
    customer_name           varchar(20),
    customer_city           varchar(20),
    customer_state          varchar(2),
    customer_region         char(1),
    item_nbr                number(5),
    quantity_sold           number(4)
)
PARTITION BY RANGE
    (order_date)
(
PARTITION
    year_1995
    VALUES LESS THAN '01-JAN-1996'
    TABLESPACE year_1995
    STORAGE (INITIAL 500M, NEXT 5M, PCTUSED 99, PCTFREE 1),
PARTITION
    year_1996
    VALUES LESS THAN '01-JAN-1997'
    TABLESPACE year_1996
    STORAGE (INITIAL 500M, NEXT 5M, PCTUSED 99, PCTFREE 1),
PARTITION
    year_1997
    VALUES LESS THAN (MAXVALUE)
    TABLESPACE year_1997
    STORAGE (INITIAL 500M, NEXT 50M, PCTUSED 60, PCTFREE 40),
);
```

Let's review this syntax. Each table partition is defined as having the **order_date** column as the partition key. The **VALUES LESS THAN** parameters determine which rows are partitioned into which tablespaces. Notice that the last partition, **year_1997**, specifies **VALUES LESS THAN (MAXVALUE)**, which means rows that do not meet any selection criteria will be placed in this partition. Also notice that even though the selection parameters for the **year_1996** partition reads **VALUES LESS THAN 1997**, the **year_1995** rows will not be stored in the **year_1996** partition because the value check is preceded by the filter for the **year_1995** partition.

Each partition in Listing 14.1 was created with different tablespace storage parameters, and it appears that only the last partition will be updated, as evidenced by the value of the **PCTFREE** parameter in the **year_1997** tablespace. At **SQL INSERT time**, the DDL is consulted, and the value specified in **order_date** determines which partition a row is stored in within a table.

With partitioned tables, the developer has a choice of either specifying the table partition by name or referencing the entire partition. Since each partition within a partitioned table can be referenced as a unique entity, the developer can save database resources by only selecting from the partitions that are of interest. Of course, the developer can query the entire table as a whole if they desire:

```
SELECT
    sum(quantity_sold)
FROM
    ALL_FACT
WHERE
    order_year = 97
AND
    customer_city = 'Albuquerque';
```

However, in most cases, it would be simpler and less resource intensive to rework this query to implicitly specify the target partition in the query. For example:

```
SELECT
    sum(quantity_sold)
FROM
    ALL_FACT PARTITION (year_1997)
WHERE
    order_year = 97
AND
    customer_city = 'Albuquerque';
```

In the same fashion, partitions can be used to limit **UPDATE** statements to a single partition. For example, let's say you have a huge employee table partitioned by department, and you want to give a 10 percent raise to the MIS department. The SQL you would use is as follows:

```
UPDATE ALL_EMPLOYEE PARTITION ('MIS')
SET
    salary = salary*1.1;
```

Migration Into Partitioned Table Structures

Migration into partitioned tables is very simple using Oracle8. Using the sample table definition displayed in Listing 14.1, you can easily migrate the data from an Oracle7 fact table into a new partitioned structure, as follows:

```
INSERT INTO ALL_FACT PARTITION (year_1995)
(
SELECT * FROM OLD_FACT
WHERE
order_year = 95
);

INSERT INTO ALL_FACT PARTITION (year_1996)
(
SELECT * FROM OLD_FACT
WHERE
order_year = 96
);

INSERT INTO ALL_FACT PARTITION (year_1997)
(
SELECT * FROM OLD_FACT
WHERE
order_year = 97
);
```

Notice that in this example, the **WHERE** clause is redundant. The partition definition will automatically filter out any rows that do not match the selection criteria for each partition.

Now that you understand how Oracle tables can be partitioned, let's take a look at how Oracle indexes can be partitioned. In many ways, the ability to partition Oracle indexes has more performance potential than table partitioning because indexes are a common source of contention within Oracle data warehouses.

Index Partitioning With Oracle8

In addition to a non-partitioned index, Oracle8 allows for two methods for the partitioning of indexes: local and global. A *local* partitioned index creates a one-for-one match between indexes and the partitions in a table. Of course, the key value for the table partition and the value for the local index must be identical. The second method, *global* partitioning, allows an index to have any number of partitions.

The partitioning of indexes is transparent to the SQL, but the Oracle8 query engine will only scan the index partition required to service a query. In addition, the Oracle8 parallel query engine will sense that an index is partitioned and fire simultaneous queries to scan the indexes.

Local Partitioned Indexes

In a local partitioned index, the key values and number of index partitions will exactly match the number of partitions in the base table. Of course, it follows that there can only be one local partitioned index for each table. This is generally done to allow the DBA to take individual partitions of a table and indexes offline for maintenance without affecting the other partitions in the table. The SQL to define a local partitioned index is as follows:

```
CREATE INDEX year_idx
    ON ALL_FACT (order_date)
LOCAL
    (PARTITION name_idx1),
    (PARTITION name_idx2),
    (PARTITION name_idx3);
```

Global Partitioned Indexes

Unlike the local partition technique that defines index partitions according to the number of table partitions, Oracle8 makes it possible to define a partitioned index according to the symbolic key values that appear in the index. A global partitioned index can be used for any symbolic key fields except those indexes used as table partition keys (such as the primary key index for the table). In OLTP applications, global partitioned indexes require fewer index probes than local partitioned indexes. In the global index partitioning scheme, an index is harder to maintain because it may span partitions in the base table (see Figure 14.3). For example, when a table partition is dropped as part of a reorganization, the entire global index is affected.

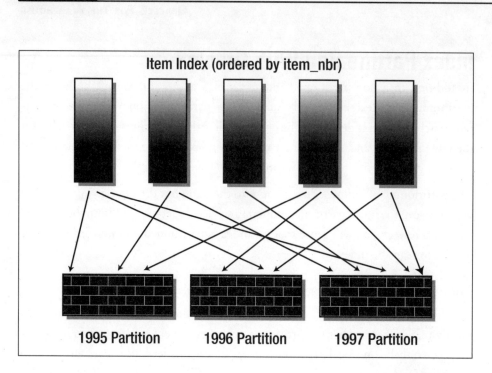

Figure 14.3
A global partitioned index.

When defining a global partitioned index, a DBA has the complete freedom to specify as many partitions for the index as desired.

Now that you understand the concept, let's examine the following Oracle **CREATE INDEX** syntax for a globally partitioned index:

```
CREATE INDEX item_idx
   ON ALL_FACT (item_nbr)
GLOBAL
   (PARTITION city_idx1 VALUES LESS THAN (100)),
   (PARTITION city_idx1 VALUES LESS THAN (200)),
   (PARTITION city_idx1 VALUES LESS THAN (300)),
   (PARTITION city_idx1 VALUES LESS THAN (400)),
   (PARTITION city_idx1 VALUES LESS THAN (500));
```

Here, you can see that the item index has been defined with five partitions, each containing a subset of the index range values. Note that it is irrelevant that the base table is in three partitions. In fact, it is acceptable to create a global partitioned index on a table that does not have any partitioning.

New Parallel Operations

Oracle8 now allows for parallel DML and parallel index scans, and provides for parallelism within the new partitioned table and index structures. The parallelism is very easy to understand if you consider an SQL operation that performs an index scan against a partitioned table:

```
SELECT
    customer_last_name
FROM
    CUSTOMER (degree 4)
WHERE
    customer_age > 45;
```

Furthermore, let's assume that the **CUSTOMER** table has been created with four partitions, with a partitioned index on the **customer_age** column. We can then visualize how a parallel query would scan only those index partitions that contained the symbolic keys for **customer_age** greater than 45. The query manager would then collect the result set from the parallel query and merge and sort it for display.

These new parallel scan features are transparent to the application, and the Oracle8 database engine takes care of all of the internal details.

Improved Join Optimization

The join optimizer has been altered to allow faster joins when utilizing partitioned tables and indexes. For example, consider a query that joins a partitioned table (with partitioned indexes) against another table:

```
SELECT
    customer_last_name
FROM
    CUSTOMER, ORDER
WHERE
    CUSTOMER.customer_ID = ORDER.customer_ID
AND
    order_total > 1000;
```

The SQL optimizer would recognize that the index is partitioned and would only access those index partitions that contain the symbolic key specified in the query. This feature is transparent to the Oracle developer and will happen automatically.

Summary

These new data warehouse features for Oracle8 continue to underscore Oracle Corporation's commitment to supporting very large data warehouse architectures. It will be very exciting to see how these features continue to improve in Oracle 8.2, when some of the object-oriented features will be available for the data warehouse. Especially exciting with be the support for class hierarchies and inheritance because these features will greatly improve the ability of the Oracle data warehouse designer to implement ad hoc classifications of data attributes.

Data Mining And Oracle

HIGH PERFORMANCE

CHAPTER

15

Data Mining And Oracle

The widespread availability of relational data warehouses has sparked renewed interest in data mining, data trolling, and other knowledge discovery tools. As little as two years ago, these terms were meaningless buzzwords meant to describe the plethora of techniques available for analyzing data warehouses. Today, if data warehouse developers want to keep pace with recent advancements, a solid definition of data mining is necessary. There has been a great deal of debate over the definition of data mining and how data mining can be used within an Oracle data warehouse. The recent interest in data warehousing has created many new techniques and tools for getting useful information out of these behemoth databases.

Defining Data Mining

It should be noted that data mining is not a new concept. Statisticians have been data mining for decades. In other words, they've been analyzing corporate information using advanced techniques to model business behaviors. What is new is the general availability of easy-to-use tools for data mining and the terabytes of online corporate data. Today's data miners, for the most part, are not required to understand multivariate statistics and neural networks in order to benefit from a data mining tool. In fact, some tools offer wizards that guide developers through the data mining process. While data mining is one area of data warehouse tools that holds a great deal of promise, many barriers remain. Despite the vendor promises to provide easy-to-use tools, sophisticated multivariate statistical analysis is inherently complex, and many data mining tools continue to require a strong background in advanced statistical techniques to properly set up and use the mining systems.

Data Mining And Data Warehouses

In traditional decision support systems, users were charged with formulating queries against databases and deciphering any trends present in the data. Unfortunately, this approach is only as good as the user of the system, and many statistically valid associations between data items can be missed. This is especially true in data warehouse systems where unobtrusive trends may be present. For example, the Psychology Department at the University of Minnesota—developers of the hugely popular Minnesota Multiphasic Personality Inventory (MMPI)—have discovered some startling patterns correlating a psychological diagnosis to seemingly unrelated, ordinary questions. The results provide unobtrusive measures of human personality. For example, they found that people with low self-esteem tend to prefer baths to showers. While no "reason" for this preference is obvious, the statistically valid correlation between self-concept and cleaning preferences remains.

These types of unobtrusive associations also plague the business world, and it is the goal of data mining software to identify these previously unknown trends and associations for warehouse users. In addition to identifying trends, some data mining software goes one step further and attempts to analyze other data to determine underlying reasons for a trend.

While basic statistical tools are adequate for doing correlation analysis among a small number of related variables, large databases with hundreds of data items are quickly bogged down in a mire of multivariate chi-square techniques that are hard to follow for even the most experienced statistician. As such, new data mining tools are meant to accept only general hints from users and then go forth into the data probing for trends.

In other cases, data mining techniques are used to prove a hypothesis based on existing data. For example, a marketing person may speculate that those with an income between $50,000 and $80,000 are likely to buy the company's products. A quick verification of this hypothesis can be run, thereby either confirming or disproving the hypothesis.

In general terms, data mining in relation to data warehousing refers to the process of "discovering" unknown information from within a data warehouse. This type of knowledge discovery may take several forms: supervised learning, unsupervised learning, and reinforcement learning.

Supervised Learning

Supervised learning is a situation where you already know the answer to a question, but you are seeking information about the environment that contributes to the answer. For example, you may have verified that computer professionals in California tend to have a high preference for blue suits, but you do not understand the reason for this association. The supervised learning tool will examine customers in related professions and locations to attempt to shed some light on the initial finding. The supervised learning tool may discover, for example, that the affinity for blue suits is shared by all professionals aged 40 through 65, and it is irrelevant whether they reside in California. Supervised learning tools work very much like decision support systems in that they rely on the intuition of the end user to guide their learning process. It is the end user, and not the software, that assigns weights to associations and guides the software through the problem resolution.

Unsupervised Learning

In unsupervised learning, you do not know the answer to a question, and you rely on the data mining software to develop a model, based on the characteristics of the data. For example, you may ask, "What is a typical customer?" or, "What classes of products are the most profitable within each region?" In addition, you may query a tool to develop a model. For example, you could use a tool to develop a model to predict a customer's propensity to purchase a Mercedes Benz based on historical data of customers who have already made similar purchases. These models can be used as general, predictive tools for entire classes of products.

Reinforcement Learning

In reinforcement learning situations, you have examples of a problem, but you do not have a model that adequately describes the answer. Commonly, this technique is used to test strategies on two-person non-zero-sum games. In chess, you may set up a problem and direct the tool to make a series of moves, and then see if you win or lose based on the moves. As a tool "learns" from experience, it becomes more proficient at recognizing valuable strategies and discarding bad strategies. In this manner, reinforcement learning is applied to data warehouses. A tool might be directed to develop a strategy for marketing a product. The tool would successively develop and test its strategies against the data warehouse, keeping track of its "wins" and "losses."

As the model becomes more sophisticated, the knowledge is saved in the tool's inference engine, and it becomes more "intelligent" about strategizing.

Information Classifications

Several types of information relative to data warehousing can be gathered from data mining. This information is generally categorized as the discovery of associations, relevant classifications, clusters of related dimension values, and predictive models, as well as the applications of predictive models to forecasting and pattern identification.

Association

The identification of associations between data items is commonly used within marketing data warehouses to locate items commonly purchased together. For example, it might not be obvious that male shoppers who buy diapers also have a high association with beer purchases. Retail stores may mine for associations between customer incomes and product preferences in order to better target their advertising.

One of the major drawbacks of association tools is the sheer volume of their output and their inability to avoid stating obvious associations between data. For example, such a tool might come up with the association that wool parkas are not selling well in Hawaii. Amidst the huge volume of output, however, there may be some jewels to be mined. For example, associations have been found between liquor preferences and the preference for expensive cigars, allowing merchandisers to place these products together where they can be purchased easily.

Classification

Data mining is used to identify new classifications of data and use these new classifications to develop behavior models. For example, a classification called *yuppie* might be created, referring to customers whose income is greater than $100,000, education is greater than grade 16, and total purchases are more than $300 per month. This new, arbitrary classification of values can then be used to predict the behaviors of the group. In some cases, the data mining tool may also determine a new classification for you. The tool can scan the data warehouse and identify commonalities among characteristics of customers based on their purchases and demographic behaviors.

Once a new classification of customers is known, further analysis can be performed to predict common buying behaviors. In many cases, management will want the data warehouse restructured to include "flags" for new classifications, so ad hoc queries can be easily executed against named customer classifications, such as *cheapskates, dinks,* or *yuppies.* This tactic is used in marketing systems for market segmentation analysis where the common characteristics of customers who buy particular products are tabulated and related to the characteristics of customers who purchase other specific products. New classifications are also used by direct marketing applications to improve the response rate to mailings.

Clustering

Clustering is the technique used to discover previously unknown associations among items in a data warehouse. The clustering software scans the data warehouse and searches for unknown relationships. For example, clustering software might discover that loan applicants who indicate that their loan is for necessities, such as home furnishing, have a default rate of 38 percent, while those who borrow for luxury goods, such as vacations, have a default rate of 2 percent.

This type of analysis involves a statistical technique known as the *K-nearest neighbor* technique. In K-nearest neighbor, the facts are plotted against many dimensions, very much like a cross-tabulation in a multidimensional database (see Figure 15.1). Then, the facts are randomly weighted to see if clusters appear (see Figure 15.2). For example, if the association dimensions are age, income, education level, and total purchases, then the tool would apply successively different weights to these dimensions, attempting to cluster the facts in some way.

Clustering is commonly used to classify customers according to the propensities of their neighbors in the cluster. For example, if your profile clusters with those who are likely to purchase ocean cruises, you might expect to receive direct mailing promoting cruise vacations.

Modeling

Modeling is the process of creating a set of rules that can be applied to a data warehouse problem. A human expert may develop a model and use the data warehouse to validate the hypothesis. For example, an expert may develop a model for predicting

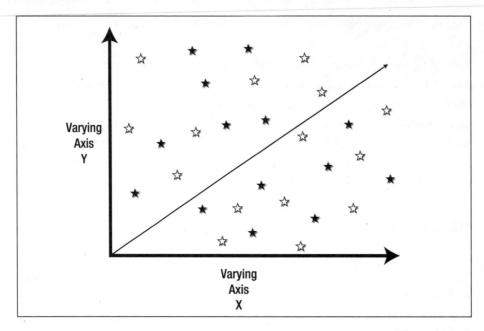

Figure 15.1
An unclustered population distribution.

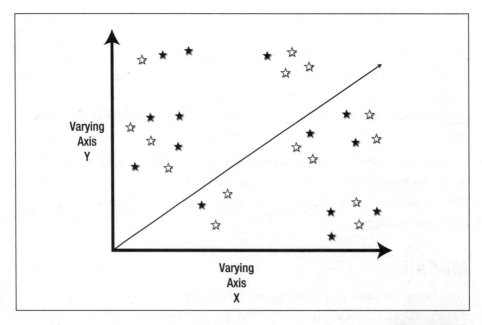

Figure 15.2
As the axes and values vary, clusters of data points may appear.

the behavior of stocks based on the robustness of the stock and the stock's covariance compared to the market as a whole. This model can be validated against the CRSP database (Consumer Reported Stock Prices—a purchasable product that provides the prices for each publicly held stock for each day since 1925). This historical data is then applied to the model, and the accuracy of the model's predictive values can be validated by using factual data. If the model accurately predicts stock price movement in the historical database, the model will, in all likelihood, predict the behavior of stocks in the future.

A model can also be generated by software programmed to recognize patterns and develop rules for the model based on historical data. This is known as the *heuristic approach* to model development, whereby the tool sweeps and resweeps the data warehouse, successively refining its model.

Modeling is closely tied to forecasting, in that a model is often used to predict the probability of a specific event. For example, a banking model may be developed to accurately predict the default rate for different classifications of customers based on historical data warehouse information.

Forecasting

Forecasting is the relatively straightforward process of taking existing information and extrapolating the data into the future. Forecasting techniques generally employ a statistical technique known as *linear regression*. In linear regression analysis, curve smoothing algorithms are employed to determine the best fit for the curve and the most likely future path for the information. One general downside of forecasting involves what is called the *confidence interval*. For example, taking a known pattern of the past 10 years and predicting behavior into the next month can be done with a high degree of confidence in the estimate. As you move further out on the time line, however, you will naturally become less confident about your estimate. This widening confidence interval has become known in data mining as the *trumpet of doom* (see Figure 15.3) because long-term forecasting, regardless of the technique, can't be highly reliable in a changing world.

Forecasting has taken on new importance in data mining when it is combined with data classification. For example, a data classification tool may identify a class of customers who share common traits and habits. By grouping customers into classes,

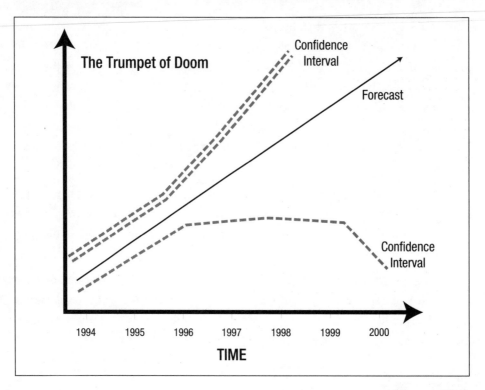

Figure 15.3
The trumpet of doom.

predictive models can be applied to each class to guess the changes in patterns over time. Once a forecasting model has been built, it can be used against a data warehouse for what-if analysis. For example, a forecasting model could be used to determine the impact of a price change on the amount sold for a product, based on the forecasting algorithm and known historical patterns of purchase behavior.

Pattern Identification

Pattern identification is used to detect patterns of behaviors within the warehouse to establish a model for behavior based on the data. For example, financial institutions use pattern identification to detect patterns of credit card fraud and the probability of bankruptcy for customers. Manufacturers use pattern identification to choose shippers who are the most likely to deliver products on time. It is interesting to note that these patterns are not predefined. The data mining software is used to create the pattern based on known facts. Banks can take transaction data from known credit card fraud cases to extrapolate a general pattern of fraudulent behavior. Psychologists can take information from known cases of schizophrenia to develop paper exams that identify the disorder in test takers. The IRS can examine known cases of tax fraud to create models of patterns to detect further fraud and trigger audits based on these patterns. And so on.

Data Mining Tools In The Marketplace

A typical data mining setup can run into the hundreds of thousands of dollars. For instance, a one-year license for BaseSAS (an enterprise-wide software system from SAS Institute that has a substantial installed base among Fortune 500 companies) costs $2,000 per client, plus $25,000 for the server.

Many data mining tools use techniques borrowed from artificial intelligence (AI), including fuzzy logic, neural networks, fractals, and a sundry of other statistical techniques. Because a number of these tools perform a huge amount of internal processing, many of them read selected information from the relational database into a proprietary, internal data representation for analysis. Neural networks, for example, use the human analogy of leaning from experience. A neural net software application is often used in reinforcement learning. A landmark experiment from the 1970s demonstrated that these types of tools can learn from their own experience. A naive computer was programmed to play tic-tac-toe with another computer that understood the rules of the game. The naive computer was also programmed with the ability to "learn" from its mistakes and refine its strategy. As we might expect, the naive computer lost miserably when the computers began playing. However, the naive computer slowly began to infer the rules for tic-tac-toe until, by the 600th game, it had completely mastered the game. The important point here is that the rules of the game were completely transferred to the naive computer. In the same fashion, neural network data mining software can be made to interact with the data warehouse and develop models based on the interaction.

No widely used data mining tools are available that run directly against the relational database, although there are several promising start-up companies (see Table 15.1). The term *data mining* is a hot buzzword, and many of the tools listed in Table 15.1

are not actually true data mining tools because they rely on a vendor's particular definition of data mining. Many of the data mining tools use a relatively straightforward exception-detection mechanism to cruise the database looking for unexpected trends or unusual patterns. Even as this list was being compiled, several new products were being introduced, and it appears that there will continue to be more entries into this potentially lucrative market in the future.

While there is still a great deal of interest in data mining applications, no single vendor has stepped up to claim market leadership. It is also true that many of these companies may disappear as market leaders emerge. It will probably be many years before all owners of a data warehouse have tools that will be able to fully exploit their data resources.

Moral And Ethical Issues In Data Mining

Because data mining provides a microscopic insight into the behaviors of customers, there are some privacy and ethics issues that need to be addressed. Since the content of a data warehouse may reveal very personal details about people, extra care must be taken to ensure that the privacy of the individual is not violated. As data warehouse technology continues to advance, data mining techniques will be able to categorize people according to their data in the warehouse.

Just as the Minnesota Multiphasic Personality Inventory (MMPI) test is able to categorize a subject's personality traits by comparing their test responses with the responses of people with known traits, data warehouse technology will evolve to gain great insight into the personality and behavior of customers. While this data is intended to be used from a purely marketing perspective, such as identifying customers with a predisposition to purchase a product, the customer profile extrapolations could be used in an unethical fashion. For example, there have been unscrupulous computer programmers who have used their companies' data warehouse information to identify potential mates.

The privacy issue also extends to family privacy. An excellent example of this problem occurred when a financial institution performed a data warehouse analysis and targeted those customers who were investing in overseas tax havens. Unfortunately, the

Table 15.1   Data mining product information.

Vendor	Tool	Description
Advanced Software Applications	ModelMax	Rule-Based
Alta Analytics	NETMAP	Neural Nets
American Heuristics	Profiler	Heuristic
Angoss International	KnowledgeSEEKER	Rule-Based
Attar Software	XpertRule Profiler	Rule-Based
Business Objects	BusinessMinder	Rule-Based
Cognitive Systems	ReMind	Inductive Logic
Cross/Z	F-DBMS	Fractals
DataMind	Database Mining Marksman	Rule-Based
Epsilon	Epsilon	Rule-Based
HNC Software	DataMarksman	Rule-Based
Holistic Systems (now owned by Seagate)	Holos	Rule-Based
HYPERParallel	Discovery	Rule-Based
IBM	Data Mining Toolkit	Fuzzy Logic
IBM	Intelligent DATA Miner	Rule-Based
Information Discovery	IDIS	Rule-Based
Information Harvester	Information Harvester	Rule-Based
Integral Solutions	Clementine	Rule-Based
Lucent Technologies	Interactive Data Visualization	Rule-Based
MIT GmbH	DataEngine	Fuzzy Logic
NCR	Knowledge Discovery Workbench	Rule-Based
NeoVista Solutions	Decision Series	Rule-Based
Nestor	PRISM	Neural Nets
NeuralWare	Predict	Neural Nets
Pilot Software	Pilot Discovery Server	Rule-Based
REDUCT & Lobbe Technologies	DataLogic	Fuzzy Sets
Silicon Graphics	MineSet	Rule-Based
SPSS	Statistical Package For The Social Sciences	Rule-Based
Thinking Machines	Darwin	Neural Nets

advertising for investments was sent to the customers' home addresses and not sent to their work addresses. This mailing caused many spouses to discover that their mates were hoarding money, and these secrets were delivered courtesy of the data warehouse.

Summary

While data warehousing is still relatively primitive in nature, the widespread availability of large Oracle warehouses is begging the industry to develop tools that can scan and extract additional useful information from these behemoth databases. In time, these tools will become increasingly sophisticated, and several market leaders will begin to dominate specific niche markets within data mining.

Oracle Warehouses And The Year 2000

CHAPTER

16

HIGH PERFORMANCE

Oracle Warehouses And The Year 2000

Oracle data warehouses are time-based; therefore, it is critical that data warehouses are properly prepared for the transition into the next century. Oracle, with all of its robust features, has a very complex strategy for managing date datatypes. As such, Oracle developers must recognize pitfalls when altering date parameters, and developers must fully understand the ramifications of any date changes they implement. Even as of this writing, Oracle has a date format (**YY**) that is programmed to automatically change behavior when the year ticks to 2000.

Oracle Date Overview

The date datatype within Oracle can be changed by setting a parameter called **nls_date_format**. Oracle's default, **DD-MON-YY**, places a **19** in front of all two-digit year values and is programmed to place a **20** in front of all two-digit years after the year 2000. **nls_date_format** accepts the following three values:

- **DD-MON-YYYY**—Four-digit years are required for query and date storage when using this value setting.

- **DD-MON-YY**—Two-digit years are used for query and date storage, and the current century is added to the date at insert time.

- **DD-MON-RR**—Two-digit years are used for queries and date storage. Where the year ranges from 00 through 49, a **20** is added for the century. For values 50 through 99, a **19** is added for the century.

523

The **nls_date_format** can be changed at the session level by using the **ALTER SES-SION** command, or it can be permanently changed by setting the **nls_date_format** parameter in the init.ora file.

Oracle provides the following two views to assist developers in displaying current date defaults:

- *V$NLS_PARAMETERS*—This view shows the current system-wide default settings for the date parameters.

```
SVRMGR> SELECT * FROM V$NLS_PARAMETERS;

PARAMETER                                         VALUE
--------------------                              -----------
NLS_DATE_FORMAT                                   DD-MON-YY
```

- *NLS_SESSION_PARAMETERS*—This Oracle view displays all of the National Language Support parameters, including the **nls_date_format**.

```
SVRMGR> SELECT * FROM NLS_SESSION_PARAMETERS;

PARAMETER                      VALUE
-----------------              -----------
NLS_DATE_FORMAT                DD-MON-YYYY
```

Date Display

There are many ways to change the date display within Oracle. Several of the popular built-in functions (BIFs), such as **to_char** and **to_date**, are commonly used to manipulate the display of Oracle dates. Of course, BIFs can never alter the internal representation of an Oracle date, but the **nls_date_format** can change the way the century portion of a date is stored within an Oracle table.

The default **nls_date_format** for Oracle is **DD-MON-YY**. Problems may arise early in the year 2000 when SQL queries may be changed to accommodate four-digit years. In the following example, a query to count all shipments after January 15, 1997 will fail to retrieve the rows because the year is interpreted as 2097, as follows:

```
SELECT count(*) FROM SHPMT
WHERE shpmt_date > '15-JAN-97';

no rows selected
```

The natural response to this failure would be to change the SQL to specify a four-digit year. Unfortunately, Oracle does not like the change, and the SQL query will fail with an error message, as follows:

```
SQL> SELECT count(*) FROM SHPMT WHERE shpmt_date > '25-OCT-1996';
ERROR:
ORA-01830: date format picture ends before converting entire
           input string

no rows selected
```

Now, it appears that you can simply change the Oracle parameter called **nls_date_format** to accommodate a four-digit year in an SQL query. Unfortunately, this change will return misleading results. When a four-digit year is used in the SQL, the query is correct, but when a two-digit year is used, an inaccurate result is returned from the SQL query. Consider the following:

```
SQL> ALTER SESSION SET nls_date_format = "DD-MON-YYYY";

Session altered.

SQL> SELECT count(*) FROM SHPMT WHERE shpmt_date > '25-OCT-1996';

  COUNT(*)
  --------
        40

1 row selected.

SQL> SELECT count(*) FROM SHPMT WHERE shpmt_date > '25-OCT-96';

  COUNT(*)
  ---------
    176858

1 row selected.
```

It appears from these tests that two events must occur in order to achieve the goal: specify four-digit dates and change the **nls_date_format**. In order to get SQL comparisons to work across the century boundary, developers could specify four-digit years in all SQL queries, as follows:

```
SELECT count(*) FROM SHPMT
WHERE shpmt_date
BETWEEN '15-JAN-2000' AND '15-DEC-1999';

  COUNT(*)
  --------
    163632

1 row selected.
```

However, a developer cannot easily change the **nls_date_format** in the init.ora file until all SQL accessing the database is converted to use four-digit years in the queries. The scariest part of this issue is that two-digit year queries do not fail, they produce misleading results. Apparently, the only solution when changing to a **YYYY** format is to carefully coordinate the change to **nls_date_format** with changes to all SQL queries that reference dates.

Date Insertion

Date insertion with the Oracle default **nls_date_format** will always prefix a year with a century of **19**, and Oracle will not allow the SQL to specify a century value. Consider the following:

```
SQL> ALTER SESSION SET nls_date_format = "DD-MON-YY";

Session altered.

SQL> INSERT INTO DT VALUES ('01-JAN-01');

1 row created.

SQL> INSERT INTO DT VALUES ('01-JAN-99');

1 row created.

SQL> INSERT INTO DT VALUES ('01-JAN-2001');
```

```
insert into dt values ('01-JAN-2001')
                     *
ERROR at line 1:
ORA-01830: date format picture ends before converting entire
          input string

SQL> INSERT INTO DT VALUES ('01-JAN-1999');
insert into dt values ('01-JAN-1999')
                     *
ERROR at line 1:
ORA-01830: date format picture ends before converting entire
          input string

SQL> SELECT * FROM DT;

DY
-----
01-JAN-99
01-JAN-01
```

Now, let's take a look at what happens if the **nls_date_format** is reset to **YYYY**. With the **nls_date_format** set to **YYYY**, developers can specify the century in the SQL **INSERT** statements. However, note that inserting the date '01-JAN-91' no longer stores the year as 1991. Instead, the year is stored as AD 91, the same year the Romans began throwing Christians to the lions! Consider the following:

```
SQL> ALTER SESSION SET nls_date_format = "DD-MON-YYYY";

Session altered.

SQL> INSERT INTO DT VALUES ('01-JAN-91');

1 row created.

SQL> INSERT INTO DT VALUES ('01-JAN-1901');

1 row created.

SQL> INSERT INTO DT VALUES ('01-JAN-1999');

1 row created.

SQL> INSERT INTO DT VALUES ('01-JAN-2001');
```

```
1 row created.

SQL> INSERT INTO DT VALUES ('01-JAN-2099');

1 row created.

SQL> SELECT * FROM DT;

DY
-------
01-JAN-0091
01-JAN-1901
01-JAN-1999
01-JAN-2001
01-JAN-2099
```

One solution can be found by using the **RR** date format in **nls_date_format**. If the **nls_date_format** is set to **DD-MON-RR**, Oracle makes some assumptions about the century. If the year is in the range 00 through 49, Oracle assumes the century is **20**, while years in the range 50 through 99 are prefixed with a **19**. This rule also remains true after the year 2000. Consider the following:

```
SQL> ALTER SESSION SET nls_date_format = "DD-MON-RR";

Session altered.

SQL> INSERT INTO DT VALUES ('01-JAN-49');

1 row created.

SQL> INSERT INTO DT VALUES ('01-JAN-50');

1 row created.

SQL> ALTER SESSION SET nls_date_format = "DD-MON-YYYY";

Session altered.

SQL> SELECT * FROM DT;

DY
------
01-JAN-2049
01-JAN-1950
```

Of course, there are some drawbacks to using the **RR** date format. For applications that need to store birth dates for anyone born before 1950, developers may have date conversion problems because 01-JAN-49 is stored as 01-JAN-2049.

Also, like the **YY** date format, the **RR** date format will not allow the century to be explicitly specified. Consider the following:

```
SQL> ALTER SESSION SET nls_date_format = "DD-MON-RR";

Session altered.

SQL> INSERT INTO DT VALUES ('01-JAN-49');

1 row created.

SQL> INSERT INTO DT VALUES ('01-JAN-1950');
insert into dt values ('01-JAN-1950')
                    *
ERROR at line 1:
ORA-01830: date format picture ends before converting entire
           input string
```

Checking Existing Century Values

The first step in year 2000 compatibility is to audit your existing databases to ensure your year values are properly stored within Oracle tables. The following code will perform this operation, selecting the distinct year values for all columns of all tables that contain date values. This query will cause full-table scans and can run for a long time, especially on data warehouses, so you may want to schedule it to run during off-hours.

```
rem  Written by Don Burleson (c) 1995

SET PAGES 9999;
SET HEADING OFF;
SET FEEDBACK OFF;

PROMPT All Distinct Year Values within all tables
PROMPT =============================================

SPOOL checkdate.sql;
```

```
SELECT 'spool date_list.lst' FROM DUAL;

SELECT 'select distinct to_char('||
       column_name||
       ',''YYYY'') FROM '||owner||'.'||table_name||';'
FROM DBA_TAB_COLUMNS
WHERE data_type = 'DATE'
AND owner NOT IN ('SYS','SYSTEM');

SELECT 'spool off' FROM DUAL;

SPOOL OFF;

@checkdate
```

A Suggested Implementation Plan

It is not enough to assume that your Oracle application is year 2000 compliant. Your database could be in trouble sooner than you think, especially if your system stores dates into the next century. For example, a system that schedules projects 24 months in advance will run into problems in January of 1998 when the 00 dates are stored as 1900 instead of 2000. To achieve year 2000 compliance, you will need to choose one of the following three options.

Option One: Do Nothing

Doing nothing when the year changes to 2000 is an acceptable alternative for applications that will never issue date queries or store dates for the years 1990-1999. As we know, the existing default of **YY** means that all dates must be specified with two digits, and that a **20** will be assumed for the century in all queries after 1-JAN-2000. This will immediately block all SQL access to dates where the century is **19**.

Option Two: Change The nls_date_format To DD-MON-RR

This option will not change the way existing queries function. However, if the application requires the storage of dates before 1950 or after 2050, then this option cannot be used because the **RR** format will not allow these dates to be stored in Oracle tables. The overriding problem is interpretive. Some SQL queries may appear backward due to the years 00 through 49 being higher than the years 50 through 99. For example, the following query will test for all rows with a date between 1998 and 2048. At first glance, it appears that this query is for rows between 1948 through 1998.

```
REM   Assume that today is 1-JAN-2001;
SELECT * FROM SHPMT WHERE DATE BETWEEN '1-JAN-48' AND '1-JAN-98';
```

In short, the **RR** option allows for an easily implemented change because no SQL changes are required and a DBA only needs to reset the **nls_date_parameter** in the Oracle init.ora file. The downside to this approach is that some of the cross-century queries may be misinterpreted by end users and programmers.

Option Three: Change The nls_date_format To DD-MON-YYYY

This option requires existing SQL to be changed to specify four-digit years and coordinating the SQL change with the change to the **nls_date_format**. In other words, if you decide to use this option, you need to develop a plan to coordinate the changing of the **nls_date_format** parameter with the changing of all SQL that accesses your database. This process requires the following procedure:

- Direct the developers to specify four-digit years in all SQL queries. This can be done before changing the **nls_date_format** parameter.

- Change the init.ora parameter **nls_date_format** to **DD-MON-YYYY**.

- Ensure that all SQL has been changed to specify four-digit years. (Remember, specifying two-digit years after making this change will result in zeros being used as century values.)

- Scan all areas where SQL might be stored, including:

  - Stored procedures and triggers.

  - Unix code libraries that contain SQL queries.

  - External program source code, such as Pro*C source libraries.

A routine to check stored procedures for two-digit dates is relatively simple to write. The following SQL can be used to interrogate all Oracle stored procedures and display the names of all stored procedures that might reference date values:

```
SET PAGES 999;
SET HEADING OFF;

PROMPT Possible stored procedures with date manipulation
PROMPT ======================================================
```

```
SELECT DISTINCT name FROM DBA_SOURCE
WHERE
    text LIKE '%date%'
OR text LIKE '%DATE%'
OR text LIKE '%dt%'
OR text LIKE '%DT%'
AND owner NOT IN ('SYS','SYSTEM');
```

Summary

Regardless of Oracle's statement that the database is year 2000 compliant, it is still the responsibility of Oracle DBAs to ensure date format changes. By following these simple steps and carefully coordinating the changes to the SQL with the change to the **nls_date_format**, you can ensure that your Oracle database will continue to function properly. It is not necessary to wait until the last minute to make changes for the year 2000. And the ramifications may be dramatic for those who do not carefully plan ahead.

Index

—E—

—F—